To the Streuli Family,

especially Hans and Pia,

Keep seeking, Keep

asking the big questions.

With all best wishes,

Tim

CROSSING PARISH BOUNDARIES

HISTORICAL STUDIES OF URBAN AMERICA

Edited by Lilia Fernández, Timothy J. Gilfoyle, Becky M. Nicolaides, and Amanda I. Seligman
James R. Grossman, editor emeritus

ALSO IN THE SERIES:

CROSSING PARISH BOUNDARIES

Race, Sports, and Catholic Youth in Chicago, 1914–1954

TIMOTHY B. NEARY

THE UNIVERSITY OF CHICAGO PRESS

CHICAGO AND LONDON

The University of Chicago Press, Chicago 60637
The University of Chicago Press, Ltd., London
© 2016 by The University of Chicago
All rights reserved. Published 2016.
Printed in the United States of America

25 24 23 22 21 20 19 18 17 16   1 2 3 4 5

ISBN-13: 978-0-226-38876-2 (cloth)
ISBN-13: 978-0-226-38893-9 (e-book)

DOI: 10.7208/chicago/9780226388939.001.0001

A version of chapter 4, "'An Inalienable Right to Play': African American Partici-
pation in the CYO," was first published in *Sports in Chicago*, edited by Elliott J.
Gorn, published by the University of Illinois Press. © 2008 Chicago History
Museum.

Library of Congress Cataloging-in-Publication Data
Names: Neary, Timothy B., 1970– author.
Title: Crossing parish boundaries : race, sports, and Catholic youth in Chicago,
    1914–1954 / Timothy B. Neary.
Other titles: Historical studies of urban America.
Description: Chicago ; London : The University of Chicago Press, 2016. |
Series: Historical studies of urban America
Identifiers: LCCN 2016001675| ISBN 9780226388762 (cloth : alk. paper) | ISBN
    9780226388939 (e-book)
Subjects: LCSH: African American youth—Illinois—Chicago. | Catholic youth—
    Illinois—Chicago. | Catholic Youth Organization—History. | Sheil, Bernard J.
    (Bernard James), 1888–1969. | African Americans—Illinois—Chicago—History—
    20th century. | Social action—Illinois—Chicago—History—20th century. |
    Chicago (Ill.)—Race relations—History—20th century. | Parishes—Illinois—
    Chicago—History—20th century. | Race relations—Religious aspects.
Classification: LCC F548.9.N4 N43 2016 | DDC 305.2350896/073077311—dc23 LC
    record available at http://lccn.loc.gov/2016001675

♾ This paper meets the requirements of ANSI/NISO Z39.48–1992
(Permanence of Paper).

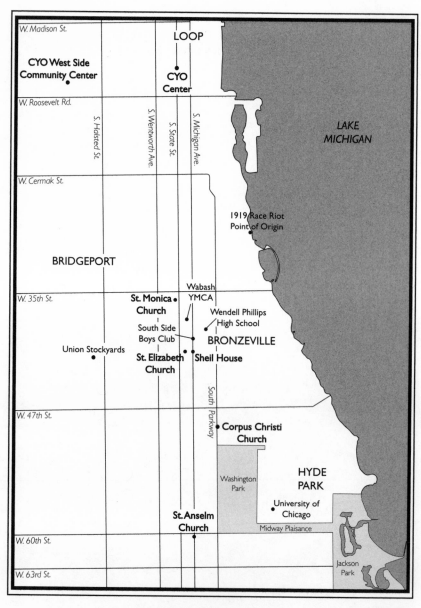

African American Parishes and the Catholic Youth
Organization in Chicago, 1914–1954. (Kevin Schuhl.)

CONTENTS

"Building Men, Not Just Fighters"

Two young men, muscles taut, eyed each other intently as they prepared to do battle on a cold, gray night in a gritty section of Chicago. During the previous day the mercury had dropped to five below zero, breaking a record for early December. While still frigid, the air temperature now was warm enough to allow a few snowflakes to blow through the streets of the city. One of the combatants was short in stature, muscular, and compact; the other, taller and leaner. Within moments, each was using his body as a weapon, pounding his fists against the head, face, chest, and stomach of the other. The goal: total domination. Because the stakes were high, they fought without restraint, using every ounce of their beings to prevail. They fought not for themselves alone, but for their communities—their neighborhoods, friends, and families. They fought for their pride and manhood. Moreover, they fought for their race. One of the young men was black, the other white.

Although they attacked each other violently, Hiner Thomas and Joseph O'Connell were not rival gang members engaged in a street fight. Rather, they were finalists in the Catholic Youth Organization's Tenth Annual Boxing Tournament. The Thomas/O'Connell matchup was one of 16 amateur bouts that attracted more than 8,500 fans to the Chicago Coliseum on the evening of 4 December 1940.[1] Located less than a mile south of downtown near the city's former red-light district, the Coliseum had served as the site of numerous national political conventions and sporting events since opening in 1899. The indoor arena at 15th Street and Wabash Avenue hosted 5 consecutive Republican national conventions between 1904 and 1920, as well as the Progressive Party's national convention in 1912. The Chicago Blackhawks professional hockey team played home games there in the late 1920s until moving at the end of the decade to the newly con-

structed Chicago Stadium on the city's West Side. Used sporadically during the Depression for events like roller derbies and wrestling matches, by
1940 the Coliseum was past its prime.[2]

On this Wednesday evening, however, the old arena was alive with excitement. Fans from throughout the city came to cheer on their favorite
Catholic Youth Organization (CYO) boxers. The 32 finalists—16 novices
and 16 competitors in the open division—fought in 8 weight classifica-
tions. The tournament had begun 6 weeks earlier with 980 entrants competing in qualifying sectionals throughout the city. Chicago newspapers
and radio stations covered the event extensively. The gate receipts, expected to reach as high as $10,000, were to be donated to the CYO Christ-
mas Fund for impoverished children. Thomas and O'Connell were fighting
for the light heavyweight championship in the evening's penultimate bout
before the heavyweight finale. Experienced boxers, they held 2 CYO titles
each: Thomas winning in 1935 and 1938; O'Connell in 1937 and 1938. Fight
fans eagerly awaited the match between 2 of the best amateur boxers in the
city. "These rivals," reported the *Chicago Tribune*, "are expected to engage
in one of the most exciting fights in the ten year history of the event."[3]

While frigid outside, the air inside the Coliseum was thick with sweat
and smoke. The sights and sounds were familiar to boxing fans—referees and coaches barking instructions, the ring of the bell announcing the
start and finish of each round, the quick feet of boxers dancing around the
ring, the thud of leather gloves pounding against flesh, cheers and jeers
from the crowd. Like the Golden Gloves and other amateur boxing tournaments, a mood of intense competition—at times even blood lust—characterized the event. Fans rooted hard for their favorites, imbuing the fighters
inside the ring with the power to embody pride in neighborhood, ethnicity, and race. Nicknames like "Kid Irish" marked boxers' ethnicities and
encouraged clannish loyalties among fans.[4] Likewise, the African American *Chicago Defender* proudly reported on "Race boys" of "our group"
winning CYO titles.[5]

The CYO event differed from other amateur boxing matches, however.
The organization demanded higher ideals from its members than simple
fair play and sportsmanship. Panethnic and interracial cooperation were
emphasized with religious and civic symbolism distinguishing the occasion. The night began with a prayer and recitation of the CYO oath,
requiring each competitor to adhere to Christian and democratic principles. Boy Scout color guards escorted the boxers into the arena. Between
contests, the hundred-piece CYO concert band performed for the crowd.
The goal of the boxing tournament was more than entertainment; its

purpose was to inspire the city's young people to be ethical, engaged, and united citizens.

The matchup between Hiner Thomas and Joe O'Connell exemplified both aspects of the CYO—ethnic competition and friendly cooperation. Standing only 5'4" and weighing 175 pounds, the 24-year-old Thomas was a powerful puncher and talented boxer.[6] Nicknamed the "Junior Brown Bomber," Thomas amassed an amateur record of 191–6, knocking out 101 of his opponents.[7] Along the way he earned numerous CYO, Golden Gloves, and Illinois Athletic Club titles. Sportswriters described him as a "rugged" fighter and "one of the most popular colored boys" in CYO boxing.[8] The blond-haired O'Connell, a "southwest side Irishman" 2 years younger than Thomas, also earned multiple amateur boxing titles in the late 1930s fighting as a welterweight. In 1940 he moved up to the light heavyweight class after gaining 25 pounds, which he attributed to working in Chicago's Union Stockyards. Although the "added weight has slowed him down a trifle, Joe is punching harder than ever since becoming a light heavyweight" reported the *Tribune*.[9]

Despite their fierce battle in the ring, Thomas and O'Connell were part of a brotherhood of CYO amateur athletes. As members of the CYO, they were expected to treat one another with dignity and respect. And as CYO titleholders, they became teammates representing Chicago, fighting against amateur CYO champions in other cities. During the second half of the 1930s and early 1940s, Thomas and O'Connell took part in integrated road trips to Midwestern cities like Cincinnati, Detroit, Dubuque, Green Bay, Kansas City, Omaha, and Racine, as well as longer trips to Pennsylvania and even Hawaii.[10] CYO publicity photographs appeared on the sports pages of Chicago newspapers showing bare-chested young pugilists—smiling broadly and wearing boxing trunks emblazoned with the CYO logo— gathered around CYO founder-director Bishop Bernard Sheil, who wore a black suit and Roman collar. Thomas and other black boxers in the photos stood shoulder-to-shoulder with white boxers like Joe O'Connell and his brother Eddie, a "frecked [sic] face Irish puncher."[11] The sight of the priest and integrated group of boxers presented an image of Catholic-sponsored interracial harmony.[12]

Inside the ring, however, Hiner Thomas and Joe O'Connell showed no mercy toward one another. The three-round bout was hard hitting, with O'Connell scoring "repeatedly with rights to the heart."[13] Absorbing the blows but refusing to fall, the sturdy Thomas—yet to suffer a knockout in his career—relied on his finely honed boxing techniques, countering with jabs and uppercuts. Thomas represented Corpus Christi, an African

American parish in the segregated Black Belt neighborhood on Chicago's South Side. Their boxers were a powerhouse in the 1930s and 1940s, winning numerous individual and team titles. Corpus Christi teammates and parishioners, along with Thomas's older brothers Bob and Jim, cheered on the Junior Brown Bomber. Indeed, nearly every black spectator in the arena or black fan listening on the radio was rooting for Thomas.

O'Connell, on the other hand, represented the Euro-American parish of St. Nicholas of Tolentine, located in the all-white West Lawn neighborhood on the city's Southwest Side. His brother Eddie, fighting in the 135-pound open class for St. Nicholas, had defeated an African American opponent earlier in the evening. Eddie now joined the O'Connell's father—and much of the audience—in cheering for Joe. John O'Connell, a city worker, was proud of his sons, boasting he had "raised a pair of champions."[14] In the end, though, the hard-fought battle came down to a decision by the ringside judges, who gave the nod to Thomas. As one sportswriter put it, the Corpus Christi boxer simply "outmauled" O'Connell.[15]

Although Thomas and O'Connell were not rival gang members, they had every reason to be on opposite sides in a fight. In Chicago and other northern cities in the mid-twentieth century, legal, political, economic, and social institutions and traditions kept blacks and whites physically separated and emotionally alienated. Racial segregation was the norm in most aspects of urban life, including housing, education, health care, and religion. Thomas and O'Connell shared many similarities—they were close in age, residents of Chicago, and both came from stable, working-class families. But because they lived in a racialized society, in most respects they occupied different worlds. In a city segregated by race, they lived on opposite sides of the color line.

Born in Oklahoma in 1915, Hiner Thomas moved with his family to Chicago during the first great wave of African American migrants from the South to northern cities during the 1910s and 1920s.[16] His family settled on the South Side, whose African American population was second in size only to New York City's Harlem. In 1934, Thomas began his boxing career at the relatively late age of eighteen, winning the CYO welterweight title in 1935. A year later, he qualified as an alternate for the 1936 U.S. Olympic boxing team, which included three boxers from Chicago's CYO. He also won the 1936 international CYO middleweight title in Honolulu, Hawaii, successfully defending it later that year when the Hawaiian team came to Chicago's Soldier Field.[17]

By the time of his light heavyweight title bout with Joe O'Connell in December 1940, the veteran boxer was coaching for the CYO and working as a porter in a downtown department store. He lived with his mother and two brothers near 95th and State streets in Lilydale, an African American neighborhood located within the Roseland community area on the Far South Side.[18] In 1944 Princeton Park Homes, described as the "largest private development in the United States occupied exclusively by Negroes," was built in Lilydale in response to the wartime housing shortage.[19] The new housing was marketed to middle-income African Americans working in Chicago's steel industry along the shores of Lake Michigan on the Far South Side and in the south suburbs. A community of modest, freestanding houses occupying small lots, Lilydale provided black families like the Thomases with the opportunity to escape the high rents and overcrowded kitchenettes of the Black Belt in order to pursue the American dream of home ownership in a semi-suburban setting. However, the expansion of private affordable housing for African Americans during the 1940s in otherwise white Roseland met with stiff resistance from local white residents.[20] Consequently, Hiner Thomas and his family lived on a black island surrounded by a sea of white, often hostile neighbors. Even though numerous Catholic churches were closer to Lilydale, Thomas traveled six and a half miles north to reach Corpus Christi, where African Americans were welcome.

The O'Connells, on the other hand, followed a path similar to many Irish American Chicagoans. As a young married couple, John and Marion O'Connell lived on the South Side in the Armour Square community area near 24th Street and Wentworth Avenue.[21] Their sons, Joe and Eddie, were born two years apart around the time of World War I. By the 1920s the O'Connell home was only a few blocks south of Chicago's emerging Chinatown and a few blocks west of the overcrowded and expanding Black Belt. Like many other white families, the O'Connells decided to leave the old neighborhood. As the Black Belt grew beyond its original boundaries and expanded into adjoining white communities, tens of thousands of white ethnic Catholics, white Protestants, and Jews abandoned their former South Side neighborhoods for new housing opportunities farther south and west.[22] By the time of World War II, the O'Connells lived in the all-white West Lawn neighborhood on the city's Southwest Side. Their two-story, red-brick home was located a block west of Marquette Park and about two miles southeast of Chicago's Municipal (Midway) Airport.[23] They were members of St. Nicholas of Tolentine parish, whose stately Gothic-style church at 62nd Street and South Lawndale Avenue stood twelve blocks to the north.[24]

Joe and Eddie attended Lindblom Technical High School in the white

West Englewood neighborhood, about three miles northeast of the O'Connell residence.[25] After graduating in 1936, Joe focused on boxing. By 1940, however, he had taken a civil service exam to become an oiler in one of the city pumping stations. He hoped to follow in the footsteps of his father, who worked at a public elementary school as a stationery engineer. In the meantime, he labored as a butcher's apprentice for the George A. Hormel and Company meatpacking firm in Chicago's Union Stockyards. Eddie, who graduated from Lindblom in 1938, also worked at Hormel.[26] The O'Connells undoubtedly found meaning in work, family, church, and sports. And as was the case for hundreds of thousands of working-class, white ethnic Catholics, their parish was central to their identity. More than the borders of West Lawn, the geographical boundaries of St. Nicholas of Tolentine defined place for the O'Connells. St. Nick's was their neighborhood.

A strong attachment to place combined with fears of racial change resulted in instances of white—often Catholic—violent resistance to residential integration in Chicago and other northern cities, especially during the years following World War II. The Airport Homes riots, for example, broke out about a mile and a half northwest of the O'Connell residence in December 1946, when hundreds of angry whites hurled bricks, broke windows, slashed tires, and tipped over cars in order to prevent two African American families from moving into temporary public housing for war veterans in the West Lawn neighborhood.[27] Two decades later, in nearby Marquette Park, Martin Luther King, Jr., was hit in the head by a rock as a vicious mob numbering four thousand attacked civil rights activists who were marching in support of fair housing legislation and residential integration. An eyewitness noted that the Marquette Park rioters became particularly enraged whenever they spotted white Catholic priests and nuns marching alongside African Americans in support of racial equality. The intensity of vitriol shocked King, a veteran of numerous violent clashes with law enforcement and counterdemonstrators in the South. "I have never seen anything like this in my life," said the civil rights leader. "I think the people from Mississippi should come to Chicago to learn how to hate."[28] West Lawn remained racially and politically conservative into the 1980s, twice producing the lowest percentage of votes of any Chicago neighborhood for the city's first African American mayor, Harold Washington.[29]

Teenagers and young adults who participated in interracial CYO programming during the 1930s and 1940s later had to choose sides during postwar battles over school integration, fair housing, and court-ordered busing. Hiner Thomas and Joe O'Connell spent hours together as teen-agers and young men, training in CYO gyms and traveling to CYO bouts around the country. But how much did such interracial cooperation carry over into other parts of their lives? Thomas, who joined the Marines in 1942, served in the still-segregated military during World War II. Remaining in uniform for twenty-one years, he saw action during the Korean War and traveled the world as a boxing instructor for the Marines. However, as an African American, he would have encountered fierce opposition if he had tried to move into the Airport Homes in 1946. Even two decades later, after retiring from the military in 1963, he likely would have met stiff resistance if he had attempted to buy or rent a house in the West Lawn neighborhood of his old CYO boxing teammate Joe O'Connell.[30]

Instead, Thomas moved to Los Angeles, where in the 1970s he opened a gym for boys called Foundations of Youth. The CYO shaped his philosophy on coaching and youth development. "I got my start right here in Chicago at the Catholic Youth Organization," recalled the former amateur boxing champion and ex-Marine in 1975, "and to this day, I've never been a smoker or drinker. And if any of my boys gets into that kind of thing . . . Out they go . . . I'm interested in building men, not just fighters. If taken seriously, boxing can build character both mentally and physically." In addition to athletics, Thomas followed in the tradition of the CYO by emphasizing religion and developing the faith lives of young people. "The only rule that I have," he said, "is that they all belong to some church, and I check to make sure they go regularly."[31]

Thomas carried with him CYO ideals throughout his life. In addition to physical, emotional, and spiritual development, those ideals included the celebration of cultural pluralism and promotion of interracial cooperation. During the mid-twentieth century, the CYO created opportunities for young people like Hiner Thomas and Joe O'Connell to cross the color line in Chicago. It is a story largely forgotten today.

CROSSING PARISH BOUNDARIES

No shortage of scholarship addresses African Americans or the Roman Catholic Church in American urban history. Beginning with W. E. B. Du Bois, scholars have studied social, political, and cultural aspects of black urban life. Some of the best works examine the large-scale migration of African Americans from the South to northern cities and its consequences.[32] Likewise, Catholic studies abound, especially those exploring the church's role in the educational, social, religious, and political lives of European immigrants in American cities.[33] Only relatively recently, however, have historians addressed the intersection of African Americans and Catholicism. Since the 1980s, a handful of historians have investigated the "minority within a minority": African American Catholics.[34] These works begin the important task of documenting the lives of black Catholics, but a gap remains in the literature—exploring interactions between African Americans and white Catholics.

Crossing Parish Boundaries describes and analyzes the little-known and largely forgotten story of Catholic interracialism prior to the modern civil rights movement. Most significant were the institutional networks that promoted interracial exchange and cooperation, most notably the CYO, which created opportunities for tens of thousands of everyday Chicagoans, black and white, to cross geographic and social boundaries in a city deeply divided by racial segregation. The mass movement in the twentieth century of African Americans from the South to the urban North led to large-scale encounters between the descendants of slaves and the offspring of European immigrants, many of whom were Catholics. *Crossing Parish Boundaries* examines how the Catholic Church in Chicago responded to population changes in the city as African American migrants settled within the geographic boundaries of parish communities that were established by earlier generations of European Americans. Covering a forty-year period between the onset of World War I and the beginning of the classical phase of the civil rights movement in the mid-1950s, the book addresses issues related to the intersections of ethnicity, neighborhood, race, and religion that influenced not only Chicago but cities throughout the North.

Crossing Parish Boundaries presents a counternarrative to the dominant historical interpretation of white ethnic Catholicism rejecting everyday interracialism in American cities. I do not deny either the intensity or prevalence of resistance by white ethnic Catholics to the racial integration of city neighborhoods. But close examination of the Catholic Youth Organization reveals a countervailing tradition of black–white interactions in certain Catholic-sponsored social, athletic, and educational settings. These interracial relationships, and the institutions that propagated them, shared similarities with better and more widely known examples of interracial cooperation found in the North among organized labor during the 1930s and 1940s.[35] In this way, *Crossing Parish Boundaries* complicates the story of northern race relations in the urban Catholic context during the first half of the twentieth century.

Historians of cities and ethnic groups have minimized or ignored interethnic and interracial cooperation. Much of the literature on Catholics and ethnicity, for example, emphasizes the violent resistance of Euro-American Catholics to African Americans moving into previously all-white, working-class neighborhoods, particularly during the period of vast racial succession following World War II. Focus on such high-profile post-war clashes over residential turf, however, obscures examples of earlier, more positive interactions between ethnic and racial groups in urban settings. Despite residential and institutional segregation, white ethnics and African Americans—particularly young people—crossed ethnic and racial lines during the Depression and World War II.[36] They found opportunities to do so in machine politics and organized labor, as well as in movie theaters, dance halls, and city parks. Likewise, institutions within the Roman Catholic Church provided young people with urban venues for inter-ethnic and interracial engagement.

The most significant was the CYO. Auxiliary bishop Bernard Sheil founded the organization in 1930 with the support of Cardinal George Mundelein, his superior and leader of the Archdiocese of Chicago. The creation of the CYO was a calculated response to growing concerns during the 1920s about the moral health of the city's young Catholics as ever-increasing consumerism, secular temptations, and materialism challenged ecclesiastical authority. Social and athletic clubs, which acted like ethnic street gangs, were of special concern, as they competed with the church for the allegiance of young men. The Irish Catholic Ragen's Colts, for example, were implicated in Chicago's 1919 race riot and 1920s "beer wars." The church used the glamour of sports, particularly boxing, to attract its target audience. Sheil modeled the CYO on Protestant reform programs like the Young Men's Christian Association (YMCA), employing modern marketing techniques to sell it. The original focus was on male teenagers from working-class, Euro-American Catholic families, but the CYO was open to "boys and girls without regard to race, creed, or color."[37]

Bishop Sheil is largely forgotten today. In the mid-twentieth century, however, he was a national figure. A former athlete and charismatic leader, Sheil was the public face of the CYO. The organization benefited from not only the steadfast support of Cardinal Mundelein but also Sheil's allies in the worlds of politics, business, labor, journalism, sports, entertainment, and the arts. By World War II, the CYO enjoyed a national reputation, with Sheil known as the "Apostle of Youth." The bishop rode the speaker's circuit, was featured in magazine articles, and spoke on nationwide radio broadcasts promoting a mixture of liberal Catholicism and American pluralism. He became the alter ego of Father Charles Coughlin,

Detroit's reactionary and anti-Semitic Depression-era "radio priest." Sheil was the antithesis, both theologically and politically, of Coughlin. Yet, while American history textbooks regularly mention Coughlin's white ethnic parochialism, evidence of Sheil's equally important cosmopolitan Catholicism is ignored and absent.[38]

African Americans participated in the CYO from its inception, a development little recognized by historians and other observers of the church. Three parishes—St. Elizabeth, Corpus Christi, and St. Anselm—founded by Irish Americans on Chicago's South Side between 1881 and 1909 provided a core of black participants. In each of the three parishes, a massive church structure towered over flat landscapes, marking the apparent permanence of its Irish American parishioners. Yet residential turnover came quickly in the 1910s and 1920s with the arrival of African Americans seeking economic and social opportunities in the industrial metropolis. St. Anselm, for instance, was the setting for James T. Farrell's *Studs Lonigan* trilogy in which the Irish Catholic Lonigan family confronts "losing" their neighborhood to African American "invasion." Racial succession, driven by the departure of whites in response to black settlement, rapidly transformed these three Irish Catholic parishes by the late 1920s into an expanding African American "ghetto," known over time by different names: the Black Belt, Black Metropolis, and Bronzeville.[39]

In American cities like Chicago, the institutional church was a paradox: it strengthened and challenged racial divisions simultaneously. On the one hand, Catholic parishes defined by territorial boundaries reinforced racial segregation by aligning parish identity with neighborhood identity. On the other hand, canon law regarded each of the more than 350 parishes throughout the city and suburbs in the Archdiocese of Chicago as equal parts of one community.

Bishop Sheil used his authority in the church's hierarchical structure and the parish/archdiocese dynamic to foster interracialism in CYO athletics. Citywide competitions in sports, such as boxing, basketball, and even swimming, meant that blacks and whites competed against one another officially as equals. At a time when the YMCA was still racially segregated, black and white athletes, including Protestants and Jews, met at the CYO Center in the city's downtown Loop district. Boxing tournaments at the old Chicago Stadium, Wrigley Field, and Soldier Field drew crowds between fifteen thousand and forty thousand, with thousands more listening live on the radio. The champions then became teammates on interracial CYO all-star squads, which traveled across the United States and abroad. The CYO promoted the panethnic and multiracial makeup of its athletes, dubbing them a "League of Nations."

The American creed—the deeply held belief that each person in the Unites States should enjoy equality of opportunity and equality before the law—was at the heart of the modern African American civil rights movement, classically defined as beginning with the 1954 *Brown v. Board of Education* decision and ending in 1968 with the assassination of Martin Luther King, Jr.[40] In recent years, however, some historians have argued for understanding the black freedom movement within the context of the "long civil rights movement," dating back to the 1930s.[41] During the Great Depression, members of the Communist Party USA critiqued economic and social inequalities in American society by linking racism with capitalism. Communists, consequently, became some of the harshest critics of racial inequalities and injustices in the 1930s. Yet card-carrying Communists were not the only northern agitators for black civil rights in the 1930s and 1940s. Mainstream civil rights organizations, like the National Association for the Advancement of Colored People (NAACP) and the Urban League, as well as socialists, religious reformers, and community activists fought for civil rights for African Americans during the Great Depression and World War II.[42]

Sheil and the CYO championed civil rights for African Americans during the 1930s and 1940s, before the classical period of the modern civil rights movement. Sheil's anticommunism stood in contrast to Communist Party members recognized by historians as civil rights pioneers during the Great Depression and World War II in the urban North. Yet, while Sheil certainly did not fit within the orthodox American Left, he did engage with members of the "Black Popular Front" and "civil rights unionism," partnering with former communist and Harlem Renaissance poet Claude McKay, Congress of Industrial Organizations leader John L. Lewis, and community organizer Saul Alinsky.[43] The bishop moved within multiple (and often oppositional) urban spheres, including those populated by the (usually conservative) American Catholic Church hierarchy; white, ethnic, working-class Catholics; African American Protestants; Catholic interracialists; Jewish American leaders; athletes; sportswriters; politicians; and popular entertainers.

Informed by Catholic social teaching, as well as by New Deal politics, Sheil adopted a progressive ideology on the issue of race in American society. He spoke out against Jim Crow segregation and racially restrictive covenants, championed the interracial Congress of Industrial Organizations, supported the Double V campaign against racial segregation during World War II, and denounced anti-Semitism in the United States and abroad. By the mid-1930s, Sheil expanded the reach of the CYO beyond sports to include summer camps, social services, and eventually adult education. The CYO concept, especially its athletic component, was copied in communities across the United States, but control remained decentralized at the diocesan level.

African Americans who participated in CYO programs (whose voices have been absent in previous studies) have admitted that their experiences took them outside their racially segregated neighborhoods and exposed them to a wider world during the 1930s, 1940s, and early 1950s. Sports, as well as nonathletic activities like checkers and marbles, allowed them to encounter and interact with whites in constructive and safe environments. Not every experience was positive; interviewees recalled racist snubs that still stung after fifty or sixty years. On the whole, however, the CYO presented opportunities to cross parish and neighborhood boundaries, move throughout the city, and, in a few cases, travel nationally and internationally. Some black participants enrolled and competed in sports at Catholic high schools and colleges, providing entrée into Chicago's Irish American Catholic business community and Democratic Party political machine.

Crossing Parish Boundaries builds upon but also departs from historical scholarship on black-white interactions in urban Catholic settings. In his pioneering *Parish Boundaries*, John McGreevy demonstrates the unique hold that urban neighborhoods had on white ethnic Catholics and their willingness to fight in defense of their home turf. In addition, McGreevy deftly shows how American Catholics in the urban North understood the concept of "race" prior to 1940.[44] McGreevy's work is supported by the rich literature on "whiteness."[45] Irish Americans, who dominated the church's hierarchy and were well established as a group in the United States by the early twentieth century, considered themselves "white." Yet they sometimes viewed more recent Catholic immigrants from southern and Eastern Europe—Italians and Poles, for example—as members of different races than themselves. African Americans—because their numbers were still relatively small in northern cities, few were Roman Catholics, and they remained segregated in clearly defined ghettos—did not yet occupy the prominent place in the racial imagination of Euro-American Catholics that they would later assume. McGreevy emphasizes the disjunction between everyday, lay Catholic parishioners and liberal theologians and religious activists. The latter sought to break down parochial isolation and promote interracial accord within the church. For these progressive thinkers who anticipated the Second Vatican Council's ecumenical and inclusive agenda, Catholicism meant reaching out to groups formerly deemed "others"—including African Americans. According to McGreevy, interracial cooperation existed as only a mere dream of liberal thinkers prior to the Second Vatican Council, as Catholics at the parish level resisted such measures. Yet Chicago's CYO offers contradictory evidence. This citywide institution, organized around the Catholic parish network, presented working-class Chicagoans from different racial and religious backgrounds opportunities to regularly interact with one another.

Along with McGreevy, Arnold Hirsch and Thomas Sugrue have emphasized conflict between working-class Euro-American Catholics and African Americans over residential space during the postwar period, as the percentage of black residents spiked in such cities as Chicago, Detroit, New York, and Philadelphia.[46] They point to the high rate of home ownership and strong identification with parish life as making white Catholics more likely to "stand and fight" against racial succession than, for instance, Jews.[47] In 1949, for example, white Catholics from the Chicago parishes of Visitation and St. Columbanus physically attacked blacks as they attempted to integrate the neighborhoods of Englewood and Park Manor, respectively.[48] Yet, during the 1930s, whites from Visitation and St. Columbanus regularly traveled to Chicago's all-black Catholic parishes to participate in CYO athletics. Likewise, black CYO participants traveled to Visitation and St. Columbanus for sports competitions.

Two key factors altered urban race relations in the Catholic context during the postwar period: a population tipping point and a changing understanding of race. The percentage of Chicago residents who were African American remained more or less steady during the Depression, increasing slightly from 7 percent in 1930 to 8 percent in 1940. During World War II and the immediate postwar years, however, the percentage of black residents almost doubled to 14 percent. And by 1960, nearly one out of every four Chicagoans identified as black.[49] As blacks composed a greater percentage of a city's population, many of its white residents, particularly those in working-class areas adjacent to African American neighborhoods, viewed the presence of blacks as an imminent threat. In the minds of many working-class Euro-American Catholics, the African American population reached a tipping point in the postwar years. Perceived racial differences among European Americans—between Irish and Italian Americans, for instance—no longer seemed relevant, as blacks appeared to be "taking over." African American participation in the CYO grew accordingly during the 1940s and early 1950s. By 1952, over 40 percent of the finalists in the CYO boxing tournament were black.[50] Angry and fearful white critics began to refer derisively to the CYO as the "Colored Youth Organization."[51]

The years of the Great Depression offered a respite of relative demographic stability in the northern cities between two periods of rapid population change. Driven by the economic catalyst of World War I, African American population growth resulted in "white flight" and neighborhood change during the 1920s in Chicago and other northern cities. Similarly, residential racial succession occurred again, this time on a much larger scale, during the postwar years of the late 1940s, 1950s, and 1960s. In the interval, a window of opportunity existed in cities like Chicago for interracial contact, as the demographic stability of neighborhoods and parishes, along with the political and social liberalism of the New Deal, created an atmosphere more conducive to interracialism than the periods immediately preceding and following it. Sheil's CYO attempted to take advantage of this opening.

Such interracialism, however, had its limits. In ways largely ignored by historians, urban Catholics in the mid-twentieth century lived a double consciousness similar to working-class Americans who accepted interethnic and interracial cooperation in the workplace but rejected it in their personal lives.[52] During the 1930s and 1940s, white ethnics participated in interracial activities outside their parishes as their homes and places of worship remained racially segregated. White Catholic parents, who may have worked with African Americans, shared public amenities with other races, and watched their children participate in interracial sports competitions, nevertheless tended to strictly guard the racial homogeneity of their parishes and neighborhoods. By the dawn of the twenty-first century, widespread urban renewal and suburbanization not only maintained residential segregation between blacks and whites, but it also made even modest attempts at interracial cooperation extremely difficult.

Yet three-quarters of a century earlier, the CYO created opportunities for Chicago's children and young adults that regularly transcended parochial and racial boundaries. Although it did not stop racism and racial segregation within the city's Catholic churches or neighborhoods, the CYO made significant contributions to interracialism in Chicago during the Great Depression, World War II, and immediate postwar period. The larger history of the American Catholic Church's encounter with African Americans, however, is fraught with generations of conflict, misunderstandings, and missed opportunities. In Chicago, African Americans in the late nineteenth and early twentieth centuries not only dealt with second-class status in the political, economic, and social aspects of city life, they also faced an exclusionary, uneven, and at times bitter history of race relations within the Catholic Church.

Minority within a Minority: African Americans Encounter Catholicism in the Urban North

If a black man is anything but a Baptist or Methodist, someone has been tampering with his religion.
—Booker T. Washington

In the late Friday afternoon of 3 January 1930, Mrs. C. Dickerson, a visiting nurse for Chicago's Department of Health, stepped out of the bitter cold into St. Elizabeth Catholic Church. Perhaps returning from work to her home in the 3800 block of South Calumet Avenue, the African American woman decided to say a few prayers. St. Elizabeth's Romanesque limestone building on the northeast corner of 41st Street and Wabash Avenue regularly offered visitors quiet refuge from the bustling streets of the surrounding Black Belt neighborhood. Upon entering, Dickerson was confronted with billowing smoke—the church was on fire! She quickly ran to the parish office and notified the pastor's secretary.[1]

The secretary phoned authorities, and the Chicago fire department responded with trucks and scores of men. As the imposing structure burned, parishioners from the surrounding neighborhood arrived on the scene, including, according to one witness, "old colored women and children, [who] stood in the maze of hose lines, saying the rosary." In disbelief, they witnessed the swift destruction of their beloved church. Longtime African American parishioner Pete Adler pulled a life-size crucifix from the burning church as the fire department chaplain rescued vessels containing the Blessed Sacrament. "The devout Negroes [on the scene]," reported the *Chicago Tribune*, "broke into a hymn as the priest reappeared, opened his slicker and displayed the sacrament, which he had carried under the garment."[2] Two hundred firemen—including Chicago's all-black

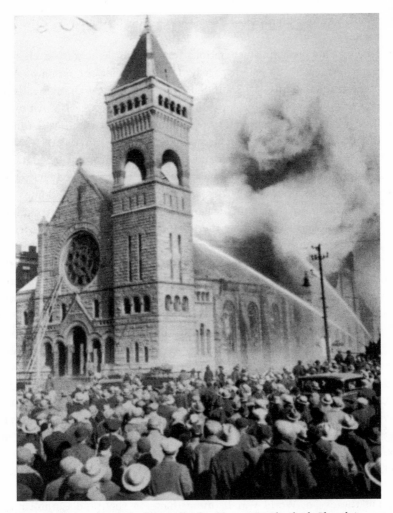

Fig. 1.1. Onlookers watch firefighters battle a blaze at St. Elizabeth Church in 1930. African Americans had taken over the parish from Irish Americans six years earlier. (Archdiocese of Chicago's Joseph Cardinal Bernardin Archives and Records Center.)

Engine Company 21—battled the consuming blaze in frigid weather, but for naught. The edifice collapsed after three hours of futile firefighting.[3]

Just a few years earlier mostly Irish Americans lived in the parish, but now St. Elizabeth's nearly four thousand parishioners were almost all African Americans. On Sunday, two days after the fire, many "former [Irish American] parishioners came as in a pilgrimage to view the ruins of their

old parish church."[4] Both blacks and whites mourned the loss of their sacred space.

During the preceding generation, remarkable demographic changes
had transformed St. Elizabeth parish. The large-scale migration of African Americans to Chicago's South Side from 1910 to 1930 dramatically altered the racial composition of the once Irish American parish. Although
most African American migrants were Protestants, a significant minority like Dickerson were Roman Catholics. In the late nineteenth century,
Chicago's black Catholics worshiped similarly to European immigrants.
Like Poles, Italians, and Bohemians, who made up segregated "national"
parishes, blacks gathered in their own separate church—St. Monica's at
36th and Dearborn streets.[5] Chicago's black parish—like other national
parishes that claimed pastors of their own ethnicity—boasted an African
American pastor for a time in the 1890s.

However, as the great influx of African Americans arrived from the
South around World War I, archdiocesan officials abandoned the national
parish model for a missionary approach. Irish American St. Elizabeth
took over the "mission" of nearby St. Monica's, and a religious order of
white priests trained to work in Africa and Asia assumed control. White
religious sisters committed to serving African Americans in the United
States operated the parish school. St. Elizabeth's numbers swelled in the
1920s thanks to the arrival of black Catholic migrants and a large number
of conversions. As Chicago's African American population grew, more and
more residents moved to neighborhoods farther south and west, leaving
those parishes adjacent to St. Elizabeth's with few white inhabitants. In
the early 1930s, Cardinal George Mundelein turned over two more South
Side parishes—Corpus Christi and St. Anselm—to religious orders to run
as missions for African Americans.

On the eve of World War II, more than ten thousand Catholics belonged to the three black parishes.[6] Each parish ran its own grade school,
while St. Elizabeth and Corpus Christi (after 1944) operated coeducational
high schools. Although they began as missionary parish spin-offs, the African American churches flourished during the decade of the Great Depression. Like their Euro-American counterparts, they worked to meet the
spiritual, educational, and social needs of their neighborhoods, and though
racially segregated, they functioned like other Catholic communities
throughout the city. They offered the sacraments of Baptism, Reconciliation, Confirmation, and Marriage. They comforted the sick and buried
the dead. Their parishioners filled large church buildings on Sundays to re-

ceive the Eucharist and attended parochial schools during the week. Like Euro-American immigrants before them, a significant number of African American migrants used urban Catholicism's resources to create a home for themselves. More specifically, between World War I and World War II, St. Elizabeth, Corpus Christi, and St. Anselm became the home of black Catholicism in Chicago. In time, they also served as the nucleus of African American participation in the CYO.

FROM NATIONAL PARISH TO MISSION FIELD: JIM CROW COMES TO CATHOLIC CHICAGO

By one account, Chicago's first African American Catholics were James and Eliza Armstrong, who arrived to the city with their daughter Rosa during the Civil War.[7] By the early 1880s, a small number of African American Catholics were worshipping in the basement of Old St. Mary's, an Irish American church at 9th Street and Wabash Avenue, just south of downtown. When the St. Augustine Society held a bazaar in 1882 to raise money for a place of worship that African Americans could call their own, an Irish American woman, Annie O'Neill, donated the substantial sum of $10,000 to begin construction on a church at 36th and Dearborn streets.[8] In addition, Archbishop Patrick Feehan donated another $1,000 to the cause. Chicago's nascent black Catholic community had formed a distinct parish community by 1885.[9] In 1889, the parish hired an African American contractor to construct a church building. Five years later, a Franciscan priest dedicated the still unfinished gray stone church to St. Monica, mother of St. Augustine, the North African bishop of Hippo.[10]

St. Monica's was distinctive for having as its pastor Augustus Tolton, the nation's first recognized African American priest.[11] Earlier in the nineteenth century, three Healy brothers—the sons of an Irish American slaveholder and mulatto mother—were prominent Catholic clergymen, but their light skin allowed them to pass for white.[12] Tolton, on the other hand, faced overt racism his entire life. Born in 1854 to Roman Catholic slaves in Brush Creek, Missouri, he grew up with his mother and two siblings as a free black and a Catholic in Quincy, Illinois. His mother and a German American priest supported his vocation to the priesthood. When Catholic seminaries throughout the United States refused to accept him, he journeyed to Rome and studied at the Sacred College of the Propaganda, where he was ordained in 1886. Tolton requested a transfer from his home diocese of Quincy after encountering racial hostility from white Catholics

Fig. 1.2. Rev. Augustus Tolton, the first recognized black priest in the United
States, was pastor of St. Monica's African American national parish, 1889–1897.
(Archdiocese of Chicago's Joseph Cardinal Bernardin Archives and Records Center.)

(including fellow clergymen). In 1889, Archbishop Feehan appointed the young African American priest to organize and lead the black Catholics of Chicago.[13]

Tolton fulfilled the traditional roles of an ethnic national pastor. African American Catholics looked up with great pride to this dynamic leader from their own race. As the only black parish priest in the United States, Tolton attracted attention far beyond the South Side. He supplemented regular Sunday collections through outside speaking engagements because his parishioners were small in number (thirty-five families) and of modest means.[14] No geographical boundaries defined the parish, since St. Monica's served blacks throughout Chicago. With its charismatic pastor and racially defined parishioners, St. Monica's fit the primary characteristics of a national parish.[15] Unfortunately, the small but growing faith community took a heavy blow on 9 July 1897.

On that midsummer day, Tolton died of heatstroke at the young age of forty-three. Suddenly, the leader of black Catholics in the United States and ethnic pastor of St. Monica's national parish was gone. Without any other black clergy, nearby St. Elizabeth Church assumed administrative control of St. Monica's. Priests from St. Elizabeth offered Mass, but activity in the church diminished, and attendance by black Catholics declined. Finally, eleven years after Tolton's death, St. Monica's received its own pastor, Rev. John Morris, a white Chicago archdiocesan priest previously stationed at St. Catherine of Siena Church on the West Side.[16] Morris's leadership improved conditions at the neglected parish, and, by 1910, nearly six hundred families worshipped at St. Monica's.[17]

In 1912, the Sisters of the Blessed Sacrament, anticipating the first great migration of African Americans, began addressing the educational needs of black children on the South Side. Katharine Drexel founded this order of white nuns in 1889 to minister to the spiritual and physical needs of American Indians and African Americans.[18] In September 1913, the Sisters of the Blessed Sacrament opened a school in the former horse stables of the 8th Regiment Armory at 37th Street and Wabash Avenue.[19] By 1915, the school boasted an enrollment of 198 pupils, with 7 nuns and one lay African American teaching.[20]

Before the mass migrations of World War I, when relatively few African Americans lived in Chicago, the primarily Irish American leadership of the archdiocese anticipated a favorable future for black Catholics, one that included integration into mainstream society. A buoyant article in the archdiocesan newspaper, the *New World*, called for white Catholics to take part in the process of assimilating African American migrants to the urban North: "To those who would like to see Africans in the process of becoming right living American citizens through the amalgamating agency of the Catholic Church, let them attend Mass at St. Monica's Church . . . and visit St. Monica's School. Such visitors cannot but be impressed with the fact that in its Christian interpretation the word 'brother' cannot be limited by race or color."[21] Ironically, these "Africans" were already American citizens with ancestors in the United States long before the arrival of most European Catholics. Despite their condescension, church leaders in 1913 saw great potential for the integration of Chicago's small African American population into Catholicism.

With the outbreak of World War I, however, thousands of African Americans began arriving weekly to work in industry. Over the next five years, this migration brought tens of thousands of African Americans to the Midwest's industrial center.[22] The massive influx of blacks prompted white Chicagoans to label their presence the "Negro problem." Likewise, the archdiocese of Chicago confronted its own difficulties brought on by the arrival of large numbers of African Americans. A 1917 New World article announced, "The whole city is obliged to take a hand in the solving of a problem that belongs to the whole city." Despite the "Negro problem," church leadership confidently predicted African American migrants from the South would embrace Catholicism: "The number of conversions will be swelled considerably when the means are provided for spreading the effective work of St. Monica's."[23]

During the migration, Rev. George Mundelein of New York became Chicago's third archbishop. Mundelein, a political ally of fellow New Yorker Franklin Roosevelt, fostered lofty aspirations for the American Catholic Church. His "Americanization plan" called for breaking up the national parish system in favor of territorial parishes. Geographic boundaries, not ethnicity, would define parish life. Mundelein disliked national parishes for two reasons. First, their insularity and homogeneity isolated them from the larger culture, thereby adding credence to the charge that Catholics held foreign allegiances and were unpatriotic. Second, ethnic pastors, often from religious orders, held the locus of power at the parish level, denying Mundelein strong influence over Chicago's Catholics.[24]

Mundelein also felt pressured by the dramatic demographic changes in his archdiocese resulting from African American migration. The small, segregated Black Belt centered around 35th and State streets could no longer contain the growing number of African Americans. Many white Chicagoans feared the burgeoning black population would spill over into other parts of the city. Rev. James Callaghan, pastor of St. Malachy's in the

2200 block of West Washington Boulevard, for example, expressed his opposition to the archbishop about changing the parish into a black church
in order to augment overburdened St. Monica's. The pastor argued that
turning his parish over to African Americans was impractical, because of
its large size and the scarcity of black Catholics in the area. "I don't know
how many Colored Catholics may be on the west side," wrote Father Callaghan, "but there are [only] five or six in this parish."[25] Mundelein chose
not to transform St. Malachy's into a black parish at that time. Rather, five
months later, he announced a policy that resulted in the effective segregation of Chicago's African American Catholics into one parish.

In October 1917, Archbishop Mundelein sought the assistance of Rev.
Adolph Burgmer, provincial director of the Society of the Divine Word.
Founded in Germany during the 1870s, the Society of the Divine Word
missionaries were a religious order of men dedicated to spreading Catholicism to non-Christian populations, especially in Africa and Asia. Their
North American headquarters were located in Techny, Illinois, just north
of Chicago.[26] Mundelein revealed to Burgmer his plan to change how the
archdiocese ministered to African Americans by transferring St. Monica's
pastor, Father Morris, to another parish and assigning "the Mission of
St. Monica" to the care of the Society of the Divine Word.

In addition to changing the leadership of St. Monica's, Mundelein forbade whites from attending services and receiving the sacraments at the
parish:

> I desire St. Monica's to be reserved entirely for the colored Catholics
> of Chicago and particularly of the South Side; all other Catholics of
> whatsoever race or color are to be requested not to intrude. It is, of
> course, understood that I have no intention of excluding colored Cath-
> olics from any of the other churches in the diocese, and particularly
> if they live in another part of the city, but simply of excluding from
> St. Monica's all but the colored Catholics.[27]

In reality, white churches in Chicago, whether Catholic or Protestant, did
not usually welcome African Americans. The *Chicago Defender* addressed
regular occurrences of Sunday morning discrimination in its pages. In one
political cartoon, a white minister, presiding over an all-white congregation, says, "Sexton, will you ask that colored gentleman in the back seat
what he wants here." The congregants turn and look menacingly at the
African American visitor, who is then forced to leave. The *Defender* asked,
"Since all of us serve the same God, why is it that a black face is unwel-

come in a church conducted by whites, and a man is forced to go miles out of his way to find a place to worship?"[28]

Mundelein justified his policy to Burgmer in three ways. First, two churches near St. Monica's provided white Catholics with the services that they needed. Second, the small church was increasingly overcrowded. Finally, because of the work of Society of the Divine Word and Sisters of the Blessed Sacrament missionaries, the growing black Catholic population no longer needed as much outside support from white Catholics in the archdiocese. The prelate went on to note that African American men "are nearly all at work and obtaining a much more adequate wage or salary." He stated that black Catholics were now in a position to support their own church and school. "Scattering" African Americans in parishes across the city, the archbishop argued, was not in their best interest.[29]

Mundelein placed the ultimate financial responsibility on the shoulders of Chicago's African American Catholics themselves. He wrote that it was their responsibility to make sacrifices, like other Catholics, in order to pay off the parish debt and build up the school. "If they do,—if we see good will, their ready response, their generous cooperation, then this will simply be the beginning of what we are prepared to establish for our Colored Catholics," he told Burgmer. "Should they fail, I would be disappointed and sadly mistaken in my judgment of them, and a parish for them would die like a poorly nourished infant. But when I consider their many good qualities, their peaceful family life, their love for their children, their strong religious spirit, I fail to see how they can fail."[30]

Confident that black Catholics could financially support St. Monica's on their own, Mundelein nevertheless acknowledged the racial prejudice facing African Americans. Yet, despite his position as head of Chicago's Catholic Church, he avoided responsibility for taking on the issue of racial discrimination: "nor will I say anything as to the justice or injustice of it . . . [for] I am convinced that I am quite powerless to change it, for I believe the underlying reasons to be more economic than social." According to Mundelein, African American Catholics bore a financial disadvantage yet were solely responsible for the economic viability of their parish. The archbishop went on to give two examples of economic success stories from impoverished peoples: blacks in New York City's Harlem, which he compared to the South Side's Black Belt; and white European immigrants who came to Chicago with little but built up their own parish communities. He believed that if they succeeded so could Chicago's black migrants.[31]

In essence, Mundelein turned over responsibility for African American Catholics to specialists from the Society of the Divine Word and Sisters of the Blessed Sacrament. At a time when he was Americanizing other parishes throughout Chicago, attempting to organize them territorially with local diocesan priests directly responsible to him, Mundelein gave control of St. Monica's to missionaries trained to work in foreign lands. In some ways, Chicago's black Catholics took on the status of the "alien peoples" of Asia and Africa. Although they worked, paid taxes, and voted like other Chicago Catholics, their church became a mission, not a church. The mission status marked a reversal of fortune from the heady days of the 1890s when an African American pastor led his own parish. Mundelein's order to white Catholics, telling them to stay away from St. Monica's, directly contradicted the *New World* article of four years earlier inviting white Catholics to come to Mass at St. Monica's. White Catholics, who used to attend services there, were no longer invited to integrate African Americans into the church. Mundelein had, in effect, introduced the color line into Chicago Catholicism.

The *Chicago Defender* quickly denounced Mundelein's new policy. The black newspaper claimed that the decision to ban whites from St. Monica's indicated that "Jim Crowism is worming its ways into Catholic circles in this city."[32] In an editorial titled "Big Step Backward," the *Defender* lamented the loss of the old St. Monica's that was composed of "men and women, black and white, who knelt to worship the same Master," a church where "colors mingled as in the rainbow."[33] Mundelein's claim that Catholics were welcome at all Chicago churches did not carry much weight, according to the editorial, because blacks knew that their children could not attend those parish schools.

Ironically, some African Americans approved of the new archdiocesan policy. After reading a copy of Mundelein's letter to Burgmer in the *New World*, Z. Withers, editor of the *Pullman Porters Review*, wrote to the archbishop. "While I as well as our staff are [sic] prodiscents [Protestants]," he commented, "never in my life time have we heard or read of such a beautiful tribute as you pay the colored race."[34] Perhaps Mundelein's call for black financial independence attracted the Pullman Porters. Most of St. Monica's African American parishioners, however, did not share the railcar workers' assessment of the new policy. Mundelein's decision to isolate Chicago's African American Catholic community devastated them. In response to Mundelein's guidelines, Chicago's black Catholic community raised their voices in protest.

The absence of African American clergy increased black Catholics' dependence on lay leadership. Joseph Madden led a group of St. Monica's parishioners calling themselves the "Colored Catholics of Chicago" against the archbishop's policy. In a virulent letter to Mundelein, Madden wrote that for blacks, "who stand erect in the panoply of their rights and privileges as righteous and self-respecting, law-abiding Catholics . . . the new policy is diametrically opposed to all real progress of faith." Moreover, he argued the policy would encourage racial prejudice and cause suffering for St. Monica's African American parishioners.[35] Black Catholics believed that the new policy would destroy many of the gains they had made over the previous thirty years in Chicago.

On 7 December 1917, a little over a month after the announcement of Mundelein's new policy, the Colored Catholics of Chicago sent a formal protest to the archbishop. The four-page, single-spaced, typed petition clearly made known their extreme dismay and disappointment over the change and appealed for the policy's reversal. Eighty-one individuals signed the memorandum with an attached note claiming that many others "share in and endorse the sentiment and protest of this appeal."[36]

The petitioners found themselves "in stupefied wonder that so uncharitable a proposition should emanate from the Chancery Office of the great Archdiocese of Chicago." The angry black parishioners wrote:

> As a bolt from the blue has come the announcement of your "new policy." The children of the bond woman shall no longer kneel at the altar with the heirs of the free. The holy wafer of the tabernacle shall rest in solemn benediction only on the tongues of Afric's [sic] sons and daughters; and proscribed and forbidden they alone shall enter into the sanctuary over whose portals is written in blazing letters of shame "SEGREGATED."[37]

The protest fell on deaf ears. The day after Christmas, Mundelein's chancellor, Bishop Edward Hoban, wrote to Madden. Hoban firmly stated, "The Archbishop bids me to say the case is closed and he desires no further correspondence on the subject." The chancellor assured Madden that Mundelein carefully considered the change in policy before acting. And in a condescending sentence, Hoban wrote that the archbishop "sought and obtained the views of ecclesiastics who were engaged in zealous work among the colored people long before many of your signatories were born."[38] The petitioners defeated, the Society of the Divine Word moved into what was now the *mission* of St. Monica's.

The new policy also attracted attention from outside of Chicago. In a letter to Hoban, Rev. Stephen Theobold, a black Catholic priest from

Fig. 1.3. Construction began on St. Monica's Church in the 1890s, but a proposed bell tower was never built. The incomplete edifice at 36th and Dearborn streets epitomized the shift in status from national parish to African American mission. (Archdiocese of Chicago's Joseph Cardinal Bernardin Archives and Records Center.)

St. Paul, Minnesota, reported the public relations damage that Mundelein's new policy created during its first weeks in effect. One of only a few black priests in the nation, Father Theobold asserted that black Protestant ministers constantly looked for indications of racist practices in the Catholic Church. Extensive religious and secular presses allowed black clergy to reach millions of African Americans. Theobold wrote that Mundelein's published letter "was immediately construed as nothing short of 'jim-crowing' [sic] the negro . . . and within a fortnight the negro [sic] press from the Atlantic to the Pacific announced the fact to their readers."[39] Mundelein refused to budge.

Racial tensions continued to grow during the late 1910s. Less than 2 years after St. Monica's change in policy, Chicago's worst case of race-related violence rocked the city. On Sunday afternoon, 27 July 1919, hostilities broke out on the South Side, along a Lake Michigan beach between 26th and 29th streets. In the midst of a stone-throwing barrage, Eugene Williams, an African American youth, drowned. Police refused to arrest a white man accused by blacks of killing the boy and instead arrested an African American man. The incident triggered a series of events leading to full-blown rioting throughout the South Side and Loop.[40] Over the course of 13 days in late July and early August, the Chicago race riot of 1919 led to the deaths of 38 people—23 blacks and 15 whites. Fighting injured an additional 537 individuals, including 342 blacks, 178 whites, and 17 persons of unknown racial background.[41] Several factors contributed to the violence. Thousands of African Americans, who migrated to Chicago during the World War I industrial buildup, competed with whites for scarce jobs in a depressed postwar economy. In addition, the racial segregation of Chicago's African American population into the strictly circumscribed Black Belt led to severe overcrowding. Finally, black men who fought in Europe to protect "freedom and democracy," returned to the United States as "New Negroes," expecting greater opportunities and more respect.

The horrific violence brought into sharp relief the level of racial discord within Chicago. Some of the heaviest fighting took place around St. Monica's. At least six deaths occurred within one block of the church at 36th and Dearborn streets.[42] Historically, the Catholic Church avoided the South's "Negro problem," because most American Catholics settled in the Northeast and Midwest rather than in the South, where the vast majority of African Americans lived prior to World War I. The events during the summer of 1919, however, made clear that race relations were a problem for the North as well. Later that year when the first annual meeting of the American Catholic hierarchy took place in Washington, DC, the church could no longer ignore the issue. In the resulting pastoral letter on postwar social reconstruction, the bishops condemned racial hatred, calling for the loving inclusion of blacks into the Catholic Church. Yet, historian Cyprian Davis writes that the letter's "failure to speak plainly, emphatically, and in detail about the racial strife of 1919 was a serious omission. Even worse was the patronizing and gratuitous reference to blacks' learning from 'their teachers the lesson of Christian virtue.'"[43]

Locally, the archdiocese's *New World* admonished African Americans for devoting their energies to ending racial segregation and instead challenged them to do more for themselves. In an editorial four months after the 1919 race riot, the Catholic newspaper noted that African Americans were making strides economically but that they still found themselves socially isolated. The editorial placed the blame for this social disconnection on Chicago's blacks themselves:

> If the prosperity . . . were given a social direction, and an earnest endeavor made to improve the present area occupied by the colored people of Chicago, there would be no racial strife. . . . Instead of battering against the wall of white determination that the races shall be kept distinct [the African American] should make an earnest endeavor to better his physical and moral surroundings.[44]

Archbishop Mundelein believed that St. Monica's mission was one such way to help blacks help themselves. Following the model of nineteenth-century European immigrant groups in Chicago, he thought that African Americans needed to build up their own community from within and earn the right to participate as equals in civic and church affairs. For Mundelein, segregation was a means for African Americans to get their house in order.

The archbishop's position evoked Booker T. Washington's "Atlanta Compromise." In 1895, the black southern leader urged African Americans to accept their socially inferior position and work to achieve economic independence through vocational training. Washington's philosophical rival, W. E. B. Du Bois, on the other hand, believed that civil rights and social equality were essential to improving conditions for African Americans. Like Washington, Mundelein argued that blacks first needed to "prove themselves" to the white world before reaping the benefits of social equality. Once African Americans demonstrated merit, so went the argument, whites would welcome them into the larger society.[45]

After World War I, St. Monica's congregation expanded as more and more African Americans moved to Chicago. The still uncompleted church building at 36th and Dearborn streets failed to accommodate the parish's increasing numbers. In particular, the Sisters of the Blessed Sacrament needed more classroom space for their school. St. Monica's neighboring parish eight blocks to the south, St. Elizabeth, conversely, lost thousands of members to white flight, as Irish Americans moved farther south and west away from the Black Belt. Consequently, in 1922, Sisters of the Blessed Sacrament missionaries began conducting grade school and high school classes for African American children in St. Elizabeth's school building.[46] Because the prevailing practice of racial segregation prohibited black and white children from attending school together, St. Elizabeth's white high school students transferred to St. James High School at 29th Street and South Wabash Avenue, and the Sisters of Mercy taught St. Elizabeth's remaining white grade school students in the former Sheridan (and Swift) Club on the southwest corner of 41st Street and Michigan Avenue. In less than a generation, St. Elizabeth experienced a swift transformation from a middle-class, Irish American congregation to a working-class, African American parish.[47]

For forty years, Irish Americans on the South Side had lived in the vicinity of St. Elizabeth. Rev. Daniel Riordan organized the parish in 1881 and the Sisters of Mercy, an Irish-dominated order of nuns, opened a school there in 1885. In 1892, Archbishop Feehan dedicated a magnificent church

building on the northeast corner of 41st Street and Wabash Avenue; this
was the structure destroyed by fire in 1930. In the last decade of the nineteenth century and first decade of the twentieth, the numbers of upwardly
mobile St. Elizabeth parishioners grew rapidly. Their wealth allowed
St. Elizabeth in 1903 to become only the second parish in the archdiocese
to pay off the entire debt on its church building.

Yet, despite these successes, Father Riordan's death in February 1922
epitomized the demise of St. Elizabeth's Irish American community.
During the previous five years, St. Elizabeth's traditional parishioners—
middle-class and wealthy Irish Catholics like meat packer Michael Cudahy
—left the area as blacks moved into the neighborhood. While the all-white
St. Elizabeth became extremely underutilized, the all-black St. Monica's
became overcrowded. A month after Riordan's death, Society of the Divine Word provincial Peter Janser informed Mundelein that "300 [African
American] children had to be turned away" from St. Monica's, eight blocks
north of St. Elizabeth, because the "school and church are absolutely in-
sufficient for the present needs."[48] Finally, in December 1924, the archdiocese transferred St. Elizabeth's to the Society of the Divine Word to run
as an African American parish. In 1926, St. Monica's closed, completing
the consolidation.[49]

By the mid-1920s, thousands of blacks made St. Elizabeth's parish
space their home, as descendants of enslaved Africans learned and worshipped in sacred spaces built by Irish Americans two generations earlier.
St. Elizabeth's 1925 annual report counted 2,500 parishioners—almost all
African Americans and many new to Catholicism. In the previous year
alone, 203 persons converted to Catholicism, and nearly 45 percent of
weddings were "mixed" marriages (i.e., unions between Catholics and
non-Catholics).[50] Many conversions began in the parish school, which required students to learn Catholic catechism and parents to attend weekly
evening courses on church doctrine. In one 1926 conversion class, for example, 96 children from St. Elizabeth School and 14 children from public
schools, along with 54 adults, entered the Catholic Church.[51] Under the
guidance of the Sisters of the Blessed Sacrament, the grade school's enrollment grew quickly. Between 1925 and 1928, the enrollment doubled from
505 to 1,016 students.[52]

In October 1926, Cardinal Mundelein came to St. Elizabeth to confirm
four hundred African American converts to Catholicism. St. Monica's
had merged with St. Elizabeth two years earlier. The prelate surveyed his
audience and said, "At a recent meeting of the Catholic bishops of this
country I told them that nowhere in the world today was there a richer

or more promising field for labor than with the colored people of the United States."[53] Understanding the demographic changes taking place in his archdiocese, Mundelein reached out to large numbers of African Americans.

Black Catholics desired the independence and self-governance of a national parish but not the isolation from society at large. Mundelein correctly understood that African American Catholics needed their own parish for a sense of racial solidarity, but forced segregation undermined the national parish's ability to empower its members. Black Catholics found St. Monica's attractive because of its history of black clerical and lay leadership. When Mundelein assigned priests and nuns trained as missionaries to the parish, black leadership took a backseat. St. Monica's was no longer one of several proud national parishes in the Chicago archdiocese that were considered distinct but equal. The change in policy branded St. Monica's and later St. Elizabeth as "different" in a pejorative way.[54] Nevertheless, St. Monica's parishioners laid foundations for black Catholic lay involvement; by the 1920s St. Elizabeth was the center of African American Catholic life in Chicago.

CORPUS CHRISTI: FROM "LACE CURTAIN" IRISH TO BLACK METROPOLIS

Corpus Christi Roman Catholic Church stood ten blocks south and four blocks east of St. Elizabeth in the Grand Boulevard neighborhood, just a few blocks north of Washington Park, which encompassed more than 350 acres on the South Side. Grand Boulevard, bounded by 39th Street on the north, Cottage Grove Avenue on the east, 63rd Street on the south, and Wentworth Avenue on the west, was home to thousands of native-born Protestants, German Jews, and Irish Catholics between 1890 and 1920. In the years immediately following World War I, however, the neighborhood underwent swift racial change. By 1930 the community was the heart of the South Side's Black Belt, later known as Bronzeville. This dramatic change in racial composition significantly affected Grand Boulevard's church communities, including Corpus Christi.[55]

At the turn of the twentieth century, wealthy and middle-class Irish Americans established Corpus Christi parish. The neighborhood's most elegant street was Grand Boulevard itself (later renamed South Parkway, and in 1968, Martin Luther King Drive). Chicago's "monied men" built an impressive wall of mansions along this "gold coast" during the 1890s. In 1901, Archbishop Feehan permitted residents to construct a chapel in the 4900 block of Grand Boulevard for the neighborhood's growing Catholic population. A dedication ceremony took place on 5 June—the feast of Corpus Christi—and workers broke ground on 22 August. In September, the Sisters of Mercy began operating a parish school. Since no school building existed, they made use of facilities at St. Agatha Academy, a day and boarding school operated by the Sisters of Mercy at 49th Street and Evans Avenue, about seven blocks east of Corpus Christi. The parish grew quickly, and in 1910 the school moved into the Corpus Christi church building on Grand Boulevard, where more than five hundred children attended classes.[56]

In 1916, fifteen years after its founding, the parish constructed an impressive church complex fitting the elegance and refinement of the surrounding neighborhood. On the feast of Corpus Christi, Archbishop Mundelein dedicated the new Renaissance-style church built from the renowned limestone of Bedford, Indiana. The elaborate structure boasted Italian-made altars, stained-glass windows from Munich, and oil paintings and murals on the walls. A three-story rectory, fountain, and school graced the spacious grounds as well. The archbishop told those ambitious parishioners assembled that "nothing is too good for God's house. That is why we bring from afar marble and gold and precious stones to build an altar and to fashion a tabernacle; we steal the colors of the rainbow to imprison them in the glass of windows and in the pictures of the walls." Yet, despite these physical signs of permanency, the Corpus Christi community faced an uncertain future. A commemorative parish history recalled, "Already before the church was completed, the affluent parish was 'threatened' by signs described by the press as 'impending danger,' 'ominous future,' meaning Blacks arriving from the South in ever-increasing numbers were moving into the district."[57]

Eight years later, most of Mundelein's audience had fled Corpus Christi. As African Americans moved into the Grand Boulevard neighborhood, the once confident and prosperous white Corpus Christi parishioners fell prey to perceived racial threats and abandoned the community in which they had invested so much. In 1924, the archdiocese assigned Rev. Frank O'Brien to the church with the mandate to "save Corpus Christi parish for the people who built it." He sought the assistance of St. Elizabeth's pastor, Rev. Joseph Eckert, a missionary from the Society of the Divine Word. O'Brien and Eckert came to the conclusion that Corpus Christi Church should minister to African Americans. Mundelein, however, refused their request, instructing them to continue directing all blacks to St. Elizabeth. The policy proved futile. Between 1924 and 1928, most of

Corpus Christi's remaining white members left, and the parish became a shadow of its former self. A 1931 article in the *New World* lamented the rapid demographic changes in the parish, "Located in the fashionable section, Corpus Christi was attended by influential and cultured people. Then came the [First World] War and the importation of negro [*sic*] laborers. Almost overnight the great parish power declined. One by one the families moved away, their homes to be taken by negroes [*sic*]."[58] In its early years, more than two thousand members worshipped at Corpus Christi, which offered five Masses on Sundays; by 1928, fewer than a hundred persons attended Sunday Mass, and only twenty-one children registered for school. The Sisters of Mercy closed the school in 1928, and O'Brien resigned as pastor in 1929.[59]

African American families continued to move into Corpus Christi parish throughout the 1920s, a decade in which Chicago's black population increased by 114 percent.[60] With a housing stock less dense and better constructed than in the blocks around St. Elizabeth, the Grand Boulevard neighborhood ranked best in "desirability" for African Americans on the South Side.[61] Although Corpus Christi officially remained a "white" church during the neighborhood's racial transformation, a few intrepid blacks attended services. An African American woman recalled her mother going to Mass at Corpus Christi in the 1920s. "When mom first started coming here it was mostly white, and they didn't want her here," she said. "But mom said, 'I don't care what they say,' and she went right down in front every Sunday. We've been coming here ever since."[62] By the end of the decade, black residents almost completely replaced whites residing in the area.

The dramatic racial change in the neighborhood led Mundelein to act in the spring of 1929. He called the Franciscan provincial to his office and invited the religious order to take charge of Corpus Christi. Mundelein's offer required the friars to assume the parish debt and convert the school building into a retreat house. The Franciscans agreed and opened a retreat center at Corpus Christi in the fall of 1929. The archdiocese advertised all-male weekend retreats at Corpus Christi as "a most invigorating vacation for the soul and a wonderful rest for the body."[63] In those early days of the Great Depression, however, the retreat house for laymen struggled and finally closed in the summer of 1930. The Franciscans managed to keep the church operating for another year, but its continued existence as a white parish proved untenable. Finally, Eckert convinced Mundelein that St. Elizabeth alone could not accommodate the South Side's black Catholic population.[64]

With permission from Mundelein, the Franciscans began ministering to African Americans in the summer of 1932 under the leadership
of Rev. Nicholas Christoffel. The friars held a two-week mission in September, organizing their first convert class of twenty-five members. Since
no formal school existed, they used parish classroom space for youth and
adult religious education. After its underutilization for several years, large
numbers of African American churchgoers now started attending Corpus
Christi Church on Sundays and participated in parish activities throughout the week.[65]

In November 1932, 40 African American laymen organized a local
chapter of the national Holy Name Society at Corpus Christi. They elected
officers and formed working groups, including a CYO committee.[66] The
Franciscan friars baptized a second convert class in December, and two
weeks later, 235 children and adult converts received confirmation.[67] For
the first time in a decade, Corpus Christi was growing, again a vibrant
church community working to meet the spiritual and social needs of the
surrounding neighborhood. Still, quality education remained an urgent
need for African American families.

Father Christoffel invited the Sisters of St. Francis of the Holy Family from Dubuque, Iowa, to operate the grade school at Corpus Christi.
The order of religious women agreed, and seven Franciscan sisters arrived in Chicago on 10 July 1933. These young women, mostly daughters
of German American farmers from Iowa, began teaching in the heart of
Chicago's Black Belt without any previous experience working in urban
areas or educating African Americans. Sister Dominica Wienecke became
the new school's first principal. In addition, Rev. Clement Martin replaced
Father Christoffel as pastor. On 5 September 1933, Father Martin opened
Corpus Christi School with an enrollment of 270 children. Within a few
weeks, the enrollment jumped to 315, and 2 additional Franciscan sisters
joined the staff. Students paid tuition of 25 cents per week.[68] Many of the
children were not Catholic, but several converted before graduating. The
school did not require them to become Catholic, but daily instruction in
Catholic theology and mandatory Mass attendance undoubtedly influenced students. In its second year, enrollment grew by over 60 percent to
492. The sharp increase in demand exceeded material and personnel capa-
bilities, forcing the school to turn away students.[69]

The Franciscan nuns originally lived within the school building in an
area dubbed the "Sisters Quarters." In 1934, however, the parish purchased
a nearby apartment building, which was converted to a convent. This
move opened up additional space for 5 new classrooms, allowing more

children to attend. Even in the midst of the Depression, the black Catholic school continued to grow. By the 1935–1936 academic year, Corpus Christi boasted 18 teachers and 678 students.[70] In 1936, 2 more classrooms were built for the 780 students now enrolled. By the end of the decade, approximately 800 students attended Corpus Christi.[71] About 25 percent of the students were non-Catholics, and many of the rest were recent converts.[72] By the late 1930s, the renewed—now African American—parish offered 6 Sunday Masses.[73]

In less than a decade, a sharp demographic shift completely transformed Corpus Christi's parish. Once the home of Chicago's South Side "lace curtain" Irish, the parish rapidly became the center of African American life in Chicago—the "Black Metropolis." Just a few blocks north of Corpus Christi's majestic twin bell towers, the famed intersection of 47th Street and South Parkway bustled with activity. Sociologists Drake and Cayton capture the neighborhood's "city within a city" quality:

> Stand on the corner of the Black Belt—at Chicago's 47th St. and South Parkway. Around you swirls a continuous eddy of faces—black, brown, olive, yellow, and white. Soon you will realize that this is not "just another neighborhood" in Midwest Metropolis. Glance at the newsstand on the corner. You will see the Chicago dailies—the *Tribune*, the *Times*, the *Herald-American*, the *News*, the *Sun*. But you will also find a number of weeklies headlining the activities of Negroes—Chicago's *Defender*, *Bee*, *News-Ledger*, and *Metropolitan News*, the Pittsburgh *Courier*, and a number of others. In the nearby drugstore colored clerks are bustling about. (They are seldom seen in other neighborhoods.) In most of the other stores, too, there are colored salespeople, although a white proprietor or manager usually looms in the offing. In the offices around you, colored doctors, dentists, and lawyers go about their duties. And a brown-skinned policeman saunters along swinging his club and glaring sternly at the urchins who dodge in and out among the shoppers. . . . On a spring or summer day this spot, "47th and South Park," is the urban equivalent of a village square. In fact, Black Metropolis has a saying, "If you're trying to find a certain Negro in Chicago, stand at the corner of 47th and South Park long enough and you're bound to see him."

Drake and Cayton note that the prominence of the approximately five hundred churches was one of the most striking features of the neighborhood. Corpus Christi was a "major community institution," and the "largest colored Catholic church in the country."[74] Church parishioners worked, shopped, and relaxed like thousands of others in Black Metropolis, the economic and cultural center of African American life in Chicago from the 1930s through the 1950s. And as the Black Belt expanded farther south, yet another Catholic parish experienced racial succession.

ST. ANSELM: FROM STUDS LONIGAN TO JESSE BINGA

Two miles south of Corpus Christi stood St. Anselm Church, just off Washington Park. Irish Americans established the parish in 1909 and promptly built a simple church building on the north side of 61st Street between Michigan and Indiana Avenues. In the fall of 1910, the Sisters of Providence from Indiana began operating a grade school for children from working and middle-class, Irish American families. Over the next fifteen years, St. Anselm's founding pastor, Rev. Michael Gilmartin, ably guided the parish, dreaming of building a new church greater than the Greek Orthodox, Episcopal, and Baptist churches standing within a block of St. Anselm. His dream came true during Advent of 1925, when Archbishop Mundelein blessed a brand-new, $350,000, Romanesque church building at the northeast corner of 61st Street and Michigan Avenue. The impressive structure included seventeen stained-glass windows from Germany, an altar rail and pulpit decorated with inlaid mosaic, and three altars sculpted from Italian marble.[75]

Despite this substantial investment, within five years hardly any Irish Americans remained in the parish as the Black Belt expanded farther south into the Washington Park neighborhood. Again, South Side Catholic space became the scene of racial transition. Sense of place and ownership permeates author James T. Farrell's descriptions of St. Anselm parish and the Washington Park neighborhood. In the Irish American novelist's trilogy *Studs Lonigan*, protagonist William "Studs" Lonigan, along with his family and friends, feels powerful attachments to his parish of "St. Patrick's" (St. Anselm), led by "Father Gilhooley" (Father Gilmartin) but fears the arrival of blacks and Jews to the neighborhood during the 1920s. They hope that their church can resist the "invasion" of African Americans, which transformed the racial makeup of St. Elizabeth and Corpus Christi parishes. Studs fears his turf turning into what he calls a "nigger neighborhood," like the one around St. Elizabeth.[76]

White resistance sometimes took violent forms. Between 1919 and 1920, for example, resentful whites repeatedly bombed the office and home of black Catholic banker and realtor Jesse Binga, because "Binga rented too many flats to Negroes in high-class resident districts."[77] Yet, in spite of white opposition, blacks eventually made Washington Park their own neighborhood and St. Anselm their own sacred space. Binga, a multimillionaire, became a St. Anselm parishioner and generous benefactor.

By the early 1930s, African Americans made up 90 percent of parishioners at St. Anselm. Nonetheless, the struggling school continued to operate as an all-white institution. In the last half of the 1920s, enrollment decreased from 500 to 175 students, "one hundred of whom come from outside the parish."[78] Like its counterparts, St. Elizabeth and Corpus Christi, St. Anselm underwent the transformation from an Irish American to African American parish seemingly overnight.

In June 1932, the archdiocese turned St. Anselm over to the Society of the Divine Word. Cardinal Mundelein believed the missionaries could best serve St. Anselm's growing African American population, just as they did at St. Elizabeth. Father Gilmartin left the parish he founded to become pastor of St. Agnes Church in the Brighton Park neighborhood. St. Elizabeth's pastor, Father Eckert, then became St. Anselm's new pastor.[79]

CATHOLICISM IN THE BLACK METROPOLIS

With the exception of Maryland and Louisiana, African Americans' first large-scale encounter with Catholicism occurred in northern cities during World War I. The American Catholic Church's record of ministry to blacks was relatively scant until the twentieth century.[80] By the early 1930s, however, African American Catholics played a significant role in the life of Chicago's Black Metropolis. The city's three black Catholic churches roughly marked the boundaries of Black Metropolis. At 49th Street and South Parkway, Corpus Christi Church stood only a few blocks from the center of Black Metropolis, while St. Elizabeth and St. Anselm fell within its respective northern and southern boundaries. Drawing on St. Monica's legacy, St. Elizabeth, Corpus Christi, and St. Anselm became home to Chicago's African American Catholics, many of whom converted to Catholicism after migrating from the South.

The encounter between African Americans and Catholicism created problems and opportunities for blacks and church officials alike. Historically an institution of European immigrants, the American Catholic Church struggled in its black ministry. Church officials attempted to address the "Negro problem"—created by widespread racial succession during the 1910s and 1920s in northern urban neighborhoods like Chicago's South Side—by using a missionary approach that did not accept African

Americans as equals. Yet large-scale conversions occurred despite this imbalanced power relationship and the unfamiliarity of Catholicism to most
black migrants. Parochial education, provided by committed women religious, and a coordinated effort to gain converts, organized by missionary
priests, attracted blacks to the "white" church. By the 1920s, significant
numbers of African Americans living in the urban North were Catholic
converts.

The South Side's three all-black parishes demonstrate the approach
taken by the Catholic Church in its ministry to African Americans. As
Irish American churches quickly lost parishioners, Mundelein turned over
their administration to religious orders specializing in missionary work.
These religious orders—the Franciscans, Sisters of the Blessed Sacrament,
and Society of the Divine Word—ministered to recently arrived African
American migrants from the South. Their mission centered on conversion to Catholicism. Working within the confines of racial segregation,
the church did not directly challenge the social and civil inequalities facing blacks in American society during the 1910s and 1920s. Nevertheless,
African Americans used their membership in the Catholic Church to confront racism. Their Catholic connection allowed them to better negotiate
the challenges of a city with a large Euro-American Catholic population.
In the process, Chicago's black Catholic population created a community
that provided the core of African American participation in the city's
Catholic interracial activities of the 1930s and 1940s.

CHAPTER TWO

"We Had Standing": Black and
Catholic in Bronzeville

> During the last ten years an intensive drive by the Roman Catholic
> Church has met with considerable success in Bronzeville.
> —St. Clair Drake and Horace Cayton, *Black Metropolis*

James Williams grew up in Bronzeville during the Great Depression. His father, frequently unemployed, worked for the Works Progress Administration to support Williams, his mother, and three siblings. When the family lacked money for groceries, they relied on the "relief wagon," which delivered government-provided food staples to neighborhood residents. Williams's parents, however, wanted a better life for their children. His father, a milliner by trade, graduated from high school, but his mother's education ended in the sixth grade. Yet, despite financial hardships, Williams and his siblings attended Corpus Christi School because his parents sought out quality educations for their children. Although Williams's great aunt was a "hard rock, hard share" Baptist, she nevertheless informed his parents about the advantages of Catholic education and encouraged them to send their children to Corpus Christi. "Black Catholics back in those days . . . it was something new," recalled Williams. "She had heard the nuns were really disciplinarians, and if you want your child to grow up with a good education and to be well behaved and not get into trouble, send them to a Catholic school." His parents took his great aunt's advice; Williams entered Corpus Christi in 1938. His two sisters and brother attended as well. Once they began school, the children were baptized as Catholics.[1]

The Williams family conversion experience was not unique in Bronzeville during the interwar period, 1919–1941. Hundreds of African American children converted to Catholicism while attending parochial schools at St. Elizabeth, Corpus Christi, and St. Anselm. Often their parents converted as well. Although some of the faithful proudly claimed "cradle Catholic" status, a whole generation of blacks embraced Catholicism after encountering the religion in Bronzeville parishes. The story of African American Catholicism in Chicago, therefore, is largely one of conversion.

ENTERING THE CATHOLIC FOLD

In 1922, the *New World* observed that St. Monica's "unusual number of converts compares most favorably with flourishing mission fields in China or in the East Indies."[2] Like missionaries in foreign lands, white priests in Chicago's Bronzeville baptized and confirmed thousands of African Americans in the Catholic Church during the 1920s and 1930s at St. Monica's, St. Elizabeth, Corpus Christi, and St. Anselm.

With the exception of Catholics from Louisiana, most African Americans who migrated from the South reached Chicago as Protestants. Southern Baptist and African Methodist Episcopal constituted the two most common denominations, but a number of "un-churched" migrants came as well. This name was often a misnomer, because many attended churches in the South that lacked nationwide affiliations. They found themselves without a specific church to attend, therefore, upon arriving in Chicago. Christian denominations, including Catholics, courted these newcomers from the South by offering them material assistance and spiritual comfort. A significant number of migrants began attending Catholic churches and sent their children to parochial schools. Between World War I and World War II, the status of Chicago's African American Catholics continued to be what Albert Raboteau has called a "minority within a minority," but substantial numbers of conversions dramatically increased their membership totals.[3]

The most successful convert-maker among Chicago's African American population was Rev. Joseph Eckert. The German-born member of the Society of the Divine Word served as pastor at St. Elizabeth from 1924 until 1932, when the society assumed administration of St. Anselm. He then led St. Anselm as pastor from 1932 until 1940. Over the course of his years in parish work, Eckert, who became known as the "second Father Tolton," baptized more than four thousand converts, almost all African Americans.[4]

In 1927, Eckert outlined six ways of reaching potentials converts: personal contact, "the lay apostolate," parochial schools, lectures and missions, church services, and prayer.[5] Because most migrants from the Protestant South arrived in Chicago unfamiliar with Catholicism, priests needed to make personal contact with Bronzeville residents if they hoped to attract churchgoers. "We often ridicule Protestant ministers and censure those pastors," wrote Eckert, "who stand at the church door and shake hands with their parishioners. In the Negro work this custom becomes a very valuable asset in getting acquainted with outsiders. In fact, the Negro would feel slighted if the priest were to pass him, unnoticed. A kind word and a hearty hand-shake [sic] will bring him to the church on the following Sunday."[6] One African American convert, Lloyd Jacobs, credited Eckert with drawing him to Catholicism. "The dynamic personality of Father Eckert is everywhere;" he said, "at the church doors between Masses with a cheery greeting; lending the aid of his presence to every assembly and personally conducting his catechism classes for converts."[7] Unlike immigrants from European nations steeped in Catholic tradition, most African Americans did not necessarily show interest in or respect for Catholic customs and authority. South Side missionaries needed to capture their attention, even if it meant changing protocol, such as shaking hands with parishioners on the church steps.

Eckert also championed the laity's role in attracting converts. He reasoned that "lay-apostles" reached far more people than a single priest. They talked to their neighbors and coworkers, sometimes bringing them to church on Sundays or on special holy days and devotions. "We have one man in our parish," Eckert wrote, "who has brought at least forty converts into the Church through his personal efforts." St. Elizabeth's pastor found that converts, in turn, did an excellent job of attracting more converts.[8] He never addressed the issue of race in conversion work, but it undoubtedly presented a challenge to white clergy attempting to convert African Americans in the 1920s and 1930s. Eckert understood that black laypeople usually related better to fellow African Americans than they did to white priests. Because of the low number of black priests in the United States, the laity by necessity played a vital role in African American Catholicism.[9]

Perhaps the most compelling attraction to Catholicism for African American families was the parish school. Bronzeville's parochial schools did not require students to be Catholic, but they received religious instruction nonetheless. "In our instructions to the children," Eckert wrote, "we impress upon their little minds these outstanding truths: that the Catholic Church is for *everybody*, and the children and their elders have a strict and just claim to the privileges and blessings of membership in the Church." Eckert invited non-Catholic children to attend Mass and included them in devotions and special services. He noted that about one-half of St. Eliza-

beth students were non-Catholics, but many converted to Catholicism by
the time they reached the upper grades. While 60 percent of children entering St. Elizabeth School during the 1920s were non-Catholics, by graduation, 95 percent were Catholics.[10] Frequently, children encouraged their
parents to convert. "They go home and tell their parents that Father has
invited both father and mother to come to church (for some special occasion) or to some entertainment of an instructive nature," wrote Eckert.
"The parents and their relatives, after a time, grow inquisitive concerning
the Church." When family members came to school functions, the pastor invited them to attend church services. "I have found that this pro-
cedure causes a wholesome relationship to spring up, as it were, between
the Church and the parents, resulting sometimes in the conversion of
whole families."[11]

Eckert stressed the importance of church services as well as missions
and lectures in attracting converts. Booking special speakers during Lent
or church missions attracted outsiders to visit the church. Funerals also led
to large numbers of non-Catholics in the church. "It is not rarely that all
the people attending a Negro funeral in our church are non-Catholics, with
the exception of the priest, altar boys, and the person over whose remains
we hold the obsequies," he wrote. The missionary priest proudly described
the beautiful and impressive qualities of church services at St. Elizabeth
and condescendingly referred to African American Protestant churches.
"It is necessary to have everything in the church in perfect order and of
extraordinary cleanliness," he wrote. Eckert claimed that black Protestant churches typically were not as well-kept as their Catholic counterparts, noting that some beautiful church buildings on the South Side had
fallen into disrepair after African American congregations took possession
of them. He emphasized the importance of creating a solemn and digni-
fied environment during Mass. Eckert's forty altar boys, for example, were
"trained to perform their functions with military exactitude." Unlike
black Protestant churches, there was "no noisy emotionalism." In Catholic services, Eckert maintained, there was only "inspiring devotion."[12]

In numerous cases, African Americans worshipped in churches and
synagogues abandoned by white Protestants and Jews. Sociologists St. Clair
Drake and Horace Cayton observe that black congregations "would take
the church or synagogue that white worshippers abandoned as they fled
from contact with their black brothers, and turn it into a worthy house of
the Lord (when they had finished paying off the mortgage)."[13] For example, First Baptist Church founded by whites in the 1870s at 31st Street and
Grand Boulevard, became the African American Olivet Baptist Church in

1917. Whites founded St. Edmund Episcopal Church (in the 5800 block of South Indiana Avenue) in 1905, but sold it to an African American congregation in 1928. Temple Isaiah, at 45th Street and Vincennes Avenue, became Ebenezer Baptist Church in 1920; Kehilath Anshe Ma'ariv Synagogue, at 33rd Street and Indiana Avenue, became Pilgrim Baptist Church in 1922; and Beth Hamedrash Hagadol Anshe Dorum Synagogue, at 5129 South Indiana Avenue, became Antioch Missionary Baptist Church in 1928.[14]

In a 1940 study of Bronzeville churches and voluntary organizations, St. Clair Drake found that South Side civic and religious institutions responded to the 1910s and 1920s "invasion" of African Americans in different ways. Previously all-white[15] institutions tended to follow four patterns when blacks moved into their neighborhoods: 1) they remained at the same site, serving both old and new residents; 2) they stayed behind but only attended to the departing group; 3) they continued at the same site but only worked with the group moving in; or 4) they abandoned the site altogether, allowing newcomers to take over.[16] Until 1917, St. Monica's served black and white Catholics under the same roof, adhering to Drake's first pattern. After Mundelein's change in policy, St. Monica's (later St. Elizabeth) followed the third pattern, ministering only to incoming African Americans. On the other hand, in most cases white Protestant and Jewish congregations initially served members who left the old neighborhood but eventually abandoned their buildings altogether and constructed houses of worship in new locations. After leaving the neighborhood, these absentee groups routinely sold churches and synagogues to African American faith communities seeking more space. Why did the "white" Catholic Church, unlike its Protestant and Jewish counterparts, stay in black neighborhoods? Roman Catholic tradition dictated that parishes must serve all those who resided within their boundaries, regardless of race or religion.[17] St. Elizabeth, therefore, did not close its doors when founding Irish American members moved outside the parish but instead changed its emphasis from diocesan priests serving a highly assimilated, Euro-American, middle-class population to missionary orders assisting a mostly migrant, African American, and non-Catholic community.

Finally, Eckert embraced prayer as a means to reach potential converts. He believed his conversion efforts in Bronzeville succeeded only through the grace of God. Conversion became the central guiding motive in his mission at St. Elizabeth. "Every Rosary which we recite before evening devotions; every Holy Hour on the First Friday of the month; and our Forty Hours' Devotions," wrote Eckert, "all are devoted to the one chief object: more converts."[18] Although the Society of the Divine Word missionary enjoyed tremendous success at St. Elizabeth and St. Anselm, carefully tracking the number of converts, some questioned Eckert's methods. In his history of the Society of the Divine Word in North America, historian Ernest Brandewie acknowledges that critics viewed the ambitious Eckert as paternalistic, overbearing, biased, and prejudiced regarding African Americans.[19]

Eckert's "dictatorial and undiplomatic" style, however, proved successful in many ways.[20] By the end of the 1920s, the priest had converted over 1,800 African Americans at St. Elizabeth. His conversion classes often numbered in the hundreds. In May 1929, the *Chicago Tribune* reported, "Five hundred colored converts to Catholicism, thought to be the largest class ever presented to a bishop for the sacrament in America, were confirmed yesterday at St. Elizabeth's church." The class consisted of 350 adults and 150 youths.[21] Although parochial schools usually attracted children and their parents to Catholicism, public school children converted as well.[22] Bronzeville's swiftly growing population, coupled with Eckert's aggressive recruitment of converts, contributed to the establish-

Fig. 2.1. Hundreds of African Americans converted to Catholicism during the 1930s and 1940s at Corpus Christi Church, 49th Street and South Parkway. (Archdiocese of Chicago's Joseph Cardinal Bernardin Archives and Records Center.)

ment of St. Elizabeth as the vital center of Chicago's African American Catholic community in the 1920s.

Like St. Elizabeth Church, Corpus Christi regularly reported large baptism and confirmation classes. In June 1937, for example, about 400 recent converts received the sacrament of Confirmation into the Catholic Church at Corpus Christi. During the half decade between 1932—when "the Franciscan Fathers threw open the doors of Corpus Christi Church to the colored people of the neighborhood"—and 1937, over 1,200 African Americans converted to Catholicism at the church. Many of the converts came from the parish school, where they took religious instruction during regular school days. Convert classes as large as 85 children received the sacrament of Baptism during a single ceremony. The Franciscans also held weeklong missions at the church, in which "all parishioners are urged to invite their non-Catholic relatives and friends to attend." Parents or other adults, who

Fig. 2.2. St. Anselm Church, 61st Street and South Michigan Avenue, was the site of hundreds of conversions of African Americans to Catholicism during the 1930s and 1940s. (Archdiocese of Chicago's Joseph Cardinal Bernardin Archives and Records Center.)

decided to convert, spent three-and-a-half months receiving instruction, usually during evening classes.[23] Between 1937 and 1939, an additional 650 African Americans converted to Catholicism at Corpus Christi.[24]

After transferring to St. Anselm, Eckert continued his fervent mission to convert Chicago's African American population. Conversion instruction classes for adults met three nights per week at 7:30 p.m. in the Sisters of the Blessed Sacrament convent at 6042 South Indiana Avenue. Announcements for conversion instruction clearly stated, "Anyone may join a class." Evening classes usually included about 30 to 40 adults, who met to learn prayers and study the Catholic catechism. In addition, Eckert gave brief talks on the students' adopted religion and drew from a "question box" in which candidates anonymously placed queries about the Catholic faith. After completing 4 months of instruction, candidates were baptized.[25] The number of baptisms at one time varied from 15 to 350 persons. In some instances, entire families entered into the Catholic Church during a single ceremony. In the spring of each year, a bishop came to confirm the newly baptized Catholics.[26]

The success of conversion classes in Bronzeville and across the urban North led one contemporary national Catholic commentator to note, "Today the apparent indifference to the spiritual well-being of the Negro on the part of Catholics has been turned into genuine enthusiasm for the Colored race."[27] Yet, despite the large number of conversions, the majority of African Americans in northern cities did not convert to Catholicism. St. Elizabeth, Corpus Christi, and St. Anselm baptized and confirmed impressive numbers of black children and adults during the 1920s and 1930s, but their numbers were small compared to Chicago's total African American population.[28] Nevertheless, a distinct black urban Catholicism arose in the city during the interwar period.

African Americans chose Catholicism for spiritual, social, cultural, and even economic reasons, but what specific benefits did they derive from their Catholic experience? At least four characteristics attracted them to Catholicism: parochial education, Catholic aesthetics and ritual, opportunities in parish life for community building and civic involvement, and, finally, the church's universality and promise of justice.

EDUCATION

Chicago's Catholic leadership expressed concern about the education of African Americans at least a decade before the large-scale resettlement of southern migrants during World War I. "A public-school Negro, as a rule, is a dangerous Negro," the archdiocesan newspaper exhorted in 1904.[29]

Schooling African Americans, however, became a more pressing concern during the 1910s. Black Catholic education in the city began in earnest in 1913 when Katharine Drexel's Sisters of the Blessed Sacrament started teaching at St. Monica's School. At the end of the first semester, a front-page article appeared in the *New World* celebrating the sisters for bringing missionary zeal to the education of first-grade "pickaninnies" (a derogatory term for black children not uncommon at the time). The sisters and St Monica's pastor, Rev. John Morris, believed they were producing good Catholics and good Americans. They also hoped to attract more blacks to the Catholic Church. The article noted that four hundred African Americans had converted to Catholicism in Chicago during "the last few years."[30]

The *Chicago Defender*, however, did not share the archdiocese's enthusiasm for the work of St. Monica's School. The paper questioned why black children needed to attend a separate facility, when white children simply attended the nearest available parish school. A scathing *Defender* editorial chastised St. Monica's segregationist policy. The newspaper demanded that Morris integrate the school or close it. "We are willing to help Father Morris in his church work," asserted the *Defender*, "but when the time comes that he objects to colored and white children being together in school we are as through with him and his church as we can be." Written four years before Mundelein's policy excluding whites from St. Monica's Church, the editorial did not, however, criticize the still integrated worship community. "We are not knocking the church, but, believe us, we are railing the devil out of that Jim Crow school and will fight it as long as a brick is left standing of such an institution."[31]

The *Defender* questioned the racial loyalty of parents who sent their children to St. Monica's: "God pity the simple-minded mother and father who would drag their children down so low as to send them to a Jim Crow school in the heart of this great city. Such Negroes should be deported back to the land of the rapists and the home of the bigamists at the South."[32] Obviously, *Defender* publisher and editor Robert Abbott believed that the segregated Catholic school was not conducted in the best interests of Chicago's African American community. Nonetheless, parents continued to send their children to St. Monica's, even if it meant traveling past white Catholic schools to get there.

Thirty years after the *Defender*'s editorial, racial segregation continued in Chicago's Catholic schools. When George Phillips and his family moved north from New Orleans in 1943, his mother tried to enroll him at Holy Angels School in the 600 block of East Oakwood Boulevard. The

Sisters of Mercy ran the school only a half block from his home at 4017 South Vincennes Avenue, but they did not accept African American children. Only those schools designated "colored" and staffed with missionary priests and nuns allowed black children. So instead of the half block to Holy Angels, Phillips and his siblings walked seven blocks to St. Elizabeth School in the 4000 block of South Wabash Avenue.[33] "There were several cases of Negro Children who were refused enrollment in the nearest parochial school," report Drake and Cayton, "although this was a violation of canon law."[34] African American doctor and Catholic interracialist Arthur G. Falls recounted sadly that his young son came to believe that public schools were for all children but Catholic schools only for whites.[35]

During the 1940s, black Catholic parents wrote to Archbishop Samuel Stritch, protesting the segregationist policies of archdiocesan schools, but the prelate took no action. One African American family, who moved from Corpus Christi to Holy Family parish on the Near West Side, wished to continue sending their children to a Catholic school. However, Holy Family's school refused admission to the children. When the children's father complained to Stritch, the archbishop weakly suggested the man be less emotional, pray about the problem, and hope for a solution in the future.[36] Only at the end of World War II did the archdiocese change its policy to allow black families to attend the nearest Catholic church and send their children to its school.[37] African American families sent their children to Catholic schools despite such segregation, in large part, because parochial schools frequently provided black children with better educational opportunities than their public counterparts.

As thousands of new families moved into the South Side during the 1910s and 1920s, the educational needs of African American children increased, but public commitment to providing quality education for them diminished. In the 1920s and 1930s, public schools in Bronzeville commonly operated in shifts. Children spent only half-days in school and the rest of their time "on the streets."[38] In addition, public schoolteachers often spurned positions in Bronzeville schools. "It is known that white teachers begin to ask for transfers when a community is 'going colored,'" note Drake and Cayton. "This results in the definition of schools in the Negro communities as 'undesirable,' and retention in such a post is interpreted as 'punishment.' There is also some evidence to indicate that teachers have been actually 'banished' to the Black Belt as a disciplinary measure."[39]

This lack of commitment to public schools in black neighborhoods negatively impacted students. The Catholic convert, four-time Olympic medalist, and U.S. Congressman Ralph Metcalfe recalled attending segregated public schools in Bronzeville during the 1920s:

> Only one or two of my teachers seemed to take any interest in us black students. The classes were overcrowded and frequently kids would be passed along, grade to grade, simply because they had good attendance records. In junior high school I learned absolutely nothing. The teachers' main concern was keeping discipline. The environment was bad: kids would be shooting craps in the toilet.

Metcalfe's educational experience only improved when his mother found a way for him to attend Tilden Technical High School, then "about 97 percent white."[40] From there, a track scholarship took him to Marquette University, where he became an All-American athlete and U.S. Olympian.

In contrast to white public schoolteachers "imprisoned" in Bronzeville schools, the Sisters of the Blessed Sacrament and Franciscan sisters voluntarily left their family homes and dedicated their lives to serving African Americans. These religious women fell into the category of those whites who remained in Bronzeville even after racial succession because of "sentimental associations or economic interests," observe Drake and Cayton. "Janitors of apartment houses, businessmen living in their commercial property, prostitutes, priests and nuns at Catholic churches, a few partners in mixed marriages—these are the types of white persons who reside permanently in the Black Belt. Their presence is not considered unusual[,] and they are generally not resented by their Negro neighbors."[41]

The Sisters of the Blessed Sacrament and Franciscan sisters set the educational tone at St. Elizabeth, Corpus Christi, and St. Anselm by wholly committing their lives to African American children. Although not black, they were not "white" in the conventional sense either. Their celibate lifestyles, religious habits, and spiritual vocations created an otherworldly quality about them.[42] The rigorous discipline of the convent and missionary work directed their lives, which they passed on to their students. James Williams, who attended Corpus Christi and St. Elizabeth, encountered the same kind of discipline serving in the military during the Korean War as he got from the Sisters of the Blessed Sacrament and Franciscan sisters. "In the Marine Corps [it was] as if they were on the same page as the nuns," he recalled. Like other graduates of Bronzeville's Catholic schools interviewed, Williams acknowledged that the sisters used corporal punishment. "But it wasn't done out of mean-spiritedness," he insisted. "It was done out of a strict sense of discipline, which I appreciate."[43]

Fig. 2.3. Society of the Divine Word priests Louis Wade (*seated*) and Vincent
Smith—visiting from out of town—meet with the first-grade class of
Sister Paulita O'Donovan, SBS. St. Elizabeth School, 1938. (Archdiocese of
Chicago's Joseph Cardinal Bernardin Archives and Records Center.)

George Phillips, who attended St. Elizabeth in the 1940s, remembered
how the authoritarian Sisters of the Blessed Sacrament established a quiet
and orderly atmosphere within the school:

> St. Elizabeth Grade School was a place [where] you knew what you
> were supposed to do. The nuns at the grade school taught and you
> learned—you actually learned something there . . . You had to do what
> you were required to do. What I remember most is we had a stairway,
> and you had to come from the yard to the first floor to get to the class-
> rooms. The rule was: "Boys on one side; girls on another." And you'd
> only hear feet. There were no voices to be heard. Throughout the whole
> time throughout that school that's all you heard was [*sic*] feet.[44]

Parochial education became Catholicism's most effective recruitment tool
in the African American community. Word spread among Bronzeville residents that Catholic schools provided individual attention, discipline, and
rigorous academic instruction often missing in public schools.

Drake and Cayton investigated why some African American parents chose Catholic education over public schools: "Interviews with Negro Catholics, and with non-Catholics whose children attend parochial schools, seem to indicate that one of the primary attractions of the Catholic Church is its educational institutions." During the interwar years, it was not unusual for Bronzeville's overcrowded public schools to run double shifts; students only attended school for half days. Many African American parents felt that Catholic schools provided a better education with personalized attention in a quiet, disciplined setting.[45]

Of course, not all African Americans adopted Catholicism. Bronzeville residents also enjoyed a wide selection of Protestant churches in the area; a 1938 report found that the Chicago district with the highest density of churches per black residents fell within St. Elizabeth parish.[46] Baptist, African Methodist Episcopal, Holiness, and Pentecostal churches dotted the neighborhood, tangible links to the black southern church so important in African American life.[47] Although black churches provided spiritual comfort and historical connectedness, Catholicism offered a unique benefit to African American families—an educational alternative to Bronzeville's substandard public schools. This promise of quality education distinguished Catholic churches from their Protestant counterparts. One African American Protestant minister lamented about his Catholic competition: "Wherever you find a . . . Catholic Church, you find their school right along with it. If you can't make a program to interest them, you can't hold the young people."[48]

Beginning in 1884, the American Catholic hierarchy mandated that each church support a parish school.[49] This commitment to comprehensive education resulted in large parish plants, operating seven days per week and staffed by scores of nuns, priests, and religious brothers. Parochial elementary schools, high schools, and in some cases, liberal arts colleges, created a significant institutional presence in urban areas that was largely absent in Protestant churches. Consequently, economic and social uplift associated with Catholic education attracted many African American families to parochial schools in the urban North. This trend continued after World War II and remains today.

In her memoirs, African American writer Rosemary Bray recounted her childhood in Bronzeville during the 1950s and 1960s. Bray's father, painfully familiar with the effects of American racism, believed that education offered African Americans the best opportunity for economic advancement and better control of their lives. Although not Catholic himself, he sent his three children to St. Ambrose Catholic Church, where they attended the elementary school and converted to Catholicism. Recognizing Rosemary's abundant intellectual gifts, St. Ambrose's School Sisters of Notre Dame arranged for a scholarship to an elite college preparatory high school on the North Side. From there she went to Yale University.[50]

While not all black Catholic school alumni reached such elite academic heights, Catholic education attained a certain reputation for excellence among Chicago's African American community. Warner Saunders, a successful television journalist in Chicago, believed class-consciousness led his mother and father to send him to Corpus Christi in the 1940s. "I think the both of them had pretty middle-class values, and I think they saw the Catholic school as getting a better education," he recalled.[51] George Phillips remembered that he and his St. Elizabeth classmates stood out as special among the youth in his area. "You were very proud to be a member of a Catholic school," he said. "I lived in a neighborhood surrounded by public school kids. They'd say, 'Oh, there goes the Catholic school kids.' They knew us. They knew who we were . . . they knew we had a standing."[52] James Williams concurred: "They would say with reverence, 'There go [sic] the Catholic school [kids].'"[53]

Discipline, individual attention, and academic rigor set Catholic schools apart from their public counterparts in Bronzeville. The nuns stressed religious training and developing fundamental academic skills necessary for successful lives, but they did not usually teach African American children about their history and culture. As in the public schools, African American heritage "was something we would pick up after school," recalled Phillips.[54] Edwin Leaner, who attended Corpus Christi School in the 1950s, agreed that black history and culture "came from *Ebony, Jet,* the *Defender,* our parents."[55] Although they worked exclusively with African American students, the religious sisters at St. Elizabeth, Corpus Christi, and St. Anselm did not develop curricula centered on race consciousness. "One thing I will say about the nuns: they instilled in us a sense of pride in ourselves," remembered Marie Davis, but "I don't recall it having anything to do with race."[56] The nuns encouraged feelings of self-esteem in their students by focusing on religion, not race. Such religious pride originated, in part, from Catholicism's rich tradition in aesthetics and rituals.

CATHOLIC AESTHETICS AND RITUALS

While parochial education generated the single greatest driving force behind the large number of conversions during the 1920s and 1930s, other

Catholic practices attracted African American Chicagoans as well. Some blacks preferred Catholicism's Old World aesthetics and ancient rituals, which stood in sharp contrast to the unadorned surroundings and "noisy emotionalism" of Bronzeville's Protestant churches. Before the Second Vatican Council of the 1960s, African American Catholics, like their white counterparts, worshipped in a quiet, conservative manner. Despite the restrained approach, the ancient symbols of the church evoked profound emotional feelings. The sight of crucifixes, smell of incense, touch of holy water, sound of Latin chants, and taste of Communion bread all created a visceral experience for congregants. Catholic symbolism, although thoroughly grounded in European traditions, appealed to many black parishioners. "Africans and African Americans process thought through the use of symbolic imagery and rhythm," writes Jamie Phelps, an African American theologian, Adrian Dominican nun, and director of Black Catholic Studies at Xavier University in New Orleans. "African linguistic expression uses analogy and metaphor extensively to reflect concrete experience and the environment, and information is relayed through descriptive images." Albert Raboteau notes that illiterate African American slaves at times found greater meaning in the symbolic rituals of Roman Catholicism than in Puritanism.[57]

Black Catholics in the twentieth century did not adopt church customs wholesale but brought African American traditions to their worship experiences. Legendary jazz artist Lionel Hampton grew up in a Holiness church in Birmingham, Alabama, until his family moved to Chicago in 1919. Concerned about safety in the public schools, Hampton's grandmother enrolled him in St. Monica's School a half block from their home. As an altar boy, he and a friend used to add a touch of African American rhythm to the solemn consecration of the Eucharist during Mass at St. Monica's. "We'd ring the bell," Hampton recalled, "and instead of the usual *bling, blong, blong,* we'd go *bling, bling-bling-bling*—we'd put a little soul into it."[58] Adapting European aesthetics and rituals to express the meaning of their lived experiences, African American Catholics found spiritual meaning in a unique Afro-Catholicism.

Since its beginnings, circumstances required Chicago's African American Catholic community to adopt and adapt sacred spaces originally meant for Euro-Americans. In the 1880s, segregation forced black Catholics to worship in the basement of a church built by Irish American immigrants. The incomplete construction of St. Monica's Church at 36th and Dearborn streets in the 1890s signified a partial victory for African American Catholics, but Father Tolton's untimely death hampered fur-

Fig. 2.4. Altar boys prepare to serve Mass at St. Elizabeth Church in 1942.
(Jack Delano, Farm Security Administration/Office of War Information, Prints
& Photographs Division, Library of Congress, LC-USW3-000155-D.)

ther efforts toward self-determination. After Mundelein's 1917 decision to
hand St. Monica's over to missionaries, Chicago's black Catholics began
worshipping in three imposing churches built and ultimately abandoned
by middle-class and well-to-do Irish Americans. The aesthetic grandeur of
these churches, although not of their making, provided inspirational settings for African Americans.

St. Elizabeth became the first adopted by African Americans. Its black
parishioners, however, lost their church to fire after only six years. Insurance policies partially covered the fire's damage, but the archdiocese did
not reconstruct the building during the lean years of the Great Depression.[59] Instead, workmen converted St. Elizabeth's assembly hall into a
new parish church. Only pews, which survived the fire, remained from the
old church. An Italian American company designed the altar and a German American company installed a new organ, but it was two large murals that signified St. Elizabeth's African American membership. One mu-
ral depicted the "Blessed Negro Martyrs of Uganda, Central Africa, who
died for their Faith in the year 1885." The other showed St. Peter Claver,
a seventeenth-century Spanish Jesuit, who reportedly baptized over three

hundred thousand enslaved Africans in Latin America and became patron saint of black Catholics.[60] By adding such cultural icons, St. Elizabeth's African American parishioners made this smaller and less imposing building their own sacred space.

To the south, Corpus Christi's impressive physical presence also commanded attention. Only a few blocks from Frederick Law Olmsted's Washington Park, the Italianate building's twin bell towers soared majestically above the surrounding neighborhood. As visitors entered the church, they saw an imposing high altar graced by fluted columns of Italian marble. A mosaic replica of Leonardo da Vinci's *Last Supper* stretched over the tabernacle. During Mass, the priest spoke from a solid bronze pulpit, and as the faithful approached the sanctuary for Holy Communion, they knelt at an altar rail carved from dark green marble. Handcrafted, stain-glassed windows from Munich allowed natural light to bathe the congregation. Because Corpus Christi's design supported a roof without columns in the nave, sightlines were excellent in this spacious church, which seated more than two thousand worshippers.[61] The architectural grandeur and ecclesiastical formality of Corpus Christi provided a haven from the bustle of Chicago's overcrowded Bronzeville. Author Richard Wright described the frequently inhumane living conditions in the South Side ghetto, yet common working people and their children could experience the transcendent beauty of a medieval cathedral within this magnificent neighborhood church.[62]

South of Washington Park, shamrocks carved in limestone on the façade of St. Anselm recalled its founders' native Ireland. The most recently constructed of the three Bronzeville Catholic churches, the brick Romanesque structure seated 1,300.[63] St. Anselm was "located in a district that . . . [was] almost entirely inhabited by the colored people, but that was once one of the best residence sections of the city." The church's beauty differed sharply from the bleakness of the surrounding neighborhood. The author of a 1931 newspaper series took readers on a tour of the five-year-old church:

> As we approach the church of St. Anselm, we are struck not only by its Romanesque beauty, but by its startling contrast to the streets about it. Swept of all grace and beauty, they are now but dusty souvenirs of the days when they were graced by the homes of people of circumstance. . . . The Rev. M.S. Gilmartin its founder, has weathered the change in population, and in spite of it has erected a church that has a haughty disdain for the changes of men and their streets.[64]

The author lamented racial transformation in St. Anselm parish but acknowledged the structure's sublime beauty and timeless appeal. The population may have changed, but the architectural beauty remained.

In addition to church aesthetics, Catholic ritual and spirituality attracted a number of Bronzeville residents. The parish school in particular steeped students in the ancient rites of Catholic tradition. For example, boys from Corpus Christi School served as acolytes, assisting the priests during Mass, while both girls and boys sang in the school choir. On Sundays, they chanted the parts of the High Mass in Latin.[65] Beginning in 1933, Corpus Christi hosted a novena each year in June to the Sacred Heart. The nine-day devotion included two Masses daily, opportunities for confession each day, public exposition of the Blessed Sacrament, and benediction. As a "local center of the Sacred Heart League" in Chicago, the parish invited Catholics from across the city to attend these devotions. Advertisements in the *New World* widely promoted the novena to whites throughout the archdiocese and informed visitors that they could easily reach Corpus Christi by automobile or by bus, streetcar, or elevated train, as the city's transportation system connected the racially ghettoized Bronzeville to the rest of the city.[66] After Mass on the Feast of Corpus Christi, the entire parish participated in a solemn procession of the Blessed Sacrament, moving outside the walls of the church onto the streets.[67] As parishioners silently processed along South Parkway followed by dozens of Franciscan sisters and friars, they must have drawn attention from the residents of Black Metropolis. The smell of incense, sound of Latin chants, and sight of priests and nuns in religious garb created a mystique around Corpus Christi distinct from the Protestant churches in the neighborhood.

In the late 1930s, Corpus Christi inaugurated a devotional practice that brought even further attention to the parish for the next three decades. Each Lent, volunteers acted out roles from the Gospel narratives of Jesus Christ's passion, death, and resurrection. In these "Living Stations of the Cross," adults and children reenacted the traditional fourteen scenes that make up the Way of the Cross. Donning period costumes, they acted the parts of Jesus, Mary, Pontius Pilate, the disciples, and others. Rev. David Rochtman, a young Franciscan friar, wrote the script and directed a cast of about forty parishioners. A *New World* reporter described their performance:

> After the Blessed Sacrament has been removed to a side chapel, the Way of the Cross begins—a priest in surplice, accompanied by the cross and candle bearers, says the introductory prayers and goes to the first sta-

tion. Then from the right sacristy comes Pontius Pilate. Accompanied by his Roman guard, he takes his seat on the platform of the altar. Claudia, his wife, follows to plead for the life of "this just Man," and Procula, his sister-in-law, is there urging Pilate to remove this trouble-maker who has dared to call Himself a King. The High Priests and Pharisees enter and with eloquent pantomime harangue the crowd; then an unobtrusive friar in his brown habit enters the pulpit and narrates the story which is being enacted before the audience with its application to the lives of his hearers.[68]

The Living Stations grew to become a great spectacle involving scores of participants undertaking weeks of preparation and rehearsal. In addition to the parish audience, Catholics from churches throughout the archdiocese made "city-wide pilgrimages" to witness the Living Stations performed weekly during the forty days of Lent. Chicago's Cardinal Francis George recalled traveling as a boy with his family in the late 1940s from his home parish on the Northwest Side to Corpus Christi to see the Living Stations. Rita Stalzer, a German American Catholic, also remembered traveling in the 1940s to see the Living Stations with her family, who lived in St. Francis Xavier parish in west suburban LaGrange.[69] The annual performance of the Living Stations left a lasting impact on visitors and parishioners alike. "It just stirred you," recalled parishioner James Williams. "It made me proud to say, 'I'm Catholic.'"[70]

Programs like the Living Stations relied on a corps of committed individuals who served the parish with their talents. Historically, the Catholic Church organized its leadership around priests and, to a lesser extent, nuns. Yet lay involvement and leadership were essential to the success of Bronzeville's "missionary" parishes. Unlike white, Euro-American national parishes, African American parishioners did not often share an ethnic or racial heritage with their priests and nuns. The burden to create ethnic leadership, therefore, fell on black laity. Corpus Christi parishioner Blanche Rodney, for example, became a mainstay in annual performances of the Living Stations. "She was one of the weeping daughters of Jerusalem," recalled daughter Marie Davis. "I was one of the children of the weeping daughters of Jerusalem. Obviously, I outgrew it . . . but Mom was in it for twenty years."[71]

Rodney's role in the Living Stations continued a lifetime of participation in the Catholic Church on Chicago's South Side. Born Blanche Young in 1903, she was baptized at St. Monica's and grew up in the parish. After her mother died when she was six years old, Rodney began attending the

Fig. 2.5. Living Stations of the Cross: Corpus Christi parishioners commemorate the crucifixion of Jesus Christ on the church's altar in the early 1940s. (Corpus Christi Church Archives.)

Illinois Technical School for Colored Girls, a Catholic boarding academy operated by the Sisters of the Good Shepherd at 4910 Prairie Avenue, two blocks west of Corpus Christi. St. Monica's Sisters of the Blessed Sacrament became her "surrogate parents" after her father died during her teenage years. Her future husband, Onezie Rodney, came to Chicago from New Orleans in 1914. He met Blanche at St. Elizabeth Church, where they married in 1926. When her daughter and four sons began attending Corpus Christi School, Rodney subsidized the cost of their tuitions by laundering clothes for the Franciscan sisters at their convent and cleaning altar linens for the church. Later in life, she moved to St. Anselm parish, where she also worked in the church.[72]

Since the time when illiterate slaves used work songs to tell Bible stories, music has held a central place in the African American church. Southern migrants brought that tradition with them when they arrived in Chicago. In the early 1930s, black composer Dr. Thomas A. Dorsey created the modern gospel sound while music director at Bronzeville's Pilgrim Baptist Church at 33rd Street and Indiana Avenue. Eight blocks to the south at St. Elizabeth, a different style of music played an important role in African American church life. The music program directed by Father Schmuelling and Sister Bonaventura was based on the classical European traditions. The parish choir of thirty to forty voices included men and women, accompanied by an organ and string orchestra of ten to twenty musicians. During its premiere concert in May 1932, the choir performed at St. Elizabeth in front of an audience of eight hundred people "from various parts of the city." Highlights included the "Hallelujah Chorus" from Handel's *Messiah* and assorted works by Mozart. Due to its successful reception, St. Elizabeth's choir repeated its performance for a Bronzeville audience in the famed Regal Theater at 47th Street and South Parkway.[73] These concerts brought attention to the parish and raised money for the primary and secondary schools.[74] Through music, South Side missionaries exposed former sharecroppers and the children of sharecroppers to "highbrow" art forms. Few Euro-American parishes in Chicago boasted such sophisticated music programs at the time.

A perception developed among African Americans of Catholicism as a middle-class faith. Private schools, disciplined classrooms, conservative worship styles, and refined aesthetics engendered status. Catholicism's cachet derived in part from its designation as a "white" religion. In many respects, Bronzeville's Protestant churches functioned differently than Protestant churches in white neighborhoods, but Catholics, regardless of race or location, more or less practiced their religion uniformly. In a city increasingly influenced by Irish Catholic political power, Catholicism connoted middle-class pretensions, if not actual wealth. James Williams remembered the class implications of attending a Catholic school in the 1930s. "Take into account that this was during the Depression," he said. "So going to a Catholic school for a poor black family wasn't so much a necessity. I guess it would be considered like a luxury that was only associated with your so-called black families that had substance."[75]

Because rich, middle-class, and poor blacks all lived within the same residentially segregated ghetto, behavioral practices, rather than wealth, often established class distinctions within the African American community. Drake and Cayton report that 80 percent of Chicago's African American population in 1945 was born in the South. Chicago's established, "respectable" blacks feared a white backlash resulting from tens of thousands of poorly educated, unsophisticated southerners pouring into a "narrow tongue of land, seven miles in length and one and one-half miles in width."[76] Robert Abbott's *Chicago Defender*, a paper with middle-class

sensibilities, instructed newcomers from the rural South on how to be-
have in the northern city. One 1923 editorial admonished newly arrived
migrants with suggestions such as, "Don't sit out on the front steps in
bare feet and undershirt," and "Don't go shopping in the Loop wearing
your overalls or dress aprons."[77]

African American Catholic styles of worship stood in sharp contrast
to the faith practices of the southern black church. James Williams remembered "Holy Rollers" meeting in tents along South State Street in
the summertime, shaking tambourines and shouting. "I figured the only
people doing that sort of thing were the ignorant blacks, who didn't know
any better," he said.[78] Whereas Pentecostal and Evangelical styles encouraged unfettered expression, Catholic practice emphasized conservative
self-control, which suggested "working within the system." Parish fellowship and city politics became two ways that African American Catholics
worked that system to their advantage.

PARISH FELLOWSHIP AND CIVIC INVOLVEMENT

Corpus Christi congregants participated in a variety of parish functions.
Each August, for example, Corpus Christi families came together in Dan
Ryan's Grove at 87th Street and Western Avenue for an annual parish
picnic. The Sunday afternoon included games for children, music, dancing, and refreshments.[79] At Thanksgiving, the women's Altar and Rosary
Sodality hosted a turkey dinner in the parish hall where members of the
community met in fellowship to enjoy a traditional meal. Significantly,
advertisements for the dinner invited former parishioners to attend. Perhaps the invitation signaled an attempt at reconciliation between former
white parishioners and current black parishioners.[80] In addition to regular
church outings, parishioners planned special events from time to time.
In June 1936, for example, the men of the Holy Name Society sponsored a
fathers and sons night meant "to bring about a better understanding and
to create a greater interest between the men and boys." Boxing stars from
the CYO—black and white—entertained those gathered with bouts inside
a ring set up in the parish hall. Three of the boxers were current Corpus
Christi parishioners. The Holy Name men also incorporated music, tap
dancing, and a guest speaker into the evening's program for boys and their
fathers.[81] Events like these involved African American laity in the leadership of a church officially led by a white clergy.

During the 1920s, Jesse Binga was Chicago's most prominent black
Catholic layman. He was also Bronzeville's most successful banker and

real estate broker. Born in Detroit, he traveled west as a railroad porter in the mid-1880s, stopping in Chicago for the 1893 Columbian Exposition. In 1898, he began his career in real estate by buying dilapidated buildings in the Black Belt and renting out rooms to working-class African Americans. Binga's wealth increased considerably in 1912 when he married Eudora Johnson, the daughter of a black underworld figure who left her with an inheritance of $200,000. The influx of migrants into the South Side during World War I only increased Binga's wealth, as he became Bronzeville's number one property owner and chairman of Liberty Life Insurance Company. By 1928, the Binga State Bank held deposits of $1.5 million, and in 1929 the black millionaire constructed the famous Arcade Building at 35th and State streets. In the course of building his wealth, Binga became a philanthropist. He gave generously to charities, especially those associated with his Catholic faith.[82]

In January 1933, Binga and a handful of black Catholic laymen reinstated the St. Anselm branch of the Holy Name Society.[83] The group sponsored various projects, such as *New World* subscription drives.[84] The organization also hosted special events, including a comedy performance that played in white parishes throughout the archdiocese and a speaker from the National Recovery Act to explain the New Deal's impact on Bronzeville.[85] In the fall of 1936, the parish began a study club, which featured "know your religion" classes and discussions on issues of the day. The clubroom included a library and furnished reading area.[86]

In addition to the all-male Holy Name Society, women's groups played important roles in parish life. In February 1933, for example, Corpus Christi's recently formed women's Altar and Rosary Sodality held its first annual "Everybody's Birthday" party. Attendees paid an admission fee of one penny for each year of age.[87] Marie Davis remembered her mother taking part in parish activities at Corpus Christi during the 1930s and 1940s. "Mom was active in the alumnae [association]," Davis recalled. "They used to have alumnae parties . . . waistline parties—you'd pay a penny an inch for your waist. They had a lot of those unique ideas."[88] Gatherings like this served two functions: they raised money for the parish and provided opportunities for women to socialize and network. This kind of basic community involvement gave participants valuable organizational experience and developed important leadership skills.[89]

Some parishioners, like Bertina Davis, used their organizational abilities within both the church and larger community. The prefect of Corpus Christi's Altar and Rosary Sodality became heavily involved in public service. After migrating to Chicago in 1919, Davis took an active role in

Chicago's Fourth Ward Democratic Party. She became a precinct captain in 1926 and began working for the Cook County Recorder's office in 1929. Her leadership roles eventually included serving as president of the West End Regular Democratic Women's Organization and sitting on a national advisory board for black Catholics. As a reward for her "outstanding work" on behalf of the Democratic Party, Chicago's Irish American civil service commissioner appointed Davis Cook County Deputy Sheriff in 1938. The only African American woman to hold this position, the "very politically connected" Davis served as an officer of the court in grand jury rooms. During the Great Depression, numerous black Chicagoans like Davis benefited from the symbiotic relationship between New Deal Democratic politics and urban Catholicism.[90]

The Irish American Democratic machine used the Catholic parish network to make inroads with different ethnic groups in political wards throughout the city. African Americans were no exception. By the mid-1930s, "Black Metropolis was a 'New Deal Town,'" according to Drake and Cayton, with most African Americans switching from the Republican Party of Abraham Lincoln to the Democratic Party of Franklin Roosevelt.[91] Democratic mayor Edward Kelly (mayor 1933–1947), an Irish American Catholic, appointed an African American to the school board, promoted a black policeman to captain, chose an African American to chair the Chicago Housing Authority, and slated a successful black candidate for municipal judge.[92] Another Irish Catholic political boss, Richard J. Daley (mayor 1955–1976), favored black Catholics for the influential job of Democratic Party committeeman in African American wards. In 1947, Christopher Wimbash became the Third Ward committeeman. Olympian Ralph Metcalfe followed him as Third Ward committeeman in 1952. In 1963, Mayor Daley chose William Shannon as the Seventeenth Ward committeeman and St. Elizabeth High School coach Joseph Robichaux as the Twenty-First Ward committeeman. And in 1968, John Stroger became the Eighth Ward committeeman and later president of the Cook County Board of Commissioners. All five men were African American Catholics.[93] In 1971, Daley tapped Joseph Bertrand—a standout athlete at St. Elizabeth High School and the University of Notre Dame—as the Democratic Party's nominee for city treasurer. Bertrand, a Catholic, became the first African American elected to citywide office in Chicago's history.[94]

In return for patronage jobs and favors, the Irish Catholic Democratic machine relied on Chicago's African American community for political support. Black Catholic Edwin Leaner witnessed the machine at work in Corpus Christi parish during the 1950s. "On Election Day, you had to turn out so many numbers," he recalled. So they sent you turkeys . . . [the] Precinct captain was trying to get people to vote . . . 'Vote for this, vote for that.' Everybody was a Democrat. Pretty much you would support any candidate that [Richard J.] Daley sent."[95] African Americans became one of the most important and reliable constituencies for Chicago's Democratic Party.[96] The black community reaped tangible rewards for its support of the machine, but critics dubbed the relationship between white party leadership and black constituents "plantation politics." Political scientist William Grimshaw calls black Catholic politicians "loyalist elites," whose "well-being was dependent on their patronage employment." Their religion provided an important connection to the Democratic machine controlled by Irish Catholics, while at the same time making it less likely that they would participate in the protest politics of the civil rights movement which were rooted in the black Protestant church.

He adds, "Their Catholicism—unusual among blacks—served to insulate them from the essentially Protestant civil rights movement, while it bound them to the machine's Irish Catholic leadership."[97] Loyalty to Daley's machine seemed out of touch by the late 1960s and 1970s, as the Black Power movement called for independence and even separatism. Yet African American Catholics fought for justice within church and society for generations. They may have "worked within the system," but they were activists nonetheless.

CATHOLICISM'S UNIVERSALITY AND THE FIGHT FOR JUSTICE

While Catholicism brought parochial education, aesthetic beauty, sacred ritual, parish fellowship, and civic involvement to Bronzeville, residents wanted more. As migrants—really refugees from the Jim Crow South, the children and grandchildren of slaves—they sought justice. Although their Catholic faith proclaimed absolute truths and promised heavenly rewards, it often delivered painful inconsistencies on earth. By definition, Catholicism professed humankind's universality through one worldwide church. Beginning in the Middle Ages, St. Thomas Aquinas and other Catholic intellectuals developed natural law theory, which argued that all persons deserved basic human rights, and in 1839 Pope Gregory XVI condemned the slave trade.[98] Still, racist thinking and practices plagued the church at the local level. Although no official policy kept African Americans from worshipping at churches throughout the Archdiocese of Chicago, de facto realities, namely the actions of parish priests and white parishioners, restricted them primarily to St. Elizabeth, Corpus Christi, and St. Anselm during the years before World War II. Following in the footsteps of their white parishioners, diocesan priests and nuns usually left these churches when African Americans moved in. The priests and nuns from religious orders who replaced them concentrated primarily on education and administering the sacraments. Trained as missionaries, they typically focused on saving souls rather than working for social justice, which was often left to the black Catholic laity.

Between 1889 and 1894, African American Catholics organized themselves nationally in five "Colored Catholic Congresses." Daniel Rudd, a black Catholic newspaperman from Cincinnati, spearheaded the national meetings, which gave African American Catholics the opportunity to show their devotion to the church while protesting against its racism at the same time.[99] Historians have described the 1890s as the nadir of U.S. race relations, but the period held potential for black Catholics: one of their own led an African American parish in Chicago, national congresses met annually, and in 1904 the Vatican wrote to American bishops instructing them to end racist practices in their dioceses.[100]

Father Tolton's death in 1897, however, left the American Catholic Church without any black diocesan priests, underscoring its failure to attract, train, and retain African American clergy. Without ordained leadership from their community, black Catholics felt neglected. "There is a universal desire of the Colored people with whom I am constantly in contact," a Baltimore funeral director wrote to Archbishop Mundelein in 1919, "to see those of their race as priest [sic] in this one, true Apostolic Church."[101] In 1920, the Society of the Divine Word opened St. Augustine Mission House in Bay St. Louis, Mississippi, a seminary for African American men. "The conviction grew upon us that the conversion of the colored RACE could not be looked for, unless there would be a COLORED CLERGY, as non-Catholic denominations had provided them ever since the Civil War," wrote a white society priest in a 1921 letter to Mundelein. He went on to contend that blacks were better as order priests—like those in the Society of the Divine Word—rather than diocesan priests. He also reminded Mundelein that the pope had called for racial harmony and indicated his belief that Catholicism would solve the "race problem" plaguing Chicago.[102]

The city's African American community demonstrated enthusiasm for religious leaders from its own race on Sunday, 28 February 1926, when a newly ordained black priest, Father Norman DuKette, sung a High Mass at St. Elizabeth Church. Originally from Washington, DC, the young priest received ordination a few weeks earlier in Detroit where he took a parish assignment. Only the second black diocesan priest since Tolton (Stephen Theobold from St. Paul, Minnesota, was the other), DuKette's arrival captivated African American Catholics and non-Catholics alike. The *Chicago Defender* described the scene:

> An air of expectancy which had hung for days over St. Elizabeth Catholic parish culminated Sunday morning in a religious celebration unique in the history of Chicago when a newly ordained Race priest chanted his first solemn high mass . . . little flower girls dressed in bridal white, wearing wreaths of orange blossoms, formed an arch down the center aisle . . . Behind the cross bearer marched 24 black robed young acolytes, bearing lighted candles, their brilliant red ties sounding an exalting note . . . clad in violet and gold embroidered vestments, walked the slim brown figure of Rev. Father Norman A. DucKete [sic] . . . As he was led up to the marble and gold altar, sparkling with beautiful lights and his soft voice began the intonation of the solemn liturgy of the Catholic church [sic], the most curious must have felt the impressiveness of the scene.[103]

The Bronzeville community, taking pride in the visiting African American priest, packed the church that morning. Members of arriving ecclesiastical hierarchy forced their way through a crowd of 10,000 to 12,000 people. Police and fire officials tried to disperse the crowd but to no avail.[104] After the Mass, "Race Catholics of Chicago" gave DuKette a gold chalice studded with jewels, and Jesse Binga presented the young clergyman with $300 collected from parishioners. Thanking his Bronzeville hosts, DuKette remarked, "I know you are happy to see one of your own come so far as to be a priest in the Roman Catholic church [sic]."[105] The intense interest in DuKette revealed a strong desire for black role models and leaders in the African American community.

Not all role models, however, needed to be black. George Clements, who in 1957 became only the second African American ordained by the Archdiocese of Chicago, credited white religious men and women for nurturing his vocation to the priesthood. "What I know as so precious in the priesthood," he later recounted, "was summed up in the Franciscans who were at Corpus Christi. There was a genuine love for people that transcended race, transcended everything, occupation, gender, whatever, you know, it was just a real love, a simple kind of love that they had."[106]

Catholicism's universality also provided African American laity with opportunities to find black role models outside the United States. St. Martin de Porres, a seventeenth-century Peruvian mulatto, became patron for North America's black Catholics. The son of a Spanish gentleman and African freedwoman, Porres worked among the poor and infirm in Lima. Until his canonization in 1962, Catholics referred to the Dominican brother as "Blessed."[107] In the fall of 1936, Pope Pius XI granted St. Elizabeth permission to publicly venerate a statue of Blessed Martin de Porres during a novena in his honor. St. Elizabeth's pastor, Rev. Bruno Drescher, invited a Dominican priest from suburban River Forest to preach about the candidate for sainthood. The special novena ended on Porres's feast day, but a perpetual novena, including veneration of one of his relics, continued to be held once a week on Sunday evenings.[108]

A month after the special novena, three members of African royalty entered into the Catholic Church at St. Elizabeth. The wife and two children of Nigerian prince Allen Adebayo Olawumi Fayoyin were baptized at the Bronzeville church during Christmas week of 1936.[109] The Adebayo family was one of three major clans in Nigeria. African American residents of Chicago's South Side shared ethnicity, or at least race, with the Nigerians, but it was Catholicism that provided the common denominator for their meeting. The universality of Catholicism created opportunities like this for African American Catholics to see a world beyond American racism. Although the larger Chicago community tended to pay little notice to such events, they helped build race pride among black Catholics.

African American Catholics belonged to a worldwide amalgamation of people missionized by the Catholic Church. Philip May, a member of Corpus Christi, represented this vision of Catholic universalism in his artwork. The young African American worked as a dishwasher in a Loop restaurant, but in his free time he created an eight-foot-by-five-foot canvas showing St. Francis with outstretched arms "gathering around him the children of all nations." The painting portrayed the slight monk clad simply in a brown robe and sandals, looking kindly over a group of multiracial children along a shoreline. The Franciscans presented May's work at the 1939 Catholic Students' Mission Crusade Convention hosted by Catholic University of America in Washington, DC. Later they displayed it at the Franciscan Missionary Union headquarters in the *Franciscan Herald* Building in Chicago's Back of the Yards neighborhood.[110] The Franciscans, like the Society of the Divine Word and Sisters of the Blessed Sacrament, saw themselves as missionaries working in foreign lands, even when those "foreign lands" were tucked within the second largest city in the United States.

Priests and nuns were not the only white Catholic Chicagoans to missionize African Americans. Despite a system of racial segregation upheld by the actions (and inactions) of the archdiocese, some white Catholics reached out to their African American coreligionists. Just as some white-led contemporary social service agencies worked with African Americans, white Catholic organizations sponsored acts of charity for the benefit of Bronzeville missions. For example, the Irish Society of Music and Drama performed a "musicale" in June 1936 at the St. Elizabeth auditorium. Proceeds from the event benefited the Sisters of the Blessed Sacrament and their work at St. Elizabeth and St. Anselm.[111] In other instances, white Catholics donated articles of clothing and financial assistance to black children on their First Communions and Confirmations.[112] In 1937, white students from all-girls Providence High School on the West Side helped outfit St. Elizabeth girls for their First Communions.[113] In addition, some white Catholics attended fundraising events sponsored by black Catholic churches, like the St. Elizabeth annual fall bazaar.[114] St. Anselm's Eckert consistently invited readers of the *New World* to visit his parish.[115] In each of these cases, white Catholics donated time or treasure to the missionary activities of the Sisters of the Blessed Sacrament, Society of the Divine Word, and Franciscan communities. While these acts of charity brought black and white Catholics into limited contact, they failed to challenge racism directly.

Nationally, a few Catholics challenged the status quo by fighting for racial justice. In 1916, Thomas Wyatt Turner, an African American Catholic from Maryland, founded the Committee for the Advancement of Colored Catholics in Washington, DC. Turner earned bachelor's and master's degrees from Howard University and in 1921 a doctorate in botany from Cornell University. He was a professor of biology at Howard from 1913 until 1924, when he began teaching at the Hampton Institute, an African American college in southeast Virginia established during Reconstruction. In response to the deadly race riots of 1919 and subsequent pastoral letter from American bishops, Turner presented a twenty-page, typewritten brief to the American Catholic hierarchy. The document condemned racism within the church and challenged religious leaders to do more for African American Catholics. In 1924, his black Catholic layman's organization transformed into the Federated Colored Catholics and began holding annual meetings in major cities in the Northeast and Midwest. The group functioned as an "action group" for black Catholic concerns.[116]

By the early 1930s, however, white involvement in the Federated Colored Catholics changed the organization. Revs. William Markoe and John

LaFarge urged Turner to shift his focus from fighting against injustices within the church to promoting interracialism among Catholics. The white Jesuits redirected the mission of the organization. Father Markoe, who published the Federated Colored Catholics' official organ, the *Chronicle*, renamed it the *Interracial Review* to reflect the changes. Some blacks within the organization supported Turner's adherence to keeping the Federated Colored Catholics an African American organization, while others favored interracialism as proposed by Markoe and LaFarge. In 1932, members of the Federated Colored Catholics voted Turner out of the presidency. Consequently, a split took place within the organization between its East Coast and Midwest branches. Turner continued to lead a weakened version of the Federated Colored Catholics in the East, while a new National Interracial Federation developed in the Midwest. In a few years, both organizations became inactive. Father LaFarge, however, took over publication of the *Interracial Review* and founded the Catholic Interracial Council of New York. Branches of LaFarge's organization then began appearing in East Coast and Midwestern cities, including Chicago.[117]

In October 1932, the Chicago District of the National Catholic Federation for the Promotion of Better Race Relations, formerly known as the Federated Colored Catholics, met at St. Elizabeth Church to discuss the topic, "Race Prejudice! What Can Catholicism Do?" Organizers characterized the conference as a milestone event for race relations in Chicago: "This meeting, open to all, Catholic and non-Catholic, colored or white, will mark the beginning of a more concerted effort in Chicagoland and is the beginning of an intensive program for the betterment of race relations within Catholic circles." The National Catholic Interracial Federation was "an organization of thinking colored and white Catholics, laity and clergy . . . interested in the improvement of race relations in Catholic circles through the stimulation of Catholic Action."[118] In his 1931 encyclical, *Quadragesimo Anno*, Pope Pius XI advanced the concept of Catholic Action to stop the growing threats of communism and fascism by directly involving laypeople in the work of the church. Favoring neither unrestricted capitalism nor communism, Pius believed a program of Catholic Action would lead to social justice. The meeting at St. Elizabeth exemplified the new emphasis on interracialism as advocated by Markoe and LaFarge. Two years later, the National Catholic Interracial Federation met again in Chicago at Corpus Christi Church.[119]

Catholicism's worldwide scope presented some unique possibilities for African Americans. Although rooted in Western tradition, it professed universality. Church leaders in Rome did not harbor prejudices against African Americans to the same degree as their Euro-American counterparts, who were tainted by U.S. racism. The Vatican repeatedly admonished American church officials to reject racial prejudices and expand African American ministries. Yet the worldwide church historically encountered non-Westerners vis-à-vis imbalanced power relationships. White missionaries typically engaged nonwhite peoples through charitable acts, which tended to place groups like African Americans in dependent positions. Nevertheless, black Catholics found ways to assume leadership roles in the church. Augustus Tolton, Stephen Theobold, and Norman DuKette became the nation's first black priests, and, perhaps more importantly, black laymen like Daniel Rudd and Thomas Wyatt Turner fought for equality in the church. By the 1930s, some white Catholics tried to move beyond the charity/dependency model by joining African Americans in the struggle for racial justice. Embracing the Catholic Action movement, these men and women advocated interracialism as a means of defeating racial prejudice. They believed that human dignity transcended national, ethnic, or racial boundaries.

A CATHOLIC BRONZEVILLE

African American migrants from the rural, Protestant South—like European immigrants before them—used Catholicism to help create a new home in Chicago. The heart of black Catholicism in the city fell within a three-mile radius on the South Side. Between World War I and World War II, a modest but significant portion of Chicago's black population adopted and adapted three parishes originally settled by Irish Americans. Several elements of Catholicism attracted Chicago's African American community. Historically denied educational opportunities, black migrants arrived in the North largely unprepared for life in a modern, industrialized society, but Catholic schools with committed teachers and high standards offered prospects for class advancement. Bronzeville's impoverished and overcrowded streets created a bleak environment, yet Catholic churches' rich aesthetics and solemn rituals brought beauty and spiritual comfort to residents in a "respectable," middle-class manner. Catholicism also provided a vital link to civic engagement in a city dominated by Irish American Catholic politicians. Finally, Catholicism's universality and program of Catholic Action offered hope for social justice. In short, black Catholics believed their religion gave them "standing" within Bronzeville and the larger Chicago community.

The church's institutional presence made a significant impact on Chicago's African American community between 1920 and 1945. As a result, thousands of black Chicagoans converted to Catholicism. By 1933, black Catholics worshipped and sent their children to school at St. Elizabeth, Corpus Christi, and St. Anselm. Drake and Cayton describe Catholicism's growth in Bronzeville between 1935 and 1945:

> During the last ten years an intensive drive by the Roman Catholic Church has met with considerable success in Bronzeville. There are three large Catholic Churches in the Black Belt, and the Masses are well attended . . . The Catholic approach to the Negroes has been aided by the establishment of a small community house, by the extensive athletic program of the Catholic Youth Organization, and by the forthright stand against race prejudice taken by an auxiliary Bishop of the Catholic diocese."[120]

The "auxiliary Bishop" was Bernard Sheil, founder of the CYO. In the 1930s, Sheil drew upon Bronzeville's three Catholic parishes to form the nucleus of black participation in the CYO. The citywide configuration of the Roman Catholic archdiocese allowed for interracial engagement across parish—and, thus, neighborhood—lines. Parishes were at once isolated (racially, geographically, socially) and at the same time part of a citywide faith community with a centralized and authoritarian organizational structure which, in the case of the CYO, was used for progressive ends. Although their numbers were relatively small, Chicago's African American Catholics played a significant role in the CYO and mid-twentieth-century race relations in Chicago.

For God and Country: Bishop Sheil and the CYO

The Catholic Youth Organization was established to promote among youth a recreational, educational, and religious program that would adequately meet the physical, mental, and spiritual needs of boys and girls without regard to race, creed, or color . . . while instilling in their minds and hearts a true love for God and country.
—Catholic Youth Organization charter (1932)

On 5 November 1937, twenty-five thousand Catholic high school and college students descended upon Loyola University Chicago's North Side campus for a giant birthday party. Color guards and marching bands led enthusiastic throngs of adolescents into the school's football stadium to celebrate the seventh anniversary of the Catholic Youth Organization. In a larger context, however, the young men and women came to exult in the distinct but complementary ideas of "God and country." Attendees included CYO founder Bishop Bernard Sheil, CYO athletic director and former University of Notre Dame football star Jack Elder, Illinois director of the National Youth Administration (NYA) and CYO secretary-treasurer William Campbell, and Chicago's Irish American Catholic mayor Edward Kelly. The guest of honor was President Franklin Roosevelt's eldest son, James. A decidedly patriotic mood with a strong dose of Catholic triumphalism characterized the event.

Speaking on behalf of his father, James Roosevelt praised the CYO for advancing American democracy during the 1930s amidst economic turmoil and threats of Communism and Fascism from abroad. He argued that the CYO embodied traditional Judeo-Christian principles, which provided the foundation for a strong nation. "We cannot achieve a stable and productive society unless we willingly believe that we are each our brother's keeper," he said. "A philosophy of . . . individualism invented to justify greed is not a society's adequate substitute for that corporate action through which alone men of good will can work out the creed of God on earth."

The Roosevelt administration counted on Catholics in northern cities for political support. Chicago's Cardinal George Mundelein was a longtime admirer of the president, actively promoting the New Deal as a means to address the shortcomings of American capitalism during the Great Depression. Mundelein, and his auxiliary, Sheil, believed that the New Deal represented an American version of the Roman Catholic Church's program for social justice as articulated in two seminal papal encyclicals, *Rerum Novarum* (1891) and *Quadragesimo Anno* (1931). "To minds trained in Catholic doctrine and steeped into the encyclicals those truths are nothing new," the junior Roosevelt continued. "What is new is that today those truths are realized by all Americans as the working principles of practical action in government." The president's wife also came to Chicago to demonstrate the administration's support of the CYO. The following day, William Campbell led First Lady Eleanor Roosevelt on a tour of the CYO headquarters, where she met scores of boys who came to train in state-of-the-art boxing facilities.[1]

Sheil founded the CYO in 1930 as a boxing league for wayward young men. Within a decade, the organization had grown into a vast network of sports leagues, clubs, camps, and social services for young people throughout the city. More than 23,000 boys and girls participated in CYO sports during 1932–1933: 10,000 in basketball, 9,000 in baseball, 2,000 in boxing, 1,200 in track and field, 900 in swimming, and 500 in golf.[2] Participation grew throughout the 1930s. By 1935, Catholic dioceses from across the nation, including New York, San Francisco, Cincinnati, Salt Lake City, Milwaukee, and Louisville, modeled their own youth organizations after Chicago's.[3] Most significant, the CYO differed from other youth leagues and organizations: from its inception, Sheil invited boys and girls regardless of ethnicity or race to participate in CYO activities.

The citywide organization opened a window of opportunity during the Depression, World War II, and immediate postwar period for interracial interaction between Euro-American Catholics and African Americans. Bronzeville's Catholic parishes—St. Elizabeth, Corpus Christi, and St. Anselm—formed the nucleus of black participation in the CYO, allowing African American boys and girls to interact with white youth for twenty-five years between 1930 and 1954. Sheil's personal commitment to providing quality recreational settings for young people regardless of race fostered these interracial opportunities.

FROM BALLPLAYER TO BISHOP

James Bernard Sheil, Jr., was born in Chicago on 18 February 1886, the only child of second-generation Irish American Catholics Rosella Bartley Sheil and James Bernard Sheil, Sr. Sometime between graduation from college in 1906 and ordination in 1910, the younger Sheil reversed the order of his first and middle names to "Bernard James," but family and friends knew him simply as "Benny." The Sheils lived near the corner of Grand Avenue and Paulina Street in St. Columbkille parish in the West Town neighborhood on the Near Northwest Side.[4] Despite later accounts (occasionally propagated by Sheil himself) of a tough childhood, Sheil grew up in a solidly middle-class family.[5] His father and paternal grandfather operated grocery, coal, wood, real estate, and insurance businesses on the West Side. Sheil's family enjoyed a prosperous life compared to most other people in the neighborhood. The skilled and unskilled laborers who lived around him worked with their hands and paid rent, whereas his entrepreneurial family owned their own home.[6]

Sheil lived in the Thirteenth Ward, about two miles north and west of Jane Addams's Hull House, but it is unlikely he ever visited the famous settlement during his childhood.[7] His life as a boy revolved around St. Columbkille's church and school, which were staffed by the Brothers of the Holy Cross and Sisters of St. Vincent. Rev. Thomas Burke, known as "Good Father Tom," ran the parish established by Irish Americans prior to the Civil War. In 1859, members of Chicago's first Irish national parish, St. Patrick's, founded St. Columbkille on the West Side's outlying "prairie." Several of the men who built the original church later served in the Union Army's 23rd Illinois Infantry, better known as Colonel James Mulligan's "Irish Brigade."[8] As a boy, Sheil doubtlessly heard stories from parish elders who fought in the war about brave service in the name of God and country. In the second half of the nineteenth century, St. Columbkille grew to become one of Chicago's largest parishes, and its members played significant roles in the city's business, political, and church affairs. In particular, the parish became known for producing men for the priesthood, thereby adding to Chicago's rapidly expanding Irish American clergy.[9]

Sheil inherited political acumen, patriotism, and eloquence from his grandfathers. His paternal grandfather, Patrick B. Sheil, moved to Chicago from New York City around the time of the Civil War and settled in St. Columbkille parish. A successful Irish American businessman, Patrick Sheil became involved in local Democratic politics, eventually serving one term on Chicago's city council as Fourteenth Ward alderman from 1869 to 1871.[10] Benny's maternal grandfather, John "Johnny" Payne, enlisted in the Union Army's Chicago Mercantile Battery in 1863 and was wounded in battle. After the war he worked as a sailor on the Great Lakes. Payne had the Irish "gift of gab" and regularly quoted poetry. "He could just look at you and rattle off some poem," remembered his sister.[11]

Sportswriter and Sheil biographer Roger Treat portrayed Sheil's home life as ideal. His parents, who "were neither rich nor poor, nor concerned about problems of finance," gave their only child abundant attention. Rosella Sheil, educated among the Catholic elite by the Religious of the Sacred Heart (often referred to as the Madams) on Taylor Street on the city's Near West Side, created a genteel Victorian home for her family.[12] In addition to his first love, baseball, Sheil took lessons in dancing, fencing, and piano. He also delivered newspapers in the neighborhood to earn spending money. Not a particularly gifted student, he produced slightly above-average work at St. Columbkille's elementary school. From his parents he learned generosity and service: James Sr. regularly helped those he encountered in need, and Rosella assisted the less fortunate by participating in parish charities.[13] In later years, she anonymously helped fund St. Joseph's Home for the Friendless on the South Side, as well as other charitable organizations.[14]

Growing up in a financially secure family removed from Sheil many of the economic excuses for bigotry common among ethnic and racial groups competing for social and economic status in the industrial order. As part of a middle-class family tied to business and politics, Sheil learned at an early age the advantages of working cooperatively with a wide range of people. He demonstrated pride in his Irish heritage but, unlike so many of his contemporaries, did not adopt a worldview that pejoratively branded non-Irish as "other." Irish and German Americans dominated his neighborhood, but Sheil encountered several other ethnic groups, including Jews. In addition, he lived within a few blocks of several African American families, who in all probability bought groceries and coal from Sheil's father.[15] By the turn of the twentieth century, a growing number of African Americans lived along Lake Street, about eight blocks to the south of the Sheil home.[16] The bishop later considered this area tougher than his neighborhood and believed that he might have ended up in jail if he had been born there.[17] Although a significant number of blacks lived in West Town, most African Americans resided on the South Side, where Chicago's black Catholic community worshipped at St. Monica's.[18]

After graduation from eighth grade in 1899, the thirteen-year-old Sheil entered St. Viator College, a Catholic boarding school for boys in Bourbonnais, Illinois, sixty miles south of Chicago. The Clerics of St. Viator—or Viatorians—founded the traditional liberal arts school in 1865. The faculty, particularly Rev. William Bergin, influenced Sheil's thinking on social issues.[19] Bergin advocated working for a just society as articulated by Leo XIII in his recent papal encyclical, *Rerum Novarum*. In particular, Bergin and his Viatorian colleagues stressed the rights of workers in an industrialized society. Bergin remained an important mentor to Sheil throughout his life. After St. Viator closed during the Depression, Bergin came to live with Sheil at St. Andrew's rectory on the North Side, where Sheil was pastor from 1935 to 1966. In addition to Sheil, the small college produced two of the twentieth century's most influential American Catholic priests: Fulton J. Sheen and John Tracy Ellis.[20]

Sheil followed a seven-year program of study at St. Viator, which led to his bachelor's degree in 1906. As was the case in elementary school, he maintained only average grades, finding more interest in extracurricular activities than academics.[21] He immersed himself in drama, debate, and public speaking.[22] In addition, he excelled on the football field as quarterback and baseball diamond as pitcher. His outgoing personality and athleticism made him popular with schoolmates, and he developed leadership skills as a class officer.[23] During the summers, he returned home to Chicago, worked at his father's businesses, and played baseball as often as possible.

During the last quarter of the nineteenth century, sports became an important form of leisure in an increasingly urbanized and industrialized United States. Spectators paid to watch professional boxing and baseball, but amateur athletics flourished as well. By the 1890s, for example, bicycling clubs became wildly popular in Chicago and other American cities and towns. As the prominence of organized athletics grew in the United States, sports like track and field and football became increasingly common on college campuses. Theodore Roosevelt, a fervent outdoorsman and sports enthusiast, believed athletics and other outdoor activities helped Americans become better citizens. "Our object," he wrote in 1890, "is to get as many of our people as possible to take part in manly, healthy, vigorous pastimes, which will benefit the whole nation."[24]

Organized religion, particularly Protestantism, used sports as an evangelizing tool in nineteenth-century America. The YMCA, founded in

England, opened its first American centers in the 1850s. The YMCA mission was to attract young American males to a "masculine Christianity," seen by many as having been "feminized" during the Victorian era.[25] Social Gospel reformers in England and the United States stressed an inter-denominational, "scientific" approach to Christian education, including athletics. Achieving salvation in this world—not just in the next—meant perfecting one's body and soul.[26] Progressive-Era reformers like Jane Addams adopted this ideology and advocated playgrounds for working-class immigrants in the nation's crowded cities.

The YMCA movement influenced James Naismith, inventor of basketball, and Amos Alonzo Stagg, father of modern football. In 1890, Naismith graduated from a Presbyterian college of theology and began teaching at the International YMCA training school in Springfield, Massachusetts. A few years later, he invented an indoor game that could be played in the winter between football and baseball seasons. Basketball went on to become one of the world's most popular twentieth-century sports. Stagg also studied theology and worked at the YMCA training school in Springfield. In 1892, one of his former professors from Yale Divinity School, William Rainey Harper, invited him to head the athletic department at the newly formed University of Chicago. Stagg built a successful football program, invented the modern "bowl" game, created numbered jerseys, and popularized the forward pass.[27] He also created the National High School Track and Field Meet (1902) and the National Catholic Interscholastic Basketball Tournament (1917).[28] Sports and religion became linked in American culture during the Progressive Era. Protestantism's "muscular Christianity," exemplified by the YMCA and so prevalent during Sheil's childhood and young adulthood, later became a model for the CYO.

In countless speeches, newspaper and magazine articles, press releases, and his authorized biography, Sheil recounted how he chose the priesthood over a promising career in professional baseball. Specifically, he often told the story of pitching a no-hitter in 1905 for St. Viator against Big Ten powerhouse University of Illinois.[29] After graduation he starred on a semi-professional baseball team, Chicago's Logan Squares. His prowess on the pitcher's mound gained him the attention of professional clubs, including Charles Comiskey's Chicago White Stockings. Sheil loved the excitement of baseball and the attention it brought to him, but he felt called to the priesthood. Many of his classmates, including his fellow baseball players, had entered seminary after graduation.[30] As Sheil pondered his vocation in the fall of 1906, he enrolled in graduate courses at the University of Illinois and practiced with the baseball team. After two months, however, he returned home and told his parents that he wanted to become a priest.[31] He entered the seminary at St. Viator in spring of 1907, and on 1 May 1910, Archbishop James Quigley presided over his ordination at Holy Name Cathedral. The following day he offered his first Mass at St. Columbkille.

Sheil quickly climbed the rungs of the Catholic Church's hierarchical ladder. He first worked as an assistant pastor for eight years at St. Mel's parish in the West Garfield Park neighborhood. During World War I, he served as chaplain at the Great Lakes Naval Training Station, thirty-five miles north of Chicago along the shores of Lake Michigan. And for three years following the war, Sheil lived in the rectory of Holy Name Cathedral on State Street, working as a chaplain a few blocks away at the Cook County Jail.[32] Archbishop Mundelein took an interest in the talented young priest and placed him on the staff of the archdiocese's central administrative offices in 1923. A year later, Sheil became archdiocesan chancellor and accompanied Mundelein to Rome, where they met with Pope Pius XI.[33] Despite reports of financial mismanagement in his later career, Sheil served successfully as treasurer for the 28th International Eucharistic Congress hosted by the Archdiocese of Chicago in 1926.[34] In 1928, as a reward for his efforts, the Vatican named Sheil an auxiliary bishop at the relatively young age of forty-two. The following year he became vicar general, second only to Mundelein in ecclesiastical powers in the Archdiocese of Chicago.

Although he chose the priesthood over a professional career in baseball, at heart Sheil remained an athlete. The prototypical muscular Christian of Sheil's childhood was William Ashley "Billy" Sunday, a professional athlete turned evangelical preacher. In 1883, the manager of the Chicago White Stockings baseball team discovered Sunday, a poor German American from Iowa, working as an undertaker's assistant. The lightning-fast runner became a successful player, stealing ninety-one bases in one season. Then, in 1886, Sunday underwent a religious conversion while cavorting with his teammates outside a Chicago tavern. He heard evangelical Christians from the Pacific Garden Mission singing and decided to accept Jesus Christ as his personal savior. In 1891, after playing professional baseball for eight years, he began working with the YMCA to spread his message of clean-living, God-fearing, hardworking Americanism. Ordained a minister in the Presbyterian Church in 1903, Sunday traveled the country giving fiery sermons at revivals in cities and towns. He became the best-known American evangelical preacher during the first two decades of the twentieth century.[35]

Sunday, like Sheil, gave up baseball to become a clergyman. Unlike the bishop, however, he rejected sports as too worldly, supported prohibition, and attacked the inherent evilness of big cities. The influence of Sunday and other evangelicals waned after World War I as more secular ideas about sports prevailed in American cities during the 1920s. By 1930, Protestants largely abandoned the idea of muscular Christianity. Little remained of American Protestantism's vigorous promotion of sports as seen in the late nineteenth and early twentieth centuries.[36]

Sheil, on the other hand, embraced muscular Christianity. His charisma, in fact, derived in large part from his vigorous athleticism. Treat's highly gendered biography describes Sheil as "no sissy priest but a rough-and-tumble scrapper," who could say "a solemn Mass at a certain moment and two hours later [be] prancing around a boxing ring—still in cassock, with boxing gloves added, slapping the ears of a fresh young punk."[37] At five feet, nine inches tall, the stocky "Little Iron Man" worked to create an image of robust virility.[38] George Drury, director of the Sheil School of Social Studies (1943–1946), recalled that Sheil—similar to an athlete—felt restless unless in motion. Like an actor on stage, he thrived in the spotlight of public attention, casting a larger-than-life presence with a magnetic smile.[39]

ORIGINS OF THE CYO

Sheil's experiences at the Cook County Jail and Great Lakes Naval Training Station left the young priest with two lasting convictions. First, society must take responsibility for juvenile delinquency. Second, the church should employ organized recreational and leisure activities to promote Christian and democratic principles among youth. As a jail chaplain, Sheil encountered young men ruined by crime, and he accompanied a number of them as they walked the "last mile" to their executions. He placed ultimate responsibility for these destroyed lives on American society, which failed to provide adequately for the social, moral, and spiritual well-being of its children. As a result of his jail ministry, Sheil committed himself to fighting the conditions that led to delinquency.[40] His days on the playing fields and time as military chaplain convinced him that athletics helped young people overcome the "problems of youth."[41] The hardships of World War I underscored sport's ability to build character among young people, and the Great Lakes Naval Training Station operated the nation's largest military athletic program during the war.[42] Working in concert with the federal government, Sheil learned how to organize and promote sports on a large scale. A personal love of athletics and experiences at Great Lakes confirmed his belief that recreational programming provided positive outlets for youthful energy. Sports taught young people discipline, teamwork, and fair play. Most of all, it occupied their time. "Idleness is my enemy," Sheil declared.[43]

Youthful idleness worried Catholic leaders, who believed that modernity along with its corollaries—secularism, materialism, and communism—seriously threatened the church. Worldly temptations, particularly in urban areas, endangered not just juvenile delinquents but all Catholic youth. Protestant organizations like the YMCA began addressing these concerns during the nineteenth century. Yet fearing Protestant influences, archdiocesan officials dissuaded Catholic young people from frequenting them.[44] In 1920, the Vatican warned American bishops about the YMCA and encouraged them to start Catholic societies to protect youth from the Protestant organization.[45]

Children and adolescents were particularly important to the American Catholic Church in the early twentieth century. Bishops viewed American-born children as providing a link between priests and their immigrant parents. The rapidly expanding nationwide network of parochial schools ensured that church representatives—especially nuns—interacted daily with children. These encounters provided opportunities to shape the hearts and minds of young people directly and thereby their parents indirectly. On the one hand, church leaders wanted to advance Americanization, integrating white ethnic Catholics into the nation's mainstream.[46] On the other hand, they desired to protect Catholics from the larger secular and Protestant cultures deemed morally unhealthy.[47] Central to this process was "training of the will." Young people needed to be taught right from wrong; they needed to internalize a moral code. While public schools could teach children reading, writing, and arithmetic, they could not teach children how to be good Catholics.[48] Schools alone, however, were not enough. Not every Catholic child attended parochial school. Catholic clubs and societies provided further avenues to reach young people.

During World War I, Mundelein instructed each parish to start a chapter of the Holy Name Society, a lay, all-male organization. By the 1920s, Holy Name men had in place a variety of religious, social, and athletic functions at the parish level. For example, a Holy Name basketball league provided opportunity for interparish competition among Catholic youth. The society also ran a big brothers program focused on preventing juvenile delinquency. The cardinal assigned his chancellor to oversee the group, but Sheil saw the need for an even more wide-ranging archdiocesan athletic program.[49] As Mundelein's protégé, he enjoyed unique access to his boss, living in the cardinal's Gold Coast mansion at North Avenue and State Parkway until 1935 when he became pastor of St. Andrew's in the North Side's Lakeview neighborhood. Sheil, with the support of Mundelein, began taking the first steps toward realizing his vision of a citywide Catholic sports league.

On 15 June 1929, just months before the stock market crash and onset of economic turmoil, the Archdiocese of Chicago chartered the CYO.[50] Mundelein instructed Sheil to "adopt a program of recreation so adequate, interesting and attractive that our youth will have a desire to partake of none other."[51] Sheil officially started the CYO on 11 June 1930, with the appointment of Rev. Raphael Ashenden as executive director.[52]

Despite his clear directive, Mundelein provided no archdiocesan funding to launch the CYO. Sheil began with an inheritance from his father, who had died a few years earlier in an automobile accident, and solicited support from Chicago's civic and business leaders. Britton Budd, president of the Public Service Company of Northern Illinois (a Samuel Insull electric utility) donated $10,000.[53] Other early supporters included Sheldon Clark of Sinclair Oil Company and Edward Doyle, president of the Commonwealth Edison Company. Arch Ward, the *Chicago Tribune* sportswriter and founder of the Golden Gloves boxing tournament and Major League Baseball's All-Star game, and *Tribune* sports editor Stuyvesant Peabody contributed organizational and promotional skills.[54]

Sheil's greatest ally aside from Mundelein was the young Catholic lawyer William Campbell. When Campbell helped Sheil create the CYO, he was only four years out of Loyola University's law school, but his firm, Campbell & Burns, counted the Archdiocese of Chicago as a major client.[55] Sheil befriended the up-and-coming young professional in the late 1920s and employed him as his personal lawyer.[56] Campbell served as CYO secretary-treasurer and legal counsel throughout the 1930s. His negotiations with Boy Scout officials at the onset of the Depression allowed the archdiocese to assume control of scouting programs for Chicago Catholics.[57] When the Roosevelt administration created the NYA, it looked to Chicago and the CYO for expertise; Sheil recommended Campbell. In 1935, Works Progress Administration (WPA) head Harry Hopkins named Campbell Illinois director of the NYA. Campbell strengthened ties between the CYO and Washington, DC, through his involvement in the New Deal. In 1938, Roosevelt rewarded Campbell for his service by naming him U.S. attorney for northern Illinois. Campbell resigned his NYA directorship to pursue prosecution full-time and in 1940 at the age of thirty-five became the youngest judge ever appointed to the federal bench.[58]

Campbell embodied Sheil's approach to managing the CYO. Instead of relying solely on the clergy, Sheil enlisted the assistance of capable laypersons like the Catholic lawyer. Campbell's professional background brought essential organizational skills to the CYO. "He was a fair administrator," recalled future U.S. federal judge Abraham Lincoln Marovitz, who met Campbell through the CYO. "He was an innovator in many ways, and he cut through a lot of red tape."[59] Those skills proved invaluable when securing New Deal public funds. Campbell regularly used his administrative proficiency to negotiate favorable agreements between the CYO and government at the federal, state, and local levels. In 1937, Mayor Edward Kelly named him to the Chicago Recreation Commission.[60]

Sheil headquartered the CYO in the downtown business Loop. The organization was incorporated with the State of Illinois in 1932. In June of that year, he signed a long-term lease for four of the seven floors of the Congress Bank Building at 31 East Congress Street. The facility, which included a large gymnasium with boxing rings, locker rooms, and fifty-two bowling alleys, served as the CYO headquarters until 1954. "We are rescuing our boys from speakeasies, gangster hang-outs, street corners, and from the other temptations that lie in wait for discontented youth," remarked Cardinal Mundelein at the center's dedication. "We hope to make this Center a school for better future citizens of Chicago."[61]

Despite an institutional foundation in Chicago's downtown, the CYO functioned primarily as an association of neighborhood youth centers at the parish level. Sheil took advantage of the comprehensive organizational infrastructure of the Catholic parish system. Each neighborhood already had an existing local Catholic church with a physical plant that often included a gymnasium and social hall. Lay and religious volunteers coached teams and chaperoned activities involving thousands of young people. After meeting on the interparish level throughout the season, teams competed citywide for championship trophies. Brackets of teams and individuals from the North, South, and West Sides determined city champions. Initially, the CYO was best known as a boxing league; three of the boxers on the 1936 U.S. Olympic team came out of the Chicago CYO.[62] By the mid-1930s, however, opportunities in an array of sports existed for both boys and girls, including basketball, baseball, softball, tennis, golf, bowling, track and field, swimming, water polo, and chess. Yet boxing remained the CYO glamour sport.

The scourge of juvenile delinquency was of great concern to the city's leaders. The rise of organized crime during Prohibition in the 1920s and the subsequent glorification of gangsters like Al Capone appealed to urban

youth, particularly adolescent boys. High unemployment during the Depression and the continued growth and influence of mass media added
still further pressure on reformers like Sheil, who were fighting to keep
kids on the straight and narrow. As consumers of mass culture, young
people in the 1930s had many choices. "The flowering of a new mass media—radio, movies, books, and comics," writes historian Howard Chudacoff, "sparked children's fantasies and consumerism in ways that had
not existed previously."[63] Facing such competition, Sheil wondered how
to capture the imagination of young people, particularly boys. Boxers, in
addition to gangsters, were the most idolized figures in American popular
culture during the 1930s. In boxing, Sheil found a hook to draw participants to his program.

"THE MANLY ART"

The "manly art of self-defense" appealed to young men from tough backgrounds, including those Sheil met in the Cook County Jail. Popular in
the nineteenth century, boxing came under attack during the Progressive
Era from reformers who thought it too violent and dehumanizing. The
sport enjoyed a resurgence after World War I, however, and by 1926 Illinois
lawmakers repealed most anti-boxing laws (in large part to allow Chicago
to host the second championship fight between Jack Dempsey and Gene
Tunney in September 1927).[64] Sportswriter Arch Ward came up with the
idea for an amateur boxing tournament in 1923, and the *Chicago Tribune*
began sponsoring the Golden Gloves in 1928. The *New York Daily News*
started a similar tournament in the East, and winners from New York and
Chicago met annually to decide the nation's best amateur boxers. Over the
years, Golden Gloves champions included a number of future professional
greats, including Joe Louis and Cassius Clay (Muhammad Ali).

Sheil modeled his CYO boxing tournament on the Golden Gloves.
He capitalized on prizefighting's power to attract urban teenagers eager
for glamour, excitement, and fame. He enlisted legendary boxing professionals—Packey McFarland in the 1930s and middleweight world champion Tony Zale in the 1940s—to coach and promote bouts. Annual CYO
championships at Chicago Stadium drew between fourteen thousand
and twenty thousand spectators, and special exhibitions at Soldier Field
and Wrigley Field attracted as many as thirty-eight thousand fans.[65] The
fights reached even larger audiences through radio broadcasts on Chicago's
WCFL.[66] Beginning in 1932 and continuing for several years, the CYO won
the Golden Gloves team trophy.[67]

Sheil viewed boxing as a means to reach teenage males: "If a boy can come to know about God through a pair of boxing gloves—swell!"[68] He believed only a glamorous sport like boxing could attract the very kind of young men who needed help. "Show me how you can lead boys from saloons with a checkers tournament," he said, "and I'll put on the biggest checkers tournament you ever saw."[69] Critics questioned the propriety of a Catholic bishop working as fight promoter, but Mundelein defended Sheil's methods in a press conference two days before the first CYO tournament:

> The church in these days, particularly in a big city like Chicago, must do some things we did not have to do a generation ago. A generation ago, when a boy had passed though the parish school and had been confirmed, we felt that we had properly prepared him for life. . . . But today we must supervise his recreation. Otherwise he may come under influence and enter into surroundings that may quickly undermine and destroy what we have built up in his soul and in his character.

The cardinal went on to support Sheil's efforts by invoking prevailing gender stereotypes. "We might as well admit that a growing healthy boy takes as naturally to boxing as a puppy does to romping," Mundelein argued. "Mothers for generations have tried to suppress it and haven't succeeded. The church doesn't try. Rather we are trying to control it . . . If done properly, it certainly helps develop the boy, it makes him alert, manly, and courageous." Mundelein also lamented the cowardly use of handguns and Chicago's high rate of violent crime during the 1920s, results of an "unmanly" culture.[70] He feared losing Catholic youth to gangsters like Al Capone, who promised fame and easy money. However, he felt confident that Bishop Sheil's CYO could "build real boys."[71]

In statements to the press, CYO official Rev. Gerald Scanlan explained the purpose behind running a boxing program. "The principal idea behind this boxing tournament," he said, "is to take the surplus time and energy of our boys and turn them into new and useful channels."[72] Scanlan also responded to charges that the CYO was simply acting as a talent agency. "We are in no sense trying to train professional boxers or prize-fighters," he maintained. "What we are endeavoring to do, is translate and emphasize through this sport, the fundamental advantages and requirements of clean-living, self-sacrifice and sportsmanship to equip our boys in the battle of life in their fight against the scourge of present-day indifferentism and the false standards of soft existence and easy money."[73]

The success of CYO tournaments allowed Sheil to reach thousands

Fig. 3.1. Bishop Sheil (*left*) holds trophy with Cardinal Mundelein (*right*) before
the first annual CYO boxing tournament, December 1931. (Archdiocese of
Chicago's Joseph Cardinal Bernardin Archives and Records Center.)

of young men throughout the city with a message of Christian morality,
civic-mindedness, and clean living, and at the same time he encouraged
Chicago's youth to adopt a civic-religious expression rooted in principles of
Catholic social teachings. Sheil followed in a long American tradition that
linked (usually Protestant) religious convictions to civic participation.[74]

Although the United States claimed no official state religion, civic-
religious expressions, like those found in the CYO, attempted to link God
and country within an urban Catholic context during the 1930s and 1940s.
The CYO represented the youth component of Mundelein's Americanization campaign to create a church that was "100 percent Catholic and
100 percent American," removing from American Catholicism the stigma
of alien customs and foreign values. Sheil took every opportunity in public
to demonstrate CYO patriotism and civic involvement. In 1935, for example, seventy-five thousand CYO supporters marched along Michigan Avenue in a three-hour parade.[75] A 1940 editorial in a secular daily newspaper

declared, "C.Y.O. has become, in ten short years, one of the most powerful influences for good citizenship in Chicago and one of the great forces for Americanism in America."[76]

On Friday evening, 4 December 1931, Bishop Sheil and the CYO hosted the first of its annual citywide boxing tournaments at Chicago Stadium. Approximately fifteen thousand fans from across the city came to watch some of the area's best amateur fighters duke it out.[77] The thirty-two CYO finalists entered the ring escorted by an honor guard of a thousand Catholic Boy Scouts from parishes throughout the city. Sheil opened with a prayer and then led participants in the CYO Pledge:

> I promise on my honor to be loyal to my God, to my Country and to my Church; to be faithful and true to my obligations as a Christian, a man, and a citizen. I pledge myself to live a clean, honest, and upright life— to avoid profane, obscene, and vulgar language, and to induce others to avoid it. I bind myself to promote, by word and example, clean, wholesome, and manly sport; I will strive earnestly to be a man of whom my Church and my Country may be justly proud.[78]

A later "My CYO Creed" was more specific:

> 1. To love God and Country; 2. To love the poor and afflicted; 3. To acquire physical and mental courage; 4. To understand myself and my group; 5. To strive for a better life for myself and my fellowmen [sic]; 6. To promote social justice by rigid application of the principles expressed in the Encyclicals of Leo XIII and Pius XI; 7. To foster the spirit of American Democracy as expressed in the deeds of Jefferson and Lincoln; 8. To abstain from excesses of any kind; 9. To emulate virtues of the victorious Apostolate of Christ; 10. To be humble in victory; undaunted in defeat.[79]

In the public venue of Chicago Stadium, the CYO tournament transformed the normally secular event of a boxing match into a celebration of religious and civic values, which made the atmosphere surrounding the occasion considerably different from professional boxing bouts or even amateur Golden Gloves matches. The CYO challenged the conventional view of boxing as a vulgar and immoral activity and in the process advanced Catholic Americanism.[80]

CIVIC PAGEANTRY AND POPULAR CULTURE

The CYO promoted Catholic Americanism on a grand scale. During 1934, it sponsored 142 amateur boxing shows; 96 were held in parishes, clubs, and societies, while 46 took place in the downtown CYO Center or the CYO Open Air Stadium on the Near West Side.[81] The CYO also hosted intercity bouts each summer.[82] In July 1935, for example, amateur boxing champions from New York City came to Chicago for competition. More than 100,000 Chicagoans welcomed the New York boxers in a huge parade with airplanes flying overhead at Garfield Park on the city's West Side. A more intimate banquet at the Midwest Athletic Club followed. Attendees included the political elites of America's two largest metropolises: Chicago mayor Edward Kelly, New York mayor Fiorello La Guardia, Illinois governor Henry Horner, and former New York governor Al Smith. Advertisements for the bouts had begun 2 weeks earlier, broadcasted on 10 different radio stations.[83] The Chicago City Council declared the intercity match a "civic event" with an official attendance of 35,000 fans at Wrigley Field.[84] Winners received prizes and scholarships,[85] and Avery Brundage, chairman of the U.S. Olympic Committee, spoke to the crowd about the following summer's Olympic Games in Berlin.[86]

Yet boxing glory itself was not Sheil's ultimate goal. Unlike the Golden Gloves or other city clubs, the CYO discouraged boxers from turning professional. CYO officials also enforced strict safety procedures. Prior to entering the ring, each boy underwent a thorough physical examination. In addition, first-time entrants took a boxing test before competing. CYO bouts were shorter than standard, and referees stopped fights at the first sign of distress.[87]

The CYO, however, did not fail to exploit publicity garnered by its few professional members.[88] In fact, Sheil established a professional boxing school in 1934 operated by Pat Kenneally, former manager of boxing great Packey McFarland. Kenneally acted as the manager for CYO champions who turned professional, but instead of taking a percentage of a boxer's winnings, Kenneally relied on his CYO salary for income. The CYO took 33.3 percent of winnings allowed to managers by law and put the money in a trust fund for the boxer.[89] A 1935 article in the *New York American* reported that unionized fight managers did not appreciate the CYO practice and noted, "C.Y.O. boxing shows have become the biggest and most popular amateur presentation of the kind."[90] The handful of boxers who went on to become professionals—Leo Rodak, Max Marek, and Harold

Dade—created a glamorous image of the CYO for adolescent boys across the country.

Sheil enjoyed the company of well-known individuals outside of boxing and used these associations to publicize CYO events. Sports personalities, popular music performers, and Hollywood celebrities promoted the CYO and raised funds for the bishop. Notre Dame great Jack Elder became a CYO sportswriter and athletic director.[91] Sportswriter Arch Ward, who came up with the idea in the 1920s for the Golden Gloves boxing tournament, supported Sheil's programs by singing the bishop's praises in his *Chicago Tribune* column. Well-known newspaperman Eddie Doherty was also a big fan of Sheil.[92] National radio broadcasts regularly covered the annual CYO boxing tournaments held each December in Chicago Stadium, as well as summer bouts at Wrigley and Soldier Fields against champions from New York City and foreign nations. *Life*, *Newsweek*, and *Time* magazines wrote approvingly of Sheil's work, while celebrities like Jimmy Durante, Danny Thomas, and Rudy Valle raised money for CYO initiatives.[93]

Sheil, who possessed many qualities of a showman, had a knack for attracting newspaper and radio coverage. His "astute understanding of popular currents in urban America" allowed the CYO to create "a highly visible, popular form of social Catholicism at the center of the industrial popular culture of America in the 1930s."[94] Sheil also drew on celebrities to reach out to the African American community. African American jazz great Lena Horne supported the CYO as did popular singer, actor, and teenage heartthrob Frank Sinatra.[95] After starring in *The House I Live In*, a 1945 film promoting racial tolerance, Sinatra performed at a CYO fundraiser in Chicago. He also spoke out on the importance of the CYO in newspaper editorials.[96] And in 1948, Sinatra donated to the CYO his earnings from playing a Catholic priest in the Hollywood film *Miracle of the Bells*.[97]

At times it must have appeared that Bishop Sheil himself was playing the role of a heroic priest in a Hollywood film. His penchant for publicity, close relationships with sports journalists, and showman's sensibilities combined to make him an attractive public figure. "Sheil loved displays of power," writes historian Steven Avella. "The smell of the crowd, the dramatic moment . . . at the scene of an accident where he would throw his coat over a victim—these were the moments he savored. These were also the moments that made his career and won him the adulation of people everywhere."[98]

Some historians believe that Catholics enjoyed a "golden age" in Hollywood from the mid-1930s to the mid-1940s, the same period that marked the height of popularity and influence for Bishop Sheil and the CYO. Indeed, popular American films during that decade often invoked strong Catholic themes, including *San Francisco* (1936), *Angels with Dirty Faces* (1938), *Boys Town* (1938), *The Fighting 69th* (1940), *Knute Rockne* (1940), *The Fighting Sullivans* (1943), *God is My Co-pilot* (1943), *The Keys of the Kingdom* (1943), and *The Song of Bernadette* (1943), to name a few. In many of these films a gutsy Catholic priest, championing the cause of social justice in the midst of an unjust society, presents to alienated urban youth an alternative to the gangster's enticements of easy money and short-lived glory.[99]

Pat O'Brien's depiction of fictional Father Jerry Connolly in *Angels with Dirty Faces* and Spencer Tracy's Academy Award–winning portrayal of real-life Father Edward Flanagan of Boys Town were evocative of Bernard Sheil. O'Brien's Father Jerry, for instance, grew up in an urban neighborhood with future gangster Rocky Sullivan (played by James Cagney) and knew how to handle himself in a fight, while Tracy's Flanagan challenged a skeptical business establishment to create opportunities for marginalized youth. Like Sheil, Flanagan did not worry himself about money and often used deficit spending to advance his enterprise.[100] Similarly, in real life, Bernard Sheil played the role of the "People's Bishop," fulfilling the public's expectations for him by exploiting symbols of patriotism, masculinity, and social justice. The prototypical urban priest of the 1930s was tough, compassionate, and championed the cause of the working class.[101] Hollywood films of the era portrayed a Catholic-led urban populism that embraced cultural pluralism and celebrated contributions of the industrial working class to American society.

The popularity of boxing in the 1930s created opportunities for African Americans and working-class whites to enter "the sporting mainstream."[102] Organized athletics no longer belonged to the exclusive purview of the middle class and college students. Programs like the CYO and Golden Gloves provided recreational outlets for youngsters from working families. Moreover, civic-religious values and close supervision promoted supervised exchanges between various ethnic and racial groups. The CYO motto, "It's more fun to fight with boxing gloves," for example, was directed at black and white youths who might otherwise meet in fisticuffs along Wentworth Avenue, the color line dividing Bronzeville and the working-class, Irish American neighborhood of Bridgeport.[103]

Basketball soon became the second most popular CYO sport. By some accounts, the CYO basketball tournament was the largest event of its kind in the world.[104] More than 250 teams entered competition during the

1931–1932 season.[105] The following year, 360 teams competed, including 110 girls teams, 110 lightweight (5′8″ and shorter) boys teams, and 140 boys heavyweight (taller than 5′8″) teams.[106] Parishes competed against adjacent parishes during the regular season, with winners advancing to playoffs where they faced the best teams in their region. Regional winners played for the championship in front of crowds of 5,000 or more in armories, university field houses, and city arenas.[107] Beginning in the spring of 1931, the CYO sponsored intercity games against New York City's Catholic champions.[108] Tournament champions, including girls teams, made all-star trips to other cities.[109] Rules required players to live inside parish boundaries, remain amateurs, and not compete in three or more games in the interparish school league.[110] As in CYO boxing matches, Sheil led players in the CYO Pledge and prayer prior to championship competition.[111]

A CATHOLIC NEW DEAL[112]

The early years of the CYO coincided with the creation of Franklin Roosevelt's New Deal. Cardinal Mundelein counted the fellow native New Yorker as a friend and supported the president's national programs and pluralistic ideology.[113] Roosevelt also developed a friendship with Bishop Sheil, who capitalized on the president's support. For example, FDR and Sheil met for the first time at a Boy Scouts meeting in New York City when Roosevelt was governor of New York. In 1933, they met a second time at the National Catholic Charities dinner, also in New York. Roosevelt told Sheil that the federal government needed the assistance of private entities like the CYO to fight social problems.[114] Mundelein and Sheil visited the White House on several occasions, and the president called on Mundelein in the cardinal's mansion in 1935 and 1937. The CYO utilized resources made available through the WPA, Civilian Conservation Corps, and NYA.[115] In addition, the CYO collaborated with local government agencies, particularly the Chicago Park District.

Six months before the first annual CYO boxing tournament in Chicago Stadium, Sheil began two experimental vacation schools on the city's Southwest Side. Like CYO sports leagues, the daily summer vacation schools took advantage of the geographical organization of Catholic parishes across the city. Children, ages five to sixteen years, primarily from working-class homes, participated in six-week camps conducted by priests and nuns. St. Rose of Lima Church in Chicago's Back of the Yards neighborhood hosted one of the two original vacation schools in 1930 but did not have enough room in its physical plant to conduct classes. Chicago's publicly funded Park District offered the use of the Sherman Park field house to the Catholic organization. By 1935, fourteen CYO vacation schools dotted Chicago's map, and the shrewdly political Sheil worked at strengthening relationships between the archdiocese and the Park District. The bishop appointed Rev. Peter Meegan as supervisor of vacation schools; his brother, Joseph Meegan, not insignificantly, was a Chicago Park District official who later collaborated with community organizer Saul Alinsky in the Back of the Yards.[116] By the summer of 1946, the CYO boasted fifty-six vacation centers serving more than forty thousand children in thirty-one public parks, eighteen parish plants, and seven settlement houses.[117]

The vacation schools, although administered by the Catholic Church, operated essentially as cooperative efforts among archdiocesan, city, and federal authorities. In organizing these programs, Sheil took advantage of personal ties to the White House and Chicago Park District. During the summer of 1939, for example, 92 WPA workers, 150 NYA members, and 149 Park District employees, along with 39 priests, 70 nuns, and 563 volunteers—mostly from Catholic high schools and colleges—administered CYO vacation schools. The vacation schools dropped Catholic instruction from their curricula after the CYO formed alliances with local and federal government entities in the mid-1930s.[118] Church and state intersected in new ways during the Great Depression. The Roosevelt administration and political leaders at the municipal level tapped into the Roman Catholic Church's expansive array of charities and social services in the urban North, partnering with organizations like the CYO to meet the widespread and acute needs of the poor, sick, unemployed, and homeless.[119]

The civic-religious expression of the CYO included love of God and country, but not sectarian dogma. About one-half of the children in the summer camps attended public schools and over 20 percent were non-Catholics, including many African Americans. Nearly one-half were children of foreign-born parents, and about one-fifth came from families receiving some kind of public assistance.[120] City and federal taxpayers supported these summer day camps administered by the Catholic Church because they emphasized "American" values and offered an existing social service infrastructure yet unparalleled by either local or national governments. Instead of emphasizing uniquely Catholic doctrine, the vacation schools advanced a more generic, civic-religious expression that championed pluralism, patriotism, and education. On one of those summer mornings, it would not have been unusual to see a Catholic nun in full habit, assisted by a New Deal government worker, reciting the Pledge of Alle-

Fig. 3.2. A Sister of Charity of the Blessed Virgin Mary supervises children attending a CYO summer vacation school. The schools were open to all races and religions, serving thousands of children throughout Chicago during the 1930s and 1940s. (Archdiocese of Chicago's Joseph Cardinal Bernardin Archives and Records Center.)

giance in a city park with children from different races, ethnicities, and religions. Civic service and religion melded during the Depression.

Roosevelt courted Catholic voters while building his New Deal coalition throughout the urban North. Prominent Catholic laymen Joseph Kennedy (chairman of the Securities and Exchange Commission and ambassador to the United Kingdom), James Farley (postmaster general), and Frank Murphy (attorney general and Supreme Court justice), held high offices in Roosevelt administrations. The Catholic Church in Chicago strongly supported the New Deal. Mundelein was Roosevelt's closest friend in the Roman Catholic hierarchy. He assisted Roosevelt by displaying unwavering support for the president and easing the administration's occasionally contentious relations with Catholics. When Roosevelt faced criticism from American Catholics over U.S. policy in Mexico, for example, Mundelein acted as an intermediary. In 1937, the cardinal hosted Roosevelt at his Gold Coast residence immediately following the president's historic "Quarantine Speech." Mundelein also defended Roosevelt during the court-packing controversy in the mid-1930s.[121] According to Harold Ickes, Chicagoan and U.S. secretary of the interior (1933–1946), the president regarded Mundelein "as one of the three greatest men in the country."[122]

Roosevelt also admired Mundelein's "right hand," Bishop Sheil. When Mundelein died in the fall of 1939, the president hoped to see Sheil appointed Archbishop of Chicago. Sheil did serve as temporary administrator of the archdiocese for two and a half months but was not promoted. Roosevelt and his advisors believed Sheil to be one of the administration's few allies in the Roman Catholic hierarchy. "He is about the only prominent churchman in the country who has even a faint coloration of liberalism," remarked Ickes. Rome's choice of Samuel Stritch for archbishop of Chicago in late December 1939 disappointed Roosevelt. "Well, you and I have had a pretty severe blow today in Chicago," he said to Ickes upon hearing the news of Stritch's appointment. Roosevelt then worked through diplomatic channels within the Vatican to get Sheil appointed to the vacant archbishopric in Washington, DC, but those efforts also failed.[123] Sheil thus remained in Chicago and continued to fight for liberal causes.

LABOR'S BISHOP

On 16 July 1939, Bishop Sheil shook the hands of labor leader John L. Lewis on stage at a union rally in Chicago's Back of the Yards. Saul Alinsky had asked the bishop to show his support publicly for the Congress of Industrial Organizations (CIO) in the union's fight against the "Big Four" meatpackers. The handshake was no small gesture. A Catholic leader had never before appeared in public with the controversial Lewis.[124] Sheil, a clergyman with strong anticommunist credentials, brought an air of respectability, a "Catholic stamp of approval," to organized labor.[125] He enjoyed the support of his superior Mundelein, who had lunched with the president at the White House just the day before the rally.[126] "[Sheil's participation] would torpedo the entire publicity campaign of the meatpackers that the CIO was a Communist conspiracy," Alinsky later wrote.[127] The stockyards workers won the strike, and Sheil secured his reputation as "labor's bishop."[128]

Just as the CIO overcame racial and ethnic divisions within the labor movement by appealing to collective values rooted in the working class, Sheil also sought the backing of workers by supporting the goals of organized labor, linking its agenda with civic-religious expression. Although liberal by the standards of his fellow clergy, Sheil was a centrist in the context of the 1930s. He supported the rather moderate assimilation of the urban working class into mainstream American culture. He never lent support to more militant, left-wing movements, such as Upton Sinclair's End Poverty in California campaign or Norman Thomas's Socialist Party. The CYO helped stave off radical labor movements in the 1930s by using competitive sports, particularly boxing, to convert potential revolutionaries to Sheil's brand of relatively moderate, Catholic social justice ideology, thereby helping to maintain the status quo of U.S. economic and political systems.[129]

Working with Chicago Park District official and Sheil associate Joseph Meegan, Alinsky solicited the bishop's help in organizing the neighborhood that Upton Sinclair dubbed "the Jungle." Located on Chicago's Near Southwest Side, the multiethnic, working-class district was variously known as New City, Packingtown, and Back of the Yards. As a young sociologist with the Institute of Juvenile Research, Alinsky became acquainted with the area while conducting a survey on criminal gang activity. Frustrated with charitable organizations that only addressed the symptoms of urban working-class social problems, Alinsky founded the Back of the Yards Neighborhood Council (BYNC) to advance self-help, participatory democracy based on cooperation across ethnic lines. Germans, Irish, Lithuanians, Mexicans, Poles, and Slovaks resided in the densely populated district in the shadows of the Union Stockyards and packinghouses. Besides employment in the meatpacking industry, what bound these workers was their shared religious affiliation. Alinsky recalled years later that "the area was 95 percent Roman Catholic, and I recognized that if I could win the support of the Church, we'd be off and running. Conversely, without the Church, or at least some elements of it, it was unlikely that we'd be able to make much of a dent in the community."[130]

Sheil endorsed the BYNC and put Alinsky in touch with prominent business leaders sympathetic to his cause, including Marshall Field III.[131] "Sheil . . . has been the godfather of the Back of the Yards Neighborhood Council from its earliest inception," noted one observer in 1940. "From the first he placed before it the benefits of his prestige, energy, and wisdom. Mr. Alinsky and Mr. Meegan had some trying days dodging the epithets 'Reds!' and 'Reactionaries!' . . . but Bishop Sheil never once wavered in his support for them."[132] The BYNC flourished, and Alinsky established the national Industrial Areas Foundation, which sought to replicate his Chicago success in cities across the country.[133]

Sheil's pro-labor stance drew criticism from some of his fellow clergymen. Cardinal Dennis Dougherty of Philadelphia, for instance, baited

Sheil, derogatorily calling him the "Red Bishop."[134] Sheil, however, never shied away from offending ideologues on either the Left or Right. He rejected, for example, offers in 1937 from representatives of the American Youth Congress to work cooperatively with Chicago's CYO. The bishop felt that the communistic leanings of the congress would compromise teenagers through its "totalitarian ideology . . . which would subvert Jeffersonian ideals and principles [adhered to by the CYO]."[135]

Yet Sheil also rejected red baiting. Instead of looking under every stone for Communists, the bishop urged business and government leaders to ensure the economic and social stability of working Americans. He agreed with the papal encyclicals of Leo XIII and Pius XI—labor rights were in truth human rights. Sheil believed a well-compensated labor force meant a safer and more democratic nation. "America need never fear Communism where economic stability exists," he argued. "Communism has a poor lure for people who are well clothed, well housed and well fed."[136] Communists and others on the Left, however, rather effectively critiqued American capitalism for its racism and class divisions. In response, the CYO promoted American pluralism.

Sheil championed Franklin Roosevelt's presidency because he believed the New Deal was in the spirit of Catholic social teaching, representing a middle path between laissez-faire capitalism and godless Communism. In particular, he also believed the New Deal was good for African Americans, who, already in a precarious economic situation before the Depression, suffered disproportionately during the 1930s. African Americans did benefit from joining New Deal coalitions found in northern cities like Chicago, but the New Deal never ended the systematic exclusion of blacks from full and equal participation in government welfare programs.[137] Indeed, Sheil recognized the limits of progressive politics when he said in the early 1950s, "The Negro has not received a square deal, an honest deal, or a new deal from white America."[138] Sheil knew more needed to be done; he envisioned the CYO as a means to promote racial justice and interracial harmony.

A HOUSE FOR ALL PEOPLES[139]

Sheil's Americanism embraced the concept of pluralism. In numerous cases, the CYO promoted the multiethnic and multiracial backgrounds of participants. "All Races and Nations Participate in the C.Y.O. Program" read a 1935 headline in the archdiocese's weekly newspaper. An accompanying photograph showed nine boys lining the ropes of a boxing ring in the

CYO gymnasium at 31 East Congress Street. This "C.Y.O. League of Nations" included boxers of various ethnicities and nationalities: Croatian, Austrian, Assyrian, Polish, Irish, Chinese, Italian, "Colored," and Mexican.[140] The following year, a similar picture showed fifteen young men from diverse backgrounds huddled around a large kettle with the banner, "The C.Y.O. Melting Pot."[141] The 1937 CYO boxing tournament in Chicago Stadium included Irish, German, Italian, Polish, Lithuanian, French, Spanish, Greek, "Colored," Austrian, Mexican, and Slovak boxers.[142] Like the Democratic Party and organized labor, the CYO formed interracial and panethnic alliances during the 1930s. The organization followed inclusive practices from the beginning, its charter promising to serve youth "without regard to race, creed, or color."[143]

The CYO employed a universal—or catholic—model that considered all youth residing within the archdiocese to be under its care. Within this model, Chicago's African American community, growing in numbers

Fig. 3.3. Members of the CYO "League of Nations" line the ropes of a boxing ring at the CYO Center in 1935. *Left to right*: Steve Press (Croatian), Frank Kainrath (Austrian), Sam David (Assyrian), Sam Zaczek (Polish), Joe Howe (Irish), Bob Chan (Chinese), Al Scarlata (Italian), Jimmy Martin ("Colored"), and Florentino Arreguin (Mexican). (Archdiocese of Chicago's Joseph Cardinal Bernardin Archives and Records Center.)

but still only 7 percent of the city's population in 1930, acted as one of several nationalities.[144] Like Irish, Polish, and Italian CYO participants, African Americans represented their own "national" parishes, three mission churches—St. Elizabeth, Corpus Christi, and St. Anselm—segregated within Bronzeville.

The CYO League of Nations embodied pluralistic values which had gained currency during the Depression and would become ingrained in the national consciousness during World War II. Several Hollywood films from the era depicted the ideal of American pluralism by casting an assortment of ethnically diverse actors, epitomized by the platoon movie *Bataan* (1943). This ideal was a new phenomenon in U.S. history. While the eighteenth-century motto *E Pluribus Unum* originally referred to thirteen states uniting to create one nation, Americans in the second half of the twentieth century began to understand the phrase to refer to one people emerging from many races, ethnicities, and religions. *Bataan*, according to cultural historian Richard Slotkin, was the "first fully articulated statement of . . . a new fable of American nationality," marking "the shift from the myth of America as essentially a white man's country, to that of a multiethnic, multiracial democracy."[145]

CYO pluralism paralleled national trends in the 1930s and 1940s that celebrated cultural diversity. Aspects of this New Deal ideology originated during World War I, when the United States confronted widespread ethnic bigotry. As war raged in Europe, American society was caught up in anti-German sentiment. Fearing for their safety, German Americans often changed surnames, business titles, and customs in an attempt to appear less German and more "American." In response, Horace Kallen, a German-born Jewish intellectual, argued for retention of ethnic differences, coining the term "cultural pluralism." Kallen favored an Americanization process that emphasized acculturation over assimilation. He believed that the prevailing "melting pot" ideology—which advocated "steaming off" ethnic distinctions so as to leave an Anglo-Saxon core—weakened the nation by eliminating the positive aspects of cultural diversity. Essayist Randolph Bourne agreed with Kallen. In his seminal 1916 essay in the *Atlantic Monthly*, Bourne described his "cosmopolitan vision" for American society. He argued that the nation benefited most from the combination of different ethnic groups. Instead of homogeneity, Bourne favored a "federation of cultures" within the United States.[146]

Cultural pluralism suffered as a result of nativism during the 1920s. Reactionary forces pushed through federal legislation placing national quotas on the number of immigrants allowed into the country, and a re-vived Ku Klux Klan attacked immigrants, Catholics, Jews, and African Americans. The American Catholic Church, led by Mundelein, conducted an Americanization campaign that sought to eliminate national parishes. The economic collapse of the 1930s, however, transformed the nation, as New Deal ideology embraced cultural pluralism. Sheil's CYO celebrated diversity, while at the same time transcending the parochialism of urban American Catholicism which tended to remain isolated within the seg-regated subcultures of its European immigrant population base. Sheil be-lieved that common links based on patriotism and shared Judeo-Christian worldviews could overcome divisions defined by race, creed, and nation-ality. Class acted as strong glue, which held together his vision for ur-ban America.

The CIO, like the CYO and Alinsky's BYNC, represented how the values of 1930s urban pluralism were transforming American social and political life. Historian Lizabeth Cohen demonstrates how a "culture of unity" allowed working-class Chicagoans to overcome ethnic differences in the cause of class solidarity.[147] The CYO, which opened a nighttime la-bor school for adults during World War II, found common cause with the CIO. Bishop Sheil felt the CIO was doing for adults what the CYO did for children and adolescents. "Thank God for the CIO," he told an organized labor rally in 1937.[148] The bishop's attacks on anti-Semitism and support of racial integration complemented the progressive labor union's efforts. Upon request, Sheil wrote an antiracist pamphlet that "became the stan-dard CIO piece on the subject in many parts of the country."[149]

The bourgeoning consumerism of the 1920s—seen in radio, music rec-ords, chain and department stores, as well as sports and leisure—provided shared experiences that transcended ethnic and racial divisions. Mass popular culture brought together working-class Americans from various ethnic and racial backgrounds, allowing them to overcome cultural differ-ence which had divided them prior to World War I.[150] They used the lan-guage of Americanism to develop a panethnic political consciousness.[151] Sheil's CYO exploited the appeal of mass popular culture, specifically sports and leisure, while at the same time invoking the language of Amer-icanism to advance a civic culture based on communal values.

Bishop Sheil is not completely unknown to historians of American Ca-tholicism, but for the most part the CYO founder-director has been rel-egated to the margins in the history of the United States and the history of American Catholicism.[152] A close examination of Sheil, however, complicates our understanding of white ethnics during the interwar period. He was as much a creation of twentieth-century urban pluralism as the CYO was the creation of the bishop.

Adhering to Mundelein's Americanization plan, the CYO advocated full participation by Catholics, Jews, and racial minorities. Included within this vision of American life were elements of fair play, religious and racial toleration, community service, pluralistic democracy, and displaying public reverence for a monotheistic deity. Likewise, the CYO fought against crime, bigotry, materialism, Communism, and secularism. With the assistance of federal and local governments, the business community, civic organizations, and members of other religions, Sheil's CYO developed a Catholic version of American pluralism that included African Americans.

CHAPTER FOUR

African American Participation in the CYO

Children have . . . an inalienable right to play.
—Bishop Bernard J. Sheil

Harry Booker, an African American teenager from St. Elizabeth parish, found himself in the finals of the second annual CYO boxing tournament by a fluke.[1] He was the substitute for another CYO boxer and future professional champion Leo Rodak, who was out with the flu.[2] Chicago boxing fans expected Rodak, representing a German American parish in the shadows of South Chicago's steel mills, to fight for the 1932 featherweight title against "Smiling" Jimmy Christy, a "puckish little Irishman" from Our Lady of Mt. Carmel on the North Side.[3] Instead, they witnessed a battle between the black Booker and white Christy. During the semifinals earlier in the evening, Booker narrowly defeated the reigning national Golden Gloves featherweight champion Joe Roman from Joliet, Illinois. Now, before sixteen thousand fans in the three-year-old Chicago Stadium, he faced Christy, the most popular boxer in the CYO. Bishop Sheil adored the redheaded Irish American, as did most of the crowd. Yet, despite his underdog status, Booker soundly defeated Christy in a three-round decision.[4]

More important, Booker's victory epitomized African American participation in the CYO, which included black members from its inception in 1930. Like each of the 1,600 entrants in the boxing tournament, Booker received a fair chance to compete and win. His racial status, a stigma in almost all other aspects of society, did not preclude him from full participation in this Catholic-sponsored event. Moreover, he represented not only St. Elizabeth but also the entire Chicago archdiocese a month later when he defeated a boxer from San Francisco in an exhibition bout at Chicago Stadium.⁵ African Americans from St. Elizabeth, Corpus Christi, St. Anselm, and after World War II other black parishes, took part in CYO activities alongside whites. Although Chicago's Roman Catholic parishes remained almost completely segregated during the 1930s, 1940s, and early 1950s, the citywide youth program provided numerous opportunities for black-white interaction. Booker enjoyed full membership in the CYO, because canon law recognized the equality of his parish—St. Elizabeth—to Christy's Our Lady of Mt. Carmel as well as to the more than 350 parishes in the Archdiocese of Chicago.⁶ Despite Bronzeville's geographic, social, and economic isolation from the rest of city, the consecrated Catholic spaces of St. Elizabeth, Corpus Christi, and St. Anselm parishes officially shared equal status with every other parish. The neighborhood may have changed from Irish American to African American during the preceding generation, but the parishes remained Catholic.

Bishop Sheil did not establish the CYO to fight racial bigotry. Over the years, however, he and his organization became one of the most prominent critics of discriminatory practices against African Americans in Chicago and the nation. The CYO, an outgrowth of the Holy Name Big Brothers program and parish athletic leagues, originally functioned as a means to counter juvenile delinquency, secularism, and antidemocratic ideologies among working-class Catholic boys during the Great Depression. Despite Chicago's black population more than doubling during the 1920s, African Americans made up only 7 percent of the city's residents in 1930, and African American Catholics accounted for less than 10 percent of the black populace. Black-white relations, therefore, did not top the list of priorities when Cardinal George Mundelein granted Bishop Sheil permission to inaugurate the CYO. Instead, Mundelein and Sheil focused on Americanization, the process whereby ethnic Catholics set aside nationalistic differences for common participation in the American church and assimilation into American society.

Within the Americanization model, African Americans like Harry Booker became, in many ways, another "ethnic"—like Irish, Poles, Germans, and Italians. In that sense, Booker did not occupy a special place in the CYO paradigm. He simply acted as another young man from one of the city's ethnic parishes participating in the tournament. With some luck (Rodak's illness), he earned his chance to win the championship. Sheil, a proud second-generation Irish American who chose green and white for the CYO colors and held annual corned beef and cabbage fundraising dinners, may have favored Christy, but he supported fair play above ethnic partisanship.⁷ For Sheil, religion trumped race. All Catholic parishes in

Fig. 4.1. Bishop Bernard Sheil and boxers promote the annual CYO tournament in 1950. (Archdiocese of Chicago's Joseph Cardinal Bernardin Archives and Records Center.)

the archdiocese, whatever their racial compositions, fell under his authority as bishop. Their members, therefore, stood as equals in the eyes of the church. This holistic approach allowed black and white young people to participate on even playing fields—if only between bells of a boxing match or whistles of a basketball game—in a city strictly divided by race.

SPORTS IN BRONZEVILLE

Race and sports shared a long history in Chicago, as well as the nation.[8] Many of the alleged culprits in the 1919 race riot were Irish American Catholic members of sporting organizations like the Hamburg Athletic Club, including seventeen-year-old Richard J. Daley, future mayor of Chicago.[9] In his 1927 study of urban gangs, sociologist Frederic Thrasher found that "the dominant social pattern for the conventionalized gang in Chicago is the athletic club." The civic commission charged with investigating the 1919 race riots blamed most of the violence and vandalism on such "athletic" and "social" clubs, which it recommended closing.[10] Nevertheless, tensions continued to worsen after 1919 between blacks and whites as the

South Side's Black Belt expanded. African American and white gangs often clashed along the Black Belt's western border, Wentworth Avenue.[11] Progressive-Era reformers believed that too much unstructured leisure time led to gang activity and advocated recreational programming as a means to avoid criminal behavior among adolescent boys. The YMCA and Boys Clubs, nondenominational Protestant movements, offered two such alternatives to gangs.

Like most American institutions prior to World War II, the YMCA operated under Jim Crow policies designed to serve African Americans in racially segregated settings. By the turn of the twentieth century, most major American cities included a black YMCA.[12] In 1910, mail-order magnate and philanthropist Julius Rosenwald pledged $25,000 to construct a building to house the African American YMCA in any community that could raise $75,000. The Sears, Roebuck and Company president eventually subsidized the construction of twenty-four "Rosenwald YMCAs" across the country. In Chicago, he convinced International Harvester boss Cyrus McCormick and prominent banker Norman Harris each to match his donation of $25,000. The resulting five-story building opened in 1913 at 38th Street and Wabash Avenue in the heart of Bronzeville. The "Wabash Y" —two blocks east and two blocks south of St. Monica's, the birthplace of Chicago's black Catholicism—assisted recent African American migrants in their acclimation to urban life. In 1915, historian Carter Woodson's Association for the Study of Negro Life and History began meeting at the South Side institution.[13] By World War I, the Wabash Y had become a hub of athletic, social, and intellectual activity in Chicago's rapidly growing African American community.[14]

In the end, however, the Wabash Avenue YMCA could not meet the ever-increasing needs of Bronzeville residents. Demand for more recreational facilities increased as the Black Belt expanded farther south during the 1920s and 1930s. "Though this district [43rd to 63rd streets between Wentworth Avenue and South Parkway] needs a YMCA, sadly there is none," noted one New Deal worker on the eve of World War II. "The Wabash Avenue YMCA at 38th Street and Wabash Avenue is overcrowded, and, apparently, would not be injured if in a city so heavily populated by Negroes another YMCA came into existence and especially to serve this district."[15] A second South Side YMCA did not open until 1949, while racial segregation continued in Chicago's YMCAs until 1950.[16]

Other institutions besides the YMCA served Bronzeville's youth. In 1924, the South Side Boys Club opened its doors on South Michigan Avenue one and a half blocks north of St. Elizabeth at the same time that the parish was undergoing its transformation from Irish American to African American. Thousands of neighborhood boys came to the club during the 1920s and 1930s.[17] Well-known alumni included singer Nat "King" Cole and Olympian Ralph Metcalfe. Wealthy white benefactors like Elliott Donnelly, president of R.R. Donnelly Publishing Company, helped keep the South Side Boys Club solvent during the economically lean years of the Great Depression.[18] In 1930, author Richard Wright got a job at the South Side Boys Club working with African American street gang members. Wright wrote in the introduction to *Native Son* that his work at the club inspired the creation of the novel's protagonist:

> The first event was getting my job in the South Side Boys' Club, an institution which tried to reclaim the thousands of Negro Bigger Thomases from the dives and the alleys of the Black Belt. Here, on a vast scale, I had an opportunity to observe Bigger in all his moods, actions, haunts. Here I felt for the first time that the rich folk who were paying my wages did not really give a good goddam about Bigger, that their kindness was prompted at bottom by selfish motive. They were paying me to distract Bigger with ping-pong, checkers, swimming, marbles, and baseball in order that he might not roam the streets and harm the valuable white property which adjoined the Black Belt. I am not condemning boys' clubs and ping-pong as such; but these little stopgaps were utterly inadequate to fill up the centuries-long chasm of emptiness which American civilization had created in these Biggers. I felt that I was doing a kind of dressed-up police work, and I hated it.[19]

Despite the good work accomplished by the Wabash YMCA and South Side Boys Club, Wright's observations pointed to the failure of most white philanthropists to challenge systematic racism within their organizations.

Not all African American teenagers, however, reacted to racism like Wright's Bigger Thomas. Many found purpose and direction in organized athletics. Public school segregation in Chicago meant that, until the mid-1930s, nearly all of the city's African American high school students attended just one overcrowded institution, Wendell Phillips High School.[20] The all-black school produced excellent basketball teams during the 1920s and 1930s. In 1926, the Phillips lightweight team advanced to the semifinals of the boys' Public League championship and two years later won the title. Racist admission practices precluded most African American athletes from competing at the collegiate level, but several Phillips basketball alumni played for the Savoy Big Five, an all-black semiprofes-

sional team on the South Side. Coach and promoter Abe Saperstein recruited players from the Savoy Big Five to create his famed Harlem Globetrotters in 1926.[21] Despite its name, the professional touring club operated
out of Bronzeville. By 1930, Phillips graduates composed the entire Globetrotter team.[22]

Some Phillips athletes attended college thanks to Katharine Drexel
and the Sisters of the Blessed Sacrament. Three years after sending her
missionary sisters to Chicago, Drexel used a portion of her fortune to establish a secondary school for African Americans in New Orleans. Two
years later, in 1917, she opened a teaching college, and the school received
its charter as Xavier University of New Orleans in 1925. By the 1930s, black
men and women from across the country attended the southern Catholic
institution, which became known for strength in the medical sciences,
especially its pharmacy program. Scores of young people from Chicago's
South Side attended Xavier. Many graduated from Catholic grade and high
schools operated by the Sisters of the Blessed Sacrament or other Catholic
religious orders, but others came from public schools, especially Phillips.
Between 1935 and 1938, Chicagoans helped the Xavier men's basketball
team compile a record of sixty-seven wins and two losses. For a time during the amazing run, all five Gold Rush starters were Phillips alumni.[23] A
virtual pipeline developed between Chicago's South Side and Xavier. Indeed, the first African American to sign with an NBA team and the first
African American to play basketball at DePaul University (and later in the
NBA) both attended Xavier on athletic scholarships after graduating from
Bronzeville public high schools.[24]

Universities closer to home did not necessarily extend the same hos-
pitality to African American athletes, as Jim Crow practices persisted in
the urban North. In 1930, the University of Chicago's athletic department
broke its longstanding practice of inviting the champion of the Chicago
Public League to its annual Amos Alonzo Stagg Basketball Tournament.
Phillips won the Public League championship that year, but university officials instead invited runner-up Morgan Park, a white high school, to its
Hyde Park campus for participation in the national tournament.[25] Because
African American athletes did not find widespread opportunities at the
collegiate level until after World War II, Xavier remained particularly at-
tractive to blacks during the 1930s and 1940s.[26]

Wendell Phillips High School, the South Side Boys Club, and the Wabash YMCA formed what one Chicago high school coach called a "golden
triangle" of "great black basketball talent" in the 1930s and 1940s.[27] Eugene Saffold, who played on DuSable High School's first basketball team

(1935–1936), recalled the importance of these institutions. "We used to meet down at the South Side Boys Club . . . That's where we all learned to play the game . . . There were only two or three places where we could go and play inside—Wabash Y and South Side Boys Club."[28] The St. Elizabeth parish plant stood only one and a half blocks to the south of the golden triangle. Bishop Sheil took advantage of the proximity by inviting black basketball players and other African American athletes to participate in CYO activities.[29] As hundreds of young people from the neighborhood, Catholics and non-Catholics, congregated at a former men's club on the grounds of St. Elizabeth, the parish-owned building became the center of Catholic-sponsored athletics in Bronzeville.

SHEIL HOUSE

After its transformation from a high school in 1944, Sheil House became a "magnet for athletes," similar to the three institutions making up the golden triangle. "Bishop Sheil more or less put the Sheil House on 41st Street for blacks to have some place to go," according to George Phillips, a standout basketball player on St. Elizabeth's teams of the late 1940s. "St. Elizabeth athletes, the public school athletes, and just about everyone in the neighborhood gravitated to this place to compete." During the day, St. Elizabeth elementary and high schools used the building's facilities for physical education and other activities. Outside of school hours, however, Sheil House operated as a community center for young people from the surrounding neighborhood. "It was just like a YMCA," recalled Phillips.[30]

Originally known as the Sheridan Club, the four-story building on the southwest corner of 41st Street and Michigan Avenue served several purposes after its completion around the time of the World's Columbian Exposition in 1893.[31] Wealthy South Side whites built the structure as a private club. Later, meatpacker Swift and Company used the building as a gymnasium and social club for its executives.[32] Between 1922 and 1926, the Sisters of Mercy operated an academy out of the old Swift Club for the remaining white children of St. Elizabeth parish. After the completion of the St. Monica's/St. Elizabeth merger in 1926, the Society of the Divine Word and Sisters of the Blessed Sacrament opened a high school for African American boys and girls in the building. During the late 1930s, the men of St. Elizabeth's Holy Name Society renovated a billiards room and bowling alley in the basement for their use.[33] Conditions became crowded as enrollment in St. Elizabeth High School grew, and in 1944 the high school moved into a more spacious building across the street.[34] This move

Figs. 4.2 and 4.3. Sheil House was formerly the Sheridan Club, the Swift Club, and—from 1926 until 1944—St. Elizabeth High School. The building on the southwest corner of 41st Street and Michigan Avenue housed Bronzeville's CYO community center between 1944 and 1954. The basement included a bowling alley. (Chicago Public Library, Special Collections and Preservation Division, CCW 15.33; Archdiocese of Chicago's Joseph Cardinal Bernardin Archives and Records Center.)

freed space in the one-time corporate club, which then took the name of the CYO founder and became an after-school destination for St. Elizabeth students and children living in the surrounding neighborhood.

Sheil House's dark granite exterior "was like a fortress" in the eyes of one South Side boy.[35] Within the walls of the nineteenth-century clubhouse, however, neighborhood children—Catholic and non-Catholic alike—took part in an assortment of athletic, educational, and social activities.[36] Students from St. Elizabeth elementary and high schools, as well as area public schools, played basketball in the second-floor gymnasium. In the basement, a game room, weight-lifting area, ping-pong tables, and bowling alley provided more recreational opportunities. Baseball, volleyball, shuffleboard, hopscotch, and jumping rope took place on the small patch of grass outside the building, as well as in an adjoining empty lot. Boy and Girl Scouts created arts and crafts projects in the third-floor workshop, and the Sheil House Players staged dramatic productions. Finally, the gymnasium functioned as a ballroom where high school dances regularly took place under the watchful eyes of the Sisters of the Blessed Sacrament and lay teachers.[37]

During the summer months, the CYO operated a day camp out of Sheil House. Scores of African American children arrived each weekday morning at the community center wearing white T-shirts emblazoned with the green CYO logo. A staff composed of laypeople, young priests, and seminarians supervised the youngsters, ages six to thirteen. The program emphasized socialization and recreation; religious instruction was generally absent. In the morning, campers might learn to minuet, polka, or square dance (decidedly non–African American dance styles), while afternoon field trips exposed them to the city's cultural resources. Edwin Leaner, who lived at 50th Street and Forrestville Avenue in Corpus Christi's parish, attended camp at Sheil House in the early 1950s with his sister. He recalled taking public transportation for outings to the zoo, museums, and the beach: "They would pile all us kids, two by two. We'd get on the el[evated train], because the el stopped right there at Indiana [Avenue] and 39th [Street]." Campers generally brought their own lunch, and parents may have paid a small weekly fee. In addition, the children learned about personal hygiene and manners. "We were pretty much a well-mannered bunch," recalled Leaner.[38]

Sheil House became a place where African American boys and girls, even those attending public schools, came into contact with the CYO. Sheil understood the importance of the nation's growing African American population in northern cities, particularly Chicago, during World

Fig. 4.4. Sheil House hosted interracial competitions like this 1950s
basketball game between St. Elizabeth and St. Patrick.

War II and the postwar years. As the war came to a close, he hired an African American G.I. with an undergraduate degree in sociology from Columbia University to be his liaison to the black community. In 1945, Joseph Robichaux became athletic director for St. Elizabeth High School and
director of the Sheil House. Robichaux, described by sportswriter Roger
Treat as "a huge tan Buddha of a man," was born in New Orleans to a
Franco-American father and Creole mother. His family migrated to Chicago, where his father worked for the railroads. Robichaux attended Catholic schools and participated in the CYO during its early years. After high
school he volunteered as a CYO coach. During World War II, he worked for
the USO to organize stateside entertainment for U.S. troops.[39]

Robichaux, who for twenty-five years was known as the South Side
"Commissioner" of youth athletics until his death in 1971, oversaw an
extensive sports program at St. Elizabeth and Sheil House. With backing
from Bishop Sheil, he recruited talented athletes from Bronzeville's golden
triangle. The densely populated, highly segregated Black Belt provided
Robichaux and his CYO associates with a rich supply of athletic talent.

Several of his protégés went on to successful careers in college athletics, business, and public life.

Robichaux's Sheil House program thrived in the years immediately following World War II, but African American participation in Catholic-sponsored athletics predated the postwar era. An entire generation of black athletes took part in the CYO prior to the formation of Sheil House. Boys and girls from St. Elizabeth, Corpus Christi, and St. Anselm participated in CYO activities from the program's beginning.

AFRICAN AMERICAN PARTICIPATION IN CYO ATHLETICS

The CYO used the popularity of black boxing champion Joe Louis to reach out to African American boys. During the 1930s, the "Brown Bomber" became a symbol of pride and solidarity in the African American community, and his triumphs in the ring presented compelling refutation to ideologies of racial superiority propagated in the United States and overseas.[40] The Detroiter got his start in competitive boxing through the Golden Gloves, winning the 1934 national amateur title at Chicago Stadium. His sixth-round knockout of Italian champion Primo Carnera in New York's Yankee Stadium in June 1935 was seen by many black Americans as retribution for Benito Mussolini's attacks on Abyssinia (Ethiopia).[41] That night black and white American pride coincided, as Louis defeated a symbol of European Fascism while upholding racial and national pride. In 1937, Louis won his first world championship by knocking out Jim Braddock at Comiskey Park on Chicago's South Side.[42] He returned to the city a year later to referee a CYO bout at Soldier Field.[43] The endorsement from Louis enhanced the CYO's standing within Chicago's black community.

The speed, power, and grace of Louis symbolized black strength for millions of African Americans. Richard Wright believed that everyday black men fought racism vicariously through the victories of Louis over white boxers, and Malcolm X later quipped, "The ring was the only place a Negro could whip a white man and not be lynched."[44] Sports historian Jeffery Sammons has emphasized how Louis "represented black pride and a nascent Pan-Africanism," while cultural historian Lewis Erenberg argues that Louis's victory over German national hero Max Schmeling "opened the door to a new conception of American identity: civic nationalism and ethnic and racial pluralism."[45] Representing the United States in title fights against Carnera (1935) and Schmeling (1936, 1938), Louis went on to serve in the U.S. Army during World War II. While not every American, especially white southerners, accepted it, Louis became a powerful symbol of the American nation. And while Carnera and Schmeling represented European Fascism and racism, Louis embodied the possibilities of American pluralism. "The acceptance of Louis as an American hero," writes Erenberg, "was only the first step for whites on the long and difficult road to redefining American national identity as ethnically and racially diverse."[46]

Joe Louis's powerful victories on the world stage and the participation of the multi-ethnic/racial/religious adolescents in the CYO "League of Nations" at the civic level were part and parcel of the same trend toward urban pluralism in American culture that began in the early twentieth century. In 1920, the Census Bureau reported that for the first time in U.S. history the majority of Americans lived in cities. By World War II, widespread urbanization changed how many Americans understood their national identity. Rather than exceptional, the diversity of cities became representative of the nation as a whole. In the process, pluralism became a characteristic of American identity.

"The American creed of a Gunnar Myrdal and the integrationist dream of a Martin Luther King Jr.," writes Gary Gerstle, "sprang from the same taproot of civic nationalism that Theodore Roosevelt espoused" in the first decade of the twentieth century during Bishop Sheil's adolescence and young adulthood. Like Sheil, "Roosevelt's civic nationalism was rooted . . . in his love of the cosmopolitan city in which he had grown up."[47] Roosevelt's "New Nationalism," as it was known, was a response to the surge of immigrants from southern and Eastern Europe, as seismic demographic changes required Americans to reconceptualize citizenship. The process of redefining American identity would continue throughout the twentieth century.

A few weeks before the Brown Bomber's knockout of Carnera in 1935, young black athletes in Chicago found similar (if less publicized) success. In four championship bouts, African Americans defeated Italians in the International Golden Gloves tournament at Chicago Stadium. One of the black boxers, Lorenzo Lovings, was a Chicago CYO member from the West Side parish of St. Malachy's. Lovings graduated from a Nashville high school in the early 1930s as economic depression gripped the nation. Unable to find employment in Tennessee, he migrated to Chicago, worked in a grocery store, and began taking boxing instruction from legendary retired fighter Paddy Kane at the CYO downtown gymnasium.[48] After just three years in Chicago, the archdiocesan newspaper dubbed Lovings "the most popular of colored [CYO] boxers."[49] He entered the CYO Professional Boxing School following his success in the Golden Gloves tournament.[50]

Ralph Leo, an Italian immigrant, antifascist, and CYO public relations director from 1934 to 1942, celebrated the victories of Lovings and the other black Golden Glovers in his tongue-in-cheek weekly sports column:

It should be quite conclusive, after the international pugilistic developments at the Stadium last week, that although Italy can put a rip-roaring argument against the world, Italy cannot lick Ethiopia . . . And, of course, it may be that the Golden Gloves results did not influence the Italian war department, but it does seem odd that forty-eight hours after Lovings, Clark, Bridges, and Pack had disposed of their Italian adversaries, Mussolini should resolve his dispute with Abyssinia . . . These international ring thrillers are indeed conducive to international amity![51]

Italian-Ethiopian peace ended five months later when Mussolini's troops invaded the East African nation. The multiracial, multiethnic CYO, however, continued to fight racist thinking. In the summer of 1936, three boxers from the CYO's League of Nations represented the United States at the Olympic Games in Nazi Germany.[52] Also at the Berlin games, African American track stars Jesse Owens and Ralph Metcalfe silenced any talk of Aryan superiority—at least on the runner's track.[53]

The CYO sought African American inclusion from its inception. A few months before the first CYO boxing tournament, an article in the archdiocesan newspaper, the *New World*, invited African American boys to enroll in free boxing lessons offered six nights a week at the "first-class" gymnasium on the grounds of St. Elizabeth. "This is an opportunity for our colored Catholics to get a splendid training in boxing, to enter the tournament and to associate themselves with some of our finest boxers," advised the weekly. A prospective boxer needed to be at least sixteen years of age, an amateur, and a Catholic. (The CYO later dropped the religion requirement.) Race, color, ethnicity, and class did not matter.[54] St. Elizabeth's pastor, Rev. Joseph Eckert, sat on the first planning committee, and the parish soon became the center of CYO boxing in Bronzeville.[55] In addition, St. Elizabeth hosted one of four sectionals within the South District of the citywide tournament.[56] Winners went on to compete in district competition at De La Salle Institute, a Catholic high school known as "the poor boy's college" for working- and middle-class Irish Catholics.[57] The CYO made black parishes an initial and integral part of its citywide organization.

In addition to annual boxing tournaments in December and large

intercity and international exhibitions during the summer, the CYO sponsored numerous smaller boxing shows around the city. These matches
included interracial lineups in both black and white neighborhoods. In
honor of "National Negro Youth Week," for example, Corpus Christi
hosted a pageant and boxing show in its parish gymnasium. The *Chicago
Defender* reported that CYO champions would display "clean sportsmanship and suberb [*sic*] boxing" in the ring, while close to one hundred boys
and girls participated in a spectacle of racial pride outside the ring.[58] Corpus Christi also sponsored Friday night fights at the famous Savoy Ballroom just two blocks north of the church.[59] Held in a popular, secular
setting offering high-caliber boxing, the entertaining exhibitions famil-
iarized Bronzeville's non-Catholic population with the CYO. The stars of
the show were more than competitive boxers, however. They served as role
models in the community, and some even became parish leaders. In 1937,
for example, two of the six officers elected to the parish board of the Corpus Christi's Young Men's Holy Name Society were CYO boxers.[60]

A range of venues provided the CYO with opportunities to promote its
brand of multiracial, multiethnic sportsmanship. African American and

Fig. 4.5. CYO boxing match circa 1950. The CYO used the glamour of boxing to
promote fair play, discipline, and American pluralism. (Archdiocese of Chicago's Joseph
Cardinal Bernardin Archives and Records Center; University of Notre Dame Archives.)

white boxers represented the CYO at athletic clubs, banquets, parish gymnasiums, even prisons.[61] During the 1933 "A Century of Progress" World's Fair, CYO boxers put on exhibition matches in the "Irish Village" on the lakefront fairgrounds.[62] The CYO Open Air Stadium located at the Mercy Home for Boys on West Jackson Boulevard became one of the city's most popular settings for amateur boxing during the 1930s.[63] More than thirty-five thousand people attended Thursday night bouts at the CYO Open Air Stadium in the summer of 1934.[64] As seasons changed, the Thursday night fights moved inside to the second-floor gymnasium at the CYO headquarters in the Loop.[65]

African American boxers found much success in CYO competition. Corpus Christi dominated CYO boxing in the 1930s, winning four team championships in the first ten years of competition (as shown in table 4.1). Harold Dade, a flyweight fighter from Corpus Christi, won two CYO titles and two Golden Gloves titles in the early 1940s. When he started boxing with the CYO at age fourteen, he did not show immediate promise, losing his first six fights. But hard work and discipline eventually paid off. After serving the United States in the Marine Corps during World War II, Dade entered the professional ranks, winning the world's bantamweight title in 1947.[66] The CYO took great pride in Dade's success. "He is one of the finest boys ever to represent the Catholic Youth Organization," declared CYO boxing director Lou Radzienda, "He is a clean-cut, hardworking young man."[67]

African Americans also played a prominent role in the CYO's second most popular sport—basketball. As with boxing, blacks participated from the beginning. St. Elizabeth fielded two teams in the first CYO season, 1931–1932.[68] The lightweight (5'8" and shorter) team began the season strong, and both the lights and heavyweights (taller than 5'8") led the South Division standings by mid-February. Although St. Elizabeth did not win either the lightweight or heavyweight title in the inaugural season, the parish's prowess foreshadowed the numerous CYO basketball championships won by Bronzeville teams in the 1930s and 1940s.[69] Corpus Christi joined St. Elizabeth in CYO competition during the 1932–1933 season. The two African American teams played most of their games (which were against white opponents) at the De La Salle Institute gymnasium and St. Elizabeth parish clubhouse (the future Sheil House).[70]

Interparish competition thus meant crossing geographical and racial boundaries. African American teams traveled to white neighborhoods, and white teams traveled to black neighborhoods. For example, during the 1932–1933 season, white teams—St. Agnes, St. Carthage, St. Mary of Perpetual Help, St. Rose of Lima, and Visitation—played games in St. Elizabeth's gymnasium against black teams from Corpus Christi and St. Elizabeth as well as against the other white teams.[71] Visitation became infamous as the site of antiblack rioting a generation later.[72] In the 1930s, however, Irish American Visitation basketball players regularly traveled to the heart of Bronzeville for Sunday afternoon games.

Conversely, African American teams from St. Anselm, Corpus Christi, and St. Elizabeth journeyed to white neighborhoods. Between 1933 and 1940, for example, St. Anselm played games at the Lady of Good Counsel gymnasium in McKinley Park, Grand Crossing Park gymnasium in Grand Crossing, Mt. Carmel, an all-boys Catholic high school in Woodlawn, and St. Rita's, a Catholic high school in Englewood, all of which were white neighborhoods.[73] Corpus Christi traveled to De La Salle, Mt. Carmel, St. Agnes, and Visitation for regular season games, while St. Elizabeth competed at De La Salle, Mt. Carmel, and St. Sabina.[74]

By the late 1930s, St. Sabina, an Irish American parish in the Auburn-Gresham/Englewood neighborhood, became one of the city's primary hubs of Catholic basketball. On 5 November 1937, Bishop Sheil dedicated the newly completed St. Sabina Community Center.[75] The state-of-the-art auditorium offered first-class facilities with enough room to accommodate large crowds. In 1938, St. Sabina began hosting an annual Amateur Athletics Union (AAU) tournament at the parish center.[76] By 1940, the tournament comprised thirty-two teams, including the Hamburg Athletic Association sponsored by Illinois state senator (and future Chicago mayor) Richard J. Daley, as well as teams from St. Anselm, St. Elizabeth, and St. Sabina.[77] The event's success prompted St. Sabina to begin an elementary school tournament in 1939, in which black Catholic schools regularly competed.[78] More than sixty years later, St. Sabina became the center of controversy surrounding interracial competition in a Catholic grade school sports league. During the Depression and World War II, however, Catholic-sponsored interracial sports flourished in the Irish American parish.[79]

African American parishes won team championships in four of the first ten years of CYO basketball competition (see table 4.1). Corpus Christi lightweights captured the 1934 title by defeating two-time champion Sacred Heart, a Jesuit parish in Pilsen.[80] The Corpus Christi team included two stars—forward Charlie Gant and guard William McQuitter—who later played on the phenomenal Phillips and Xavier teams of the 1930s. Such young men became minor celebrities in Bronzeville, often mentoring, for example, the next generation of athletes. Gant and Andy Summerlin, Corpus Christi's center, returned to the parish after World War II and coached.[81] The Corpus Christi basketball program set a high standard surpassed only by neighboring St. Elizabeth.

St. Elizabeth's heavyweight team dominated the South District during the 1935–1936 season, becoming one of four teams favored to capture the league's trophy.[82] The Collegians did not win the championship that year but the following season garnered the first of two back-to-back titles.[83] St. Elizabeth's stars—Agis Bray, Hillary Brown, and William "Iron Man" McKinnis—were some of the best basketball players in the country.[84] Under the leadership of a young Joe Robichaux, St. Elizabeth's "heavies" won CYO titles in 1937 and 1938, suffering only one pair of losses in two seasons.[85] St. Elizabeth won the CYO heavyweight title for a second year by defeating St. Stanislaus Bishop and Martyr, a Polish American parish in the white, Northwest Side, Belmont-Craigin neighborhood in front of six thousand fans at the 132nd Infantry armory on the West Side.[86]

St. Elizabeth Church was described by one reporter as the "pride of Chicago's south side [sic]," and "one of the greatest cage aggregations in the country."[87] Success brought opportunities for exposure and travel. In 1937, St. Elizabeth competed in a CYO fundraiser against St. Viator College (Bishop Sheil's alma mater) before eleven thousand fans in Chicago Stadium.[88] The following year, the Collegians traveled to Denver for a national AAU tournament.[89] St. Elizabeth standouts Agis Bray and Iron Man McKinnis played on the CYO all-star team against Chicago's B'nai B'rith Youth Organization (BBYO) at Lane Tech High School in 1939.[90] The CYO beat the BBYO with Bray leading all scorers.[91] The Collegians even defeated the 1936 U.S. Olympic team.[92] A third consecutive championship title eluded St. Elizabeth, however, when St. Anthony's, a Lithuanian American parish in west suburban Cicero, defeated the Collegians in the 1939 CYO tournament.[93]

St. Anselm also followed along the successful path of Corpus Christi and St. Elizabeth. During the 1939–1940 season, the African American lightweights amassed a 56–3 record, winning the 1940 CYO title by upsetting reigning champion St. Sylvester, a white parish in the Logan Square neighborhood on the city's Northwest Side.[94] Postseason competition included an intercity CYO all-star game against Detroit at the St. Sabina Community Center and an interfaith contest with the Albany Park Boys Club BBYO. A week later, St. Anselm traveled with CYO athletic director Jack Elder and the St. Columbanus heavies to Cleveland for a second intercity all-star game.[95] St. Columbanus, an Irish American church ten blocks

TABLE 4.1. African American team champions in three major CYO sports, 1931–1949

Year	Basketball	Boxing	Track & Field
1931	Tournament not yet started		Tournament not yet started
1932			
1933	St. Elizabeth girls*		
1934	Corpus Christi (lights)		
1935		Corpus Christi	St. Elizabeth (jr.)
1936			St. Elizabeth (sr. & jr.)
1937	St. Elizabeth (heavies)	Corpus Christi	St. Elizabeth (jr.)
1938	St. Elizabeth (heavies)	Corpus Christi	St. Anselm (sr.) St. Elizabeth (jr.)
1939			St. Anselm (sr.) St. Elizabeth (jr.) St. Elizabeth (grammar)
1940	St. Anselm (lights)	Corpus Christi**	St. Anselm (sr.) St. Elizabeth (jr.)
1941			St. Anselm (sr.) St. Elizabeth (jr.) St. Elizabeth (grammar)
1942			St. Elizabeth (jr.)*
1943	St. Anselm (heavies)		unknown champion
1944			Olde Tymers (sr.) Olde Tymers (grammar)
1945		St. Elizabeth (high school)	Olde Tymers (sr.)
1946	St. Elizabeth (heavies)*	St. Elizabeth (high school)	Olde Tymers (sr.) Sheil House (jr.)† Olde Tymers (grammar) Sheil House (grammar)*
1947			Olde Tymers (sr.)* Olde Tymers (jr)

Year	Basketball	Boxing	Track & Field
1948			Olde Tymers (sr.)
			Madden Park (jr.)
1949			CYO (sr.)‡
			CYO (jr.)‡

Note: From 1941 to 1943, the annual boxing tournament was scaled back due to World War II. It is unclear if team championships were awarded. The CYO adopted the Chicago Catholic League's system for dividing basketball players into lightweight and heavyweight divisions. Despite their names, it was height that defined membership. Lights were players 5'8" and below. Heavies were the taller players. In track and field, the CYO defined juniors as participants 18 years and younger. Seniors were over 18.
Sources: Chicago Tribune and *New World*, 1931–1949. Compiled by the author.
*Runner-up
**In 1940, a team champion was not reported in the newspapers, but Corpus Christi had twice the number of individual champions as the next closest competitor, thereby qualifying them as team champions.
†Tied with Green & Gold Athletic Club
‡ All CYO athletes, including African Americans, competed as one team

south and four blocks east of St. Anselm in the white Park Manor neighborhood, became infamous in the late 1940s for stiff resistance to African Americans. White parishioners viciously attacked the home of a black Catholic married couple who moved into the parish in 1949.[96] Nine years earlier, however, St. Columbanus teenage boys made an out-of-town, interracial trip with African American teenage boys from St. Anselm without incident under the auspices of the CYO. In the 1930s, Bishop Sheil's organization used sports to transcend Catholic parochialism so evident in postwar housing conflicts.

In addition, the CYO challenged gender norms in modest ways. Unlike boxing, basketball offered an opportunity for girls to take part in CYO competition. More than ninety girls teams competed in the first CYO basketball season, 1931–1932.[97] A female team from St. Elizabeth entered the second season, playing most of its games at Our Lady of Good Counsel gymnasium in the white McKinley Park neighborhood three and a half miles west of St. Elizabeth.[98] Corpus Christi entered the girls league during the 1933–1934 season, competing at St. Agnes's, an Irish American parish in the white Brighton Park neighborhood.[99]

The CYO may have included girls, but it did not give them equal attention. Boys sports dominated CYO athletics coverage in the archdiocesan and city newspapers. The CYO reflected Sheil's version of muscular Christianity. In the early 1930s, an African American mother expressed concern to Bishop Sheil about her son boxing in the CYO because he suffered nosebleeds easily. The CYO founder replied curtly, "That's good . . . He'll learn how to protect himself."[100] A college athlete as well as military and prison chaplain, Sheil exuded a certain macho persona. Yet he strove to include girls in CYO programming. When the bishop negotiated with the Boy Scouts of America to assume responsibility for sponsoring Catholic Boy Scouts, for example, he also began sponsoring Catholic Girl Scouts. Girls participated; they just did so with less fanfare than boys. That changed, however, when girls track became the premier CYO sport of the 1950s.

African American boys dominated CYO track starting in the mid-1930s. St. Elizabeth's juniors (eighteen and younger) won seven consecutive CYO titles between 1935 and 1941, while St. Anselm seniors (nineteen and older) won four consecutive titles between 1938 and 1941 (see table 4.1). Championship meets took place at Loyola University's campus in the Rogers Park neighborhood on the Far North Side of the city and at Ogden Park in the white Englewood neighborhood on the Southwest Side.[101] Talented CYO athletes, like Agis Bray and Iron Man McKinnis, competed in multiple sports, running track in the spring after participating in boxing and basketball in the fall and winter.

As much success as Bronzeville's young men enjoyed in track and field, the CYO young women eventually surpassed them. During the CYO's first ten years, female athletes struggled to gain much notice. They could not use most of the facilities at the CYO Center until 1943, when large numbers of men went away to serve in World War II.[102] By the late 1940s, however, girls commanded their fair share of the CYO spotlight. After taking charge of Sheil House and St. Elizabeth athletics, Joe Robichaux assembled an extremely talented group of female athletes. The CYO girls track team soon became a national powerhouse. Instead of individual parish teams, Robichaux coached a citywide squad—blacks and whites together—that competed in AAU meets across the country. The interracial approach did not play well everywhere, especially in the South. The sight of black and white CYO girls draping their arms over each other's shoulders after a 1950 race scandalized spectators at a national AAU tournament in Freeport, Texas. Two men standing next to Robichaux, recoiled in disgust, one saying to the other, "Now I've seen everything. Let's get out of here." Natural camaraderie and easy give-and-take between blacks and whites remained a radical notion to most Americans.[103]

The CYO girls track team produced two great individual talents in the 1950s. Sheil House's Mabel Landry was a four-time national AAU champion in the long jump and two-time champion in the 50-meter sprint,

Fig. 4.6. Members of the 1950 CYO girls track team. *Seated from left to right*:
Dorothy Jacobs, Mildred Martin, Betty Lou Casper, and an unidentified girl.
Standing from left to right: Veronica Fickling, Geraldine Culp, and Eva Pikal.
(Archdiocese of Chicago's Joseph Cardinal Bernardin Archives and Records Center.)

while Barbara Jones was a two-time winner in the 100 meters.[104] Their victories brought widespread attention to Robichaux's program and garnered unique opportunities for the young women. In 1952, Landry traveled to Helsinki, Finland, where she represented the United States in the long jump competition at the Olympic Games. Barbara Jones also competed at the Helsinki games and became the youngest female ever (at age fifteen) to win an Olympic gold medal in track and field, capturing a second gold medal as a member of the U.S. 4 × 100-meter relay team at the 1960 games. She later credited the CYO with providing her the opportunity to become a world-class competitor regardless of race. "CYO was mixed, so, you know, I didn't know anything about segregation," recalled Jones, who grew up in Chicago's Ida B. Wells public housing project and received a full athletic scholarship to track-and-field powerhouse Tennessee State University.[105]

More than fifty years later, Mabel Landry Staton reflected on the social significance of the CYO girls track team: "We were the only inter-racial team running at that time. And we beat everybody." She remembered disregarding local laws as she encountered Jim Crow in the South while traveling for AAU competitions. In Georgia, for example, she refused to sit in a bus station waiting room designated for "coloreds," noting that "it was fun going into the white bathrooms when we weren't supposed to."[106] Landry Staton credited the Sisters of the Blessed Sacrament at St. Elizabeth's school with instilling self-esteem and confidence in their students. "Living in the era of segregation wasn't a bed of roses," she recalled. "What helped me was my faith and the support of family, coaches, and teammates. I'll never forget the time I raised my hand in first grade. 'Sister, why are we different from everyone else?' I had asked. The nun replied: 'God gave you color because he loves you more.' There wasn't any stopping me after that."[107]

In 1949, Landry was kicked out of a train's sleeping car when a conductor informed her that they were crossing the Mason-Dixon Line and that she would have sit in the all-black section. Her coach, Joe Robichaux, was furious. The CYO sued the Illinois Central Railroad and won.[108] The black and white young women on the CYO track and field team not only made their mark athletically but also made the case for a different approach to race relations in Chicago and the nation.

LASTING IMPRESSIONS

The CYO experience frequently left lifelong impressions on its members, who in turn "gave back" to the community. Jacob "Jake" Lampkins, born

in Mississippi, came to Chicago as a child. His family lived on the Near
West Side in St. Joseph's parish, an African American mission operated by
the Jesuits of Holy Family Church on Twelfth Street (later Roosevelt Road).
Even though his father was a Baptist minister, the Catholic Lampkins (his
mother was a "cradle" Catholic) became involved in CYO sports. In 1936,
"Two Town" Lampkins won the 147-pound CYO championship representing Holy Family. The following year, he began instructing younger boxers
at Corpus Christi's gymnasium on Indiana Avenue. He remained involved
in boxing even as he supported his family by working at Campbell's Soup
and International Harvester's McCormick Works. Lampkin's son remembered his father taking him and other children on field trips outside of
their neighborhood near 47th Street and Cicero Avenue. The racially segregated LeClaire Courts Housing Project where they lived did not offer
much in the way of recreational opportunities for kids in the early 1950s.
Lampkins, however, transported groups of neighborhood boys to the downtown CYO gymnasium where they enjoyed access to the best equipment
and finest instruction. The excursions taught the boys the sport of boxing
(not just fighting), exposed them to positive influences, and occupied their
time while keeping them out of trouble. Through his ongoing involvement
in youth sports, Lampkins gave back to his community.[109]

George Phillips remembered interracial friendships he made through
sports. While playing high school basketball for St. Elizabeth, Phillips became good friends with Johnny Lattner, a football star at Fenwick High
School who later went on to win the Heisman Trophy at the University
of Notre Dame. Phillips also made several lasting friendships with other
white athletes. Even when he did not become friends with his white competitors, he got to know them on a basic level. "If you played against these
guys, you had to know them," Phillips said, "It wasn't a close relationship, but it was a competitively friendly relationship."[110] This kind of exposure helped Phillips and his peers later in life as they entered into the
larger world.

INTERRACIAL FUN AND GAMES

Boxing, basketball, and track and field made up the big three CYO sports,
but African Americans competed in other activities as well. For example,
St. Elizabeth's girls played volleyball against white parishes across the
city, and boys from Corpus Christi competed in CYO horseshoes tournaments in Lincoln Park on the North Side.[111] Bronzeville children were exposed to a greater variety of games after the CYO expanded its mission

in 1938 to include social services. Sheil wanted to reach more than just the star athletes; he wanted everyday young people to get involved. Consequently, boys from St. Elizabeth, Corpus Christi, and St. Anselm participated in the first annual CYO marbles tournament in 1938. The divisional playoffs took place in Jackson Park on the South Side, and the finals were held downtown in Grant Park. A boy from St. Elizabeth finished in fourth place in the citywide competition.[112] While defending the Catholic Church's sponsorship of boxing, Sheil once quipped, "Show me how you can lead boys from saloons with a checkers tournament, and I'll put on the biggest checkers tournament you ever saw."[113] Apparently, someone convinced him. In 1939, the CYO held its first annual checkers tournament at the CYO Center in the Loop with youth from Bronzeville among the more than five hundred entrants.[114] Finally, boys and girls from the Black Belt found success in CYO table tennis tournaments.[115] Richard Wright may have questioned ping-pong's ability to affect social change, but St. Anselm took great pride in its 1939 table tennis team championship at the CYO Center.[116] By playing everyday games with white children—table tennis, checkers, marbles, horseshoes, or volleyball—African Americans crossed social boundaries. It was one thing to punch a black opponent in a boxing ring; it was quite another to rub shoulders with him while lining up a shot in marbles.

The most formidable boundary, however, was the swimming pool, as American society held a longstanding taboo against interracial swimming.[117] The 1919 Chicago race riot erupted from an incident along the shores of Lake Michigan, and some of the ugliest confrontations in the modern civil rights movement took place around public pools.[118] It was as if whites thought African Americans "polluted" water with their "blackness." Yet, African Americans swam in CYO meets as early as the mid-1930s. When the CYO held its sixth annual swim meet in 1936 on the seventeenth floor of the Illinois Club for Catholic Women's North Michigan Avenue building, a boy from St. Elizabeth came in third in the 40-yard breaststroke.[119] District playoffs took place at Mt. Carmel High School's pool with finals often held at Loyola University's Rogers Park campus on the Far North Side of the city.[120] The CYO, however, did not confine interracial swimming to competitive meets. Marie Davis, an African American woman who grew up in Corpus Christi parish, swam in 1942 with white girls at a CYO camp in Libertyville, Illinois.[121]

In 1950, the CYO established its own citywide team to compete against area swim clubs. The first open meet was held in the Washington Park swimming pool at 56th Street and South Parkway.[122] Whites and blacks

Fig. 4.7. The 1950 CYO swim team poses in the second-floor gymnasium
of the CYO Center, 31 East Congress Street. Coaches Dorothy Ziegler
(*left*), John M. Walsh (CYO athletic director; *center*), and Udell Weathers
(*right*) stand in the center of the swimmers. (Archdiocese of Chicago's
Joseph Cardinal Bernardin Archives and Records Center.)

swam and dove in the same pool, including a white girl from the Gage
Park neighborhood, which later became infamous for white Catholic racism.[123] The Lake Shore Club from the tony Gold Coast neighborhood captured first place, while Portage Park, a white neighborhood on the Northwest Side and the Lawson YMCA on the Near North Side took second and
third, respectively. Teams from Back of the Yards and Washington Park
also competed.[124] At a time when de jure racial segregation ruled the South
and de facto segregation existed almost everywhere else, the CYO defied
conventions by bringing blacks and whites together—even in water.

PLAYING TO THE CROWD

Although Sheil's inclusive policies guaranteed African American participation in the CYO, black athletes did not always receive support from
majority-white crowds. The CYO boxing team, undefeated for seven
consecutive years in intercity and international competition, received a
scare during an international tournament at Soldier Field in the summer
of 1938. Entering the second-to-last bout of the night, the CYO and Ire-

land were tied, four wins apiece. The CYO light heavyweight champion from St. Cecilia's, a white parish east of the stockyards in the Fuller Park neighborhood, won in a decision. The win guaranteed the CYO would not lose the tournament, but the final bout offered a chance to win it outright. Clarence Brown, an African American heavyweight champion from St. Nicholas parish in suburban Evanston, represented the CYO. His Irish opponent was Matt Lacey, described by a sportswriter as a "dock worker and able seaman." Brown knocked Lacey to the canvas in the first round, where he stayed a full eight counts. In the final round, though, the Irishman recovered and pummeled Brown with punches that "had the big colored boy staggering almost helpless around the ring."[125] The Chicago crowd booed when officials announced Brown the winner, even though his triumph ensured a tournament victory for the CYO, which retained its undefeated record.[126]

Crowds usually cheer for the hometown competitor. In this case, however, loyalty shifted away from the African American heavyweight. It is difficult to determine whether the booing resulted from racist thinking or a sincere difference of opinion with the judges. Still yet another possibility might explain the crowd's reaction: ethnic allegiance. During the 1930s, fight promoters often appealed to ethnic loyalties by highlighting the nationality of boxers. Some fighters even changed their name to appeal to certain ethnic groups. The CYO, playing up its League of Nations theme, publicized boxers based on their national origins. Perhaps the undoubtedly large number of Irish American spectators at Soldier Field that night simply chose ethnic allegiance over loyalty to their city and the CYO. Whatever the case, the incident underscored a harsh reality for black athletes—success did not necessarily translate into acceptance.

While individual whites harbored racist feelings toward African American CYO participants, Bishop Sheil's organization still provided black athletes with opportunities to compete on a level playing field—at least within the confines of organized athletics, where the long-cherished principles of sport included fair play and equal opportunity. Yet, every so often, racist behavior poisoned supervised competition. St. Elizabeth alumnus George Phillips recalled his eighth-grade basketball team encountering racial bigotry during a 1947 tournament at St. Sabina, an Irish American parish. St. Elizabeth was routing its opponent (not St. Sabina), when the opposing coach, a white priest, ordered St. Elizabeth to "take the good niggers out." With the game out of reach for the opposing team, St. Elizabeth coach Melvin Cash sat Phillips and the other starters on the bench. After the game, the same priest then offered to buy ice cream as payoff to those he called the "good niggers." In response, an enraged Phillips challenged the priest, even threatening to throw a basketball at him. Cash quickly restrained Phillips. "You're going to encounter this," Cash explained to Phillips. "You can't fight everybody."

Phillips found it particularly difficult to accept that a priest could be racist, since, in his experience, the German American missionaries at St. Elizabeth were "authoritative" but "not racist." The incident taught Phillips that all priests were not necessarily as enlightened on race as the members of the Society of the Divine Word. "Just because you wear a Roman collar," he decided, "doesn't mean you're what you're supposed to be." In the end, St. Elizabeth won the tournament. Phillips said the experience taught him to ignore race-baiting tactics and concentrate on his own successes.[127]

Phillips's painful experience underscored the prevalence of racism among Chicago's white Catholics. Sheil used his authority as bishop to include African American parishes in CYO competitions, but he could not change the hearts and minds of racists living in white parishes. Black CYO teams, therefore, regularly faced hostilities while traveling in white neighborhoods for competitions. Since the archdiocese included the entire city, black athletes traveled into white neighborhoods throughout Chicago.[128] African Americans competed in CYO contests downtown, in the stockyards district, in the suburbs, and in white neighborhoods on the South, West, and North Sides of the city.[129] Basketball teams or boxing squads from St. Elizabeth, Corpus Christi, or St. Anselm often met near their local streetcar or elevated train stop and traveled together into white neighborhoods for protection.[130] As the second great migration of African Americans arrived in Chicago during World War II and the immediate postwar years, mutual distrust grew between blacks and whites.

"LEAGUE OF NATIONS" TO "COLORED YOUTH ORGANIZATION"

Unlike the rapid growth of 1920s, Chicago's African American population increased little during the 1930s—due primarily to the economic depression. By 1940, therefore, only 8 percent of the city's residents were black, an increase of just 1 percent since 1930.[131] As a result, African American CYO participants, in many respects, acted as another ethnic group, like German Americans, Italian Americans, or Polish Americans.[132] Sheil and the CYO attempted to downplay interethnic and interracial differences as part of Mundelein's Americanization of Chicago Catholicism—the plan to create a church "100 percent American and 100 percent Catholic."

Yet the second great migration of African Americans that began during World War II dramatically affected race relations in Chicago. By 1950, African Americans composed 14 percent of the city's residents, and that number increased to 23 percent by 1960 (as shown in figure 4.8). As Chicago's black population expanded, the participation levels of African Americans in the CYO grew. In 1932, Harry Booker was the only African American to make it to the finals of the CYO boxing tournament, but by 1940, nine of the thirty-two finalists were African American. And when the CYO held its final boxing tournament under Bishop Sheil in 1953, more than 40 percent of the finalists were black (see figure 4.9).

African American teams also found success in the CYO. Between 1931 and 1949, 46 percent of team champions in CYO basketball, boxing, and track and field were African American (as shown in figure 4.10). In 1937, for instance, Corpus Christi won the team boxing championship; St. Elizabeth took the boys heavies basketball championship and won the junior track title; and a St. Elizabeth athlete won the men's singles title in tennis.[133] Bronzeville parishes dominated the CYO again in 1938, when Corpus Christi won the team boxing championship, St. Elizabeth took the boys heavies basketball championship, and St. Anselm won the senior track title, while St. Elizabeth took the junior track title (see table 4.1).[134] The trend continued through World War II and the postwar period, with Latinos joining African Americans in large numbers. In 1948, nine boxers

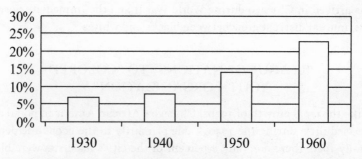

Fig. 4.8. African Americans as a percentage of Chicago's total population, 1930–1960. (from Campbell Gibson and Kay Jung, *Historical Census Statistics On Population Totals By Race, 1790 to 1990, and By Hispanic Origin, 1970 to 1990, For Large Cities And Other Urban Places In The United States*, Popular Division Working Paper No. 76 [Washington, D.C.: U.S. Census Bureau, February 2005].)

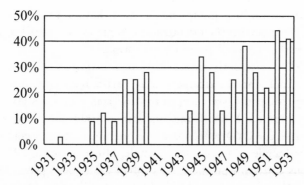

Fig. 4.9. Percentage of CYO boxing finalists who were African American, 1931–1953. From 1941 to 1943, the annual boxing tournament was scaled back. It is unclear how many African American champions were crowned during those years. (*Chicago Tribune*, 1931–1953. Compiled by author.)

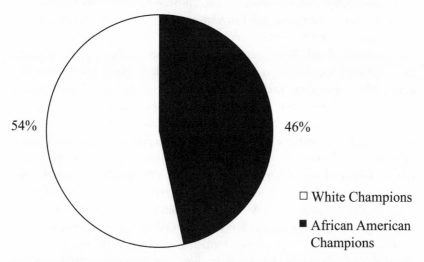

Fig. 4.10. The races of CYO boys team champions in basketball, boxing, track & field, 1931–1949. (*Chicago Tribune* and *New World*, 1931–1949. Compiled by author.)

from St. Francis Mexican Youth Center qualified for the CYO finals—the largest number ever from one parish.[135] The Mexican Americans won the team championship.[136]

As African Americans and Latinos (particularly Mexican Americans and Puerto Ricans) played more prominent roles in CYO athletics, many white Catholics began to believe the CYO had reached a racial tipping point. They no longer saw black involvement in the CYO as the participation of just one ethnic group among many. Rather, they felt that racial minorities had overrun the organization. Some even referred to the CYO derisively as the "Colored Youth Organization."[137]

The CYO consistently depicted its members as "clean, honest, and upright."[138] Such characterizations were particularly crucial for African American participants, stereotyped in American society as lazy, untrustworthy, and immoral. Sheil and his staff portrayed African American members, like all CYO participants, as virtuous citizens committed to Christian principles. In 1940, for example, Hiner Thomas, a black boxer from Corpus Christi, won the CYO Club of Champions prize. The award recognized Thomas for "upholding the C.Y.O. principles of fair play and sportsmanship."[139] CYO public relations director Ralph Leo often used his weekly column in the archdiocesan newspaper to promulgate accounts of honorable young men living out CYO ideals.

In one Depression-era account, Leo chose Westerfield Millen, an African American boxer who lived in Corpus Christi parish, to serve as the model CYO youngster of the week. One night, Millen found himself far outside of the Black Belt (near Wrigley Field on the North Side) without fare for the elevated train ride home. "Westerfield solved his dilemma by doing what any other intelligent young man would have done—walked into the Town Hall Police Station, smiled at the sergeant and proceeded to explain his predicament," Leo recounted in an idealized narrative. "By way of adducing further evidence as to his bona-fide status in the community, Westerfield mentioned the fact that he was a member of the C.Y.O. boxing club and knew Boxing Director T. F. O'Connell personally." According to Leo, this piece of information carried great weight with the desk sergeant, who gave the African American teenager a dime for carfare. Millen promptly returned the ten cents to O'Connell, who kept it on his desk in the CYO headquarters, promising to return it to the policeman the next time they met. The sergeant, however, forgot about the loan and never asked for the money. When the exceptionally conscientious Millen insisted that the loan be repaid, O'Connell went so far as to send a note written by Millen to the police station with the dime enclosed.[140]

The tale, however contrived, captured several dynamics at work in the CYO. First, the organization had established citywide prominence by the mid-1930s. Therefore, Millen garnered immediate respect from the police officer when he revealed his connection to the sports league. Second, the desk sergeant's friendship with boxing coach O'Connell suggested Chicago's influential network of Irish American Catholics. Irish Americans dominated police and fire departments, politics, and leadership positions in the Catholic Church. As a black teenager alone in a white neighborhood at night, Millen himself did not command much respect, but his association with the CYO improved his standing. Finally, Millen's behavior and the police response exemplified the organization's approach to fighting racism: Millen showed respect for authority and worked within the system, demonstrating his personal integrity by conducting himself in a manner beyond reproach, and for that he was treated with respect. The story encapsulated an optimistic view of race relations, for despite the prevalence of bigotry and discrimination, African Americans could find protection within the city's Euro-American Catholic fold through association with the CYO. A number of African Americans took advantage of their connection to Catholic-sponsored athletics to gain access to Chicago's influential network of Irish American contacts in business and politics. Their link to Catholicism and the Democratic Party often mitigated the effects of racism and gave them connections to power and influence.

THE CLUB

Black Catholics composed a relatively small part of Chicago's African American population. Yet, by the mid-twentieth century, they were leaders in business, politics, and the professions in numbers disproportionately higher than their share of the black population. Sociological studies demonstrate that African American Catholics attained higher levels of education, income, and influence than their black Protestant counterparts.[141] But in Chicago, black Catholics had a particular advantage. In a city dominated by Irish American Catholic leadership and power, connections to the Roman Catholic Church and the Democratic Party helped African Americans gain access to areas otherwise off limits. For many black men, Catholic-sponsored sports provided one entry into the world of Irish American Catholic power and influence.

Two-time Olympian Ralph Metcalfe epitomized this process. Born in Atlanta in 1910, Metcalfe's family relocated to Chicago during the first great migration of African Americans to the urban North around the time of World War I. A track star at Tilden Technical High School, Metcalfe received an athletic scholarship to Marquette University in Milwaukee, where he won the national collegiate championship in the 100- and 220-yard dashes for three consecutive years. The phenomenal sprinter earned international fame as a member of the U.S. track team, winning silver medals in the 100-meter dash at both the 1932 and 1936 Olympic Games. At the Berlin games, Metcalfe joined Jesse Owens on the historic

4 × 100-meter U.S. relay team that dramatically refuted Aryan theories of physical superiority.[142]

While at Marquette, Metcalfe converted to Catholicism. Chicago's Catholic *New World* proudly reported on "one of their own," using Metcalfe's story to evangelize African Americans. A gentleman, scholar, and athlete, he became a kind of Catholic Paul Robeson.[143] He allowed Sheil to use his athletic fame for promoting youth activities. Metcalfe, for example, came to Chicago and ran exhibition races during CYO track meets.[144] CYO members must have felt great pride when it was reported that Metcalfe received Holy Communion on the morning of his gold medal victory in Berlin, making the sign of the cross just prior to the race.[145] After coaching track and field at Xavier University in New Orleans and serving in the U.S. Army during World War II, Metcalfe returned to Chicago. He became the first African American appointed to the Illinois State Athletic Commission and served as an assistant to the Chicago Board of Examiners under Mayor Martin Kennelly. In 1952, political boss Richard J. Daley helped the former track star secure the job of committeeman for the city's Third Ward. Loyal to Chicago's Democratic machine, Metcalfe in 1970 was elected to the U.S. Congress, representing the First District of Illinois after African American Congressman William Dawson vacated the seat shortly before dying.

Metcalfe became the most prominent member of Mayor Richard J. Daley's "loyalist black elites."[146] They also included John Stroger, later president of the Cook County Board of Commissioners. A native of Helena, Arkansas, Stroger converted to Catholicism in elementary school. After graduating from Xavier University, he moved to Chicago in 1955. He plugged into the black Catholic network and began attending Mass at Corpus Christi. Then he met Metcalfe, who once taught and coached track at Xavier. "So when I came up, people suggested that I should go and talk with Ralph, and I went up and talked with him," Stroger remembered. "We developed a relationship."[147] That relationship led to a fifty-year career in Chicago politics. A staunch machine loyalist, Stroger became the Eighth Ward committeeman, later Cook County commissioner, and eventually president of the Cook County Board. In 2001, the first Mayor Daley's son, Mayor Richard M. Daley, appointed Stroger's son Todd, also a Xavier graduate, to fill the vacated aldermanic seat representing the Eighth Ward. Following in his father's footsteps, Todd Stroger served as president of the Cook County Board between 2006 and 2010.

In addition to acting as the "commissioner" of South Side athletics, Joe Robichaux was also a loyalist black elite in Richard J. Daley's machine. In

1963, Daley named Robichaux committeeman of the Twenty-First Ward. The president of an ice cream company, Robichaux integrated politics, sports, and business into his South Side leadership. Through programs at St. Elizabeth and Sheil House, he groomed numerous future leaders in the African American community. His most famous protégé was Joseph Bertrand, a standout athlete at St. Elizabeth High School. Bertrand starred on the St. Elizabeth's "Iron Man" team that won the 1950 National Negro Basketball Championship and received an athletic scholarship to the University of Notre Dame.[148] In 1971, Mayor Daley chose Bertrand as the Democratic Party's nominee for city treasurer. A Catholic, he became the first African American elected to citywide office in Chicago's history. Bertrand's son, Jason, described the network of black men involved in Democratic Party politics, sports, and Catholicism as a "club," an association that continued to function in the twenty-first century.[149]

Eugene Saffold, not as well-known as Metcalfe, Stroger, or Bertrand, was nonetheless representative of Chicago's black Catholic network. Saffold graduated from DuSable High School in 1937 and attended Xavier University on a basketball scholarship. Raised in a Methodist family, he converted to Catholicism as a young adult. After World War II, he went to work for Joe Robichaux as a program director at Sheil House. When he decided he could not raise his young family on low CYO salaries, Bishop Sheil arranged for Saffold to get a job with Anheuser Busch beer distributors. Saffold said that Sheil secured jobs for several African Americans at Chicago companies; many times they were the first blacks to work in managerial positions at these firms. Saffold enjoyed a long career as a business executive. In 1995, Mayor Richard M. Daley appointed Saffold's son Gene to the Chicago Public School Board. Gene Saffold later served as Mayor Daley's chief financial officer from 2009 to 2011.[150] Catholic contacts made as a young man influenced the rest of Eugene Saffold's life, as well as the lives of his family members.

THE IMPORTANCE OF SPORTS

Chicago's multifaceted CYO was more than a series of youth athletic leagues, but sports were indeed central to the organization's origins, operations, and identity. Therefore, the question—How important were sports to race relations?—is significant. On the one hand, the persistence of racial segregation in northern housing, education, and social life—even as interracial athletic opportunities expanded—suggests that sports may not have made much of a difference in race relations in northern cities during the mid-twentieth century. On the other hand, throughout the twentieth century, sports repeatedly symbolized and dramatized issues of race relations and racial justice, particularly for African Americans.

Jesse Owens, Joe Louis, Jackie Robinson, Muhammad Ali, and Arthur Ashe—to name some of the most prominent examples—became cultural icons not only because of their great athletic accomplishments but because they embodied the ongoing national struggle to achieve racial justice and interracial harmony. The accomplishments of exceptional black female athletes, such as Althea Gibson, Wilma Rudolph, and Venus and Serena Williams, also spoke to the issue of race but brought the added dimension of the struggle for women's social and legal equality. The stories of these black men and women captivated the American public because at their root they were narratives about the search for fairness. Unlike so many other aspects of society, sports—at its best—allowed for the objective measure of individual accomplishment on a "level playing field" within the parameters of a uniform set of rules. In such a meritocratic context, racial discrimination's fundamental unfairness stood out prominently.[151]

INTERRACIALISM A GENERATION BEFORE *BROWN*

A common theme that emerged in interviews with African Americans who participated in the CYO was "exposure." Interviewees repeatedly mentioned how their experiences in the CYO opened new worlds. They described how the CYO offered exposure to white people, to various parts of the city, to different economic classes, and, at times, to rejection and hatred based on race. Often positive and sometimes negative, interracial contact shaped lives, affecting where they attended high school and college, where they worked, and how they understood their role in a city dominated by the Irish American political machine and the Roman Catholic Church.[152] Some even obtained membership in "the club," a tight-knit fraternity of politically connected former athletes who traversed the boundaries of race, religion, and ethnicity; built successful careers; and achieved prominence in Catholic and African American communities alike.

Yet the interracial process often proved difficult. In their 1945 classic *Black Metropolis*, sociologists St. Clair Drake and Horace Cayton found in interviews with African American youth that many preferred all-black schools. The social life was better. For example, black students frequently were not welcome at dances held in mixed-race schools. They ran into problems when trying to participate in dramatics or swimming. When traveling for school sports, they worried about embarrassing their white

Fig. 4.11. CYO summer camp, August 1954. Beginning in 1941, more than a decade
before *Brown v. Board of Education*, interracial lodging and swimming were
common at Doddridge Farm, the CYO camp near Libertyville, Illinois. *Left to
right, in foreground*: Teddy Stoklosa, of Chicago's Humboldt Park neighborhood,
reads a comic book, while Leonard Pusateri of Old Town and Anthony Jones
of Lawndale sweep the cabin floor. (Courtesy of Sun-Times Media.)

teammates if they were denied lodging because of their race. Other black
students, however, wished for full integration. Drake and Cayton conclude
that generalizations are tricky.[153] CYO officials attempted to protect African American participants from such hardships, but they were not always
successful. Yet, despite challenges, CYO alumni credited their exposure to
worlds outside of Bronzeville with enhancing their lives.

In 1954, just as the CYO experiment in interracialism ended, the U.S.
Supreme Court ruled in *Brown v. the Board of Education of Topeka, Kansas* that "separate but equal" was in fact "inherently unequal." Desegregation of public schools, and eventually other public facilities, became law.
Yet Bishop Sheil and the CYO anticipated the legal ruling by twenty-five
years, opening its programs to children and adolescents of all races in
1930. "Full recognition of his inalienable rights to life, liberty and the pur-
suit of happiness is the legitimate expectation of every American child,"

declared Sheil. "That is his heritage, and it is his regardless of the 'race,' the creed or the position in life of his parents. . . . Children have therefore an inalienable right to play."[154] Whether in boxing rings, on basketball courts, at summer camps, or in swimming pools, between 1930 and 1954, the CYO created opportunities for thousands of young Chicagoans to cross racial boundaries in a Catholic context.

CHAPTER FIVE

The Fight Outside the Ring:
Antiracism in the CYO

Jim Crowism in the Mystical Body of Christ is a disgraceful anomaly.
—Bishop Bernard J. Sheil

In the summer of 1946, George Phillips, an African American teenager representing the CYO, won a citywide checkers tournament yet did not receive first place. Instead, the runner-up, a white boy, was awarded the top prize: a new bicycle and an expenses-paid trip to New Jersey to compete in a national playoff. Tournament officials ostensibly disqualified Phillips because of his age (his birthday surpassed the cutoff date by less than a week). Sheil House director Joe Robichaux, however, believed racism motivated the strict, retroactive, and selective enforcement of the age requirement against the black CYO entrant among a field of white competitors. Bishop Sheil "was livid" when he heard about the incident and argued with tournament organizers on behalf of Phillips, but to no avail. Despite the bishop's inability to overturn the decision, his passion impressed the young CYO checkers player. "To me [Sheil] was a very great man," he later declared.[1]

The checkers tournament story underscores a harsh reality facing Sheil and the CYO during the 1930s and 1940s: fair play within the confines of organized competition did not necessarily apply outside the ring, basketball court, or playing field. The United States remained a profoundly racist society. Jim Crow continued in the South, and persistent de facto racial segregation in the North, including Chicago, prevented African Americans from gaining access to opportunities afforded to most whites. Sheil became more aware of and sympathetic to the unique plight of African Americans as the CYO sponsored recreational programming in Chicago's black community throughout the Depression and World War II. During

135

those years, three key factors affected Sheil's evolving views on race: the creation of the CYO Department of Social Services, his steadfast commitment to organized labor, and continued exposure to liberal ideologies from both secular and theological realms.

The CYO attained nationwide attention by the mid-1930s for its recreational programming. High-profile boxing extravaganzas, extensive radio coverage, and celebrity endorsements made Sheil and his organization recognizable names in Catholic (as well as many non-Catholic) households across the United States. Although widely regarded as one of the largest and most successful sports leagues in the nation, the CYO network also included an aeronautics technical school, Boy and Girl Scouts troops, homes for orphaned boys and parolees, and daily vacation schools. Held each summer in public parks, the vacation schools served as an intensive six-week delivery of social services to neighborhoods throughout the city.

Yet when Americans thought of the CYO, they first and foremost envisioned boxing and basketball. By the late 1930s, Sheil believed CYO sports programming had reached a "state of saturation" and decided the organization needed to expand its agenda to meet the city's social service needs in a more comprehensive, permanent way.[2] With the backing of Cardinal George Mundelein, he applied for CYO membership in the Welfare Council of Metropolitan Chicago. "The C.Y.O. is not only a Catholic Organization [sic]," wrote Sheil in the 1938 application, "but a community organization and, therefore, wishes to participate in a coordinated program for community planning."[3] Moving beyond the purview of sports and moral instruction, the CYO positioned itself as a social service provider serving the city's general youth population. The principles of Catholic Social Action guided this new endeavor.

CATHOLIC ACTION

Catholic Action—defined as "active participation of the laity in the apostolate of the Church under the guidance of the hierarchy"—gained prominence during the pontificate of Pius XI (1922–1939).[4] Central to Catholic Action was the Pauline notion of the Mystical Body of Christ, which held that Catholics were united in the literal body of Christ through their reception of the Eucharist. The movement called upon laypeople to take responsibility for building the kingdom of God on earth; the church could not rely solely on the actions of clergy to achieve social justice. The Catholic Action movement spread rapidly across Europe during the years of social instability following World War I. In the United States, Peter Muldoon, a progressive Chicago priest who became Bishop of Rockford, Illinois, oversaw the Social Action Department in Washington, DC, and liberal activist Msgr. John Ryan served as its director from 1919 until his death in 1945.[5] However, "not until the Great Depression first caused immense suffering to millions of parishioners and then triggered massive protest movements among working-class Catholics did the American Catholic Church show sustained interest in issues of social reform." At that point, writes historian Gary Gerstle, "The Catholic Church responded to the Depression with an unprecedented commitment to social reform."[6] In 1931, on the fortieth anniversary of *Rerum Novarum*, Pius XI issued *Quadragessimo Anno*, an encyclical reasserting the importance of protecting basic human rights in industrialized societies, including the rights of workers. Chicago's Catholic Church, under the leadership of Cardinal Mundelein, was a national leader in this area, with Bishop Sheil's CYO a high-profile manifestation of the principles of Catholic Action. The U.S. Catholic Church sponsored its first National Catholic Social Action conference in 1938—the same year in which the CYO began its program of expanded social services.[7]

Catholic Action was predicated on a corporate understanding of society. Catholic corporatism dated from the Middle Ages, when the guild system organized precapitalistic economies by classifying groups based on crafts. Corporatism emphasized cooperation over competition, with the goal of providing security for its constituent members. The Catholic Church played the role of mediator, overseeing relationships between urban merchants, workers, and the crown. Centuries later, Catholic corporatism provided an alternative to fascist and communist ideologies of the 1920s and 1930s that critiqued American capitalism for its racism, economic class divisions, and excessive individualism. Corporatism's adherents viewed it as a middle ground between the evils of unregulated capitalism and godless communism. The idea was to organize the main occupational groups (capitalists, workers, farmers, professionals, small businessmen) into "guild-like bodies"; each would promote its own group but would also increase awareness of interdependencies.[8]

As the Catholic Social Action movement in the United States reached its peak during the 1930s and 1940s, Chicago became a center of Catholic Action activities. Cardinal Mundelein, who embraced the spirit of social justice found in the papal encyclicals of Pius XI, endorsed a wide array of lay groups involved in what became known as "specialized Catholic Action." Adopting the kind of zeal associated with religious missionary orders, lay associations like the American Catholic Trade Unionists (ACTU),

Chicago Inter-Student Catholic Action Organization (CISCA), Friendship House (an interracial settlement house), and the Young Christian Workers (YCW), took actions to advance social justice in Chicago. In the summer of 1938, Rev. Reynold Hillenbrand, a leader in the liturgical movement, began conducting his nationally recognized Summer School of Social Action for Priests at the archdiocesan seminary. The intensive course of study introduced pastors and assistant pastors to practical applications for introducing the laity to Catholic Action. One class, for example, taught priests how to promote sportsmanship in a Catholic context among children participating in parish athletics.[9] Over the next six summers, Hillenbrand educated a generation of Chicago clergy in the precepts of Catholic Action.[10]

The CYO operated within this progressive Catholic milieu. Initially, the organization focused on problems of juvenile delinquency, specifically among the city's Catholic males. Sheil believed the CYO had turned the corner in the war on delinquency during its first five years. "[Former juvenile delinquents] have substituted Catholic for worldly ideas, the Holy Name pledge for profanity," the bishop triumphantly reported to the 1934 meeting of the National Council of Catholic Men, "and they now wave boxing gloves, baseball bats, and troop emblems in the place of the Communists' red flag and the gang's machine guns."[11] Sheil's rhetoric surely exaggerated the success of the CYO antidelinquency program, but it clearly articulated the fight between secularism and Catholic Action for the allegiance of Chicago's young people.

Catholic Actionists also tackled the problem of racism, the nation's most fundamental and enduring social injustice. For example, a white member of CISCA, the social action group made up of Chicago's Catholic high school students, expressed concern in 1937 about the effects of antiblack racism. "Limited to very few fields of employment, no matter what be [sic] their ability or education, and excluded from most of the labor unions, the Negroes are the lowest paid group in the country," she wrote. "They are too, 'the last to be hired and the first to be fired.'" She went on describe how racial segregation in housing forced African Americans to live in rundown neighborhoods. The CISCA activist called on the U.S. Congress to appropriate funds for new federal housing projects in the nation's urban black ghettos.[12]

Like members of Chicago's CISCA, a select group of white students in Catholic schools across the country grappled with consequences of Depression-era racism. At a Catholic Action forum in 1933, for instance, students at Manhattanville College of the Sacred Heart in New York City adopted a series of resolutions calling for better treatment of African Americans by white Catholic students.[13] A student speaking at a 1938 Catholic Action meeting in Chicago noted that African American priests enjoyed the singular privilege of changing bread and wine into the body and blood of Jesus Christ. "If they're good enough for God," she asserted, "they're good enough for me."[14] (Ironically, the Archdiocese of Chicago did not ordain its first African American priest until 1949. Prior to World War II, the seminaries of religious orders tended to train the few African American candidates for the priesthood.)[15] While these progressive students did not speak for all white Catholics, they represented far more voices than the handful of liberal theologians and national Catholic commentators who typically receive credit for advancing antiracism among Catholics.

A few Catholic Action disciples, Sheil among them, went beyond racial toleration and espoused interracialism. Furthering Catholic interracial work begun by Jesuits John LaFarge and William Markoe, they believed that racial divisions prevented the Mystical Body of Christ from attaining full unity as God intended.[16] A medieval understanding of community informed Catholic thinkers and social critics, who advocated mutual responsibilities for each member of society. For them, "racialist ideologies destroyed hopes for a genuinely corporate community, one united through faith."[17]

By adopting the idea of corporatism, Catholic Action supporters understood society as a collection of groups, not individuals. They even proposed an amendment to the U.S. Constitution for the establishment of "occupational groups," variations on the guilds of medieval European towns.[18] Corporatism broke down, they believed, when the majority culture excluded entire categories of people—based on race, class, or ethnicity—from full membership in society. Catholic Action principles required its adherents to heal such societal wounds. The CYO Department of Social Services worked to fulfill the Catholic Action mission by reaching out to several groups marginalized and alienated from mainstream society, including Chicago's African American community.

CYO SOCIAL SERVICE DEPARTMENT

"There is no 'youth problem,' only problems of youth," Bishop Sheil liked to say.[19] The CYO mission was to solve such problems. Athletics provided an outlet for many physically and mentally healthy children, but more complicated "problems of youth" required further attention. Building on the success of daily summer vacation schools and juvenile delinquency programs, the CYO Social Service Department began operations

on 1 August 1938. With offices in the CYO Center, the department provided an array of services to children and adolescents referred by parents,
priests, and teachers from schools throughout the city.

Since its beginnings in the United States, the Roman Catholic Church
performed charitable acts at the parish level. Priests oversaw Catholic
charities, but religious brothers and sisters did the hands-on work, most
of which focused on children. Not until the postbellum second wave of
nineteenth-century Euro-Catholic immigration, however, did the church
formally organize its charitable activities in response to the "threat" of
secular organizations like the American Red Cross and Protestant organizations like the YMCA "taking our poor." Influenced by Protestant reformers, Catholic laywomen led a Progressive-Era movement culminating
in the formation of the National Council of Catholic Charities in 1910.
After World War I, American Catholic bishops assumed tighter control of
the organization, further consolidating the hierarchy's control of Catholic
Charities. By the 1930s, Catholic Charities, particularly in northern cities,
was a vital part of private social services as the church formed partnerships with federal New Deal programs and municipal welfare agencies.
Such public-private partnerships allowed CYO summer vacation schools
to flourish during the Depression and World War II. Despite its growth in
size and influence, however, Catholic Charities remained supplemental to
government aid to the poor.[20]

The CYO followed many of the traditional Catholic Charities practices, but also differed in key respects. Sheil's staff, for instance, adopted
a "scientific" method of professional social work, which originated with
elite Protestant settlement house pioneers like Chicago's Jane Addams.[21]
Yet Catholic ideologies heavily influenced their approach as well. Several
CYO caseworkers received their training at Chicago's Loyola University,
home of the nation's first Catholic school of social work, which opened
in 1912. Ever open to new ideas (some would say a dilettante), Sheil embraced the field's latest advances, especially psychiatric social work. In
particular, he was interested in using psychological evaluative techniques
to understand and subsequently prevent deviant behavior in children and
adolescents. In June 1940, the CYO began the Juvenile Delinquency Prevention Service, which aimed to stop youth embarking on lives of crime.[22]
The Social Service Department also provided support to offsite CYO projects, including Chicago's West Side Community Center.

In 1938, the CYO assumed control of operations at the West Side Community Center founded three years earlier by the Chicago Area Project.[23]
The four-story brick building on the city's Near West Side served "poor

Italian families, with other racial groups heavily represented" in the area bounded by Halsted Street on the east, Ashland Boulevard on the west, Van Buren Street on the north, and Roosevelt Road on the south. Activities included basketball, table tennis, crafts, shop work, weaving, dancing, sewing, singing, story hours, and radio engineering.[24] The CYO worked with the Chicago Police Department, YMCA, Juvenile Protection Association, juvenile courts, public schools, Hull House, and other Near West Side groups. This neighborhood youth center presented a model for Sheil House, which opened six years later. WPA workers helped staff the operation. By 1939 the facility served five thousand children weekly.[25]

The center continued to operate through World War II, but a 1945 evaluation by the Council of Social Agencies reported disorganized operations managed by a staff with little professional training.[26] Underfunding created most of the problems. "There was never enough money," complained Ernest "Ernie" Giovangelo, director of the West Side Community Center from 1948 to 1952.[27] In addition to lack of finances, the center, like much of Catholic Charities, suffered from parochialism and antiprofessionalism.[28] Sheil hired Giovangelo, a college graduate, war veteran, and Near West Side native, to bring professionalism to the center's operations.[29]

Giovangelo, who grew up attending programs at Jane Addams's Hull House, gathered together a talented staff willing to work with neighborhood young people for little pay. African Americans lived in the area, but Giovangelo did not recall blacks visiting the CYO West Side Community Center in the late 1940s and early 1950s. Whites on the West Side took a "racist approach" toward African Americans, according to the former director.[30] Although blacks frequented the Sheil House on the South Side, boxed in the gymnasium at the CYO Center in the Loop, and participated in interracial CYO and Catholic League sporting events in white parishes throughout the archdiocese, local neighborhood youth centers—even those with official policies of nondiscrimination—remained as racially segregated as the neighborhoods in which they were located.

The unprecedented influx of African Americans into the relatively fixed boundaries of Black Metropolis during World War II led to extremely congested conditions. Public schools consistently suffered from overcrowding. Some adolescents took to the streets, often finding themselves in trouble with the law. Consequently, juvenile delinquency rates skyrocketed in the South Side ghetto. The CYO Social Service Department began a special program in 1942 for the prevention of juvenile delinquency. Working with local agencies and the Chicago Police Department, the CYO offered counseling services to youth in trouble with the law.[31] Monthly

records indicated that police made use of the program by regularly refer-
ring delinquents to the CYO. In the ten-month period between March
1943 and January 1944, law enforcement officials made more referrals to
the CYO Social Service Department from Bronzeville's Fifth District than
all but four of the twenty-five participating police districts. The most referrals came out of the Nineteenth District located in the Irish Catholic
neighborhood of Bridgeport, adjacent to Bronzeville.[32]

The CYO, however, did not work only with juvenile delinquents. Children and adolescents received care from the Social Service Department for
a range of educational, emotional, developmental, psychological, and social problems. In his quest for the modern, Sheil sought to employ the latest techniques in helping children. Medical doctors, dentists, trained psy-
chologists, and psychiatrists volunteered at the Social Service Department
with a few hired as full-time staff. Clients received assistance regardless
of race. Between 1943 and 1944, 7.9 percent of referrals were for African
American children, and increased to 9.4 percent for the period between
1945 and 1947.[33] The Social Service Department served African American
young people from the Bronzeville parishes of St. Anselm, Corpus Christi,
St. Elizabeth, and St. James.[34]

Sheil's organizational successes relied in part on convincing up-and-
coming professionals to work intensely for a few years with the CYO.
Drawing upon the missionary nature of specialized Catholic Action, Sheil
persuaded young talent to offer their services for little compensation. One
former employee recalled that he "worked for peanuts."[35]

The bishop, acting in accordance with Catholic Action ideology, did
not, however, discriminate based on race or gender in his choice of employees. Dora Somerville, an African American social worker, began
working for Sheil in 1942. Described as "kind . . . very intelligent . . . [and]
demure," Somerville was born in Greensboro, Alabama, grew up in Cleveland, and attended Ohio's Ursuline College.[36] In 1938, she received a BA in
sociology from the Catholic University of America in Washington, DC,
and earned a MSW degree from the same institution in 1940. After graduation, she worked at the Catholic Home Bureau in New York City for a
year. In 1942, Sheil recruited her to Chicago, where she served as assistant
director of the CYO Parish Service Bureau. Somerville, who lived in the
Woodlawn neighborhood, immediately south of the University of Chicago,
then earned a second master's degree in psychiatric social work, becoming
associate director of the Sheil Guidance Clinic in 1947 and its director in
1948.[37] The CYO opened the Sheil Guidance Clinic in 1945 to serve emotionally disturbed children "without regard to religion, race or economic

status." By 1953, the clinic served more than three thousand children annually.[38]

Somerville enjoyed working for Sheil, whom she admired. If there were concerns about money, she was unaware of them. "We never felt financial strain," she recalled of her years working in the Social Service Department.[39] Sheil did not let his employees worry about finances; fundraising was his job. When a CYO public relations director questioned him about the lack of available funds to pay employees, the bishop snapped, "It's no concern of yours. . . . I'll raise the money."[40] Despite his assurances to the contrary, money problems plagued the CYO, particularly after World War II as Sheil continuously committed the organization to take on new projects. CYO staff members were overworked and underpaid, and some became disgruntled with their boss. Ironically, "Labor's Bishop" squashed a 1946 attempt by CYO employees to unionize. In 1948, the CYO's "competent and long-suffering" controller resigned in frustration.[41] While Sheil's management style was improvisational and autocratic, his inclusive policies were far ahead of his time. His choice of a black laywoman to direct a Catholic clinic for children of all races anticipated the Second Vatican Council, the modern civil rights movement, and the modern women's movement by twenty years.

Most Irish American Catholics like Sheil found a place in mainstream society by the 1930s.[42] Some looked at African Americans and saw another minority group competing for working-class jobs.[43] Others, recalling the troubled past of their ancestors, empathized with historically oppressed groups and saw blacks as potential allies in the fight against social inequalities. An Irish American priest writing in his weekly Catholic Action column in 1938, for example, implored readers to "wake up to the Negro problem." He chided those who said, "The Negro doesn't mind being obliged to live in squalor," for forgetting how "the English used to say the Irish didn't mind being poor and dirty."[44] The author told his Catholic readers that, as members of a religious minority, they should concern themselves about difficulties faced by other minority groups, especially African Americans. In order to take Catholic Action, he argued, individuals first needed to try to put themselves in the shoes of those they sought to help. Bishop Sheil, in particular, regularly took opportunities to express his solidarity with African Americans.

Chicago publisher John Johnson turned to Sheil when assembling the first issue of Negro Digest, a monthly periodical targeted to African American readers and the precursor to Ebony magazine. In "A Bishop Looks at Race Bias," Sheil emphasized the importance of dealing immediately

Fig. 5.1. Dora Somerville, Director of the Sheil Guidance Clinic
(*far end of table*), confers with members of the CYO Social Service
Department during a 1949 staff meeting. (Archdiocese of Chicago's
Joseph Cardinal Bernardin Archives and Records Center.)

with the nation's crisis in race relations: "The time has come to apply the
remedies and to apply them quickly." African Americans, he warned in
the 1942 article, "are no longer satisfied with weasel words and insincere
promises."[45] Three months later, Sheil wrote another piece for *Negro Digest* as part of a regular series entitled, "If I Were a Negro," in which well-
known white Americans, including First Lady Eleanor Roosevelt, weighed
in on the state of blacks in America. "If I were a Negro," wrote Sheil, "I
would be thankful for my heritage, for the traditions of my people, for a
culture which presents such a hopeful contrast to the artificial and material elements now dominant in our modern civilization." Although blunt
in his assessment of race-based inequalities and scathing in his critique of
those who perpetrated them, Sheil took an optimistic position informed
by faith on the future of African Americans in the United States. "Finally,
if I were a Negro," the bishop concluded, "I would fix my eyes steadily
on the horizon of the future. The past is dead . . . It is the future and the

future alone which holds out to us the sustaining hand of hope and the reward for courage, devotion to ideals, for trust in our common Father and Creator."[46]

By the early 1940s, Sheil had become a "Race man" in the parlance of early-twentieth-century black civil rights activist Robert Abbott, founder, publisher, and editor of the *Chicago Defender*. Abbott used the term to describe African Americans who proudly represented the black race while battling racism. The Irish American Sheil embraced black causes as his own throughout the 1940s and in the process gained the esteem of African Americans in Chicago and across the country. For example, Sheil lobbied for antilynching legislation and pushed for fair and equal labor practices for black workers.[47] In 1953, the *Defender* honored Sheil with the Robert S. Abbott Memorial Award, which recognized him for "giving American youth, regardless of color, greater opportunities to develop their minds and bodies for a quarter of a century of unremitting struggle against racial bigotry."[48]

How did a bishop of the nation's most segregated city arrive at such enlightened positions on race a generation before the modern civil rights movement and the Second Vatican Council? Sheil's commitment to organized labor, opposition to Fascism and anti-Semitism, and exposure to Catholic interracialism shaped his views on race.

LABOR AND RACE

Much of Sheil's progressive politics, including his views on race, stemmed from his background in organized labor. He often cited experiences growing up in a largely working-class neighborhood on Chicago's West Side as providing the basis for his interest in labor issues. During his teenage years, the priests at St. Viator College steeped Sheil in church teachings on labor, placing the concerns of the American working class within a Catholic context. The height of Sheil's prestige as a moral leader during the first decade of the CYO corresponded with the 1930s American labor movement. During those years, the bishop earned national praise (as well as scorn) for his resolute stance on the rights of workers to organize. The CYO and the labor movement shared the same base constituency of white ethnic, working-class urban Catholics. As was the case in the labor movement, Sheil expanded that constituency to include African Americans, Jews, and other minorities. Historian Lizabeth Cohen describes the Congress of Industrial Organizations (CIO) "making a New Deal" by crossing

ethnic and racial boundaries in Chicago during the 1930s.[49] Sheil's CYO
followed a similar path by building coalitions between blacks and whites,
Christians and Jews, and church and state.

African Americans had worked in Chicago since the city's founding
in the 1830s. By the 1930s, blacks comprised a significant portion of workers in the stockyards, rail yards, factories, and mills. Sheil's involvement
with labor issues exposed him to the challenges facing Chicago's working
families of color. Leo XIII, in his 1891 papal encyclical *Rerum Novarum*,
compared modern industrial capitalism's "wage slavery" to the subjuga-
tion of Africans in the transatlantic slave trade.[50] On the one hand, Leo
criticized the excesses of modern liberalism and unrestricted capitalism
and on the other warned against the evils of statism and socialism. In order to protect human dignity in modern Western societies, the pope recommended adopting a variation of the medieval guild system. Although
Sheil did not equate slavery and wage labor, he did understand that two
types of "slavery"—race and class—burdened black workers, and he believed the labor union, a kind of twentieth-century guild, provided the
best protection for workers. Another pope, Pius XI, issued a follow-up to
Rerum Novarum during the CYO's first year of operation. Reiterating the
principles of corporate responsibility and workers' rights found in its late-
nineteenth-century precursor, *Quadragesimo Anno* urged national leaders
facing economic depression and political instability in their countries to
choose a middle path between fascism and communism.

In the United States, church leaders, including Sheil, worried about
radical ideologies from both the left and right threatening American democracy. A major concern centered on the Communist Party's ability to
exploit racial inequalities in its attempt to recruit black members.[51] Communists gained the admiration of many African Americans, for example,
after International Defense Fund lawyers worked to free the "Scottsboro
Boys."[52] Fascism, on the other end of the ideological spectrum, also threatened the church. Sheil embraced the organized labor movement as a middle way to affect reform within the capitalist system without threatening participatory democracy. "Workers of the World—Unionize," urged
Church leaders who asked working-class Americans discouraged by the
Depression to "try the Catholic solution."[53] Chicago's Catholic Labor Alliance grew out of participation in Dorothy Day's Catholic Worker movement. Ed Marciniak, a Catholic Worker and "active crusader in [sic] behalf
of labor and racial minorities," began publishing a small journal, *Work*, in
1943 with the support of Father Reynold Hillenbrand.[54] The publication

advocated a nationwide minimum wage, federally built public housing, and the termination of race-based discrimination in labor unions.[55]

Sheil understood the connection between civil rights and workers' rights. During World War II, he supported the federal Fair Employment Practices Committee (FEPC). The result of a compromise between Franklin Roosevelt and African American labor leader A. Philip Randolph, the FEPC gave black workers the opportunity to obtain defense industry jobs. After the war, Sheil used his political and moral influence to champion a state FEPC in Illinois. One of the first broadcasts on the new CYO radio station (WFJL) in 1949 was a Sheil speech voicing support of the Illinois FEPC.[56] President Franklin Roosevelt had considered appointing Sheil to the national FEPC, but the post ended up going to Msgr. Francis Haas, a well-known organized-labor advocate and bishop of Grand Rapids, Michigan. Sheil's superior, Cardinal Samuel Stritch, opposed an Illinois FEPC.[57] Governor Otto Kerner eventually signed it into law in 1961.

Sheil's friend John Yancey personified the convergence of labor activism, Democratic Party politics, civil rights, and Catholicism in mid-twentieth-century Chicago. The black Catholic labor leader served as secretary-treasurer, and later executive vice president, of the United Transport Service Employees of America, a CIO union representing Red Caps (railway station porters). He also supported the Catholic-sponsored interracial Friendship House, taught at the Sheil School of Social Studies, and served on the board of the Chicago Urban League. Between 1950 and 1957, Yancey was the only African American commissioner of the Chicago Housing Authority (CHA). Paradoxically, he blocked efforts of CHA executive secretary Elizabeth Wood to promote racial integration in Chicago's public housing projects.[58] Perhaps Yancey's conservative stance resulted from feelings of indebtedness to the city's Irish Catholic Democratic machine, which opposed Wood's integrationist efforts.

Yancey earned his credentials as a champion of racial and labor rights in the early 1930s, when he traveled to Mississippi to organize African American workers. "I had three strikes against me before I stepped off the train," he recalled, "I was a union organizer, black, and a Catholic."[59] He continued to organize in the South during the 1940s.[60] According to longtime Chicago alderman Leon Despres, Yancey "took Catholicism very seriously," employing Catholic Action principles for more than three decades in his fight for labor and civil rights.[61] In 1945, Yancey and Rev. Daniel Cantwell, an archdiocesan priest trained by Reynold Hillenbrand, founded the Chicago Catholic Interracial Council.[62] Yancey's successes resulted from taking advantage of Chicago's fusion of Catholicism, Democratic Party politics, and union activism. In 1972, the CHA named a Washington Park community/daycare center three blocks southwest of St. Anselm for Yancey.[63]

Yancey undoubtedly influenced Sheil's understanding of the interconnectedness between race and class. He realized that without equal opportunities for quality education and meaningful employment, African Americans would remain at the bottom of the nation's socioeconomic system. Blacks, however, found success when they gained access to resources; they simply needed a chance to succeed. In a commencement speech given in Bronzeville to DuSable High School's class of 1943, Sheil dismissed the notion of "scientific racism" and African American inferiority:

> If there is any one thing which modern anthropology has utterly exploded by severely scientific methods, it is the vain pretension of superior and inferior races. *There are no superior races; there are only superior opportunities.* Granted equal opportunities over a sufficient period of time, every race is equal to every other race. The Negro people are living, tangible refutation of the un-Christian, unscientific, philosophy of racism. In proportion to their numbers, and considering the grievous handicaps under which they have labored, they have contributed as much to the well-being and happiness of the [human] race as any other people whatsoever.[64]

Recognizing historic injustices, Sheil advocated assisting black Americans in realizing their human potential. He argued that racist categorizations belonged to the morally bankrupted Nazis. American ideology, conversely, rested on egalitarian principles of freedom and equality. Therefore, the bishop supported a national minimum wage, fair and open housing, and desegregated schools.[65]

DEFENDING PLURALISM

Sheil's fight against racism predated his work on behalf of black civil rights. The Roman Catholic bishop consistently fought against Fascism and anti-Semitism throughout the 1930s. Community organizer Saul Alinsky, founder of the Back of the Yards Neighborhood Council and later the Industrial Areas Foundation, was "starry-eyed" about Sheil, according to one observer.[66] In a 1951 tribute to the CYO founder, Alinsky called Sheil the "prelate of the people." He recounted the story of Sheil's encounter with a representative of the rightwing "Christian Front" following a speech by the bishop. As Sheil walked from the podium, an angry woman blocked his path. "I'm a Catholic," she yelled, "but you, you—You're not a Catholic Bishop. God damn you! Nigger lover! Jew lover! A Bishop! Ha Ha! Rabbi Sheil!" With that she spat on one side of his face. Sheil literally turned the other cheek and after a silence replied, "Rabbi? That is what they called our Lord."[67]

Sheil worked closely with local and national Jewish leaders to fight the rising tide of anti-Semitism worldwide during the 1930s. The CYO, from its earliest years, cooperated with Jewish organizations in sponsoring youth programming. The B'nai B'rith Youth Organization and the Jewish People's Institute, which sponsored programs similar to those of the CYO, met the Catholic organization regularly in all-star athletic contests held across the city during the 1930s and 1940s.[68] Urban pluralism encouraged such ecumenical cooperation. For example, when St. Charles Borromeo Catholic Church on the West Side built a new CYO center in 1933, a Jewish dentist who lived within the parish boundaries donated $700 toward remodeling the adjacent playground.[69] The benefactor wanted the neighborhood children engaged in safe and productive activities; and the center and playground benefited the whole neighborhood, as children of different creeds and ethnicities used the facilities. Faith distinctions in a pluralistic society did not necessarily mean religious isolation.

Cardinal Mundelein actively supported the interfaith work of his protégé and the CYO. The archdiocesan newspaper, for example, denounced Adolf Hitler's anti-Semitism four months before the dictator assumed control of Germany. The 1932 editorial compared Hitler's anti-Semitism to the anti-Catholicism and antiblack racism perpetrated by the Ku Klux Klan.[70] New Deal civic-religious pluralism did not call upon Catholics to de-emphasize religious differences but rather accept Jews as fellow citizens rooted in a shared Judeo-Christian tradition. A 1938 editorial in the same newspaper told its Catholic readers that the Jew "is a brother. He has an inalienable right to worship according to his conscience. Even if we disagree with him theologically we must socially admit the status of our fellow man under God."[71]

Bishop Sheil's pro-Jewish positions put him at odds with another prominent Catholic clergyman using mass media in the 1930s to engage working-class Americans: Rev. Charles Coughlin, Detroit's "radio priest." Unlike Sheil, Father Coughlin appealed to fear and bigotry rather than hope and cooperation. His vigorous support of the American working class turned over time into anti-Semitic diatribes.[72] Coughlin's radio show drew large national audiences as he tapped into the frustrations of many working-class Americans during the Depression. Because he cited some of the same Catholic social teachings as Sheil, Coughlin was able to shroud his increasingly anti-Semitic rants in a cloak of ecclesiastical respectability.

Alinsky blamed the largely conservative American Catholic Church for allowing "a little two-bit Hitler like Coughlin" to stay on the airwaves. While he was disappointed with the church overall, Alinsky found "Chicago in those days a peculiar exception." The community organizer recalled in a 1972 interview only months before his death that "under Cardinal Mundelein and Bishop Sheil, it was the most socially progressive archdiocese in the country. Sheil was a fine man, liberal and prolabor [sic]."[73] As early as 1935, Mundelein criticized Father Coughlin publicly.[74] Speaking on behalf of Mundelein in 1938, Sheil roundly condemned Coughlin's anti-Semitism, telling a national radio audience, "Father Coughlin does not reflect the official opinion of the Catholic Church."[75]

Sheil aggressively challenged anti-Semitism. "It is an irreconcilable contradiction for a true Christian to be anti-Jewish," he told members of Chicago's Temple Shalom in 1942, "because the spiritual essence of Christianity dogmatically excludes anti-Semitism."[76] In 1937, Cardinal Mundelein became the first major American Catholic official to speak officially against Hitler and question American isolationism.[77] Just hours after Mundelein's unexpected death in 1939, Sheil announced the cardinal's intention to endorse Roosevelt's "cash and carry" policy, the first step toward intervention in Europe.[78] In 1940, the United Jewish Appeal for Refugees donated $125,000 on Sheil's behalf to Pope Pius XII, and after World War II the bishop raised money for the organization.[79] In addition, a wealthy Jewish family bequeathed to Sheil a mansion along Sheridan Road in north suburban Evanston; its land later became the site of Northwestern University's Sheil Center for Catholic students.[80]

"Beloved" by the Jewish community, Sheil received much recognition for his work to promote interfaith dialogue.[81] In 1947, New York City's Jewish Institute of Religion granted its first honorary degree to a Catholic bishop, calling Sheil "a true and fearless servant of man" and "bishop of the American people."[82] In 1951, B'nai B'rith gave Sheil its "Service to Humanity" award at a Chicago ceremony.[83] In his acceptance speech, the bishop linked Jewish and African American concerns. "Segregation, beyond any doubt, is now the cornerstone of the discrimination which is so widely proclaimed in the United States," Sheil told the Jewish audience gathered to honor him. "The plea that all facilities are separate 'but equal' is a complacent and silly myth concocted by people who are afraid to face reality," he declared three years before the U.S. Supreme Court found racial segregation in public schools unconstitutional.[84]

This ecumenical approach invited Protestants to support CYO programming as well. The CYO and YMCA, for example, competed in boxing matches as early as 1932.[85] And in 1940, Rt. Rev. George Craig Stewart, Episcopal Bishop of Chicago and founder of the World Council of Churches, donated to Sheil Doddridge Farm near Libertyville, Illinois. The site, which included twenty-one buildings on more than a hundred acres of land, became a CYO summer camp.[86]

Sheil's defense of pluralism included fierce battles against antidemocratic forces. Throughout the 1930s and 1940s, he fought vigorously against fascist ideologies taking root at home and abroad. Sheil and Mundelein, for example, opposed the Fascists in the Spanish Civil War.[87] While "almost to a man the hierarchy and the American Catholic press supported the Franco side," Chicago's archdiocesan newspaper officially remained neutral but ran articles supporting the Spanish Loyalists.[88] Sheil acknowledged threats to the church posed by godless Communism, but he also recognized the dangers of Fascist totalitarianism, a form of government antithetical to the communal values of Catholicism and the individual freedoms of American democracy. In addition, he saw the relationship between Fascism and racism, warning, "race bigotry . . . [is] the first step toward full-blown Fascism."[89] The bishop developed a reputation as a different kind of Catholic leader, one who denounced antidemocratic forces not only on the Left but from the Right as well. When the *New York Post* ran a postwar profile on Sheil, a large headline read, "Fascists Hate This Man."[90]

As the United States fought against the forces of Fascism in Europe and Asia, Sheil exposed fascist aspects of American society in speeches throughout the country. "Evidently, not all the Hitlers are in Germany," he charged in 1943 after a summer of race riots unparalleled since 1919 swept across the nation. Sheil recognized that antiblack sentiment at home drew upon the same kind of racial hate driving anti-Semitism and other kinds of racism abroad. He compared the fallacies of Nietzsche's "Super Man" theory with historical forms of racism in the United States, including Anglo-Saxon nativism in the nineteenth century and white supremacy in the twentieth.[91]

The societal consequences of racial discrimination became more pronounced during the 1940s as the second great wave of African Americans migrated to northern cities seeking wartime labor opportunities, and the influx put greater demands on overcrowded, segregated neighborhoods like Bronzeville. The publication of Gunnar Myrdal's large-scale sociological study *An American Dilemma* underscored the destructive effects of racism on both blacks and whites. Although thousands of black soldiers fought to protect American democracy from the racist regimes of Italy, Japan, and Germany, antiblack racism remained prevalent in the United States. Obvious contradictions existed between the Constitutional promise of participatory democracy for all citizens and the reality of one in ten Americans denied basic civil rights on a regular basis because of skin color. Over time, a number of liberal social commentators denounced the hypocrisy of federal, state, and local laws and policies that upheld racial discrimination. They called on American political leadership to end Jim Crow practices immediately in the areas of education, employment, and housing. The *Pittsburgh Courier*, an African American weekly, dubbed this wartime crusade the "Double V Campaign": a campaign for victory abroad against Fascism and at home against racism.[92]

Sheil made the case that that the war effort would be in vain if the United States continued to deny civil rights to African Americans. "It is the most dangerous kind of hypocrisy to wage a war for democracy and at the same time to deny the basic benefits of democracy to any group of citizens," he told a Kansas City audience in 1942.[93] Three years later, as Allied forces neared victory in Europe, Sheil bemoaned that Americans sacrificed immense amounts of human and material resources to preserve democracy abroad yet denied it to African Americans at home.[94]

Following the liberation of German concentration camps, Sheil challenged American society. "We recoil with horror from Buchenwald and from Dachau," he noted. "We cannot find words adequate to describe our revulsion. Yet, are our hands quite clean? Can we denounce the appalling atrocities in Germany and ignore our own practices? Our own hands are stained with the same brush. We decry racism and its fiendish injustices; yet we participate blandly in similar practices in our own nation. We have not erased racism from the conscience of the world by defeating Germany."[95]

No other American Catholic of Sheil's stature—a nationally recognized public figure—took up the Double V campaign so intensely. Other members of the church hierarchy, including Cardinal Samuel Stritch, Sheil's superior after 1939, opposed antiblack racism; but none of them reached popular audiences like Sheil, who spoke to labor unions, boxing fans, and national radio audiences.

Moving freely among the worlds of politics, popular culture, and religion, Sheil represented what Antonio Gramsci called an "organic intellectual."[96] Although Sheil was not an intellectual in the conventional sense (he did not pursue graduate studies, do much serious reading, or write most of his own speeches), he attracted intellectuals with his enthusiasm for putting ideas into action. Plus, he captivated people with his personal magnetism. "When he walked into a room, everybody stopped," recalled former CYO public relations director Robert Burns. An aura of celebrity surrounded the bishop. Sheil, for example, hosted a small dinner party in honor of Jacques Maritain on the occasion of the French theologian's acceptance of a CYO award. The evening included distinguished guests Robert Hutchins and Mortimer Adler from the University of Chicago, French philosopher Yves Simon and community organizer Saul Alinsky. Clare Booth Luce, wife of *Time* publisher Henry Luce, allegedly petitioned unsuccessfully for Catholic television personality Fulton Sheen to secure for her an invitation to the dinner. Alinsky later recalled that Sheil impressed Maritain.[97]

Sheil's credibility with intellectuals came in part because he did not shy away from criticizing members of his own church (including the hierarchy) for inaction in the face of social injustice. "Christianity [in its origins] was the most radical and uncompromising revolution that men had ever experienced," he wrote. "And one of the truly tragic happenings of the modern age is that the same Christianity, because of fear and human respect, has been allowed to become synonymous with conservatism. It is impossible to correlate conservatism with Christianity . . . There is no longer place for the fainthearted, for the so-called conservative Catholic in this world-wide battle for justice, for the cause of the oppressed, of the common people everywhere."[98]

Sheil routinely criticized Catholic institutions, such as schools and hospitals, for racial segregation, especially in light of the wartime sacrifices of African American soldiers.[99] "If the Negro is worthy to die with the white men," Sheil declared, "then he is worthy to live with him [sic] on terms of honest, objective equality."[100] Creating an environment for interracial contact, however, proved more difficult than delivering stirring speeches. As the United States entered World War II, a Catholic settlement house on Chicago's South Side undertook this challenge.

FRIENDSHIP HOUSE

Sheil began networking with liberal Catholic activists from around the country after the CYO gained national prominence in the mid-1930s. John LaFarge's Catholic Interracial Council of New York published the *Inter-*

racial Review, a monthly journal supporting interracialism and New Deal trends in pluralistic tolerance. Moreover, articles in Catholic periodicals like *America* and *Commonweal* advocated labor and civil rights for the nation's working class and racial minorities. Catherine de Hueck, a Russian refugee, garnered the attention of such Catholic interracialists when she opened Catholic settlement houses in African American ghettos. Born into a wealthy noble family around the turn of the twentieth century, Baroness de Hueck fled Russia during the revolution of 1917. After traveling for a decade through Europe and North America, she committed her considerable financial and organizational resources to promoting relations between black and white Americans. Abhorrence to the threat of "Reds" motivated her to work on behalf of African Americans, whom she supposed were particularly vulnerable to Communist recruitment. In 1938, she started the first American Friendship House in New York's Harlem.[101]

Four years later, Bishop Sheil invited the baroness to open a Friendship House on the South Side. The dedication ceremony at 43rd Street and Indiana Avenue, three blocks southeast of St. Elizabeth, garnered national attention in the African American press. Attendees included University of Chicago sociologist Horace Cayton, coauthor of *Black Metropolis* and director of Bronzeville's Parkway Community Center; Vincent Smith, an African American priest from the Society of the Divine Word assigned to St. Elizabeth; and Sheil, the operation's financial benefactor.[102] Ann Harrigan, a white college graduate, and Ellen Tarry, an African American feature writer for Harlem's *Amsterdam News*, came from New York City to codirect the Chicago settlement. Father Daniel Cantwell served as chaplain. Seven full-time workers and about twenty volunteers staffed the library, supervised a children's center, and taught evening classes in English literacy, African American history, and Catholic Action principles.[103] Well-known newspaperman Eddie Doherty, who married de Hueck after interviewing her for a story, wrote flattering pieces in the popular print media about Sheil and the work of Friendship House.[104]

Friendship House complemented the CYO mission of ministering to Bronzeville residents by promoting interracialism and fighting against Communist inroads into the African American community. Russell "Russ" Marshall, a black college graduate and volunteer at Friendship House, recalled the settlement's unique role:

> I worked with the groups who were interested in unemployment, and the people who were being put out of their homes, and in the ones who

were picketing the gangs working in the streets who did not employ
Negroes. These people, these young Communists, were quite active on
the South Side [of Chicago]; in fact they were the only ones active on
the South Side in the early days of the Depression and in the late '30's
[sic], I'd say. So that when Friendship House came in '42, for the first
time those other than the Communists were actively engaged in some
of the problems brought on by segregation.[105]

Racial discrimination forced Marshall, a philosophy major at the University of Chicago, to accept working as a postal deliveryman for nearly forty
years. Friendship House, however, provided a social and intellectual outlet for this gifted man, who later taught in the Chicago Public Schools,
received ordination as a Roman Catholic deacon, and worked as a prison
chaplain.[106]

Baroness de Hueck became a Sheil confidant during the 1940s, pressing the bishop to take bolder stances on issues of racial justice. A long-

Fig. 5.2. *Left to right:* John Yancey, Bishop Sheil, Catherine de Hueck, and Ann
Harrigan celebrate with an unidentified boy at Friendship House during the 1940s.
(Archdiocese of Chicago's Joseph Cardinal Bernardin Archives and Records Center.)

time advocate of organized labor, critic of anti-Semitism, and opponent of Communism, Sheil began taking unyielding positions against antiblack racism that went beyond the inclusion of African American teenagers in archdiocesan-sponsored athletic competitions. He realized that African Americans were no longer just another member of the CYO League of Nations. Rather, in a city swelling with southern migrants and facing contentious race relations, African Americans, by World War II, had become key social and political players. Relatively few were Roman Catholics, but Sheil saw himself as bishop of all Chicago residents, regardless of religious affiliation. Moreover, the numbers of conversions among African Americans increased during the 1940s, and Sheil believed Catholicism's educational and social benefits would continue to attract blacks. The postwar creation of Sheil House reflected in the CYO a new attention to African Americans and an increased commitment to antiracism.

INTERRACIALISM AT SHEIL HOUSE

Sheil House provided a clubhouse for the after-school recreational activities of St. Elizabeth's students and other youth from Bronzeville, but the community center also served as a social service agency and hub of Catholic interracial activity during the postwar period. Joe Robichaux oversaw a paid staff of African American laypeople who managed the multipurpose facility. Xavier University of New Orleans graduate Eugene Saffold served as program director from 1946 to 1953.[107] Beatrice Simms, a social worker trained in psychology, ran the extended school program for children.[108] In 1949, she became director of the Sheil House Day Nursery, a daycare center for preschool children. Both programs met childcare needs of working mothers in the neighborhood.[109] Finally, John Hawthorne, a 1936 CYO boxing champion, supervised the game room in the basement.[110]

Sheil House served the area bounded by 31st Street on the north, 51st street on the south, Lake Michigan on the east, and Wentworth Avenue on the west. This neighborhood was densely populated, highly segregated, and poor. Postwar urban renewal and the construction of public housing projects placed further stress on the community, and Sheil House could not meet the demand for services. A 1954 report on the community center conducted by the Welfare Council of Metropolitan Chicago concluded, "Community need continues to exceed the present capacity."[111] The report, however, praised Sheil House for establishing two committees composed of thirty-six area residents who provided input on community conditions.[112]

In addition to these social services, Sheil House became, along with Friendship House, a center for Catholic interracial activity on the South Side. The Sheil House Players, for example, staged a live theater production in 1948 promoting interracialism. George Dunne, a Jesuit who grew up in Chicago, authored the play in 1945 at about the same time that St. Louis University expelled the scholar-priest for his support of campus integration.[113] A year later, Dunne wrote a scathing critique of American Catholic racism in *Commonweal*. He argued that not only overt acts of racial discrimination, but racial segregation itself, constituted sin in the eyes of the church.[114] "Dunne's essay, which attracted wide attention and was reprinted more often than any other article that ever appeared in *Commonweal* magazine," writes historian Philip Gleason, "put the expression 'sin of segregation' into general circulation among Catholic intellectuals."[115]

In the spring of 1948, Sheil House sponsored the Chicago production of Dunne's play, *Trial by Fire*, which told the story of a postwar African American family confronting the bombing of its house after moving into a white Los Angeles neighborhood. The play also ran in Los Angeles and New York City between 1947 and 1948.[116] In Chicago, supporters included University of Chicago faculty members Paul Douglas and Louis Wirth.[117] The Sheil House production so moved stage actress and future motion picture and television star Jan Sterling that she financially supported its extended run in Chicago. Bishop Sheil also paid for an extra staging at the Wabash Theater in the Loop and offered to cover the production expenses of any Chicago organization willing to host the play. "On this basis," Dunne recalled, "*Trial by Fire* played two or three times a week for more than a year in Chicago and its environs."[118]

By providing cultural-intellectual opportunities like the presentation of *Trial by Fire*, the CYO exposed everyday people to interracial ideologies that might otherwise have remained hidden within the rarified pages of papal encyclicals, academic treatises, or even *Commonweal* magazine. A popular sports and social organization serving hundreds of thousands, the CYO reached far more working-class Chicagoans than specialized organizations like the Catholic Interracial Council or Friendship House. Not all CYO participants attended plays and lectures on interracialism, of course, but they certainly knew where Bishop Sheil and his organization stood on the issue of antiblack racism.

Trial by Fire followed in the tradition of New Deal community theater, which provided a platform for working-class politics unparalleled in U.S. history. The Federal Theater Project of the WPA supported the production of numerous plays that examined social issues facing everyday Ameri-

Fig. 5.3. The Sheil House Players perform a scene in the 1948 production of *Trial
by Fire* by Rev. George Dunne, S.J. (Archdiocese of Chicago's Joseph Cardinal
Bernardin Archives and Records Center; University of Notre Dame Archives.)

cans. The program provided work and artistic opportunities for thousands
of aspiring actors, writers, and directors.[119] Chicago icon Studs Terkel, for
example, began his career in the Federal Theater Project. The Federal Arts
Project likewise brought funds from the U.S. Congress for urban cultural
enrichment.

Bronzeville native Margaret Burroughs helped establish the Southside
Community Art Center in 1941 with such funds. The WPA-supported ven-
ture employed artists and exposed working-class African Americans to the
fine arts. "Minority people got a chance to develop in arts and culture,"
Burroughs recalled. "It's just unfortunate that after the Roosevelt era, the
reactionaries came in and cut it out. They figured poor people didn't need
anything like that."[120] Burroughs, an African American Catholic and graduate of St. Elizabeth elementary school, later founded Chicago's Du Sable
Museum of African American History and served on the board of commissioners for the Chicago Park District.[121]

The leftist leanings of the WPA Federal Theater Project coincided with
the radical nature of Catholic interracialism in the 1940s. The Sheil House
production of *Trial by Fire* exemplified this syncretism of progressive poli-

tics and Catholic Action. Leftist Catholics, like Burroughs, did not necessarily see contradictions between radical politics and their religious faith.
In May 1945, the performer-activist Paul Robeson spoke at Corpus Christi's
parish center, the former Sinai Temple at 46th Street and South Parkway. In
the speech, "San Francisco and Planning the Negro's Future," he addressed
the implications of the charter conference of the United Nations then taking place in California and the role of African Americans in the postwar
world. Attendees included Burroughs and African American communist
Ishmael Flory. A year earlier, in the same building, Burroughs attended the
Interracial South Side Cultural Conference, which addressed "The Present
Day Problems of South Side Poets, Writers, Painters, Sculptors, Dancers,
Singers, Musicians, Actors, Entertainers, and Playwrights."[122]

Catholic interracialism obviously appealed to leftists like Burroughs,
but what about centrist New Deal Democrats? Did interracial ideologies
appeal to the CYO base of white urban Catholics? Sheil's speeches to labor unions, charitable organizations, schools, and radio audiences brought
such ideas to mainstream audiences. And, of course, CYO policies on athletic and social events supported interracial contact among youth. Sheil's
most tangible manifestation of Catholic interracialism, however, was a
program he founded largely for adults.

SHEIL SCHOOL OF SOCIAL STUDIES

On 1 February 1943, a little more than a year after the United States entered World War II, the CYO opened the Sheil School of Social Studies
on the sixth floor of its headquarters building at 31 East Congress Street.
Sheil championed the "labor school"[123] as an experiment in participatory
democracy that endeavored to "give to people, to all people, an even fuller
knowledge of the truths of reason and revelation to enable them to build
a better world. The time is apt for such instruction. The American government—and the people are the government—is faced with making tre-
mendously important decisions in the very near future." The school was
open to all regardless of "education, 'race,' color, creed or money." There
was no tuition.[124] Because so many men were away at war, the enrollment of the school consisted of about 75 percent women. In its first year,
5–9 percent of the students were African Americans.[125] Courses addressed
topics important to working people during the war years—labor, race relations, and the impact of international affairs on the U.S. domestic economy. Classes on social justice and Catholic encyclicals were also offered.
Course titles included "Reconstructing the Social Order," "Interracial Jus-

tice," and "Problems of a Wartime Economy."[126] Guest lecturers, such as
University of Chicago sociologist Horace Cayton, American Federation of
Labor leader George Meany, CIO head Walter Reuther, and NAACP executive director Walter White, spoke on pressing social concerns.[127] Faculty
from DePaul University, Loyola University, the University of Chicago,
the University of Illinois, and the University of Notre Dame volunteered
time and expertise. When South Side blacks had difficulty making it to
downtown classes, the Sheil School began conducting extension courses
in Bronzeville.[128] By the 1948–1949 academic year, over 1,800 students attended the school.[129]

The Sheil School provided a forum for working people to discuss issues
of the day in an atmosphere charged with Catholic Action principles and
Western intellectual traditions. As Chicago's "Catholic Times Square,"
the school bustled with mostly young adults attending classes in the evenings and on weekends.[130] The demands of World War II had temporarily
interrupted debates over controversial issues facing the American public,
including labor and race relations. Once an Allied victory was in sight,
however, Americans began considering the organization of the postwar
world. Communism and Fascism had ravaged the world, but the Sheil
School explored ways to promote a pluralistic democracy committed to
the welfare of the urban working class.

The nation-state's vast expansion during the Great Depression and
World War II affected the lives of all Americans. The Sheil School curricu-
lum attempted to address the ramifications of such changes, particularly
with regard to American citizenship in the postwar period. Widespread
participation in the war effort during the 1940s created new expectations
among citizens for the federal government in the areas of civil rights, labor protections, and economic security. In particular, the "citizen soldier"
of World War II embodied sacrifices that millions of Americans made for
the state. In turn, they expected more from their national government
than ever before. "Americans began to visualize themselves as full citizens," writes historian James Sparrow, "comrades of the soldiers, patriotic
members of a nation whose government owed them, as their due, a diffuse
but powerful right, the opportunity to attain the 'American standard of
living.'"[131]

The Sheil School specifically advanced the notion that the national
state owed African Americans the full protections and privileges of American citizenship. The school's largely volunteer faculty included several
African Americans. A 1945 class bulletin bragged, "Did You Know . . . that

while only five major colleges or universities [in the United States] have one Negro faculty member, Sheil School has had Negro teachers consistently since its beginning in 1943?"[132] John Yancey lectured on organized labor. Madeline Morgan, a Chicago public school teacher, taught African American history. And Dora Somerville led workshops on social justice issues. Course titles included "The Negro in America," "History of the Negro People," "American Negro Literature," and "The History of Race Prejudice in America."[133] At a time when most elementary schools, high schools, and even colleges and universities ignored African American history and culture, these courses were far from ordinary.

The school's best-known African American faculty member was Harlem Renaissance poet and former Communist Claude McKay.[134] Living in virtual poverty and facing declining health, the Jamaica native took an interest in Catholicism toward the end of his life.[135] His circumstances "touched" Bishop Sheil, who heard McKay's story through contacts at Harlem's Friendship House.[136] While few whites understood the black poet, "Bishop Sheil came close," according to historian Tyrone Tillery.[137] Sheil invited McKay to Chicago, where he went to work for the CYO in April 1944. Six months later he was baptized into the Roman Catholic faith at Old St. Mary's in the Loop. Catholic labor activist Ed Marciniak was his godfather.[138] McKay taught courses in African American literature and international relations (drawing on his experience with Russian affairs). He also lectured on important black political and artistic figures, such as Countee Cullen, W. E. B. Du Bois, Langston Hughes, Jacob Lawrence, Mary McLeod Bethune, and Ethel Waters.[139]

Catholic Action idealism met working-class politics at the Sheil School. The institution did not focus exclusively on interracialism, but the study of race relations, along with labor, public policy, and religion, was central to its mission. After expanding the CYO to include social services in 1938, Sheil took the organization a step further in the 1940s with the explicitly political "workingman's college." The school represented the amalgamation of numerous CYO trends: organized labor objectives, Democratic Party politics, Catholic teachings on social justice, New Deal social welfare principles, lay involvement in church affairs, ecumenism, and interracial cooperation. Like the rest of the CYO, the school continued into the early 1950s, but it became increasingly clear that American society was turning in a different direction.

"PROPHET WITHOUT HONOR"

When Cardinal Mundelein died unexpectedly in 1939, Sheil seemed a likely candidate for Archbishop of Chicago. The fifty-three-year-old senior auxiliary bishop and vicar general was second in command of the archdiocese and since the early 1920s had enjoyed a close working relationship with his superior. In return for Mundelein's mentorship and support, Sheil became the cardinal's public persona and mouthpiece on social and political issues. Mundelein biographer Edward Kantowicz compared their symbiotic relationship to the dissimilar but complementary personalities of a gregarious athlete and a reserved administrator.[140] Unlike the stern and aloof Mundelein, Sheil's energy, charisma, and regular presence at parish Confirmations, speeches, fundraisers, and sporting events endeared him to the general public and Chicago press. He also drew considerable national attention as the "apostle of youth," a loyal ally of the Roosevelt administration, and a vocal advocate for organized labor.[141] In 1938, the Vatican's newspaper, L'Osservatore Romano, showered praise on Sheil's CYO.[142] In the end, however, Rome chose Milwaukee's scholarly archbishop, Samuel Stritch, to lead the church in Chicago.[143] Officials most likely passed over Sheil because of his political liberalism and reputation for imprudent spending.[144]

Without Mundelein's patronage, Sheil no longer occupied a favored position in the American Catholic hierarchy. Historian Steven Avella argues that Stritch wanted to distance himself from Mundelein's legacy and, therefore, from Sheil. As chairman of the National Catholic Welfare Council's administrative board, Stritch prevented Sheil from nationalizing the CYO in 1939. When he became Archbishop of Chicago, Stritch refused to renominate Sheil for the position of vicar general, leaving the post empty for two years.[145] After a decade of ascent, Sheil's ecclesiastical career plateaued. Yet his successful youth programs and outspoken positions on social and political issues continued to enhance his public prominence.[146] Throughout the 1940s, speculations surfaced in the press that the Vatican would appoint Sheil to head another archdiocese somewhere in the United States.[147] Ultimately, they were nothing but rumors.

As the national mood shifted toward conservativism in the postwar period, Sheil continued to speak out on behalf of civil liberties and economic opportunity for African Americans. In 1946, he addressed the Chicago Council Against Racial Discrimination (of which he was co-chair) in a speech entitled "Restrictive Covenants vs. Brotherhood." Sheil called for the complete elimination of restrictive covenants. He admitted that clergy often remained silent on the issue of racial discrimination. "Too often in the past," he said, "religious leaders, under the plea of prudence have failed to appreciate or to teach fearlessly what the Brotherhood of Man means in terms of simple justice and charity toward the poor, the underprivileged and the oppressed. Too much respect for the local banker, industrialist, realty operator, or politician has caused them to be silent when the teachings of Christ should have been literally shouted from the house-tops."[148] Sheil urged white Catholics to see African Americans as their "brothers and sisters," not neighborhood intruders.

Some aspects of Sheil's vision materialized, such as the U.S. Supreme Court's ruling against racial restrictive covenants and the desegregation of the military, but for the most part, the decade after World War II was more conservative than the Roosevelt years.[149] The federal government stepped back from advancing the New Deal's progressive agenda as a Republican Party majority controlled both houses of Congress after the midterm elections of 1946. In addition, labor unions lost bargaining advantages gained during wartime production. In 1947, Sheil testified on Capitol Hill against replacing the Wagner Act with the Taft-Hartley labor relations bill, which he believed gave too much power to employers.[150] He warned that a national retreat toward conservatism would make Communism more attractive to the working class.[151] Sheil also extended his scope beyond the United States. In efforts to promote human rights, he supported the fledgling United Nations and other forays into international governance, preaching humanity's imperative to assure international peace in the wake of World War II. In early 1946, at the request of President Harry Truman, Sheil toured postwar Germany, met with the former head of the Hitler Youth movement, and floated ideas about establishing the Boy Scouts in Germany.[152]

While Stritch did not embrace Sheil, he did not directly challenge the popular Chicagoan either. Faced with the unenviable task of overseeing a subordinate more famous and more loved than himself, the new archbishop simply adopted a policy of benign neglect. Consequently, the CYO "empire" continued to expand in the 1940s with little supervision from the chancery's office.[153] Sheil took on more and more programs without any clear system or rationale. For example, he began operating an FM radio station without Stritch's approval even as the CYO went into debt.[154] During a 1949 awards banquet in which the Sheil School of Social Studies honored Stritch with its annual Pope Leo XIII medal, the cardinal teasingly drew attention to his lack of knowledge concerning the affairs of his own auxiliary.[155]

Sheil's empire reached its zenith in the early 1950s as the CYO continued to sponsor a wide range of sports: basketball, track and field, volleyball, swimming, and, of course, boxing. In 1950, nearly fifteen thousand
spectators came to Chicago Stadium for the twentieth annual CYO boxing
tournament to see eight young men crowned citywide champions, including three African Americans, two Latinos, and one Asian American.[156] In
addition to athletics, a myriad of social and educational programs fell under the CYO umbrella.[157] Such a vast array of programs required considerable funding. Consequently, the CYO annual operating budget increased
by more than 50 percent between 1948 and 1953.[158]

Yet, to the chagrin of both superiors and subordinates, Sheil appeared
not to worry about money. "Very often his dreams were far larger than his
pocketbook," recalled *Chicago Tribune* sportswriter Dave Condon.[159] Sheil
took sole responsibility for CYO fundraising, somehow coming up with
the money to keep the organization afloat. In essence, Sheil ran a one-man
show. The bishop and the CYO were one and the same. He never created
an endowment or established long-term planning. When he became ill
with pneumonia in 1951 and 1952, for instance, CYO income dramatically
declined.[160] The demands began to take their toll on Sheil, then in his late
60s. One associate believed that he wanted to resign as early as 1952.[161]

In addition to financial concerns, Sheil's New Deal liberalism isolated him politically in an increasingly conservative post–World War II
America. His opposition to restrictions on organized labor and support of
an increase in the national minimum wage exposed Sheil to red-baiting
tactics.[162] In 1946, Los Angeles radio newsman Upton Close accused Sheil
of Communist sympathizing.[163] In another instance, the president of the
Armour meatpacking company in 1948 charged Sheil with aiding Communists through his pro-union positions.[164] And during the same year, the
CYO resisted pressure to withdraw from Chicago's Youth Week because
supposed Communists from Roosevelt University were participating.[165]

Despite such Red Scare hysteria, Sheil's anticommunist credentials,
dating to the 1930s when he opposed the leftist American Youth Congress, remained securely intact. Few institutions opposed communism
as staunchly as the Roman Catholic Church. Nevertheless, advancing the
progressive agenda of Catholic Social Action proved incredibly hard in the
1950s. Concentration on private life and anticommunism made social programs and group work difficult. Individualism won out over corporatism.

Sheil's precarious political position came to a head in 1954 when he
roundly challenged U.S. Senator Joseph McCarthy (R-Wis.) in a speech to
members of the United Auto Workers, a CIO union. The bishop's criti-

cism of McCarthy epitomized the conflict between the conservative Cold War and progressive New Deal versions of American Catholicism. Sheil scolded the Roman Catholic "junior senator from Wisconsin" for "phoney anti-Communism that mocks our way of life."[166] The bishop did not consult with Cardinal Stritch prior to making his remarks. The speech garnered widespread national attention, coming only days after the nation's most prominent Catholic prelate, New York's Cardinal Francis Spellman, appeared with McCarthy at a fundraiser.[167] McCarthy enjoyed the support of Catholics nationwide, including those in Chicago. After Sheil's speech, an American Legion post in Chicago passed a resolution introduced by a "prominent Catholic layman" supporting McCarthy and opposing Sheil.[168] And in a speech in Chicago, Rev. Edward Lodge Curran, Catholic priest, pastor of St. Joseph Church in Brooklyn and president of the anticommunist Catholic Truth Society, publicly criticized Sheil's attack on McCarthy.[169]

A few months later, Look magazine published a swan song written by Sheil entitled "Should a Clergyman Stay Out of Politics?" In the article, Sheil insisted that he did his duty as priest by speaking out on social issues.[170] Few religious leaders took such a position prior to the Second Vatican Council and civil rights movement of the 1960s. They tended to focus on personal morality. Sheil was different. Former CYO staff member Mary Elizabeth Carroll declared him "a prophet without honor in his own Church." She wrote: "Bishop Sheil is not a saint, not a genius, probably not even a wise man in the ways of his Church. But he is a man wholly in the American tradition of democracy and Christian tradition of hope."[171]

On 2 September 1954, Sheil resigned from directorship of the CYO. It is unlikely he resigned specifically because of the McCarthy incident. Financial difficulties, isolation from church hierarchy, and failing health played larger parts in the decision.[172] By the time of his resignation, the CYO had accumulated an estimated debt of $429,000.[173]

Sheil's resignation led to a policy of "decentralization" by the archdiocese.[174] His successor as CYO director, Msgr. Edward Kelly, "was critical of the whole 'liberal philosophy' of the CYO program."[175] Immediately following Sheil's resignation, Cardinal Stritch dismantled the CYO, either terminating programs or parceling them off to different archdiocesan offices. The CYO headquarters relocated from the spacious Congress Bank Building to smaller offices at 1122 South Wabash Avenue. The entire board of directors, including Sheil, resigned. And the CYO program of social services became part of Catholic Charities.[176] Twenty-five years earlier, the archdiocesan newspaper heralded the CYO for "organizing all parish activities in the Archdiocese into one efficient, extensive unit."[177] By 1955, however, the CYO empire had fallen.

Sheil spent the remainder of his career at St. Andrew's parish, where he had been pastor since 1935. Although he remained a prelate, even receiving the honorary title of archbishop from the Vatican in 1959, Sheil's power in the American hierarchy severely declined. He effectively became persona non grata among his ecclesiastical superiors, cardinals Albert Meyer and John Cody. To most of the city's residents, however, Sheil remained "the people's bishop." Anne Lyons, Sheil's secretary at St. Andrew's, recalled scores of individuals filling the waiting room outside the bishop's office several days a week. They came to ask for help—money, jobs, contacts.[178] Sheil continued to enjoy a good relationship with sportswriters and members of Chicago's business and philanthropic communities from the mid-1950s to the mid-1960s.[179] His participation in church affairs, however, dropped off considerably.[180] Steven Avella describes Sheil in retirement as a "sad, pathetic figure . . . thoroughly embittered with the diocese and the Church he had so faithfully served."[181]

In May 1966, Cardinal Cody required Sheil, age eighty, to step down as pastor of St. Andrew's, citing the age and declining health of the auxiliary archbishop. The action "was widely regarded as a brutal show of power" by Sheil supporters who communicated their displeasure to the cardinal.[182] After thirty-eight years as bishop and thirty-one as pastor of St. Andrew's, Sheil, a lifelong Chicagoan, moved to Arizona with his secretary. For many everyday Chicagoans, Sheil's exile into obscurity was a loss. Upon his resignation from the CYO in 1954, Mary Elizabeth Carroll wrote, "Those who know the solid work done behind the façade of Sheil's follies may well wonder if the Church can *afford* to let all of them go."[183] The costs, indeed, were high for church and society.

"Ahead of His Time": The Legacy of Bishop Sheil and the Unfulfilled Promise of Catholic Interracialism

I just wanted to play basketball against different types of people.
—Isaac Glover, student at St. Sabina Academy

Bernard James Sheil died of heart failure in a Tucson hospital on 13 September 1969, at the age of eighty-three. His mourners ranged from Mayor Richard J. Daley to Lincoln Smith, an African American butcher's assistant. Although high-level church, government, and business officials attended the funeral, "most of the mourners were people Archbishop Sheil devoted his life helping—workers, youngsters, blacks, poor people."[1] Longtime personal friends, like the Jewish politician Jacob Arvey, Irish Catholic community organizer Joseph Meegan, and African American physician Theodore Lawless, served as pallbearers. Honorary pallbearers included the Catholic federal judge and early CYO official William Campbell; the Jewish lawyer, philanthropist, and Boy Scouts of America backer Leonard Ettelson; Sheil's chauffeur Gunnar Larson; the Catholic athletic director at St. Andrew's parish school and former CYO boxer Al Prislinger; and the Catholic commercial real estate broker and president of the Chicago Board of Education Frank Whiston.[2] The diversity of mourners represented the wide range of racial, ethnic, class, and religious groups of people that befriended and worked with Sheil during his lifetime.

A nationally known figure from the mid-1930s to the mid-1950s, Sheil spent his last years in quiet retirement. From the obscurity of desert exile, the CYO founder and champion of liberal causes witnessed dramatic transformations in American society and Catholicism. Time and again the modern civil rights movement and Second Vatican Council produced changes that confirmed his foresight. Sheil had advocated for greater involvement of laity in church affairs, campaigned on behalf of organized labor, preached racial tolerance and civil rights, worked for ecumenism, and stressed the importance of investing in youth. His progressive agenda for American society during the Great Depression and World War II often created controversy and resentment among his coreligionists, especially the church hierarchy. Upon his death, however, Cardinal John Cody called him a leader "ahead of his time." Although the CYO and countless other Sheil initiatives never fully met their objectives, the Catholic bishop's leadership proved visionary. At the end of his life, Sheil undoubtedly found satisfaction in watching Americans adopt reforms that he had championed a generation earlier.

Like Franklin Roosevelt's New Deal, Sheil's civic-religious urban coalition crossed lines of ethnicity, race, and religion. Collaborating with labor, government, and business, the bishop exploited the archdiocese's extensive network of parishes to build "a house for all peoples." In addition to his base constituency—Euro-American Catholics—Sheil brought African Americans, Jews, and Protestants into the CYO alliance. Socially outgoing, he formed relationships with hundreds of individuals whom he called on to support his undertakings. He seemed to know everyone—from U.S. presidents to business executives to newsboys. As Sheil's body lay in repose for two and half days in the nave of St. Andrew's on the North Side, thousands paid homage to the people's bishop. Black and white mourners knelt side by side in prayer at Sheil's casket even as racial unrest plagued Chicago and other American cities.[3] The nation had entered a new era of race relations by 1969, with Black Power and group rights replacing New Deal liberalism. Nevertheless, those touched by Sheil remembered him. John Hawthorne, a fifty-six-year-old African American cab driver from the South Side Englewood neighborhood, paid his respects. "He was very good to me in the [19]30s—very helpful," recalled Hawthorne, who won the CYO light heavyweight boxing championship in 1936 and later coached boxing for the CYO, working at the Sheil House in the 1940s.[4]

Sheil's supporters remembered him as "the apostle of youth," "champion of little guys," a "shirt-sleeve bishop."[5] They loved his passionate, no-nonsense style and praised his social-religious network of programs, which reached thousands of everyday Chicagoans. Throughout his public life, Sheil also enjoyed mostly favorable coverage by local and national media. "It could be said that his influence on the moral character of Chicago was probably greater than any other man of his time," asserted a *Chicago Daily News* editorial.[6] The *Chicago Defender* remembered him as a "noble and valiant Catholic clergyman," who took a "forthright stand against racial discrimination."[7]

Sheil's bold denunciations of racism, anti-Semitism, McCarthyism, and unrestricted capitalism, however, created enemies. "The outspoken prelate's career bristled with controversy," noted the *New York Times*.[8] In addition to intrepid stances on social and economic issues, he often alienated fellow priests and members of the church hierarchy with an autocratic leadership style and financial liberality. "He was the last of the big spenders," derided one archdiocesan associate. Despite these failings, Sheil was a dynamic figure who made significant contributions to American society by taking bold, prophetic positions on important moral and social issues. Community organizer Saul Alinsky, a friend and collaborator, effusively recalled, "There were a number of times when he literally touched the stars."[9]

The CYO experiment in citywide Catholic interracialism ended as the modern civil rights movement began its transformation of American society. Sheil's resignation in September 1954 came a few months after the U.S. Supreme Court issued its unanimous *Brown v. Board of Education* decision outlawing racial segregation in public schools. The Archdiocese of Chicago had dismantled the CYO by the time the court issued its "Brown II" ruling in 1955 calling for desegregation of the nation's public school systems with "all deliberate speed." Rosa Parks's refusal to give up her seat on a bus in Montgomery, Alabama, later that year set in motion a mass protest movement that, along with international pressures on the U.S. government, ultimately resulted in the enactment of momentous federal legislation in 1964 and 1965 protecting the civil and voting rights of African Americans. Yet legislation did not end racial conflict. Vicious mobs confronted Martin Luther King, Jr., in 1966, as he visited the white Catholic neighborhoods of Gage Park and Marquette Park on Chicago's Southwest Side; and CYO interracial cooperation seemed long forgotten when the Roman Catholic priest Francis Lawlor urged residents of those neighborhoods to "hold the line" against black encroachment.[10]

Historians Gerald Gamm, Arnold Hirsch, John McGreevy, and Thomas Sugrue, among others, have documented the pattern of working-class, white Euro-American Catholics resisting the movement of African American residents into previously all-white, urban areas during the mid-twentieth century. High rates of home ownership as well as deep psychological and financial investments in parishes created strong neighborhood ties for white Catholics. While Protestants and Jews commonly fled, many Catholics remained in the old neighborhoods. In several cases, Euro-American Catholics in the urban North used violence to intimidate African Americans from moving into their parishes. Typically, historians have accepted such racist behavior as representing everyday urban Catholics.

The little-known story of the CYO complicates this history, offering a counternarrative to the literature on white Catholic racism in twentieth-century urban America. A story of ultimate decline but not failure, the CYO reached hundreds of thousands of Chicagoans with its message of equality and universalism between 1930 and 1954. The CYO name continued as a way to describe Catholic intramural sports, but neither Chicago nor any other American city again witnessed the same kind of commitment to Catholic-sponsored citywide interracialism as seen in Chicago during the Great Depression, World War II, and immediate postwar period. Liberal Catholic activists like Chicago's Msgr. John Egan and organizations like the Chicago Catholic Interracial Council fought for racial justice in the 1950s and 1960s, but they did not possess the authority of Bishop Sheil or the comprehensive scope of the CYO.

BLACK CATHOLIC NUCLEUS

In creating interracial opportunities, the CYO relied on Catholic inroads in Chicago's African American community. Parishioners from St. Elizabeth, Corpus Christi, and St. Anselm comprised the core of black CYO participation. Like their white counterparts, African Americans experienced Catholic space within a multifaceted context. Their parishes were not simply religious spaces; they encompassed political wards, commercial districts, and industrial areas.[11] The economic and cultural center of Black Metropolis at 47th Street and South Parkway, for example, fell within Corpus Christi's parish boundaries. Corpus Christi, therefore, shaped the development of Black Metropolis and in turn was shaped by it.

African Americans encountered dynamic parish complexes offering an array of educational, recreational, social, and spiritual opportunities. Just as Drake and Cayton described a city within a city, Bronzeville residents successfully made use of Catholic space by creating distinctly black ethnic parishes. This intersection of African American society and Catholic space resulted in the creation of a Catholic Bronzeville. Despite wholesale departure of whites, Catholic institutions—churches, schools, and hospitals—continued serving black neighborhoods. African Americans, like their Euro-American predecessors, adopted and adapted these Catholic spaces to meet their needs, educating their children and worshipping in the Catholic built environment. The black Catholic experience, however, did not remain isolated within the residentially segregated borders of Bronzeville. Citywide associations like the CYO, the Democratic Party, and the CIO presented opportunities for interracial interaction within Catholic contexts. Through such organizations, significant numbers of African Americans took advantage of the institutional reach of Chicago's Catholic Church. Catholicism created a link to the city's Irish American Democratic machine, allowing black Catholics to participate in ward politics and secure patronage jobs. In addition, some graduates of parochial grade schools gained exposure to the majority-white culture by attending Catholic high schools and colleges. Such Catholic-sponsored interracial cooperation during 1930s and 1940s contrasts with images of postwar racial violence. Addressing cooperation as well as conflict complicates historical interpretations of U.S. urban race relations.

NEW DEAL COSMOPOLITANISM

Bishop Sheil modeled the CYO on nondenominational Protestant movements like the YMCA, Jane Addams's Hull House, and Boys Clubs, as well as Jewish organizations like the Chicago Hebrew Institute (known as the Jewish People's Institute after 1922), which embodied the reform values and Americanization agenda of the Progressive Era. By 1930, the presence of mainline Protestantism in urban America was on the decline, as many Protestant congregations uprooted and relocated to the expanding suburbs during the previous two decades. The migration of hundreds of thousands of African Americans to northern cities during and following World War I precipitated the white flight of middle-class Protestants, Catholics, and Jews alike. What distinguished Catholic churches from Protestant congregations and Jewish synagogues was the territoriality of the Catholic parish. Middle-class Irish American Catholics left Chicago's South Side in droves during the 1920s as the city's Black Belt expanded, but the institutional presence of Catholicism remained. Each inch of the South Side continued to fall within the boundaries of Catholic parishes. Individual Catholics might leave a parish, but the parish itself would remain. Consequently, Catholic leaders like Sheil felt that such neighborhoods fell within their jurisdiction, regardless of the religion, race, or ethnicity of the inhabitants.

The CYO, an expansive array of public-private, interracial, and ecumenical programs, flourished between 1930 and 1954 because church and state supported its goals. "Thank God for Franklin D. Roosevelt," proclaimed Sheil.[12] During the Great Depression and World War II, the CYO shared a common liberal ideology with political leaders, like Roosevelt, and ecclesiastical ones, like Cardinal Mundelein. The New Deal's emphasis on pluralism corresponded with the height of Catholic Action in the United States. The popularity of New Deal ideology and a wartime patriotism that emphasized civic involvement in American society, the Catholic Church's strong institutional presence in Chicago, and Sheil's connections to local and national political leaders created incomparable opportunities for crossing parish boundaries, including the color line.

New Deal ideology advocated American pluralism and working-class corporatism in the 1930s. The CYO worked with the National Youth Administration to run summer vacation schools for underprivileged children and coordinated wartime leisure activities for military personnel with the Civilian Conservation Corps. At the local government level, the CYO partnered with the Chicago Park District. Sheil's CYO also allied itself with the CIO and community organizer Saul Alinsky's Back of the Yards Neighborhood Council and Industrial Areas Foundation. These partnerships embodied a societal commitment to corporate and pluralistic values that bolstered Catholic Social Action.

The CYO brands of Catholicism and Americanism were singularly urban; for it was in the modern American city where pluralism was a lived reality. Even though redlining practices of banks, restrictive covenants of neighborhood associations, and outright verbal and physical intimidation of hostile homeowners in almost every case strictly segregated Chicago's residential zones by race, ethnicity, and religion in the 1930s, certain public spheres did operate as "open spaces" where peoples of diverse backgrounds interacted.[13] In the case of the CYO, those spaces were boxing rings, basketball courts, running tracks, and even swimming pools. Working under the assumption that he was responsible for all of Chicago's people—Catholic and non-Catholic alike—Bishop Sheil involved each one of the archdiocese's more than 350 parishes in the CYO, covering the entire city. His League of Nations characterization of Chicago's multiethnic young people revealed Sheil's underlying commitment to the principle of cosmopolitanism. This milieu provided a more conducive context for interracialism in an urban Catholic setting than the postwar period centered on individualism, suburbanization, and the nuclear family.

POSTWAR CONSERVATISM

The late 1940s and 1950s was "an era of hidden violence."[14] Clashes erupted in Chicago and other American cities during the postwar period when white Catholics took extralegal measures to "protect" their parishes from African American "invasion." Working-class whites, angry and frustrated by the impending movement of African Americans into their neighborhoods, lashed out in instances of communal rioting. Violence sometimes broke out as white parishes faced the prospect of racial integration. When African Americans moved into a previously all-white public housing project in the South Deering neighborhood in 1953, they were met with vicious resistance. The Trumbull Park Homes riots continued for months, drawing national attention to the steel mill district on the city's Far South Side. Recognizing the crucial intersections of race, religion, neighborhood, and class in the conflict, the director of the Federal Housing Authority called on Mayor Martin Kennelly, labor leader Walter Reuther, and Bishop Sheil to mediate the dispute.[15]

Despite sometimes-violent resistance, African Americans integrated a series of Euro-American parishes on the South and Southwest Sides of the city after World War II. In many cases, these parishes "turned" quickly. St Anne's parochial elementary school on Garfield Boulevard in the Back of the Yards, for instance, enrolled its first African American student in 1945; 75 percent of the students were black by 1949. Likewise, St. George's on the South Side admitted its first African American student in 1947; 100 percent of the student body was black by 1949.[16]

Rapid racial succession gave rise to white backlash, including two high-profile communal riots in Chicago in 1949. Parishioners from Visitation and St. Columbanus attacked African Americans as they attempted to integrate the neighborhoods of Englewood and Park Manor, respectively. White children from both of these parishes had participated in interracial CYO sports just a few years earlier. In fact, during the Depression and war, thousands of white Catholics took part in interracial programs sponsored by the CYO.

What changed? The CYO brand of social corporate responsibility, rooted in pluralistic values, did not fare well in postwar America. The Catholic Church, as well as American society generally, turned attention away from social concerns like race relations and focused primarily on the nuclear family, personal piety, and anticommunism.[17] Moreover, postwar economic expansion and government spending, which included the building of superhighways and federal subsidies for home loans, paved the way for the rapid growth of American suburbs.[18] Not only the "push" factor of racial succession but also the "pull" factor of suburban living led many white Catholics to leave their old neighborhoods.

ORGANIC INTELLECTUAL

Bishop Sheil and the CYO were synonymous, the man and organization inseparable. A lifelong Chicagoan with an outgoing personality, the athlete-priest provided Cardinal Mundelein with the ideal individual to lead the American Catholic Church's response to the muscular Christianity of Protestant youth ministries. Sheil followed Mundelein's mandate by advancing Americanism among working-class Euro-Americans who comprised the heart of Chicago's Catholic constituency. Yet the auxiliary went beyond his superior, urging blacks and whites to cross racial boundaries. Sheil's ability to move back and forth between ecclesiastical and secular realms allowed him to create unique partnerships that provided the driving force behind the CYO. The bishop was as comfortable (if not more so) among the laity as he was among the clergy. He crossed boundaries of race, gender, and class to build multifaceted coalitions. African Americans, women, and laypeople played crucial roles in building and operating the CYO. In these respects, Sheil anticipated the Second Vatican Council and modern civil rights movement by more than twenty years.

While the black-white divide was the toughest boundary to cross, the CYO also addressed other racial divisions. "No one but a naïve child, or an adult fool," said Sheil, "would claim that Negroes, Mexicans, Filipinos, or Jews have the same opportunities as their fellow white Americans."[19] In the post–World War II years, the CYO ran programs for Chicago's Filipino, Japanese, and Puerto Rican populations and supported the St. Francis Mexican Youth Center on the Near West Side. Sheil also continued his work with the Jewish community, advocating the creation of the state of Israel during the late 1940s. In addition, he championed the rights of the physically handicapped. CYO programs provided assistance to scores of blind youngsters over the years.[20] In speeches across the country, the bishop advocated the rights of the disabled forty years prior to passage of the Americans with Disabilities Act.[21]

On the one hand, Sheil deserves credit for the boldness, dynamism, and success of the CYO. On the other hand, blame for the organization's financial fluctuations, frequent shifts in programming, and staff instability falls squarely on his shoulders. The CYO crumbled upon his resignation in part because its leadership relied exclusively on Sheil himself. Yet the organization's collapse also resulted from decisions made by Sheil's superiors. After the death of Mundelein in 1939, Sheil never again enjoyed the full backing of church hierarchy. Cardinal Stritch largely ignored the CYO and, upon Sheil's resignation, acted quickly to downsize it.

Sheil's critics faulted him for poorly administering the CYO and alienating his fellow clergy. They blamed the CYO's decline on his overspending, lack of strategic planning, and sizable ego.[22] Admittedly, Sheil lacked the patience and organizational skills of a proficient administrator. Following his resignation, however, Stritch might have tapped the manifold talents of Chicago's clergy and laity to continue the interracial work of the CYO. Instead, he dismantled the CYO and distributed the surviving parts among various archdiocesan departments. Those decisions in the mid-1950s marked a retreat from everyday Catholic interracialism. The Catholic Church in Chicago and across the nation largely neglected the postwar urban crisis in race relations. Much of the damage was irreparable by the time the church introduced antiracism reforms after the Second Vatican Council (1962–1965).

A WORKING-CLASS DOUBLE CONSCIOUSNESS

The CYO interracial movement of the Great Depression and World War II never advocated racial integration, per se, and racial segregation in residential areas defined by parish boundaries continued. Yet in certain recreational, educational, and work environments, blacks and whites cooperated. African Americans and Euro-Americans involved in Catholic-sponsored interracial activities held what Ira Katznelson describes as a double consciousness—individuals worked or played in interracial settings but lived and developed intimate relations with members only of their own race.[23] The racial integration of sporting events, public transportation, or workplaces was quite different from sharing one's neighborhood and place of worship. Coalitions like the CIO and CYO, although fragile, nevertheless transformed American society with their commitments to pluralism and corporatism, values that called for communal responsibility.

Urban America experienced comparative racial stability during the Depression and World II, as economic stagnation and the national war effort led to relative neighborhood stability. Incidents of racial conflict erupted, as in the summer of 1943, but the period witnessed nothing like the wholesale racial successions and violence of the 1920s and 1950s, when flush economies encouraged new housing developments and white flight to outlying neighborhoods and suburbs. Black and white Chicagoans lived in segregated neighborhoods during the 1930s and 1940s, but those neighborhoods bordered one another. Thus, Euro-American Catholics and African Americans shared workplaces, public transit, and select recreational and social venues, such as those provided by the CYO. Bishop Sheil's coalition of parishes representing all sections of the city created the opportunity for inter-neighborhood contact among young people. Postwar suburbanization, conversely, produced geographical, municipal, and psychological barriers that severely limited such possibilities. Catholic-sponsored interneighborhood, interracial, and cross-class interactions became nearly impossible without the comprehensive coverage of an archdiocese-wide program under a strong authority like Sheil. Yet a window of opportunity existed during the Depression and World War II for urban interracialism. The current historical literature misses this complex aspect of American race relations.

PUBLIC MEMORY

Bishop Bernard Sheil is largely forgotten today. Catholic interracialism in Chicago took place on a large scale a generation before the modern civil rights movement and Second Vatican Council. Yet the public, like historians, has little memory of Sheil and the CYO. The politics of racial stratification in the 1950s and 1960s overshadowed the CYO pluralism of an earlier period. African Americans and whites—many of whom were Catholics—clashed over housing and schools, as well as parks and recreational facilities in Chicago and other northern cities. In 1965, national television audiences saw white Catholic priests and nuns (along with rabbis and white Protestant ministers) join African Americans hand in hand walking over the Edmund Pettus Bridge in Selma, Alabama. For many Americans, this alliance between white Catholics and African Americans was novel, but Chicago had experienced Catholic interracialism more than three decades earlier.

After World War II and the second great migration of African Americans to the urban North, Chicago's African American community, emboldened by legal victories over racially restrictive covenants, civil rights legislation, and a growing middle class, expanded far beyond Bronzeville's former borders. African American parishes proliferated throughout the city, but Chicago's original black Catholic spaces—St. Elizabeth, Corpus Christi, and St. Anselm—remained distinctive cradles of black Catholicism in Chicago. Many African Americans, even after moving away, retained strong emotional ties to the "old neighborhood," attending parish reunions where former parishioners gathered in Catholic spaces and visited the nuns and priests who had influenced their lives. These black Catholics recalled Sheil's steadfast antiracism and opportunities created by the CYO. They remembered the bishop plainly speaking out against racial injustices.

Chicago's larger community, however, remembers little of Sheil and the CYO. Northwestern University's Catholic student center is named for the bishop, but the archdiocese does not celebrate his legacy. Similarly, Sheil has received little civic recognition with the exception of a public park facility near St. Andrew's named in his honor.

In the second half of the twentieth century, African American families in northern cities continued to send their children to Catholic schools in significant numbers, seek health care at Catholic hospitals, and utilize Catholic service agencies. Into the twenty-first century, nonwhite and non-Catholic students composed majority enrollments in numerous inner-city parochial schools, and African Americans—as well as Hispanic and Asian immigrants—commonly encountered Catholic spaces in urban settings. As reformers and politicians debate the merits of faith-based initiatives and parental vouchers for parochial education, it is useful to examine the place of Catholic institutions in American cities.

Exploring the interactions of African Americans and Euro-American Catholics in the CYO during the Great Depression and World War II broadens our conception of interracial and ecumenical possibilities for America's urban youth in the twenty-first century. Cities still struggle to find ways to meet the educational, social, and spiritual needs of young people. Many African American parents, seeking environments that offer security, discipline, and moral instruction, send their children to parochial schools. Parents, educators, and policymakers weigh historical commitments to separation of church and state against society's desire for "value-based" educational instruction. Programs link schoolchildren to the larger community by assigning adult mentors who act as role models for their young partners, and educators champion programs that advocate multiculturalism. The CYO story, therefore, is particularly relevant.

Influenced by New Deal ideology and liberal Catholic teachings, Sheil's CYO—religious but not rigidly sectarian—crossed parish boundaries. A pluralistic people strongly committed to religious values, Americans continue to face challenges associated with race and faith. Chicago's Southside Catholic Conference controversy during the summer of 2001—in which a majority of parishes in the predominantly white Catholic sports league initially denied membership to St. Sabina, an African American Catholic parish—demonstrated the continuation of racial conflict in the twenty-first century.

"LET THE KIDS PLAY"

On 31 May 2001, a front-page headline in the *Chicago Sun-Times* proclaimed, "You Can't Play with Them: Black Catholic Grammar School Denied Membership in White League." The daily newspaper revealed that the Southside Catholic Conference (SCC), a mostly white sports league administered by parents of children in twenty-one parochial elementary schools, had denied admission to St. Sabina, a fellow Roman Catholic parish. St. Sabina, like its SCC counterparts, functioned under the authority of the Archdiocese of Chicago with an athletic program complementing its academic and religious curricula. Located in the Auburn-Gresham neighborhood on the city's Southwest Side, St. Sabina's nearly seventy-year-old parish plant stood only a few miles from most SCC member schools. Yet in many ways, its students and parishioners lived in another world. The overwhelming majority of St. Sabina's students were African American.[24]

The league's rejection of the black school began an emotionally charged public controversy. Although St. Sabina already ran a successful basketball league and sponsored football, volleyball, and track for its schoolchildren, membership in the SCC promised unique opportunities for the parish. Pastor Michael Pfleger and athletic director Chris Mallette believed that their students would benefit from competing in an athletic league made up of children from diverse backgrounds. "St. Sabina's not setting out to be the Jackie Robinson and integrate this thing," said Mallette, an attorney who quit his job to work full-time directing St. Sabina's youth programs. "Our motivation is to try to increase the opportunity and exposure of our kids."[25] In the spring of 2001, Mallette expressed St. Sabina's interest in joining the SCC to Hank Lenzen, conference chairman. Lenzen then sent a letter to league members recommending St. Sabina's admission into the SCC. On 17 May, Mallette addressed the conference board, answering questions about safety in the neighborhood around St. Sabina's gymnasium. In a secret vote on 24 May, athletic directors from twenty of the conference's twenty-one schools cast their ballots, eleven to nine against admitting St. Sabina. An indignant Father Pfleger sent a letter of protest to pastors of SCC member schools and on 29 May informed a reporter about the situation. The results of the vote appeared two days later in the *Sun-Times*.[26]

Auxiliary Bishop Joseph Perry, head of St. Sabina's Vicariate VI, called the vote "terribly embarrassing and disconcerting." Sister Anita Baird, director of the archdiocese's Office of Racial Justice, spoke out against the league's action. "We are disturbed by a decision that appears to be racially motivated and flies in the face of Cardinal George's recent pastoral letter on racism," stated Baird, while adding that the archdiocese would "rectify this injustice that has been committed against the children and families of St. Sabina's School."[27]

Just weeks earlier on the thirty-third anniversary marking the assassination of Martin Luther King, Jr., Chicago's Cardinal Francis George released a pastoral letter on racism in the church—*Dwell in My Love*. The impetus for the letter came from the 1997 brutal beating of a thirteen-year-old African American boy, Lenard Clark. When Clark and a black friend entered Chicago's Bridgeport neighborhood on bicycles, a group of white Catholic teenagers attacked them. Clark nearly died and ultimately sustained permanent brain damage.[28] "Spatial racism," Cardinal George wrote, "refers to patterns of metropolitan development in which some affluent whites create racially and economically segregated suburbs or gentrified areas of cities, leaving the poor—mainly African Americans, Hispanics, and some newly arrived immigrants—isolated in deteriorating areas of the cities and older suburbs." He went on to say that racism "can be seen in most of our institutions," including sports teams.[29] The prelate's letter appeared prophetic two months later when the SCC/St. Sabina controversy erupted.

Ironically, many SCC members traced their roots to St. Sabina parish. A handful of families founded St. Sabina on the largely vacant "prairie" of Auburn-Gresham in 1916. By the early years of the Great Depression, a growing number of Irish American parishioners built an impressive church plant at 78th and Throop streets. Modest bungalows and small three-flats lined the streets of the working-class, white ethnic parish. Through the 1940s and 1950s, St. Sabina's famous basketball tournament became a favorite event among Catholic schools throughout Chicago, as the church boasted one of the best athletic facilities in the city. By 1957, the vibrant parish claimed more than ten thousand members with nearly three thousand families.[30]

Then, in the 1960s, racial change swept over Auburn-Gresham as African American families moved into the neighborhood. Whites fled St. Sabina for the Far Southwest Side and south suburbs. Businesses moved out, city services declined, and crime increased; the neighborhood became an impoverished ghetto. Michael Pfleger, a white priest who came of age during the civil rights movement and Second Vatican Council, reached out to the African American community upon being assigned to St. Sabina. Afrocentric liturgies and repeated clashes with his archdiocesan superiors made him a controversial figure, but his leadership transformed the parish.[31] When Pfleger arrived in 1975, he found only 80 regular parishioners attending church. Over the next two decades, his activism and community organizing helped resurrect the neighborhood. By 2001, more than 2,500 members belonged to St. Sabina, 110 children participated in the parish athletic program, and its fully occupied school had a waiting list for applicants.[32]

Parents and grandparents of many SCC members, who raised their families in St. Sabina during its "golden age," left the parish harboring bitter feelings when African Americans began arriving in the 1960s. Nancy Angus, mother of children in Most Holy Redeemer Catholic School (a SCC member) in suburban Evergreen Park, said her parents once lived near St. Sabina, but she did not go back to visit. "It's a shame that the neighborhood went the way it did. Just from what I've heard, it's not safe," she said.[33] SCC parents who avoided Auburn-Gresham missed positive changes taking place in the neighborhood since the 1980s. The St. Sabina of the 1960s—plagued by racial unrest and violent turmoil—remained firmly entrenched in their memories.

In the week following the announcement of the vote against St. Sabina, bishops and pastors as well as athletic directors and parents met to work out the dispute. They agreed that a second vote would take place on 20 June.[34] On Sunday, 17 June, Cardinal George celebrated the feast of Corpus Christi in a Mass at Corpus Christi Church. On this day, Corpus Christi—one of the oldest African American Catholic parishes in the city—marked its one hundredth anniversary. In his homily, George spoke about visiting the black parish in the late 1940s as a white boy from St. Pascal Church in the Portage Park neighborhood on the city's Northwest Side. "It was a long way, in distance and time, from the Northwest Side to Corpus Christi; but it was a longer way culturally and racially," remembered the cardinal. "We went because we knew our faith was the same faith, and that was enough."[35] He promised St. Sabina's schoolchildren would play in the SCC.[36] Three days later, the SCC board voted twenty-one to zero in favor of St. Sabina entering the conference. The controversy seemingly came to an end.[37]

Yet problems remained. Although SCC leadership promised to place St. Sabina on all of its athletic schedules, some coaches and parents threatened to forfeit games hosted by the black school. In a letter to the *Daily Southtown*, Bob Gorman of St. Catherine School in south suburban Oak

Lawn rejected promises to provide a safe environment around St. Sabina by its pastor and Chicago's superintendent of police and neighborhood resident Terry Hillard. "As a seventh-grade girl's [sic] basketball coach for the past five years," he wrote, "I can promise Fr. Pfleger and Mr. Hillard that St. Sabina will beat my team each time we play at their facility. They will win by forfeit." In response, Pfleger made it clear his parish would not join the SCC if some parents and coaches planned to forfeit games scheduled to be played at St. Sabina. "I'm not going to put kids through that," he said. "It's humiliating. It's demoralizing. We won't be a part of that."[38]

During the week of 9 July, talks between St. Sabina and the league broke down. While SCC officials continued to express concerns about neighborhood safety, Mallette and Pfleger worried about protecting their students from white racist behavior at athletic competitions. On 19 July, St. Sabina withdrew its membership in the league after the SCC refused to meet specific demands meant to safeguard against racist incidents.[39] Cardinal George, however, did not let the issue drop. The next evening he called together Pfleger and the SCC pastors, pressing both sides to reach common ground.

Two days later, on Sunday, 22 July, the vitriolic words of racial bigots raised the stakes. After Sunday Masses at several Southwest Side churches, parishioners found racist leaflets on their car windows. The National Alliance, a white supremacist group based in Hillsboro, West Virginia, distributed 1,400 fliers to 11 parishes. The leaflets read, "Before you let your children and spouses visit St. Sabina, please consider . . . ," then listed statistics supposedly showing that black men posed a danger to whites. Some SCC members may have harbored racist feelings, but they certainly did not see themselves allied with such extremists. Nevertheless, the public relations cat was out of the bag. "Unfortunately, sick folks like the National Alliance rise up on things like this and fuel it and take ownership of it," said Pfleger. "This goes to show what we've said all along. Race is embedded in this. It's at the root of this."[40]

This latest incident attracted the attention of Chicago's African American religious and political leaders. Three days after the racist leaflets were distributed, Rev. Jesse Jackson and more than thirty black leaders met for a press conference at St. Sabina. "The challenge here is much bigger than a ballgame," Jackson told news reporters and St. Sabina's faithful assembled in the parish gymnasium. Echoing Martin Luther King, Jr., he asked, "Shall we learn to live together as brothers and sisters or shall we die apart as fools?"[41] In a statement released later that day, George weighed in on the controversy, ending his neutrality in the dispute. Addressing St. Sabina's

demands, the cardinal wrote, "These are legitimate and necessary conditions, clarified for us all by Father Michael Pfleger to assure respect for all
those playing." George expected St. Sabina to be an equal member in the
SCC. "If organizations such as the Southside Catholic Conference cannot be used as a vehicle for social change," he wrote, "the young people
will not be able to live in a world any better than our own. . . . Let the
kids play."[42]

On 1 August, St. Sabina and SCC representatives reached an oral agreement. "I'm extremely optimistic," said Chris Mallette. "We sat down
and addressed issues before us. We met each other where we were."[43] Yet
St. Sabina objected days later when the conference released a written account of the accord. It included an anti-forfeiture clause but did not require signatures from parents or coaches. St. Sabina's representatives felt
betrayed, but Cardinal George prohibited them from withdrawing. Therefore, they voted in favor of the new agreement.[44] At last, St. Sabina was in
the conference.

The SCC/St. Sabina saga of 2001 embodied the contested meanings
of ethnic, religious, and neighborhood identities in everyday urban life.
Historically, labels like "Irish Catholic from Bridgeport" or "Russian
Jew from the Near West Side" acted as shorthand to many Chicagoans,
communicating social, political, and economic standings. In the SCC/
St. Sabina controversy, however, a fourth identity trumped all others:
race. St. Sabina's parishioners practiced the same religion as SCC members. They also lived in the same neighborhood, worshipped at the same
church, and attended the same school as the grandparents of many SCC
children. Yet racial classification set St. Sabina's parishioners apart from
the members of twenty-one nearby Catholic churches. As African Americans—even African American Catholics—they were different. They lived
in a neighborhood that was seen to be off-limits to nonresidents (i.e.,
white people). Law enforcement officials may have posted high crime
rates for Auburn-Gresham, but race, not safety, most clearly distinguished
St. Sabina from other SCC parishes.

Parents and coaches of the mostly white SCC did not consider themselves to be racists, because they did not adhere to ideas of racial supremacy or teach their children to hate others. Nevertheless, a racial divide between St. Sabina and its sister parishes isolated both sides. St. Sabina stood
only a few miles from the geographic center of the Southside Catholic
Conference, but its parishioners lived in a world apart. Nearly half a century after *Brown v. Board of Education*, four decades following the civil
rights legislation of the 1960s, and more than a generation since court-

mandated desegregation of public schools, racial segregation remained. Although members of St. Sabina and their counterparts in SCC parishes shared a faith tradition and many of the same middle-class values, neighborhood boundaries and parochial attitudes separated them. The SCC/St. Sabina controversy became a case of "us versus them" centered on the issue of race.

In his pastoral letter, Cardinal George condemned spatial and institutional racism, words that turned out to be particularly relevant in the SCC/St. Sabina conflict. St. Sabina's parishioners encountered spatial racism, because they lived in Auburn-Gresham, a neighborhood cut off, in effect, from the rest of the city. In addition, institutional racism—rejection from a Catholic sports league—threatened to isolate them even further. In the end, however, the two sides came together. After an arduous summer of intense debate and negotiations, the adults "let the kids play" and struck a blow against institutional racism.

St. Sabina's first league basketball game in the late fall of 2001 generated widespread attention. Newspaper photographers and television crews captured the scene in St. Sabina's gymnasium as black and white boys held hands in prayer before tip-off. "Thank God we can play together," remarked St. Sabina fifth-grader Jonathan Morris.[45] The St. Sabina Saints enjoyed great success in their inaugural basketball season. The eighth-grade boys team amassed a perfect 13–0 record by March, while the seventh-grade boys went 12–1.[46] Under the guidance of Cardinal Francis George, it appeared that St. Sabina and the SCC had achieved Catholic interracialism.

Yet racial problems remained. St. Sabina's coaches and parents complained of hostility from other teams in the league, including an incident in January 2002, in which a player from a mostly white parish allegedly called a St. Sabina player a racial epithet. As a result, the leadership of the African American parish felt it could no longer participate in the league. Two days before the beginning of the playoffs, St. Sabina permanently pulled out of the SCC.[47] The decision shocked Chicagoans and garnered front-page coverage in the *New York Times*.[48] Two months later, the network television news program *Nightline* devoted an episode to the SCC/St. Sabina controversy. In the fall of 2002, St. Sabina joined the Chicago Public Schools League. The Chicago Board of Education allowed the Catholic parish to participate as long as St. Sabina paid for its own expenses.[49] Catholic interracialism had failed. "Something's not right," Chicago Auxiliary Bishop Joseph Perry told *Nightline*'s audience. "We should be able to play together."[50]

Perry, an African American clergyman, personified the collective disappointment of a city and nation still entangled in a web of racial divisiveness. If young people could not participate in interracial sports, what hope remained for the future of American race relations? "The church," wrote Martin Luther King, Jr., in 1963, "must be reminded that it is not the master or the servant of the state, but rather the conscience of the state."[51] Between 1930 and 1954, Chicago's CYO provided a model of citywide, faith-based programming that allowed thousands of children and adolescents a chance to cross parish boundaries.

During the SCC/St. Sabina controversy in 2001, the children themselves best seemed to understand what was at stake. Twelve-year-old Vincent Lewis, the child of a white mother and black father, wanted St. Sabina to join the conference. "This is a Catholic school and we love each other, and need to set an example," he said. His white teammate, Brian Jucas, agreed and declared that African Americans like Vincent were an essential part of life. "You need them in order to live," he said, "or life would be uncool." The initial decision to exclude St. Sabina's from the SCC insulted Vincent and Brian, who were best friends. "I was very offended the Catholic conference was practically saying bad stuff about blacks, and I'm black," said Vincent. Brian agreed: "It hurts inside. Vinnie's not the only one being hurt since he's black. I'm hurt." The two boys appreciated interracial opportunities within a Catholic setting and wanted the same for others. Vincent even understood the issue's historical context. "If I were living 50 years ago, Brian wouldn't be able to be my friend," he said. "That would affect my whole life."[52] Paradoxically, it may have been more likely for the boys to encounter one another in Catholic-sponsored youth athletics during an earlier era. Despite persistent racism in society and in the church, Sheil's CYO created opportunities during the mid-twentieth century for friendships like the one between Vincent and Brian by crossing parish boundaries in a segregated city. Eighty years later, it is a model worth reexamining.

ACKNOWLEDGMENTS

W riting this book took me a long time. I am now grateful to see *Crossing Parish Boundaries* finally go to print. A happy result of such a long project is that I have been privileged to work with many talented and generous individuals along the way.

I first met historians Suellen Hoy and Ellen Skerrett at the Urban History Seminar at the Chicago Historical Society (now Chicago History Museum). They encouraged me to investigate the history of Bishop Bernard Sheil and the Catholic Youth Organization when I told them that I was interested in black-white relations in urban Catholic settings. Since that first meeting, Suellen and Ellen have supported me professionally and personally in countless ways. I am forever indebted to them for their expert guidance, encouragement, and friendship.

Timothy Gilfoyle was my mentor at Loyola University Chicago and has remained so to this day. In addition to being a leading historian in the field of U.S. urban history, Tim is a superb reader and editor. Time and time again he returned my chapter drafts with lightning speed, filled with thoughtful comments, precise edits, and historiographical insights. I am thankful moreover for his personal kindness and friendship, including the countless conversations we enjoyed during meals for which he generously picked up the tab.

Salve Regina University has been a wonderful place to teach. For their support, I thank my colleagues in the Salve Regina History Department: John Buckley, the late Christopher Kiernan, William Leeman, and John Quinn, who carefully read a full draft of *Crossing Parish Boundaries*, offering numerous helpful comments and suggestions. Salve Regina staff members Grace Cleary and Daniel Titus provided crucial technical support with preparing charts and photos for the book, while my students

Timothy Lamperelli and Sara Thurber helped with proofreading. I also thank the staff of McKillop Library for their assistance with interlibrary loans. Provosts Dean de la Motte and Scott Zeman made professional development funds available for research and conference attendance. Finally, Salve Regina University President Jane Gerety, RSM, provided a Presidential Faculty Award and granted me a course reduction in the spring semester of 2012 for the purpose of revising the book manuscript.

I was fortunate to have the opportunity to present parts of my manuscript to colleagues across the United States. I thank participants of the American Catholic Studies Seminar at the Charles and Margaret Hall Cushwa Center for the Study of American Catholicism at the University of Notre Dame (November 2004), the Boston Immigration and Urban History Seminar at the Massachusetts Historical Society (April 2011), the panel session "Catholicism in the City of Big Shoulders" at the Annual Meeting of the American Catholic Historical Association (January 2012), and the panel session "Race, Religious Histories, and the Taboos of the Spiritual" at the Annual Meeting of the Organization of American Historians (April 2015). In addition, I benefitted from the expert feedback from the following individuals who read sections of the manuscript: Howard Chudacoff, Lewis Erenberg, Elliott Gorn, Suellen Hoy, Cheryl Johnson-Odom, John McGreevy, Patricia Mooney-Melvin, Steve Rosswurm, and Ellen Skerrett.   .

I thank *U.S. Catholic Historian*, *American Catholic Studies*, and the Cushwa Center at the University of Notre Dame for allowing me to include previously published materials in *Crossing Parish Boundaries*. Some of the material in chapters 1 and 2 was originally published in "Black-Belt Catholic Space: African-American Parishes in Interwar Chicago," *U.S. Catholic Historian* 19, no. 4 (Fall 2000): 76–91. Some of the material in chapters 3, 4, and 5 was originally published in "Crossing Parochial Boundaries: Interracialism in Chicago's Catholic Youth Organization, 1930–1954," *American Catholic Studies* 114, no. 3 (Fall 2003): 23-37; and "Taking it to the Streets: Catholic Liberalism, Race, and Sport in Twentieth-Century Urban America," Working Paper Series, Charles and Margaret Hall Cushwa Center for the Study of American Catholicism, University of Notre Dame, ser. 36, no. 2 (Fall 2004).

Throughout the many years it took to finish this book, a large group of colleagues and friends supported me in a multitude of ways. I thank the late Felix Armfield, Wallace Best, Joe Bigott, Randi Barnes Cox, Kathleen Sprows Cummings, the late Peter D'Agostino, Cyprian Davis, Marie Davis, Nancy Davis, Laura Milsk Fowler, Gerald Gems, Elliott Gorn, Rebekah Gross, Carole Heath, D. Bradford Hunt, Karen Joy Johnson, Barbara Kathe, Christopher Kaufman, Ann Durkin Keating, James Kraeger, Timothy Lacy, Ronald Martin, Malachy McCarthy, Margaret McGuinness, Cecilia Moore, Diane Batts Morrow, Walter Nugent, Dominic Pacyga, Douglas Pfeister, Stephen Power, Robert Pruter, Christopher Ramsey, David Richmond, Kristin Richmond, and Rima Lunin Schultz.

Research for this book was possible only through the assistance of talented and generous archivists and librarians. I thank Meg Romero Hall and Julie Satzik at the Archdiocese of Chicago's Joseph Cardinal Bernardin Archives and Records Center; the late Archie Motley at the Chicago History Museum; Marcus Berry and Glenn Humphreys at the Chicago Public Library; Maureen O'Donnell and Toby Roberts at the *Chicago Sun-Times*; Chris Barbuschak and Elaine Varvatos at the *Chicago Tribune*; Rev. Anthony Ita Bassey, MSP, and Dolores Williams at Corpus Christi Church; Jeff Bridgers and Michelle Wright at the Library of Congress; and Kevin Cawley, Charles Lamb, and Jean McManus at the University of Notre Dame. In addition to archival research, I conducted a number of oral history interviews for this book. I thank the numerous individuals who agreed to sit down with me and share their stories: Jason Bertrand, Bob Bigott, Timuel Black, Stephen Carter, Marie Davis, Leon Despres, Ernest Giovangelo, James Lampkins, Edwin Leaner, Anne Lyons, Ed Marciniak, George Phillips, Eugene Saffold, Warner Saunders, Rita Stalzer, Hon. John Stroger, James Williams, and John Woodford.

It has been a great pleasure working with the University of Chicago Press. Acquiring editor Robert Devens first encouraged me to submit a book proposal to the Historical Studies of Urban America series. When Robert left for the University of Texas Press, I was fortunate that his successor, Timothy Mennel, likewise was patient and encouraging. I thank Tim for his professionalism, kindness, and enthusiasm. Mary Tong expertly edited the manuscript, and editorial associates Nora Devlin and Rachel Kelly cheerfully helped a first-time author navigate the editorial process. I also thank the University of Chicago Press for recommending the services of Kevin Schuhl, who designed the book's map. Historical Studies of Urban America series editors James Grossman, Becky Nicolaides, and Timothy Gilfoyle helped make *Crossing Parish Boundaries* a better book by pushing me to situate my work within the most relevant twentieth-century U.S. urban historiography. Finally, I thank the three anonymous outside readers for their insightful, challenging, and helpful comments.

I end by thanking my family. My father John Robert Neary and late mother Colleen Brennan Neary provided me with a loving home in which they fostered learning, particularly about history. I thank my siblings, Maureen, Jack, Michaela, Patty, Brian, and Sheila—along with their own families—for their love and support. My in-laws, Jean and Claire Carré, have welcomed me into their French home as one of their own children: *merci*.

To Aïda, my love, words cannot convey my gratitude. Thank you for sharing your life with me. Thank you for Langston and Claire. May their generation face fewer boundaries.

NOTES

INTRODUCTION

1. Frank Mastro, "Two Retain Title in C.Y.O. Boxing Meet: Al Noto, Wells Triumph Again Before 8,563," *Chicago Tribune*, 5 December 1940.

2. Paula Lupkin, "Places of Assembly," in *Encyclopedia of Chicago*, ed. James R. Grossman, Ann Durkin Keating, and Janice L. Reiff (Chicago: University of Chicago Press, 2004), 609–10.

3. Frank Mastro, "C.Y.O. Boxers Battle for Titles in Coliseum Tonight: 9,000 to See Bouts in Open, Novice Classes: Three '39 Champions Defend Crowns," *Chicago Tribune*, 4 December 1940.

4. "Stadium Calls Off Ring Show; Purses Too High," *Chicago Tribune*, 18 January 1933; "Candidates for C.Y.O. Team Open Camp Training," *Chicago Tribune*, 7 September 1941.

5. "Five Corpus Christi Boxers are C.Y.O. Boxers: Lightweight Crown Won by Goldsmith: Willie Moon Looks Like Another Armstrong in the Ring," *Chicago Defender*, 17 December 1938; Fred Downer, "Bray, Thomas Capture C.Y.O. Ring Crowns," *Chicago Defender*, 14 December 1935.

6. French Lane, "Rabbit's Foot and Punches Do William Wrong: Charm Doesn't Work in Golden Gloves," *Chicago Tribune*, 13 February 1937.

7. Norman O. Unger, "Ex-Marine Boxing Teacher Still Building Young Men," *Chicago Defender*, 2 September 1975.

8. French Lane, "19,000 Watch C.Y.O. Boxers Take Championships: Adler Scores Technical K.O. Over Camber: Scrivani Wins His Third Title," *Chicago Tribune*, 5 December 1935; "Semi-Finals in C.Y.O. Tourney Open Tomorrow: Winners Qualify for Finals Dec. 2," *Chicago Tribune*, 22 November 1936.

9. Frank Mastro, "C.Y.O. Finalists Near Finish of Training Grid: But O'Connell Brothers Won't Slow Down," *Chicago Tribune*, 1 December 1940.

10. "C.Y.O. Boxing Squad Wins in Cincinnati," *Chicago Tribune*, 15 December 1936; "C.Y.O. Boxers Win, 11 to 5, from Detroit," 21 October 1937; "C.Y.O. Boxers Defeat Dubuque, 5 to 3," 18 June 1937; "179 C.Y.O. Boys Pass Physical Test for Golden Gloves

Bouts," 25 January 1938; "C.Y.O. Boxers Go to Kansas City for Team Match," 19 March 1939; "Chicago C.Y.O. Team Battles Omaha to a Draw," 16 March 1937; "Chicago C.Y.O. Defeats Racine, 5 to 1," 24 May 1938; "C.Y.O. Triumphs, 7 to 3, in Wilkes-Barre," 2 August 1938; "Ex-C.Y.O. Champ on Furlough," *Chicago Defender*, 27 January 1945.

11. "C.Y.O. Boxers Battle Way into Finals," *Chicago Tribune*, 23 November 1937.

12. For example of photos, see "And May the Better 16 Men Win!" *Chicago Tribune*, 4 December 1935; "C.Y.O. Finalists Wear that Victory Smile," *Chicago Tribune*, 29 November 1936; "Be Ready Win you Return, Boys," *Chicago Tribune*, 10 August 1937; "They Fight for Fun and What Fun!" *Chicago Tribune*, 18 January 1939.

13. Mastro, "Two Retain Title in C.Y.O. Boxing Meet."

14. Joe Rein, "C.Y.O. Aces Clash Tonight in Title Battles: Fight at Coliseum on Christmas Fund Program," *Chicago Daily News*, 4 December 1940.

15. Clair Kelly, "Crown New C.Y.O. Ring Champions," *Chicago Herald-American*, 5 December 1940.

16. 1940 U.S. Federal Population Census, Sheet Number 8, Sheet B, Line Number 75, NARA Microfilm Roll Number 959, NARA Publication Number T627, http://www .archives.com/1940-census/hiner-thomas-il-87359498, accessed 9 June 2015; "Hiner Thomas, 1915–2000, Military Grave Location, US Marine Corps," http://findgrave.org/ hinerthomascalifornia478843/, accessed 12 June 2015.

17. "Ex-C.Y.O. Champ on Furlough."

18. On Lilydale, see Jeffrey Helgeson, *Crucibles of Black Empowerment: Chicago's Neighborhood Politics from the New Deal to Harold Washington* (Chicago: University of Chicago Press, 2014), 152–58.

19. "O'Toole to Speak at Realtors Meet," *Milwaukee Sentinel*, 18 June 1944.

20. Janice L. Reiff, "Roseland," in Grossman et al., *Encyclopedia of Chicago*, 722–23.

21. 1917–1918 World War I Draft Registration Cards, John H. O'Connell, Draft Board Chicago City no 2; M-X; NARA Publication Number M1509, http://www.archives .com/, accessed 26 June 2015.

22. The Bukowskis are one example. In the mid-twentieth century, the Polish American family left the South Side Bridgeport neighborhood for the "bungalow belt" on Chicago's Southwest Side, relocating in the Gage Park neighborhood; Douglas Bukowski, *Pictures of Home: A Memoir of Family and City* (Chicago: Ivan R. Dee, 2004). I thank Ellen Skerrett for this reference.

23. 1940 U.S. Federal Population Census, Sheet Number 6, Sheet B, Line Number 31, NARA Microfilm Roll Number 948, NARA Publication Number T627, http://www .archives.com/, accessed 26 June 2015.

24. On St. Nicholas of Tolentine, see Rev. Msgr. Harry C. Koenig, *A History of the Parishes of the Archdiocese of Chicago* (Chicago: The Archdiocese of Chicago, 1980), 659–62.

25. The West Englewood community area was 97 percent white in 1930; Franklin Forts, "West Englewood," in Grossman et al., *Encyclopedia of Chicago*, http://www .encyclopedia.chicagohistory.org/pages/1337.html, accessed 26 June 2015.

26. Mastro, "C.Y.O. Finalists Near Finish of Training Grind."

27. "Rocks Injure 8 in Disturbance at Vets' Homes: Crowd Makes Protest as Negroes Move In," *Chicago Tribune*, 6 December 1946.

28. Gene Roberts, "Rock Hits Dr. King as Whites Attack March in Chicago: Felled Rights Leader Rises and Continues Protest as Crowd of 4,000 Riots," *New York Times*, 6 August 1966.

29. Douglas Knox, "West Lawn," in Grossman et al., *Encyclopedia of Chicago*, 872.

30. The 1960 U.S. census shows only five African Americans living among 26,893 whites in West Lawn; Knox, "West Lawn," in Grossman et al., *Encyclopedia of Chicago*, http://www.encyclopedia.chicagohistory.org/pages/1339.html, accessed 26 June 2015.

31. Unger, "Ex-Marine Boxing Teacher Still Building Young Men."

32. For Chicago examples, see Davarian L. Baldwin, *Chicago's New Negroes: Modernity, the Great Migration, and Black Urban Life* (Chapel Hill: University of North Carolina Press, 2007); St. Clair Drake and Horace Cayton, *Black Metropolis: A Study of Negro Life in a Northern City* (New York: Harcourt Brace, 1945); Adam Green, *Selling the Race: Culture, Community, and Black Chicago, 1940–1955* (Chicago: University of Chicago Press, 2009); James R. Grossman, *Land of Hope: Chicago, Black Southerners, and the Great Migration* (Chicago: University of Chicago Press, 1989); Allan H. Spear, *Black Chicago: The Making of a Negro Ghetto, 1890–1920* (Chicago: University of Chicago Press, 1967).

33. For examples, see Jay P. Dolan, *The Immigrant Church: New York's Irish and German Catholics* (Baltimore, MD: Johns Hopkins University Press, 1975); Andrew M. Greeley, *The American Catholic: A Social Portrait* (New York: Basic, 1977); Robert A. Orsi, *The Madonna of 115th Street: Faith and Community in Italian Harlem, 1880–1950* (New Haven, CT: Yale University Press, 1985); Charles Shanabruch, *Chicago's Catholics: The Evolution of an American Identity* (Notre Dame, IN: University of Notre Dame Press, 1981); Evelyn Savidge Sterne, *Ballots and Bibles: Ethnic Politics and the Catholic Church in Providence* (Ithaca, NY: Cornell University Press, 2003).

34. Albert J. Raboteau, "Minority within a Minority: History of Black Catholicism in America," chap. 6 in *A Fire in the Bones: Reflections on African American Religious History* (Boston: Beacon, 1995), 117–37. See also Dorothy Ann Blatnica, *"At the Altar of Their God": African American Catholics in Cleveland, 1921–1961* (New York: Garland, 1995); Cyprian Davis, *The History of Black Catholics in the United States* (New York: Crossroad, 1990); Gary Wray McDonogh, *Black and Catholic in Savannah, Georgia* (Knoxville: University of Tennessee Press, 1993); Diane Batts Morrow, *Persons of Color and Religious at the Same Time* (Chapel Hill: University of North Carolina Press, 2002); Marilyn Wenzke Nickels, *Black Catholic Protest and the Federated Colored Catholics, 1917–1933: Three Perspectives on Racial Justice* (New York: Garland, 1988); Stephen J. Ochs, *Desegregating the Altar: The Josephites and the Struggle for Black Priests, 1871–1960* (Baton Rouge: Louisiana State University Press, 1990).

35. For example, see Lizabeth Cohen, *Making a New Deal: Industrial Workers in Chicago, 1919–1930* (New York: Cambridge University Press, 1990).

36. James R. Barrett, *The Irish Way: Becoming American in the Multiethnic City* (New York: Penguin, 2012), 52–53.

37. CYO Charter quoted in Welfare Council of Metropolitan Chicago, "Catholic Youth Organization," January 1954, p. 1, box 257, folder 3, Welfare Council of Metropolitan Chicago Papers, Chicago History Museum.

38. Bishop Sheil's politics are not easily labeled; he was at once a staunch anticommunist, staunch antifascist, proponent of the State of Israel, and harsh critic of U.S. Senator Joseph McCarthy. His ideology did not follow the typical Left-Right political spectrum, but rather was rooted in the social justice teachings of the Roman Catholic Church. Specifically, Sheil's thinking was shaped by Pope Leo XIII's encyclical *Rerum Novarum*, or "Rights and Duties of Capital and Labor" (1891), which argued for the amelioration of "the misery and wretchedness pressing so unjustly on the majority of the working class." Sheil's interracialism is better understood in this context because his support of the rights of labor to form unions, rejection of communism and unrestricted capitalism, and affirmation of the right to private property were at the heart of *Rerum Novarum*. On the influence of *Rerum Novarum* on Catholics in the United States, see John T. McGreevy, *Catholicism and American Freedom: A History* (New York: W.W. Norton, 2003), 127–65.

39. Historian Christopher Reed argues that the term "ghetto"—with the connotation of dysfunction as used by social scientists since the 1960s—inaccurately describes all-black communities, like Bronzeville, in the first half of the twentieth century; Christopher Robert Reed, *The Rise of Chicago's Black Metropolis, 1920–1929* (Urbana: University of Illinois Press, 2011), 2, 12, 27, 30, 32.

40. In his classic 1944 study, the Swedish economist and sociologist Gunnar Myrdal shined a light on the hypocrisy of a society which held up such a creed as a model for the world while at the same time subjecting millions of its citizens to the injustices of Jim Crow; Gunnar Myrdal, *An American Dilemma: The Negro Problem and Modern Democracy* (New York: Harper & Row, 1944).

41. Jacquelyn Dowd Hall, "The Long Civil Rights Movement and the Political Uses of the Past," *The Journal of American History* 91.4 (March 2005): 1233–63. For a critique of the "long civil rights movement" thesis, see Eric Arnesen, "Reconsidering the 'Long Civil Rights Movement,'" *Historically Speaking* 10.2 (April 2009): 31–34.

42. Thomas J. Sugrue, *Sweet Land of Liberty: The Forgotten Struggle for Civil Rights in the North* (New York: Random House, 2008).

43. On the "Black Popular Front," see Martha Biondi, *To Stand and Fight: The Struggle for Civil Rights in Postwar New York City* (Cambridge, MA: Harvard University Press, 2006). On "civil rights unionism," see Robert Rodgers Korstad, *Civil Rights Unionism: Tobacco Workers and the Struggle for Democracy in the Mid-Twentieth-Century South* (Chapel Hill: University of North Carolina Press, 2003).

44. John T. McGreevy, *Parish Boundaries: The Catholic Encounter with Race in the Twentieth Century Urban North* (Chicago: University of Chicago Press, 1996).

45. For examples, see Eric Arneson, "Whiteness and the Historical Imagination," *International Labor and Working-Class History* 60 (Fall 2001): 3–31; Noel Ignatiev, *How the Irish Became White* (New York: Routledge, 1996); Matthew Frye Jacobson, *Whiteness of a Different Color: European Immigrants and the Alchemy of Race* (Cambridge, MA: Harvard University Press, 1999); Ira Katznelson, *When Affirmative Action Was White* (New York: W.W. Norton, 2006); David R. Roediger, *The Wages of Whiteness:*

Race and the Making of the American Working Class (New York: Verso, 1991) and *Working Toward Whiteness: How America's Immigrants Became White: The Strange Journey from Ellis Island to the Suburbs* (New York: Basic, 2005).

46. Arnold R. Hirsch, *Making the Second Ghetto: Race and Housing in Chicago, 1940–1960* (Chicago: University of Chicago Press, 1998); Thomas Sugrue, *The Origins of the New Urban Crisis: Race and Inequality in Postwar Detroit* (Princeton, NJ: Princeton University Press, 1996).

47. Institutional differences between Catholicism and Judaism explain much about how the two groups responded to racial change. The Catholic attachment to place was rooted in the tradition of territorial parishes and a strong hierarchy, while Jewish survival historically relied on portability and autonomy; Gerald Gamm, *Urban Exodus: Why the Jews Left Boston and the Catholics Stayed* (Cambridge, MA: Harvard University Press, 1999).

48. McGreevy, *Parish Boundaries*, 93–97; Hirsch, *Making the Second Ghetto*, 88–93. Sugrue gives similar examples of white Catholic resistance in postwar Detroit; Sugrue, *The Origins of the New Urban Crisis*, 235–41.

49. Campbell Gibson and Kay Jung, *Historical Census Statistics On Population Totals By Race, 1790 to 1990, and By Hispanic Origin, 1970 to 1990, For Large Cities And Other Urban Places In The United States*, Popular Division Working Paper No. 76 (Washington, DC: U.S. Census Bureau, February 2005), Table 14, http://www.census.gov/population/www/documentation/twps0076/ILtab.pdf, accessed 14 May 2014.

50. See figure 4.9.

51. "Roman Catholics: Winning the Kingdom of God," *Time*, 26 September 1969, 63.

52. Ira Katznelson describes such double consciousness leading to a "radical separation . . . of the politics of work from the politics of community"; Ira Katznelson, *City Trenches: Urban Politics and the Patterning of Class in the U.S.* (New York: Pantheon, 1981), 6.

CHAPTER ONE

1. A thief rifling through poor boxes knocked over lit candles and started the fire, according to one newspaper account; "To Rebuild Catholic Edifice," *Chicago Defender*, 11 January 1930. A parishioner recalled years later that dried Christmas trees inside the church caught fire from the heat of electrical lights adorning a crèche; John Woodford, interview by author, Chicago, Illinois, 26 April 2002.

2. "Flames Damage St. Elizabeth's; Priests Heroes," *Chicago Tribune*, 4 January 1930.

3. "St. Elizabeth's Old Historic Church Burns: Blessed Sacrament Saved After Several Unsuccessful Attempts," *New World*, 10 January 1930. The number of firemen and length of conflagration from "Community History," archives, St. Elizabeth Convent, Chicago, Illinois (hereafter, SEC). Information on Pete Adler from Marie C. Davis, interview by author, Chicago, Illinois, 6 July 2001. Adler is also described in Caroline Hemesath, *From Slave to Priest: A Biography of the Rev. Augustine Tolton (1854–1897), First Afro-American Priest of the United States* (Chicago: Franciscan Herald, 1973), 147.

4. "St. Elizabeth's Old Historic Church Burns." Number of St. Elizabeth's parishioners in 1930 from *New World*, 19 December 1930.

5. The national parish was a Catholic congregation composed of immigrants from one national background (e.g., Polish or Italian). Typically, the pastor shared the ethnicity of his parishioners. Parish organizations and activities supported the retention of ethnic heritage. In 1787, German Americans founded the nation's first national parish, Holy Trinity, in Philadelphia; Jay P. Dolan, *The American Catholic Experience: A History from Colonial Times to the Present* (Notre Dame, IN: University of Notre Dame Press, 1992), 130.

6. Parish annual reports for 1941 list "about" 3,000 members for St. Elizabeth's, 2,400 for Corpus Christi, and 3,850 for St. Anselm; Parish Annual Reports Collection, box ADMN/P0170/140; folder 1941, Archdiocese of Chicago's Joseph Cardinal Bernardin Archives and Records Center (hereafter, AAC). One historian estimates the city's total black Catholic population in 1938 to be 16,000; James W. Sanders, *The Education of an Urban Minority: Catholics in Chicago, 1833–1965* (New York: Oxford University Press, 1977), 215.

7. St. Elizabeth Church, "The Beginning of an Era: History of the Work of the Catholic Church Among the Negroes of Chicago: Silver Jubilee of the Ordination of Rev. William S. Brambrink, SVD," Chicago, Illinois, 1952, AAC (this booklet was found on a shelf in the reading room; it is not a part of a specific collection). The Armstrongs, however, were not the first black Catholics to live in the area. In 1779, Jean Baptiste Pointe Du Sable, a Roman Catholic Afro-French fur trader established a permanent trading post on the spot where Euro-Americans founded Chicago in the 1830s.

8. This is approximately $225,000 in 2012 real dollars.

9. Glen E. Holt and Dominic A. Pacyga, *Chicago: A Historical Guide to the Neighborhoods, The Loop and South Side* (Chicago: Chicago Historical Society, 1979), 88.

10. Harry C. Koenig, *A History of the Archdiocese of Chicago* (Chicago: Archdiocese of Chicago, 1980), 248.

11. Tolton's name is alternatively spelled "Augustine" and "Augustus." At times it is listed as "John Augustine." I follow the practice of Cyprian Davis, who uses "Augustus" in his excellent book on the history of black Catholics; Davis, *The History of Black Catholics in the United States* (New York: Crossroad, 1990), 297n25.

12. Alexander Sherwood Healy was a priest at the cathedral in Boston and worked in the Vatican; James Augustine Healy became bishop of Portland, Maine; and Patrick Francis Healy, S.J., became the president of Georgetown University. On the Healy brothers, see James M. O'Toole, *Passing for White: Race, Religion, and the Healy Family, 1820–1920* (Amherst: University of Massachusetts Press, 2002); Albert S. Foley, *God's Men of Color: The Colored Catholic Priests of the United States, 1854–1954* (New York: Farrar, Straus, 1955), 1–31.

13. Koenig, *A History of the Archdiocese of Chicago*, 248. For the only book-length biography of Tolton, see Hemesath, *From Slave to Priest*; see also Foley, *God's Men of Color*, 32–41.

14. An analysis of the annual parish reports of St. Monica's and neighboring St. Elizabeth demonstrates Tolton's alternative fundraising methods. In 1890, for example, Tolton earned $315 for the parish through lecturing (presumably drawing crowds in part

because of his uniqueness), almost equaling his annual salary of $385.50. The 1890 Sunday and holiday collection total for St. Monica's was only $255.76, and special outside fundraising collected by parishioner Lincoln C. Vallé totaled $306. Therefore, special fundraising methods more than doubled weekly collection totals in 1890; "St. Monica's Annual Report," 1890, Parish Annual Reports Collection box ADMN/P0170/164, folder 1890, AAC. Conversely, nearby St. Elizabeth 1890 revenues came almost exclusively from a total of $5,453.95 in weekly collections. St. Elizabeth's parishioners were greater in number and wealthier individually; "St. Elizabeth's Annual Report," 1890, Parish Annual Reports Collection box ADMN/P0170/164, folder 1890, AAC.

15. John McGreevy writes, "African American Catholics, like Poles, Italians, and other Euro-American groups, were expected to worship in their own parishes, receive the ministrations of religious-order priests specially trained for work in their community, and learn from nuns who were devoted to working in their parochial schools"; John T. McGreevy, *Parish Boundaries: The Catholic Encounter with Race in the Twentieth Century Urban North* (Chicago: University of Chicago Press, 1996), 29.

16. Koenig, *A History of the Archdiocese of Chicago*, 249.

17. Sanders, *The Education of an Urban Minority*, 205.

18. Born in 1858, Mary Katharine Drexel was the second daughter of Philadelphia millionaire Anthony Joseph Drexel. She entered religious life in 1889 and used her share of the family fortune to found the Sisters of the Blessed Sacrament. Pope John Paul II canonized her on 1 October 2000; for more on Drexel, see Consuela Marie Duffy, *Katharine Drexel: A Biography* (Philadelphia: P. Reilly, 1966).

19. The 8th Regiment was an African American army unit from Illinois that fought in the Spanish American War; "Community History," SEC. A former St. Monica's student remembered the lingering smell of horses in the school; Woodford, interview by author.

20. "St. Monica's Annual Report," year ending 31 December 1915, Parish Annual Reports Collection, box ADMN/P0170/130, folder 1915, AAC.

21. "Catholicity Among Chicago Negroes: Growing Membership Gives Allegiance to the Universal Church," *New World*, 19 December 1913.

22. For a full account of the first great migration of African Americans to Chicago, see Grossman, *Land of Hope: Chicago, Black Southerners, and the Great Migration* (Chicago: University of Chicago Press, 1989).

23. "Increasing Negro Population New Catholic Problem," *New World*, 4 April 1917.

24. Mundelein is discussed fully in Edward R. Kantowicz, *Corporation Sole: Cardinal Mundelein and Chicago Catholicism* (Notre Dame, IN: University of Notre Dame Press, 1983).

25. Father J. F. Callaghan to Archbishop George W. Mundelein, 3 May 1917, Madaj Chancery Correspondence Collection, box EXEC/V2530/141, folder M-327, AAC.

26. For more on the Society of the Divine Word, see Ernest Brandewie, *In the Light of the Word: Divine Word Missionaries of North America* (Maryknoll, NY: Orbis, 2000).

27. Archbishop George W. Mundelein to the Very Rev. J. A. Burgmer, SVD, 26 October 1917, box EXEC/V2530/143, folder 5-17, AAC.

28. *Chicago Defender*, 14 October 1922.

29. Mundelein to Burgmer, 26 October 1917; Sanders, *The Education of an Urban Minority*, 213.

30. Mundelein to Burgmer, 26 October 1917.

31. Ibid.

32. "St. Monica's Church Again the Scene of Discrimination," *Chicago Defender*, 17 November 1917.

33. "Big Step Backward," *Chicago Defender*, 17 November 1917.

34. Z. Withers to Archbishop Mundelein, 13 November 1917, box EXEC/V2530/141, folder M-166, AAC.

35. James S. Madden to Archbishop Mundelein, 20 November 1917, box EXEC/V2530/142, folder M-77, AAC.

36. "AN ADDRESS to the ARCHBISHOP OF CHICAGO protesting against A POLICY OF SEGREGATION in the administration of the AFFAIRS OF ST. MONICA'S MISSION," 7 December 1917, Madaj Chancery Correspondence, box EXEC/V2530/142, folder M-77, AAC.

37. Ibid.

38. Bishop Edward P. Hoban to Joseph S. Madden, 26 December 1917, box EXEC/V2530/142, folder M-77, AAC.

39. Father Stephen L. Theobold to Bishop Edward P. Hoban, 9 February 1918, box EXEC/V2530/139, folder H-270, AAC.

40. A 1919 coroner's report found that Williams drowned after letting go of a railroad tie that was keeping him afloat. In 1969, an eyewitness told historian William Tuttle that a rock hit Williams in the head and he drowned; Chicago Commission on Race Relations, *The Negro in Chicago: A Study of Race Relations and a Race Riot* (Chicago: University of Chicago Press, 1922), 4; William M. Tuttle, Jr., *Race Riot: Chicago in the Red Summer of 1919* (New York: Atheneum, 1970), 3–8.

41. Chicago Commission on Race Relations, *The Negro in Chicago*, 655–67.

42. Ibid., 658, 661–62.

43. Davis, *The History of Black Catholics*, 216–17.

44. "Business and the Negro," *New World*, 12 December 1919.

45. On the Washington/Du Bois split, see David Levering Lewis, "Clashing Temperaments," chap. 10 in *W. E. B. Du Bois: Biography of a Race* (New York: Henry Holt, 1993), 238–64.

46. The building was at 4052 South Wabash Avenue.

47. Koenig, *A History of the Archdiocese of Chicago*, 245–48.

48. Peter F. Janser, SVD, to Archbishop George W. Mundelein, 13 March 1922, box EXEC/V2530/128, folder M-38, AAC.

49. Koenig, *A History of the Archdiocese of Chicago*, 245–48.

50. Annual report, St. Elizabeth Church, 1925, Box 17, Parish Annual Reports, box ADMN/P0170/156, folder 1925, AAC.

51. "Historical Account," typewritten manuscript, SEC.

52. Koenig, *A History of the Archdiocese of Chicago*, 249.

53. St. Elizabeth Church, "The Beginning of an Era."

54. For more on the negative effects of Mundelein's policy on Chicago's black Catholic community, see Karen Joy Johnson, "The Universal Church in the Segregated

City: Doing Catholic Interracialism in Chicago, 1915–1963" (PhD diss., University of
Illinois at Chicago, 2013).

55. For a description of this change, see Dominic A. Pacyga and Ellen Skerrett, *Chicago: City of Neighborhoods, Histories and Tours* (Chicago: Loyola University Press, 1986), 335.

56. *Corpus Christi Parish: Our History, 1901–1977*, 4920 Dr. Martin Luther King Drive, Chicago, Illinois (Hackensack, NJ: Custombook, Inc., 1977), 2–3, Parish Commemorative Books: Hist/C5700/13, folder 15, AAC. Koenig, *A History of the Archdiocese of Chicago*, 216–17.

57. *Corpus Christi Parish: Our History*, 6–7.

58. "Sunday Walks: XIX, The Old and New in Church Architecture," *New World*, 9 January 1931.

59. *Corpus Christi Parish: Our History*, 6–7; Koenig, *A History of the Archdiocese of Chicago*, 218.

60. Campbell Gibson and Kay Jung, *Historical Census Statistics On Population Totals By Race, 1790 to 1990, and By Hispanic Origin, 1970 to 1990, For Large Cities And Other Urban Places In The United States*, Popular Division Working Paper No. 76 (Washington, DC: U.S. Census Bureau, February 2005), table 14, http://www.census.gov/population/www/documentation/twps0076/ILtab.pdf, accessed 14 May 2014.

61. St. Clair Drake, *Churches and Voluntary Associations in the Chicago Negro Community* (Chicago: Work Projects Administration, 1940), 192–93.

62. Susan Kuczka, "George is Confident St. Sabina Will Play," *Chicago Tribune*, 18 June 2001.

63. "Why Laymen's Retreat?" *New World*, 18 April 1930.

64. *Corpus Christi Parish: Our History*, 8.

65. Apparently some whites continued to attend the church. The archdiocesan newspaper reported the baptisms of "converts of both races" at Corpus Christi on 4 June 1933; "Converts Baptized Sunday at Corpus Christi Church," *New World*, 16 June 1933.

66. The officers in the fall of 1932: Rev. Nicholas Christoffel, OFM—spiritual director; George R. Holland—president; George Adams—vice-president; Cassius Foster—secretary; Usher Davis—treasurer; Eugene Marshall and Thomas Bryan—Big Brother committee; Henry Boone, MD, and Albert Taper—CYO committee; and Severin Langlois—entertainment committee; "Corpus Christi Men Organize Branch," *New World*, 18 November 1932. The officers in the fall of 1933: Rev. Clement Martin, OFM—pastor and spiritual director; George R. Holland—president; Cassius J. Foster—secretary; Eugene J. Marshall—Big Brother committee; R.A. Skinner—CYO Committee; and H.L. Jennings—librarian; "Corpus Christi," *New World*, 6 October 1933.

67. *Corpus Christi Parish: Our History*, 10. "Baptism of 50 Adults at Corpus Christi Church," *New World*, 16 December 1932.

68. By November, the enrollment increased again to 325 "mostly colored" students; "Benefit Bazaar for Imposing Center of Faith," *New World*, 17 November 1933.

69. *Corpus Christi Parish: Our History*, 10.

70. A newspaper article put the number at 680; "Administer Baptism to Class of 127 Converts—Corpus Christi Church Scene of Important Events in May," *New World*, 29 May 1936.

71. *Corpus Christi Parish: Our History*, 10.

72. "Large Convert Class to be Confirmed Tonight by Bishop Sheil," *New World*, 2 June 1939; "Converts at Corpus Christi Total 1,200 in Five Years: Franciscan Fathers Instruct Large Number in Faith; Bishop Sheil to Administer Confirmation June 8," *New Word*, 4 June 1937.

73. *Corpus Christi Parish: Our History*, 11.

74. St. Clair Drake and Horace Cayton, *Black Metropolis: A Study of Negro Life in a Northern City* (New York: Harcourt, Brace, 1945), 379–81.

75. Koenig, *A History of the Archdiocese of Chicago*, 72; Agnes T. Ryan, "Bringing Down to Date the Histories of the Parishes of the Archdiocese of Chicago," *New World*, 2 October 1936.

76. James T. Farrell, *Studs Lonigan: A Trilogy Comprising* Young Lonigan, The Young Manhood of Studs Lonigan, *and* Judgment Day (New York: Penguin, 2001), 93 (the books were originally published in 1932, 1934, and 1935, respectively); see also Charles Fanning and Ellen Skerrett, "James T. Farrell and Washington Park: The Novel as Social History," *Chicago History* 8.2 (summer 1979): 80–91.

77. Chicago Commission on Race Relations, *The Negro in Chicago*, 125–26.

78. "Sunday Walks: XXV. From St. Anselm's to St. Raphael's," *New World*, 20 February 1931.

79. Koenig, *A History of the Archdiocese of Chicago*, 74; "Chicago Pastors Begin Service in Their New Fields of Labor: Recent Appointees Begin Duties," *New World*, 10 June 1932.

80. Outreach to African Americans did take place in the nineteenth century, especially in the heavily Catholic states of Maryland and Louisiana. The Oblate Sisters of Providence were established in Baltimore in 1829 to minister to African American girls, and several black women eventually joined the order. The Josephites, originally an English order of priests and brothers, came to Baltimore in 1871 for the purpose of missionizing African Americans, particularly those recently freed from slavery; Diane Batts Morrow, *Persons of Color and Religious at the Same Time* (Chapel Hill: University of North Carolina Press, 2002); Stephen J. Ochs, *Desegregating the Altar: The Josephites and the Struggle for Black Priests, 1871–1960* (Baton Rouge: Louisiana State University Press, 1990).

CHAPTER TWO

1. Williams's older sister, Lucy E. Williams, became the first African American nun in the Sisters of St. Francis of the Holy Family, Dubuque, Iowa; James J. Williams, interview by author, Chicago, Illinois, 29 June 2001.

2. "St. Monica Parish Good Record: Eighty Adult Converts Since September; Home Missions as Demonstrated by Zealous Pastor and His Aides," *New World*, 26 May 1922.

3. Albert J. Raboteau, "Minority Within a Minority: History of Black Catholicism in America," chap. 6 in *A Fire in the Bones: Reflections on African-American Religious History* (Boston: Beacon, 1995), 117–37.

4. Ernest Brandewie, *In the Light of the Word: Divine Word Missionaries of North America* (Maryknoll, NY: Orbis, 2000), 210. The "second Father Tolton" quotation is

taken from Caroline Hemesath, *From Slave to Priest: A Biography of the Rev. Augustine Tolton (1854–1897), First Afro-American Priest of the United States* (Chicago: Franciscan Herald, 1973), 17.

5. Joseph F. Eckert, "Methods of Convert-Making among the Negroes of Chicago," in *The White Harvest: A Symposium on Methods of Convert Making*, ed. John A. O'Brien (New York: Longmans, Green, 1927), 95–109.

6. Ibid., 99–100.

7. "St. Anselm's Home of Hundreds of Converts: Rev. Joseph F. Eckert, S.V.D. is Leader of Missionary Work Among Colored: Modern Disciples Push Forward in Hot-Bed of 'Isms,'" *New World*, 20 March 1936.

8. Eckert, "Methods of Convert-Making," 101.

9. Cyprian Davis, *The History of Black Catholics in the United States* (New York: Crossroad, 1990), 229; see also Marilyn Wenzke Nickels, *Black Catholic Protest and the Federated Colored Catholics, 1917–1933: Three Perspectives on Racial Justice* (New York: Garland, 1988).

10. James W. Sanders, *The Education of an Urban Minority: Catholics in Chicago, 1833–1965* (New York: Oxford University Press, 1977), 214.

11. Eckert, "Methods of Convert-Making," 102–4.

12. Ibid., 104–7.

13. St. Clair Drake and Horace Cayton, *Black Metropolis: A Study of Negro Life in a Northern City* (New York: Harcourt, Brace, 1945), 81.

14. Dominic A. Pacyga and Ellen Skerrett, *Chicago: City of Neighborhoods—Histories and Tours* (Chicago: Loyola University Press, 1986), chaps. 9 and 10.

15. Contemporaries often considered Jews, as well as Poles and Italians, to be different races than native-born "white" Americans; but for dichotomous purposes, I here refer to all nonblacks as "white."

16. St. Clair Drake, *Churches and Voluntary Associations in the Chicago Negro Community* (Chicago: Work Projects Administration, 1940), 153.

17. John T. McGreevy, *Parish Boundaries: The Catholic Encounter with Race in the Twentieth-Century Urban North* (Chicago: University of Chicago Press, 1996), 11; see also Gerald Gamm, *Urban Exodus: Why the Jews Left Boston and the Catholics Stayed* (Cambridge, MA: Harvard University Press, 1999); Mark T. Mulder, *Shades of White Flight: Evangelical Congregations and Urban Departure* (New Brunswick, NJ: Rutgers University Press, 2015).

18. Eckert, "Methods of Convert-Making," 108.

19. Brandewie, *In the Light of the Word*, 201–3.

20. Ibid.

21. "Bishop Sheil Confirms 500 Colored Converts: Record Class," *Chicago Tribune*, 6 May 1929.

22. In May 1934, for example, eighty-nine children received First Holy Communion at St. Elizabeth. Thirty-five of these children attended public school; "Baptize 40 Children at St. Elizabeth's Friday, May 4th," *New World*, 4 May 1934.

23. "Converts at Corpus Christi Total 1,200 in Five Years," *New World*, 4 June 1937; "1200 Colored Converts in Five Years; Is Accomplishment of Franciscan Fathers in Chicago," *New World*, 17 December 1937; "Corpus Christi Church Scene of Important

Events in May: Impressive Example of Home Mission Work Carried on in Chicago," *New World*, 29 May 1936; "Corpus Christi Parish Mission, Sept. 15 to 22: To Inaugurate New Class of Converts to Be Ready for Baptism Before Christmas," *New World*, 6 September 1935.

24. "Large Convert Class to Be Confirmed Tonight by Sheil," *New World*, 2 June 1939.

25. "St. Anselm's Home of Hundreds of Converts."

26. See *New World*, 9 December 1932, 8; 3 February 1933, 8; 26 May 1933, 8; 2 February 1934, 7; 16 March 1934, 8; 11 May 1934, 2; 15 June 1934, 8; 28 September 1934, 2; 1 March 1935, 8; 10 May 1935, 11; 7 June 1935, 8; "Solemn Baptism of 40 Converts at St. Anselm's: New Evidence that Chicago is Becoming More Mission-Minded," *New World*, 20 September 1935; "Eighty-One Converts in Record Class at St. Anselm's, *New World*, 8 May 1936; "Group of 131 Converts Receive First Communion," *New World*, 7 May 1937; "Convert Class of 30 Baptized Sept. 12 at St. Anselm's," *New World*, 10 September 1937; "Class of 120 to Be Baptized at Saint Anselm's: Brings Total to 2,550 All Instructed by Rev. Joseph F. Eckert, S.V.D.," *New World*, 29 April 1938; Vincent I. Murphy, "A Local Mission Field," *New World*, 6 May 1938; Murphy, "Work for Colored Catholics Progresses in Chicago," *New World*, 27 May 1938; 6 January 1939, 3; "Many Converts to Be Confirmed on Oct. 29 at St. Anselm's," *New World*, 27 October 1939.

27. Theodore A. Thoma, "Changing the Color Line," *Extension* (February 1929), clipping file, archives, St. Elizabeth Convent, Chicago, Illinois (hereafter, SEC).

28. In 1927, there were about 3,000 black Catholics in Chicago, including 225 black Catholic families and 250 black families with one Catholic parent. Out of 1,133 children attending St. Elizabeth's, 461 were Catholic; "Survey of the Negro Population in Chicago, 1927," Madaj Chancery Collection, box EXEC/V2530/92, folder S-23, Archdiocese of Chicago's Cardinal Joseph Bernardin Archives and Record Center (hereafter, AAC). In 1940, around 6 percent of Chicago's African American population was Catholic. Out of 277,731 African Americans, about 16,000 were Catholic; Drake and Cayton, *Black Metropolis*, 8; Sanders, *The Education of an Urban Minority*, 215.

29. Sanders, *The Education of an Urban Minority*, 206.

30. "Catholicity Among Chicago Negroes: Growing Membership Gives Allegiance to the Universal Church," *New World*, 19 December 1913.

31. "That Jim Crow School," *Chicago Defender*, 22 March 1913.

32. Ibid.

33. George Phillips, interview by author, Chicago, Illinois, 10 August 2001. In 1942, the pastor of Holy Angels told a woman that her children could only attend the parish school if they could "pass" for white; Sanders, *The Education of an Urban Minority*, 216. Ironically, Holy Angels would become one of the largest and most prominent black Catholic parishes in the United States during the 1970s and 1980s.

34. Drake and Cayton, *Black Metropolis*, 196–97.

35. Karen Joy Johnson, "The Universal Church in the Segregated City: Doing Catholic Interracialism in Chicago, 1915–1963" (PhD diss., University of Illinois at Chicago, 2013), 50–51. On Falls, see Johnson, "The Universal Church in the Segregated City," as well as Lincoln R. Rice, "Confronting the Heresy of 'The Mythical Body of Christ': The Life of Dr. Arthur Falls," *American Catholic Studies* 123.2 (2012): 59–77.

36. Sanders, *The Education of an Urban Minority*, 216.

37. Drake and Cayton, *Black Metropolis*, 196–97; Sanders, *The Education of an Urban Minority*, 217.

38. In 1938, thirteen of the fifteen public schools in Bronzeville ran on either double or triple shifts; Drake and Cayton, *Black Metropolis*, 202; see also Michael W. Homel, *Down from Equality: Black Chicagoans and the Public Schools, 1920–41* (Urbana: University of Illinois Press, 1984), 76–84.

39. Drake and Cayton, *Black Metropolis*, 123.

40. Earl and Miriam Selby, *Odyssey: Journey through Black America* (New York: G. P. Putman's Sons, 1971), 315. Historian Timuel Black recalled that his brother, a star athlete, was the only African American on the Tilden basketball team in the 1940s; Timuel Black, interview by author, Chicago, Illinois, 27 February 2003.

41. Drake and Cayton, *Black Metropolis*, 197.

42. Restrictions placed on St. Elizabeth's Sisters of the Blessed Sacrament nuns indicate their "otherworldliness." Their superior usually forbade reading secular newspapers and listening to the radio except in cases where classroom instruction necessitated it; correspondence, Sisters of the Blessed Sacrament, SEC.

43. Williams, interview by author.

44. Phillips, interview by author.

45. Drake and Cayton, *Black Metropolis*, 412–15.

46. District 12, which fell within St. Elizabeth's parish boundaries, claimed the highest percentage of churches per black residents in Chicago; "Density of Negro Churches by Desirability of Neighborhood for 23 Negro Districts: 1938," in Drake, *Churches and Voluntary Associations in the Chicago Negro Community*, 172.

47. In *Roll Jordan, Roll: The World the Slaves Made* (New York: Pantheon, 1974), Eugene Genovese writes that enslaved African Americans relied heavily on Christianity for resistance against white oppression. Sterling Stuckey, in *Slave Culture and the Foundations of Black America* (New York: Oxford University Press, 1987), argues that blacks retained much of their non-Christian, African religious traditions in America. While the relative influences of European Christianity versus native African religion are arguable, religious experience undoubtedly played an important part in African American life.

48. Drake and Cayton, *Black Metropolis*, 685. A Catholic perspective indicated agreement with this proposition that children were the key to attracting new church members: "It is the opinion of those who have labored among them that increase in Colored converts will be accomplished chiefly by winning over the children, and training them to grow up as good Catholics"; Thoma, "Changing the Color Line."

49. See section 34, "Need for More Catholic Schools," in the pastoral letter issued by the Third Plenary Council of Baltimore, 7 December 1884. Hugh J. Nolan, ed. *Pastoral Letters of the United States Catholic Bishops* Vol. I, 1792-1940 (Washington, DC: National Conference of Catholic Bishops, United States Catholic Conference, 1984), 225.

50. Rosemary L. Bray, *Unafraid of the Dark: A Memoir* (New York: Random House, 1998). Sociological evidence supports the contention that parochial education produced a positive correlation between religious affiliation and higher educational levels and

greater wealth among African American Catholics; J. L. Alston and E. Warrick, "Black Catholics: Social and Cultural Characteristics," *Journal of Black Studies* 3.2 (December 1971): 245–55; William Feigelman et al., "The Social Characteristics of Black Catholics," *Society and Social Research* 75.3 (April 1991): 133–43; Larry L. Hunt, "Religious Affiliation Among Blacks in the United States: Black Catholic Status Advantages Revisited," *Social Science Quarterly* 79.1 (March 1998): 170–92.

51. Warner Saunders, interview by author, Chicago, Illinois, 24 August 2001.

52. Phillips, interview by author.

53. Williams, interview by author.

54. Phillips, interview by author.

55. Edwin W. Leaner III, interview by author, Chicago, Illinois, 27 June 2001.

56. Marie C. Davis, interview by author, Chicago, Illinois, 6 July 2001.

57. Jamie T. Phelps, "Black Spirituality," in *Taking Down Our Harps: Black Catholics in the United States*, ed. Diana L. Hayes and Cyprian Davis (Maryknoll, NY: Orbis, 1998), 181; Barry A. Kosmin and Seymour P. Lachman, *One Nation Under God: Religion in Contemporary American Society* (New York: Harmony, 1993), 129.

58. Lionel Hampton with James Haskins, *Hamp: An Autobiography* (New York: Amistad, 1993), 20.

59. The *Chicago Defender* reported a week after the fire that "immediate steps will be taken to rebuild St. Elizabeth's"; "To Rebuild Catholic Edifice," *Chicago Defender*, 11 January 1930. But a year later, the *New World* argued, "To rebuild the destroyed church would have involved a tremendous expense. This the parishioners could not have borne because of poverty, brought about especially by the [Great] depression"; "Bishop Sheil Dedicates New St. Elizabeth's," *New World*, 30 January 1931. Like many South Side African American Catholics, St. Elizabeth parishioner John Woodford remained convinced that the church could have been rebuilt with a stronger commitment from the archdiocese; John Woodford, interview by author, Chicago, Illinois, 26 April 2002.

60. St. Elizabeth's Old Historic Church Burns," *New World*, 10 January 1930.

61. "Corpus Christi, Gem of Church Architecture, Scene of Novena," *New World*, 20 May 1932.

62. Richard Wright, *Native Son* (1940; New York: Perennial, 2001). Historian Ellen Skerrett has shown the impact of Catholic aesthetics on otherwise austere working-class neighborhoods; Skerrett, "The Irish of Chicago's Hull-House Neighborhood," *Chicago History* (Summer 2001): 22–63.

63. Agnes T. Ryan, "Bringing Down to Date the Histories of the Parishes of the Archdiocese of Chicago," *New World*, 2 October 1936.

64. "Sunday Walks: XXV. From St. Anselm's to St. Raphael's," *New World*, 20 February 1931.

65. R. Augustine Skinner, "Corpus Christi's Rapid Growth Under Spiritual Guidance of Father Clement Martin, OFM," *New World*, 3 April 1936.

66. Despite its "city within a city" fame, Bronzeville did not exist in a vacuum. St. Elizabeth, Corpus Christi, and St. Anselm parishioners lived and worked in a society connected to Chicago's overall economy and culture. Many African American men worked outside Bronzeville in the stockyards district to the west and steel mills to the

south. Black women—more likely to work outside the home than white women—often traveled to private homes on the North Side to labor as domestic servants.

67. "Corpus Christi Parish Observes Patronal Feast," *New World*, 9 June 1933; "Novena Corpus Christi Church May 31 to June 8: Devotions In Honor of the Sacred Heart," *New World*, 18 May 1934; "Novena to Open at Corpus Christi on June 20th: Sermons to be Preached by Franciscan Missionary Rev. L. Johntges, OFM," *New World*, 14 June 1935; "Solemn Novena at Corpus Christi Church: Devotions in Honor of the Sacred Heart of Jesus to be Held May 27 to June 4," *New World*, 14 May 1937; "Novena at Corpus Christi Church: Series of Devotions in Honor of the Sacred Heart of Jesus June 16–24," *New World*, 10 June 1938. The solemn procession on the Feast of Corpus Christi of the Blessed Sacrament continued into the twenty-first century. Cardinal Francis George participated in the procession on 17 June 2001.

68. "Stations Enacted During Lent at Corpus Christi: South Side Church Presents Unique Lenten Program," *New World*, 24 February 1939.

69. It is unclear whether the Living Stations began in 1937 or 1938. A parish history lists the start date as 1937; *Corpus Christi Parish: Our History, 1901–1977*, 4920 Dr. Martin Luther King Drive, Chicago, Illinois (Hackensack, NJ: Custombook, Inc., 1977), 6–7, Parish Commemorative Books: Hist/C5700/13, folder 15, AAC. *New World* articles indicate that the tradition began in 1938. "Corpus Christi Group to Re-Enact Drama of Passion Weekly," *New World*, 4 March 1938; "Stations Enacted During Lent at Corpus Christi: South Side Church Presents Unique Lenten Program," *New World*, 24 February 1939. A *Chicago Daily News* article lists 1938 as well; Ben Holman, "Corpus Christi Church: A Busy Gem in Stone: Soaring Landmark is Area Hub, Former Franciscan Retreat House," *Chicago Daily News*, 7 November 1957; Francis George, "Corpus Christi: The Parish, the Feast and the Doctrine," *New World*, 24 June 2001; Rita Stalzer, CSJ, interview by author, Chicago, Illinois, 3 May 2002.

70. Williams, interview by author.

71. Davis, interview by author.

72. Ibid. For Blanche Rodney's involvement in the Illinois Technical School for Colored Girls, see Suellen Hoy, "Illinois School for Technical Girls: A Catholic Institution on Chicago's South Side, 1911–1953," *Journal of Illinois History* 4.2 (Summer 2001): 116n29. Historian Caroline Hemesath described Blanche Rodney as a "pioneer member" of St. Monica's Parish; Hemesath, *From Slave to Priest*, 43.

73. "Colored Catholic Choir is Praised for Artistic Program," *New World*, 6 May 1932.

74. *New World*, 25 March 1932, 2; *New World*, 17 February 1933, 7; "St. Elizabeth's Choir in Christmas Concert Sunday, December 18th," *New World*, 16 December 1932, 11; *New World*, 22 December 1933, 8.

75. Williams, interview by author.

76. Drake and Cayton, *Black Metropolis*, 99, 12; For a discussion of class distinction in Bronzeville, see pp. 710–14.

77. "Don'ts for Newcomers," *Chicago Defender*, 14 July 1923.

78. Williams, interview by author.

79. "Corpus Christi Parish Picnic Sunday, August 22: Rev. Clement Martin, OFM, Pastor, Plans Outing August 22," *New World*, 13 August 1937.

80. "Parish Events," *New World*, 23 November 1934; "Parish Events," *New World*, 30 October 1936.

81. "Corpus Christi Branch," *New World*, 12 June 1936.

82. Binga's success ended when he lost everything in the Depression. In 1933, a jury convicted him of fraud, and a judge sentenced him to ten years at Joliet State Prison. Attorney Clarence Darrow, church officials, and community leaders, however, successfully petitioned for his parole in 1938. Penniless, he worked as a custodian at St. Anselm. He died in 1950. On Binga, see Inez V. Cantey, "Jesse Binga," *Crisis*, December 1927, 329, 350, 352; Carl R. Osthaus, "The Rise and Fall of Jesse Binga, Black Financier," *Journal of Negro History* (January 1973): 39–60; Nicholas A. Lash, "Binga, Jesse," in *Encyclopedia of African American Business History* (Westport, CT: Greenwood, 1999), 68–70; June Skinner Sawyers, "Jesse Binga," in *Chicago Portraits: Biographies of 250 Famous Chicagoans* (Chicago: Loyola University Press, 1991), 31–32.

83. "St. Anselm Branch," *New World*, 10 February 1933.

84. William Quane, "St. Anselm's in Good Showing in Press Sunday: Two Hundred Heads of Families Enroll as New World Boosters," *New World*, 28 April 1933. St. Anselm's participation in the 1933 *New World* subscription drive earned the parish a spot on the newspaper's "Roll of Honor"; 1 September 1933.

85. "St. Anselm's Branch," *New World*, 5 May 1933; "St. Anselm's Branch," *New World*, 2 February 1934.

86. *New World*, 13 September 1936, 9.

87. *New World*, 10 February 1933, 8.

88. Davis, interview by author.

89. In his study of black Protestant churches in the post–civil rights era, political scientist Frederick Harris found that church activity among African Americans prepared them for involvement in electoral politics; Frederick C. Harris, *Something Within: Religion in African-American Political Activism* (New York: Oxford University Press, 1999). I argue that Catholicism during the mid-twentieth century acted in a similar way to help African Americans develop political skills and contacts in Chicago.

90. *New World*, 10 February 1933, 8; "Mrs. Bertina Davis is Named Deputy Sheriff," *Chicago Defender*, 30 September 1939, 5; Woodford, interview by author. On the political relationship between New Deal Democrats and African Americans, see Alan Brinkley, *The End of Reform: New Deal Liberalism in Recession and War* (New York: Vintage, 1995), 165–70; William J. Grimshaw, *Bitter Fruit: Black Politics and the Chicago Machine, 1931–1991* (Chicago: University of Chicago Press, 1992), 47–68; William E. Leuchtenburg, *Franklin D. Roosevelt and the New Deal, 1932–1940* (New York: Harper & Row, 1963), 185–87; Harvard Sitkoff, *A New Deal for Blacks: The Emergence of a National Issue: The Depression Decade* (New York: Oxford University Press, 1978); Nancy J. Weiss, *Farewell to the Party of Lincoln: Black Politics in the Age of FDR* (Princeton, NJ: Princeton University Press, 1983).

91. Drake and Cayton, *Black Metropolis*, 88.

92. Ibid., 353.

93. Grimshaw, *Bitter Fruit*, 81, 108, 131–33.

94. Bertrand served as treasurer from 1971 to 1975. "Daley Enters Mayor Battle for 5th Term," *Chicago Tribune*, 18 December 1970; Adam Cohen and Elizabeth Taylor,

American Pharaoh: Mayor Richard J. Daley: His Battle for Chicago and the Nation (New York: Little, Brown, 2000), 506–7.

95. Leaner, interview by author.

96. Under the leadership of the powerful African American Congressman and Second Ward committeeman William Dawson, blacks produced the margin of victory for at least three of Mayor Richard J. Daley's six victories between 1955 and 1975.

97. Grimshaw, *Bitter Fruit*, 118.

98. Pope Gregory XVI, *In Supremo Apostolatus Fastigio*, 1839. A debate exists about whether Gregory XVI condemned slavery as well. The slave trade had already been condemned by Pope Pius VII in 1815; John F. Quinn, "'Three Cheers for the Abolitionist Pope!' American Reaction to Gregory XVI's Condemnation of the Slave Trade, 1840–1860," *American Catholic Historical Review* 90.1 (January 2004): 67–93.

99. Cyprian Davis, "Catholic African Americans: A Historical Summary," in Committee on African American Catholics, National Conference of Catholic Bishops, *Keep Your Hand on the Plow* (Washington, DC: United States Catholic Conference, 1996), 14.

100. Davis, *History of Black Catholics*, 195–98. The 1904 letter led to the creation of the Catholic Board of Negro Missions in 1907.

101. Clarence C. Wright to Archbishop George W. Mundelein, 16 October 1919, box EXEC/V2530/135, folder M-201, AAC.

102. Father Peter F. Janser, SVD, to Archbishop George W. Mundelein, 25 November, 1921, box EXEC/V2530/130, folder M-231, AAC.

103. Evangeline Roberts, "Packed Church to Hear New Priest Chant First Mass," *Chicago Defender*, 16 March 1926.

104. St. Elizabeth's Church, "The Beginning of an Era: History of the Work of the Catholic Church Among the Negroes of Chicago: Silver Jubilee of the Ordination of Rev. William S. Brambrink, SVD," 1952, AAC.

105. Roberts, "Packed Church to Hear New Priest Chant First Mass."

106. George Clements, transcribed interview, 4 September 1999, Fr. Marty Zielinski Oral History Project/Clergy Exhibit, box HIST/H3300/364, folder Clements, AAC.

107. "Blessed" refers to a deceased person who has been beatified by the Roman Catholic Church. Beatification is the third of four steps on the path to sainthood.

108. "Honor Bl. M. De Porres at St. Elizabeth Church," *New World*, 2 October 1936; "Begin Novena to Bl. Martin De Porres: St. Elizabeth's First to Honor Pious South American Youth," *New World*, 16 October 1936; 30 October 1936, 8.

109. "Family of African Prince Baptized Here," *New World*, 8 January 1937.

110. "Spare Time Work a Masterpiece," *New World*, 25 August 1939.

111. "Benefit Musicale for the Blessed Sacrament Nuns," unattributed newspaper piece, June 1936, SEC.

112. "Picturesque Ceremonies During Easter Season at St. Elizabeth's," *New World*, 28 April 1933; "First Communion and Confirmation at St. Elizabeth's," *New World*, 22 May 1936.

113. "First Communicants, St. Elizabeth School," *New World*, 28 May 1937.

114. "Thirty Converts to be Baptized at St. Elizabeth's: Sunday, Sept. 25th and Oct. 2nd Special Services; Forty Hours' Devotion," *New World*, 23 September 1932.

115. *New World*, 30 March 1934, 8; "Eighty-One Converts in Record Class at

St. Anselm's," *New World*, 8 May 1936, 3; "Many Converts to be Confirmed on Oct. 29 at St. Anselm's," *New World*, 27 October 1939, 1.

116. Davis, *The History of Black Catholics*, 220; 214–29. The definitive work on Turner and the Federated Colored Catholics is Marilyn Wenzke Nickels, *Black Catholic Protest*; see also McGreevy, *Parish Boundaries*, 38–47.

117. Chicago's Catholic Interracial Council was founded in 1945.

118. "Federation to Hold Symposium on Racial Bias: Meeting Sunday at St. Elizabeth's; Aim: To Promote Better Relations with Colored People," *New World*, 21 October 1932. For more on African American lay involvement in the Federated Colored Catholics and successor groups in Chicago, see Johnson, "The Universal Church in the Segregated City," chaps. 3 and 4.

119. "Interrace Session Scores Treatment Accorded Negro: Meeting Sponsored by N.Y. Laymen's League Flays Discrimination," *New World*, 25 May 1934.

120. Drake and Cayton, *Black Metropolis*, 412–15.

CHAPTER THREE

1. "The Last Best Hope of Earth," *New World*, 12 November 1937; Annamarie Masterson, "President's Son Urges CISCA, C.Y.O., to Aid in Securing Peace: Mystical Body Principles Pointed Out as Basis of Democracy," *New World*, 12 November 1937.

2. Bernard J. Sheil, speech to Youth Session of the 13th annual convention of the National Council of Catholic Men, Congress Hotel, Chicago, 1933, box 1, folder 2, Bishop Bernard J. Sheil Papers, Archdiocese of Chicago's Joseph Cardinal Bernardin Archives and Records Center (hereafter, AAC). During 1948–1949, the numbers were: 2,640 in basketball; 1,728 in softball; 992 in boxing; and 396 in volleyball; Welfare Council of Metropolitan Chicago, "Catholic Youth Organization," November 1949, p. 14, box 11, folder 1, Edward Victor Cardinal Papers, (hereafter, CCRD), University of Notre Dame Archives, Notre Dame, Indiana (hereafter, UNDA). The number of participants declined considerably by 1953 in every sport except boxing, which had greatly increased: 965 in basketball; 1,756 in softball; 490 in baseball; 28,104 in boxing; 702 in track and field; 1,103 in volleyball; 1,004 in ice skating, 130 in the regatta club; and 35 in the cycling club; Welfare Council of Metropolitan Chicago, "Catholic Youth Organization," January 1954, pp. 9–10, box 257, folder 3, Welfare Council of Metropolitan Chicago Papers (hereafter, WCMC), Chicago History Museum (hereafter, CHM).

3. Ralph C. Leo, "Success of Inter-City Boxing Meet Points to Brilliant Future for C.Y.O.," *New World*, 9 August 1935; for New York, see "Catholics Launch a New Youth Movement: Activities to be Centralized in an Association for the New York Archdiocese: Crime Curb is Sought," *New York Times*, 20 January 1936; "Cardinal Hayes Promotes C.Y.O. in New York Archdiocese: Changes Name of New York Youth Association and Names Fifteen Priest-Moderators. Each Parish to be Organized," *New World*, 1 January 1937. In 1934, Catholic representatives from Chicago, Los Angeles, San Francisco, and more than a dozen other dioceses met in San Francisco to create a national CYO; Ralph C. Leo, "Formation of National C.Y.O. Climaxes Three Years' Work by Bishop Sheil for Youth," *New World*, 19 January 1934.

4. Rosella Bartley and James B. Sheil both grew up in St. Columbkille parish. Five

years before their marriage, census records show eighteen-year-old Rosella Bartley living with her aunt and uncle at 639 West Indiana Street (renumbered 1912 West Grand Avenue after 1910)—just a few blocks west of the church; 1880 U.S. Census, roll 195, enumeration district 132, page 35, stamped page 584, Chicago, Cook County, Illinois, dwelling visitation number 241, family visitation number 328, enumerated 11 June 1880. James and Rosella were married at St. Columbkille on Tuesday, 19 May 1885. Their marriage license is dated the next day; James B. Sheil and Rosella Bartley, Cook County, May 20, 1885, license number 00092096, Illinois Statewide Marriage Index 1763–1900, Illinois Secretary of State. Nine months later, Rosella gave birth to a son. According to archdiocesan records, Bernard Sheil was born at 163 North Paulina Street (renumbered 502 North Paulina Street after 1910); Bernard J. Sheil personnel file, AAC. The Sheils lived near the corner of Paulina Street and Grand Avenue for at least the next forty years. In 1900, the Sheil family lived at 546 and 548 West Grand Avenue (renumbered 1700 block of West Grand Avenue after 1910); 1900 U.S. Census, roll 260, ward 13, enumeration district 384, sheet number 9, stamped page 76A, Chicago, Cook County, Illinois, dwelling visitation number 115, family visitation number 177, enumerated June 8, 1900. At the time of Sheil's ordination in 1910, his family lived at 550 West Grand Avenue (renumbered 1725 West Grand Avenue after 1910); Sheil personnel file, AAC.

5. According to Mark Sorvillo, Sheil came from a "conventional middle class home"; Mark B. Sorvillo, "Bishop Bernard J. Sheil: Hero of the Catholic Left" (PhD diss., University of Chicago, 1990), 43.

6. Of the thirteen households in the 500 block (renumbered the 1700 block after 1910) of West Grand Avenue, only four—including the Sheils—owned their own home in 1900. Head-of-household occupations included baker, cabinetmaker, cigar maker, day laborer, engineer, housepainter, motorman, piano maker, saloonkeeper, shoemaker, and teamster; 1900 U.S. Census, roll 260, ward 13, enumeration district 384, sheet number 9, stamped pages 76A and 76B, Chicago, Cook County, Illinois, enumerated June 8, 1900.

7. The Thirteenth Ward boundaries were Chicago Avenue on the north, Lake Street on the south, Reuben Street (later known as Ashland Avenue) on the east, and 40th Avenue (later known as Crawford Avenue and eventually Pulaski Avenue) on the west.

8. Agnes T. Ryan, "Bringing Down to Date the Histories of the Parishes of the Archdiocese of Chicago: St. Columbkille's—1859," *New World*, 8 January 1937. "Mulligan's Brigade," or the "Western Irish Brigade," won fame for fighting courageously at the battle of Lexington, Missouri, in 1861. The brigade later guarded Camp Douglas in Chicago and fought battles in Virginia, Maryland, and Washington, DC. Mulligan, a Chicago businessman and politician, died while in Confederate custody in 1864.

9. "St. Columbkille Parish Reunion Arranged for April 15," *New World*, 26 March 1937; "St. Columbkille's Bids Welcome," 29 October 1937. In addition to Sheil, St. Columbkille's produced another member of the Catholic hierarchy. Parishioner Edward Hoban became a Chicago auxiliary bishop. In 1928, Hoban left Chicago and became bishop of Rockford, Illinois, paving the way for Sheil's rise to auxiliary bishop of Chicago; "Msgr. B.J. Sheil Named Bishop; Cardinal Home: New Official to Fill Hoban Vacancy," *Chicago Tribune*, 1 April 1928.

10. Frederick Rex, *Centennial List of Mayors, City Clerks, City Attorney, City Treasurer, and Aldermen, Elected by the People of the City of Chicago, From Incorpo-*

ration of the City on March 4, 1837 to March 4, 1937, Arranged in Alphabetical Order Showing the Years During which Each Official Held Office (Chicago: Municipal Reference Library, 1937), 24. In 1880, the Fourteenth Ward became the Thirteenth Ward. The name changed, but the boundaries remained the same. Therefore, Sheil grew up in the same ward that his grandfather represented. (Interestingly, between 1910 and 1923, it was known as the Fourteenth Ward once again.)

11. From the Payne family website, http://www.fitmaurice.info.payne/payne_we2 .html, accessed 1 April 2004.

12. Ibid.

13. Roger L. Treat, *Bishop Sheil and the CYO: The Story of the Catholic Youth Organization and the Man Who Influenced a Generation* (New York: Messner, 1951), 20–23.

14. From the Payne family website, http://www.fitzmaurice.info/payne_we2.html, accessed 1 April 2004.

15. In 1880, a few African American families, whose heads of household worked as barbers, bartenders, and waiters, lived on Ashly Street (the 1900 block of West Race Avenue after 1910)—four blocks to the west of the Sheil home; 1880 U.S. Census, roll 195, enumeration district 132, page 26, Chicago, Cook County, Illinois, enumerated 11 June 1880. In 1900, eleven African American families lived along the 600 and 700 blocks of West Carroll Avenue (the 1800 and 1900 blocks of West Carroll Avenue after 1910)—four blocks to the south and two blocks to the west of Sheil home; 1900 U.S. Census, roll 260, enumeration district 415, pp. 234B, 235A, 235B, 237A, and 238B, sheets 2, 4, 5, Chicago, Cook County, Illinois, enumerated June 1900.

16. In Sheil's ward, 2 to 3 percent were African American in 1900; Allan H. Spear, *Black Chicago: The Making of a Negro Ghetto, 1890–1920* (Chicago: University of Chicago Press, 1967), 12, map 1.

17. Treat, *Bishop Sheil and the CYO*, 45.

18. Sheil perhaps knew through the Catholic press about the nation's only African American priest during the 1890s, Augustus Tolton, leading Chicago's black Catholics across the city at St. Monica's.

19. Robert E. Burns, interview by Steven Avella, 4 January 1988, box 1, tape 1, Rev. Steven Avella Oral History Project, AAC.

20. Fulton Sheen graduated in 1919 from St. Viator, and after a successful academic career at the Catholic University of America earned international fame for his popular books and television shows. Father Bergin is credited with convincing Sheen to enter the priesthood. John Tracy Ellis graduated from St. Viator in 1927, joined the Catholic University of America faculty, and became the twentieth century's most influential historian of U.S. Catholicism. St. Viator College permanently closed during the Great Depression due to financial difficulties.

21. Sorvillo, "Bishop Bernard J. Sheil," 34.

22. "Honor Bishop Sheil on Sacerdotal Silver Jubilee: Bishop Sheil to be Honored on Silver Jubilee—Pontifical Mass of Thanksgiving to Mark Twenty-Five Years as Priest," *New World*, 17 May 1935.

23. "Souvenir of the First Open Meeting and Smoker, given by the Class of 1906 of St. Viator's College at Bourbonnais Town Hall, Friday, April 27th 1906," program in

author's possession. Sheil also spoke at his commencement ceremony; Sorvillo, "Bishop Bernard J. Sheil," 36.

24. Theodore Roosevelt, "Professionalism in Sports," *North American Review* (August 1890): 187–91. In 1906, the year Sheil graduated from college, President Roosevelt oversaw the establishment of the National Collegiate Athletic Association (NCAA).

25. For discussions of gender in American Protestantism, see Gail Bederman, "'The Women Have Had Charge of the Church Work Long Enough': The Men and Religion Forward Movement of 1911–1912 and the Masculinization of Middle-Class Protestantism," *American Quarterly* 41.3 (September 1989): 432–65; Paul Boyer, *Urban Masses and Moral Order in America, 1820–1920* (Cambridge, MA: Harvard University Press, 1978), 113–15; Allan Stanley Horlick, *Country Boys and Merchant Princes: The Social Control of Young Men in New York* (Lewisburg, PA: Bucknell University Press, 1975), 249–54.

26. Clifford Wallace Putney, "Muscular Christianity: The Strenuous Mood in American Protestantism, 1880–1920" (PhD diss., Brandeis University, 1994), 76–77.

27. Although Stagg came from a religious tradition, his tremendous success in Chicago developed secular big-time college sports, including special athletic scholarships, preferential treatment of players, and aggressive recruiting tactics. On Stagg, see Erin A. McCarthy, "Making Men: The Life and Career of Amos Alonzo Stagg, 1862–1933" (PhD diss., Loyola University Chicago, 1994).

28. Albert G. Applin, "From Muscular Christianity to the Market Place: The History of Men's and Boys' Basketball in the United States" (PhD diss., University of Massachusetts, 1982), 155–56.

29. Ironically, St. Viator lost the game 0–1 due to three errors in the bottom of the ninth inning. Robert Burns, a CYO employee, told historian Steven Avella that he inspected the score books and found no evidence of a no-hitter; Steven M. Avella, *This Confident Church: Catholic Leadership and Life in Chicago, 1940–1965* (Notre Dame, IN: University of Notre Dame Press, 1992), 22, 352n9.

30. Three members of Sheil's 1905 St. Viator team went on to play professional baseball. The remaining players all entered the priesthood; "Odds and Ends," *New World,* 20 July 1934.

31. Treat, *Bishop Sheil and the CYO,* 24–25.

32. The old Cook County Jail was at Illinois and Dearborn streets.

33. In recognition of the Archdiocese of Chicago's growing importance, Pius XI named Mundelein a cardinal in 1924. Sheil greatly admired Pius XI, who would later author *Quadragesimo Anno* (1931), an encyclical upholding and expanding the principles articulated in *Rerum Novarum* (1891).

34. The first Eucharistic Congress held in the United States proclaimed Chicago as an internationally important archdiocese and announced Mundelein's ascension to the top of American Catholic hierarchy; Edward R. Kantowicz, "Cardinal Mundelein of Chicago and the Shaping of Twentieth-Century American Catholicism," *Journal of American History* 68.1 (June 1981): 58–59, and *Corporation Sole: Cardinal Mundelein and Chicago Catholicism* (Notre Dame, IN: University of Notre Dame Press, 1983), 166–68.

35. June Skinner Sawyers, "Billy Sunday: Evangelist," in *Chicago Portraits:*

Biographies of 250 Famous Chicagoans (Chicago: Loyola University Press, 1991), 239–40; for more on Sunday, see Robert Francis Martin, *Hero of the Heartland: Billy Sunday and the Transformation of American Society, 1862–1935* (Bloomington: Indiana University Press, 2002); Roger A. Bruns, *Preacher: Billy Sunday and Big-Time American Evangelism* (New York: Norton, 1992); Lyle W. Dorsett, *Billy Sunday and the Redemption of Urban America* (Grand Rapids, MI: Eerdmans, 1991); William G. McLoughlin, Jr., *Billy Sunday Was His Real Name* (Chicago: University of Chicago Press, 1955).

36. Tony Ladd and James A. Mathisen, *Muscular Christianity: Evangelical Protestants and the Development of American Sport* (Grand Rapids, MI: Baker, 1999), 101.

37. Treat, *Bishop Sheil and the CYO*, 7–8, viii; see also Edward R. Kantowicz, "Bishop Sheil and 'Muscular Christianity,'" chap. 12 in *Corporation Sole: Cardinal Mundelein and Chicago Catholicism* (Notre Dame, IN: University of Notre Dame Press, 1983), 173–88.

38. Charles Carroll Smith, "Father of the C.Y.O," *Esquire*, July 1942, 122. Smith worked in the CYO public relations department during the 1940s and eventually became CYO executive director.

39. George Drury, interview by Steven Avella, tape recording, box 1, Rev. Steven Avella Oral History Project, AAC. At the age of sixty, Sheil was described as "still an athlete," playing golf and handball; Thomas B. Morgan, *Speaking of Cardinals* (New York: G. P. Putnam, 1946), 169.

40. Over the years, Sheil often recounted a dramatic story about the origin of his commitment to fighting juvenile delinquency. Fifteen minutes after witnessing an execution as jail chaplain, he supposedly looked at the prison walls and promised to fight for youth, saying, "This I pledge you; this I will not forget." If the story's veracity is questionable, the sentiment is clear; Treat, *Bishop Sheil and the CYO*, 37–39.

41. Bernard J. Sheil, "Problems of Youth," *Catholic Mind* (22 September 1936): 368.

42. Applin, "From Muscular Christianity to the Market Place," 176, 185. George Halas (University of Illinois and Chicago Bears), Paddy Driscoll (Chicago Bears and Chicago Cubs), and Jimmy Conzelman (Chicago Cardinals) played on the Great Lakes football team that won the 1919 Rose Bowl. Driscoll and Halas also played on an all-star basketball team that toured the country. During World War I, strong ties developed among athletes involving patriotism, sport, and religion, particularly Catholicism. During World War I, Catholics composed a much larger percentage of the Army (35–40 percent) than their share of the overall U.S. population (about 15 percent); Putney, "Muscular Christianity," 342.

43. Treat, *Bishop Sheil and the CYO*, 38.

44. James T. Farrell's Irish American protagonist Studs Lonigan, for example, felt out of place visiting his neighborhood YMCA in 1924; James T. Farrell, *Studs Lonigan: A Trilogy Comprising Young Lonigan, The Young Manhood of Studs Lonigan, and Judgment Day* (New York: Penguin, 2001), 338–46.

45. P. J. Lydon, *Ready Answers in Canon Law* (New York: Bensiger Brother, 1937), 481; cited in John P. Ly, "A Comparative Study of the Young Men's Christian Association and the Catholic Youth Organization" (MA thesis, Loyola University Chicago, 1951), 47.

46. Robert Orsi, *Between Heaven and Earth: The Religious Worlds People Make and the Scholars Who Study Them* (Princeton, NJ: Princeton University Press, 2005), 84.

47. James W. Sanders, "American Catholic Education," *History of Education Quarterly* 30.1 (Autumn 1990): 383.

48. "Reasons for the Existence of Catholic Schools," *National Catholic Welfare Bulletin* 4.4 (September 1922): 28.

49. Gerald R. Gems, *Windy City Wars: Labor, Leisure, and Sports in the Making of Chicago* (Lanham, MD: Scarecrow, 1997), 142; *New World*, 6 April 1920, 5; 20 May 1921, 10; 16 February 1923, 5. Not only worldly vices but, by 1930, economic depression threatened young people by producing debilitating social and economic effects, especially for the city's African American community. Although they composed less than 10 percent of Chicago's population in 1931, African Americans made up 16 percent of the total unemployed and 25 percent of the city's relief cases; from an Urban League study published in March 1931, cited in Rita Werner Gordon, "The Change in the Political Alignment of Chicago's Negroes During the New Deal," *Journal of American History* 56.3 (December 1969): 591.

50. Alice Mary Burns, "A Study of the Catholic Youth Organization Home for Boys, 2944 South Michigan Avenue, Chicago, Illinois" (MA thesis, Loyola University Chicago, 1935), 7.

51. Sheil, speech to the Youth Session of the 13th annual convention of the National Council of Catholic Men.

52. Known as "Father Ray," Ashenden was killed in a car accident on 11 February 1931. "Tribute to Leader of Catholic Youth Most Impressive," *New World*, 20 February 1931.

53. Carter Horsley, "Archbishop Bernard Sheil Chicago Dies at 83: 'Apostle of Youth,'" *New York Times*, 14 September 1969. Sheil reportedly started with $112 of his own money and a "sizeable gift"; *Chicago Daily News*, 17 September 1969, 3; "Historical Survey of the Catholic Youth Organization," p. 12, box 11, folder 9, CCRD. According to Steven Avella, Sheil's inheritance was $100,000; Avella, *This Confident Church*, 22; see also "J.B. Sheil, Father of the Chancellor, Passes Away: Cardinal Mundelein, Bishop Hoban, and Bishop Deschamps Officiate at Obsequies, Monday Last," *New World*, 7 October 1927.

54. Dora B. Somerville, "A Study of the Juvenile Delinquency Prevention Service of the Social Service Department, Catholic Youth Organization, Chicago, Illinois" (MSW thesis, Loyola University Chicago, 1947), 4; Ly, 15.

55. "William J. Campbell, 83; Ex-Chief District Judge," *Chicago Tribune*, 21 October 1988.

56. Sheil officiated at Campbell's wedding; "William J. Campbell and Miss Cloherty Married in New York City Church," *New World*, 12 February 1937.

57. The Boy Scouts of America subsequently named Campbell to its national executive board in 1934; "Wm. J. Campbell Now On Executive Board of Boy Scouts: Nominated for Membership by Col. Theodore Roosevelt," *New World*, 8 June 1934; on Campbell, see Avella, *This Confident Church*, 23–26.

58. "President Names W. J. Campbell U.S. Attorney," *New World*, 2 December 1938; "William J. Campbell Relinquishes State NYA Directorship," 1 March 1940. Campbell was the presiding judge in the "Chicago Seven" trial of 1960s radicals. Chicago's triangular-shaped U.S. courthouse annex at 71 West Van Buren Street, designed by noted architect Harry Weese, is named for Campbell.

59. "William J. Campbell, 83; Ex-Chief District Judge."

60. "Youth Leader," *New World*, 20 August 1937.

61. "The Cardinal Dedicates New Youth Center: Colorful Ceremonies Monday Afternoon Inaugurate Week of Special Activities," *New World*, 16 September 1932; Katherine Kelley, "Bishop Visits Gymnasium of Catholic Youth: Teach Boys to 'Take It on the Chin,'" *Chicago Tribune*, 27 August 1932. Columbia College Chicago currently owns and occupies the building.

62. Winners of the 1931 CYO boxing championship were given the opportunity to qualify for the 1932 Olympic Games. "Boxing Tournament Winners to Qualify for Olympic Games," *New World*, 13 November 1931; Leo, "Looking 'Em Over," 15 May 1936.

63. Howard P. Chudacoff, *Children at Play: An American History* (New York: New York University Press, 2007), 122.

64. On the history of nineteenth- and early-twentieth-century boxing in the United States, see Elliott J. Gorn, *The Manly Art: Bare-Knuckle Prize Fighting in America* (Ithaca, NY: Cornell University Press, 1986).

65. Attendance figures for CYO championships in Chicago Stadium as reported in the *Chicago Tribune*: French Lane, "16,000 See Catholic Youth Ring Champions Crowned: Title Bouts in Stadium Ring Draw $50,000: West Side Wins Team Honors," 5 December 1931; Wilfred Smith, "C.Y.O. Boxing Champions Crowned Before 16,000," 3 December 1932; Lane, "17,000 See 16 C.Y.O. Boxing Champions Crowned," 6 December 1934; Lane, "19,000 Watch C.Y.O. Boxers Take Championships," 5 December 1935; Smith, "20,000 See 16 C.Y.O. Champions Crowned," 3 December 1936; Charles Bartlett, "16,258 See C.Y.O. Ring Champions Crowned," 2 December 1937; Charles Bartlett, "C.Y.O. Crowns 16 Boxing Champions: 12,000 See Finals," 10 December 1938; Howard Barry, "14,000 See Eight C.Y.O. Ring Champions Crowned," 30 November 1939. Attendance figures for CYO exhibition fights at Soldier Field and Wrigley Field as reported in the *Chicago Tribune*: Smith, "C.Y.O. Boxers Defeat New York: Goldenglovers [sic] Help Win Title Before 35,000," 1 August 1935; Smith, "C.Y.O. Defeat New York Boxers, 11–5, Before 38,000," 23 July 1936; Barry, "C.Y.O. Conquers South American Fighters, 11 to 5: 32,000 See International Boxing Carnival," 26 August 1937; Smith, "C.Y.O. Boxers Defeat Irish, Six Bouts to Four: Retain Perfect 7 Year Record Before 30,000," 15 July 1938; Smith, "Irish Boxers Tie C.Y.O., 5–5, Before 35,372," 20 July 1939.

66. *New World*, 12 October 1934, 13. WCFL was Chicago's pro-labor radio station; Nathan Godfried, *WCFL: Chicago's Voice of Labor, 1926–78* (Urbana: University of Illinois Press, 1997). In 1934, the CYO began broadcasting a daily sports review on radio station WSBC. The station also aired CYO boxing on Thursday nights; "C.Y.O. Sportscast," *New World*, 12 January 1934.

67. "C.Y.O. Praised for Splendid Achievements: Catholic Youth Work in Varied Sports Is Outstanding," *New World*, 18 March 1932.

68. Arch Ward, "Bishop Bernard J. Sheil: Everyone's Champ," Chicago's Tribute to His Excellency Most Rev. Bernard J. Sheil, D.D. on the Twenty-Fifth Anniversary of his Consecration, 29 April 1953, box 4, folder 3, Sheil Papers, AAC.

69. "'People's Bishop' Has a Silver Jubilee: Chicago Gives Its Beloved 'Benny' Sheil a Well-Earned Celebration," *Life*, 18 May 1953, 63.

70. Lane, "Cardinal Tells Aims of Catholic Youth's Tourney," *Chicago Tribune*, 2 December 1931.

71. See Rev. Edward V. Dailey, "Wanted, A Boy! The Catholic Youth Organization Seeks to Build Real Boys," *New World*, 18 March 1932.

72. "Second Annual Boxing Show is Now in Preparation: Three Thousand Will Try for Honors in Boxing Tourney," *New World*, 23 September 1932.

73. "Boxing Tournament Winners to Qualify for Olympic Games," *New World*, 13 November 1931.

74. Since the nation's beginnings, civic-religious expression has played a central role in public discourse, usually in the form of a vaguely nondenominational Protestantism. Examples include prayer before each session of Congress and the swearing of an oath to God and country at presidential inaugurations. In 1954, the words "under God" were added to the Pledge of Allegiance, and in 1956, the United States adopted "In God We Trust" as its official motto.

75. "Historical Survey of the Catholic Youth Organization," p. 3, box 11, folder 9, CCRD, UNDA.

76. *Chicago Herald-American*, 9 July 1940.

77. Twenty years later, Treat put the attendance at 18,000; *Bishop Sheil and the CYO*, 70; the *Chicago Tribune* estimated 16,000; Lane, "16,000 See Catholic Youth Champions Crowned"; the *New World* gave the number 15,000; 11 December 1931, 1.

78. Treat, *Bishop Sheil and the CYO*, 70–71. Even the traditionally anti-Catholic *Chicago Tribune* described the recitation of the CYO oath as a "real thrill"; Lane, "16,000 See Catholic Youth Champions Crowned."

79. "CYO History and Information" folder, box 4263, CYO Papers, AAC.

80. The *New World* described the first annual CYO boxing tournament as "good, clean amateur boxing," 4 December 1931, 12.

81. Leo, "Looking 'Em Over."

82. "Civic Leaders are Committee Leaders for Boxing Show—New York-Chicago Inter-City Bouts to be Witnessed by 50,000—Present, Past Champs to Gather For Match," *New World*, 5 July 1935.

83. Leo, "150,000 to Welcome New York Boxing Team: Plan Huge Reception July 24 at Garfield Park Band Stand," *New World*, 12 July 1935.

84. "New York-Chicago Boxing Matches Declared a Civic Event by the City Council," *New World*, 19 July 1935; Wilfred Smith, "C.Y.O. Boxers Defeat New York, 10 to 6: Goldenglovers Help Win Title Before 35,000," *Chicago Tribune*, 1 August 1935.

85. For example, in 1935, awards included "Cardinal Mundelein diamond-studded medals, Bishop Sheil scholarships to either high school or college, individual trophies and a trip to California"; "Fourth Annual C.Y.O. Boxing Tournament Dec. 5: Sixteen Bouts to Be Staged in Ring Classic," *New World*, 30 November 1934.

86. "Chicago Greets Team of Boxers from New York," *Chicago Tribune*, 25 July 1935.

87. "Boxers Return; Recall Safety of C.Y.O. Bouts: Careful Supervision of 1,500 Boxers Reflect Strict Care Taken in C.Y.O. Tournament," *New World*, 24 February 1933. Bob Bigott, who boxed in the CYO as well as other South Side boxing leagues, confirmed that the CYO protected its boxers better than any other organization, including the Golden Gloves; Bob Bigott, interview by author, South Holland, Illinois, 9 March 2000.

88. The 1930s *New World* sports pages regularly profiled former CYO boxers who turned professional; Leo Rodak, 8 September 1933; Jimmy Christy, 3 May 1935; Max Marek, 28 June 1935.

89. *New World*, 17 August 1934, 16.

90. Damon Runyon, "Both Barrels: Wait Till U.F.M. Hears About This! Promoters Who Take No Money!" *New York American*, 6 December 1935, repr. in *New World*, 13 December 1935.

91. "Throng Will Cheer C.Y.O. Athletes Next Sunday: Catholic Youth to Vie for Honors In a Great Athletic Tournament," *New World*, 11 March 1932; "Jack Elder, Played for Notre Dame," *Chicago Tribune*, 8 December 1992.

92. See, for example, Eddie Doherty, "The Bishop and the Wolves: A Heart-Warming True Story of Drama and a Death House That Gave Rise to a Stirring Adventure in Human Salvage," *Liberty*, 26 March 1938, 18–20.

93. Robert E. Burns interview by Steven Avella, 15 June 1989, box 1, tape 2, Rev. Steven Avella Oral History Project, AAC.

94. Anthony Burke Smith, *The Look of Catholics: Portrayals in Popular Culture from the Great Depression to the Cold War* (Lawrence: University Press of Kansas, 2010), 29.

95. Burns interview.

96. Julie Young, *The CYO in Indianapolis and Central Indiana* (Charleston, SC: History, 2011), 12.

97. Avella, *This Confident Church*, 140.

98. Ibid., 148.

99. Anthony Burke Smith, *The Look of Catholics*, 45.

100. Ibid., 51.

101. Ibid., 55–56.

102. Gems, *Windy City Wars*, 158–59.

103. Somerville, "A Study of the Juvenile Delinquency Prevention Service," 11.

104. Gerald R. Gems, "Sport, Religion, and Americanization: Bishop Sheil and the Catholic Youth Organization," *International Journal of the History of Sport* 10.2 (August 1993): 236.

105. "Throng Will Cheer C.Y.O. Athletes Next Sunday."

106. Jack Elder, "C.Y.O. Basketball Tournament Will Open Sunday, December 11," *New World*, 9 December 1932.

107. "Catholic Youth Basketball League Championship Finals" [advertisement], *New World*, 27 March 1931; "C.Y.O. Praised for Splendid Achievements: Catholic Youth Work in Varied Sports Is Outstanding," *New World*, 18 March 1932; "C.Y.O. Crowns 3 New Champs in Basketball: Cicero Five Wins Title in Heavyweight Class," *New World*,

12 March 1934; "C.Y.O. Champions Crowned in Finals: Season Closes at Loyola with Record Attendance," *New World*, 8 March 1935; Elder, "Final Elimination in C.Y.O. Basketball League Play, *New World*, 28 February 1936; "Play in 132nd Armory, Sunday, March 7," *New World*, 5 March 1937; Gene Kent, "Expect 5,000 Spectators at Armory Sunday: Four Divisions Mix for 1938 Cage Crowns: First Game Starts 2:00 p.m.," *New World*, 4 March 1938; Dan Ryan, "Six Squads Await Climax of C.Y.O. Cage Meet Sunday," *New World*, 17 March 1939; Mike Murphy, "St. Columbanus, St. Anselm Win C.Y.O. Basketball Titles," *New World*, 22 March 1940.

108. "New York vs. Chicago! Catholic Youth Inter-City Basketball Championship" [advertisement], *New World*, 4 March 1931.

109. Elder, "C.Y.O. Basketball Tournament Will Open Sunday, December 11."

110. "Basketball Rules," *New World*, 11 November 1932. A new rule was added during the 1937–1938 season; individuals playing on non-Catholic church teams were disqualified from CYO competition; Gene Kent, "C.Y.O. Adopts New Rule for 1937 Cage Tourney," 3 December 1937.

111. "CYO Cages Open Slate with 3 'P's'—Pray, Pledge, Play," *New World*, 16 December 1949.

112. I borrow this phrase from Kenneth J. Heineman, *A Catholic New Deal: Religion and Reform in Depression Pittsburgh* (College Station: Pennsylvania State University Press, 1999).

113. For an account of Mundelein's relationship with Roosevelt and Americanization strategies, see Kantowicz, *Corporation Sole*. For Americanization in the CYO, see Gems, "Sport, Religion, and Americanization," 233–41.

114. Sorvillo, "Bishop Bernard J. Sheil," 318.

115. In the spring of 1933, for example, the CYO ran the recreational programming at Fort Sheridan on Chicago's North Shore for forty thousand to fifty thousand men in the CCC "Reforestation Army"; *New World*, 12 May 1933, 4.

116. Margaret Mary Pembroke, "Vacation Schools of the CYO" (MA thesis, Loyola University Chicago, 1940), 8.

117. Somerville, "A Study of the Juvenile Delinquency Prevention Service," 9.

118. Pembroke, "Vacation Schools of the CYO," 16, 9. Until then, students learned the basics of Catholic faith by studying the *Baltimore Catechism*.

119. For example, see Heineman, *A Catholic New Deal*.

120. Pembroke, "Vacation Schools of the CYO," 21, 23, 25.

121. David J. O'Brien, *American Catholics and Social Reform: The New Deal Years* (New York: Oxford University Press, 1968), 55. Roosevelt delivered the Quarantine Speech on 5 October 1937 at the dedication of Chicago's Outer Drive Bridge, a WPA project. In his remarks, the president called for an international "quarantine of aggressor nations," challenging U.S. isolationism in foreign affairs.

122. James Delmage Ross, who Roosevelt appointed in 1937 as the first administrator of the Bonneville Dam Administration, was one of the other two. Ickes wrote that he could not recall the third person; Harold L. Ickes, *The Secret Diary of Harold L. Ickes*, vol. 3, *The Lowering Clouds, 1939–1941* (New York: Simon and Schuster, 1954), 53.

123. Ibid., 35–36, 55–56, 63–65, 110–11, 114, 154, 382–83, 403–4; Thomas J. Reese,

Archbishop: Inside the Power Structure of the American Catholic Church (San Francisco: Harper & Row, 1989), 11–12.

124. "C.I.O. Threatens Packer Strike on Wage Pacts: Lewis Issues Warning to Industry's Big Four," *Chicago Tribune*, 17 July 1939.

125. Burns interview.

126. "Cardinal Mundelein at White House," *New World*, 21 July 1939.

127. Saul Alinsky, "Prelate of the People," *Progressive* 15.6 (June 1951): 7.

128. "Labor's Bishop," *Newsweek*, 15 July 1946, 82. A story circulated that anti-union forces tried to violently intimidate Sheil. A bullet allegedly went through the window as the bishop lunched in a downtown restaurant on the day of the rally. It remains unclear whether the story is apocryphal or not. CYO public relations director Robert Burns corroborated the story with several people; Burns interview. Roger Treat repeated the story in his 1951 biography of Sheil; Treat, *Bishop Sheil and the CYO*, 169. Journalist Robert Lasch wrote, "Gunmen had sprayed bullets through windows of a restaurant where he usually ate"; Lasch, "Bishop Sheil of Chicago Runs a Cartel—of Charitable, Social-Service, Educational, Pro-Labor Enterprises," *Reporter* 1.6 (5 July 1949): 25.

129. Gems, "Sport, Religion, and Americanization," 237.

130. Eric Norden, "Saul Alinsky: A Candid Conversation with the Feisty Radical Organizer," *Playboy*, March 1972, 72.

131. On Alinsky's relationship with Chicago's Catholic Church, see Saul Alinsky, *Reveille for Radicals* (New York: Vintage, 1946); Sanford D. Horwitt, *Let Them Call Me Rebel: Saul Alinsky—His Life and Legacy* (New York: Knopf, 1989).

132. Kathryn Close, "Back of the Yards: Packingtown's Latest Drama: Civic Unity," *Survey Graphic: Magazine of Social Interpretation* 24.12 (December 1940): 615.

133. On the Back of the Yards Neighborhood Council, see Slayton, *Back of the Yards: The Making of a Local Democracy* (Chicago: University of Chicago Press, 1986).

134. Joseph Dever, "Bishop Sheil: "You Need a Bull Neck," *National Catholic Reporter*, 18 May 1966; Lasch, "Bishop Sheil of Chicago Runs a Cartel," 26.

135. "Historical Survey of the CYO," 18, box 11, folder 9, CCRD.

136. Sheil to Benjamin Weintraub, president, General Motors Coach Company, 4221 Diversey Avenue, Chicago, 23 February 1946, box 136, folder 11, Hillenbrand Printed Materials, UNDA.

137. Lizabeth Cohen argued that 1930s unionism and New Deal politics presented blacks with opportunities for economic advancement by forming coalitions with white ethnic workers in northern cities like Chicago; Lizabeth Cohen, *Making a New Deal: Industrial Workers in Chicago, 1919–1930* (New York: Cambridge University Press, 1990). More recently, Ira Katznelson has questioned the claims of racial progress made by the New Deal, demonstrating how programs like Social Security and the G.I. Bill in fact exacerbated economic and racial divides in the United States; Ira Katznelson, *Fear Itself: The New Deal and the Origins of Our Time* (New York: W. W. Norton, 2013) and *When Affirmative Action Was White* (New York: W. W. Norton, 2006).

138. Sheil, quoted in Saul Alinsky, "Prelate of the People," *Progressive* 15.6 (June 1951): 9.

139. Mayor Anton Cermak used this phrase to describe Chicago's multiethnic Democratic Party political machine in the 1930s.

140. "All Races and Nations Participate in C.Y.O. Program," *New World*, 29 November 1935. Again, in 1939, the paper touted the "C.Y.O. 'League of Nations.'" Participants included "Jesse Garcia, Mexican; John Leahy, Irish; Matt Jachec, Polish; Eldie Miller, German; Jack McNeil, Scotch; Tony Bausone, Italian; and Harold Dade, colored"; *New World*, 3 November 1939.

141. "The C.Y.O. Melting Pot," *New World*, 20 November 1936. The caption listed the boys as Polish, Italian, Ukrainian, Bohemian, Mexican, Greek, Chinese, Slovak, Spanish, German, English, "Colored," Irish, and French.

142. Mike Murphy, "21,000 to See C.Y.O. Boxing Finals Dec. 1: Proceeds of the Bouts Will Aid Poor Youngsters," *New World*, 26 November 1937.

143. Treat, *Bishop Sheil and the CYO*, 54.

144. In 1930, Chicago's total population was 3,376,438, while its African American population was 233,903. Campbell Gibson and Kay Jung, *Historical Census Statistics On Population Totals By Race, 1790 to 1990, and By Hispanic Origin, 1970 to 1990, For Large Cities And Other Urban Places In The United States*, Popular Division Working Paper No. 76 (Washington, DC: U.S. Census Bureau, February 2005), table 14, http://www.census.gov/population/www/documentation/twps0076/ILtab.pdf, accessed 14 May 2014.

145. Richard Slotkin, "Unit Pride: Ethnic Platoons and the Myths of American Nationality," *American Literary History* 13.3 (Fall 2001): 470.

146. Horace M. Kallen, "Democracy versus the Melting-Pot: A Study of American Nationality, Part I," *Nation*, 18 February 1915, 190–94; Horace M. Kallen, "Democracy versus the Melting-Pot: A Study of American Nationality, Part II," *Nation*, 25 February 1915, 217–20; Horace M. Kallen, *Culture and Democracy in the United States: Studies in the Group Psychology of the American Peoples* (New York: Boni and Liveright, 1924); Horace M. Kallen, *Cultural Pluralism and the American Idea: An Essay in Social Philosophy* (Philadelphia: University of Pennsylvania Press, 1956); Randolph S. Bourne, "Trans-National America," *Atlantic Monthly*, July 1916, 86–97.

147. Lizabeth Cohen, *Making a New Deal*, 333–349.

148. "Thank God for CIO, Prelate Tells Rally," *People's Press*, 27 November 1937.

149. Slayton, *Back of the Yards*, 200.

150. Cohen, *Making a New Deal*, 357.

151. Gary Gerstle, *Working-Class Americanism: The Politics of Labor in a Textile City, 1914–1960* (New York: Cambridge University Press, 1989), 331.

152. For examples of Sheil receiving scholarly attention in recent years, see Robert A. Orsi, "U.S. Catholics between Memory and Modernity: How Catholics Are American," in *Catholics in the American Century: Recasting Narratives of U.S. History*, ed. R. Scott Appleby and Kathleen Sprows Cummings (Ithaca, NY: Cornell University Press, 2012), 37; Anthony Burke Smith, *The Look of Catholics*, 6, 29, 47, 112; William J. Baker, *Playing with God: Religion and Modern Sport* (Cambridge, MA: Harvard University Press, 2007), 175–180; Amy L. Koehlinger, *Rosaries and Rope Burns: Boxing and Manhood in American Catholicism, 1880–1970* (Princeton, NJ: Princeton University Press, forthcoming).

CHAPTER FOUR

1. The 1930 U.S. census shows only one "Harry Booker" in Chicago. He is listed as sixteen years old, "Negro," born in Iowa, living at 1442 West Washburne, and working as a broom-maker. This person would most likely be eighteen years old in December 1932, a typical age for CYO boxing finalists. Also, although his address is on the West Side, it was not unusual for blacks to travel to St. Elizabeth, Chicago's only black Catholic parish before 1932; 1930 U.S. Federal Population Census, Sheet Number 7, Sheet B, Line Number 83, NARA Microfilm Roll Number 456, NARA Publication Number T627, http://www.archives.com/, accessed 25 June 2015.

2. Rodak—from Saints Peter and Paul parish at 91st Street and South Exchange Avenue—was Golden Gloves champion in 1931 (112 lb.), 1932 (118 lb.), and 1933 (126 lb.). He became a professional in 1933 and won the 1938–1939 National Boxing Association Featherweight Championship.

3. A favorite of Sheil, Christy turned professional in 1935, but left boxing after one year to pursue a career in graphic arts. He was killed in action serving as a private in the U.S. Army Air Corps during World War II; Roger L. Treat, *Bishop Sheil and the CYO: The Story of the Catholic Youth Organization and the Man Who Influenced a Generation* (New York: Messner, 1951), 81–82, 191–94.

4. *New World*, 2 December 1932, 1. A sportswriter recounted that the "hard hitting colored youth . . . waded into Christy and in the last round had Christy staggering"; Wilfrid Smith, "C.Y.O. Boxing Champions Crowned Before 16,000," *Chicago Tribune*, 3 December 1932. CYO Athletic Director Jack Elder wrote, "Perhaps the most interesting battle of the evening was that in which Harry Booker, St. Elizabeth star, defeated Smiling Jimmy Christy by coming with a rush in the last round to put little Jimmy in distress near the middle of the round"; Elder, "The Tournament Finals Reviewed for the Record," *New World*, 9 December 1932.

5. The tournament between the CYO and all-star boxers from Californian Catholic youth organizations celebrated the upcoming 1933 Chicago World's Fair; "Inter-City Bouts Draw Interest: Civic Reception for Pacific Coast Teams Who Will Meet C.Y.O. Champs," *New World*, 30 December 1932; Jack Elder, "Capacity Attendance Expected at C.Y.O. Inter-City Tournament," 6 January 1933; Elder, "Coast Teams Say Good-Bye," 13 January 1933. A few weeks later, Booker led the CYO team to victory at the Illinois Athletic Club's annual tournament. "Harry Booker, C.Y.O. Champ, Continues String of Victories," *New World*, 27 January 1933.

6. Canon 208, *Code of Canon Law*, http://www.vatican.va/archive/ENG1104/_PU .HTM, accessed 21 June 2015.

7. Historian Timuel Black, who grew up in Bronzeville during the 1930s, played basketball at St. Elizabeth's gymnasium, and briefly attended Xavier University in New Orleans, recalled that Sheil was simply "fair"; Timuel Black, interview by author, Chicago, Illinois, 27 February 2003.

8. On the relationship between African Americans and sports, see Othello Harris, "African Americans," in *Encyclopedia of Ethnicity and Sports in the United States*, ed. George B. Kirsch, Othello Harris, and Claire E. Nolte (Westport, CT: Greenwood Press, 2000), 3–23.

9. No evidence is available to either confirm or deny that Daley took part in the rioting. The best works on Chicago's 1919 race riot are William M. Tuttle, Jr., *Race Riot: Chicago in the Red Summer of 1919* (New York: Atheneum, 1970); Dominic A. Pacyga, "Chicago's 1919 Race Riot: Ethnicity, Class, and Urban Violence," in *The Making of Urban America*, ed. Raymond A. Mohl (Wilmington, DE: Scholarly Resources, 1997), 187–207.

10. Members of one club, "Ragen's Colts," learned how to box from a Roman Catholic priest; Chicago Commission on Race Relations, *The Negro in Chicago: A Study of Race Relations and A Race Riot* (Chicago: University of Chicago Press, 1922), 16.

11. Frederic M. Thrasher, *The Gang: A Study of 1,313 Gangs in Chicago* (Chicago: University of Chicago Press, 1968), 43, 52, 139–40.

12. Some early opposition surfaced in Chicago's African American community to the organization of an all-black YMCA; "Gag Law in the Church: Desperate Attempt of Some Fossils to Organize a Colored Y.M.C.A., Disgraceful Proceedings," *The Appeal*, 30 November 1889, 1; "Object to the Color Line: Negroes of Chicago Who Oppose the Formation of an African Y.M.C.A.," *Chicago Herald*, 9 December 1889; "Is Jim Crowism Growing in Chicago?" *Broad Ax*, 31 December 1910, 1. Although opposition existed, Alan Spear noted that most African Americans in Chicago fully supported an all-black YMCA; Allan H. Spear, *Black Chicago: The Making of a Negro Ghetto, 1890–1920* (Chicago: University of Chicago Press, 1967), 100. I thank historian Suellen Hoy for directing me to these sources.

13. This group organized Negro History week, which eventually became Black History Month.

14. For more on the Rosenwald YMCAs, see Nina Mjagkij, *Light in the Darkness: African Americans and the YMCA, 1852–1946* (Lexington: University Press of Kentucky, 1994), 74–83. See also Mjagkij, "A Peculiar Alliance: Julius Rosenwald, the YMCA, and African-Americans, 1910–1933," *American Jewish Archives* 44.2 (fall/winter 1992): 584–605; Mjagkij, "True Manhood: The YMCA and Racial Advancement, 1890–1930," *Men and Women Adrift: The YMCA and the YWCA in the City*, ed. Nina Mjagkij and Margaret Spratt (New York: New York University Press, 1997); Mjagkij, "Young Men's Christian Association, Colored Work Department," in *Organizing Black America: An Encyclopedia of African American Associations* (New York: Garland, 2001), 707–10. For more on the Wabash YMCA, see James R. Grossman, *Land of Hope: Chicago, Black Southerners, and the Great Migration* (Chicago: University of Chicago Press, 1989), 81, 116, 128–29, 134, 140–43, 150, 200–202, 228–29, 235, 240.

15. Margaret Brennan, "Recreation Facilities in Chicago's Negro District," Federal Writers' Project: Negro Studies Project, Box A875, Library of Congress, quoted in *Bronzeville: Black Chicago in Pictures, 1941–1943*, ed. Maren Stange (New York: New Press, 2003), 189.

16. The Washington Park YMCA at 50th Street and South Indiana Avenue (three blocks east and one block south of Corpus Christi) opened in 1949 and closed in 2003. A 1945 YMCA internal report recommended desegregating Chicago's YMCAs. A policy of nonsegregation was adopted in 1948, but compliance took two more years; "Y Integrated—After Five Years," *Chicago Defender*, 10 June 1950, pp. 1–2.

17. The boys club movement began in England during the 1850s. The first U.S. club

opened in 1860 in Hartford, Connecticut. In 1906, clubs from across the country formed the Boys Club Federation of America. In 1990, the U.S. Congress rechartered the nationwide association under its current name, Boys & Girls Clubs of America. For more on boys clubs in Great Britain and the United States, see Frank Victor Dawes, *A Cry from the Streets: The Boys' Club Movement in Britain From the 1850s to the Present Day* (Hove, UK: Wayland, 1975); Gerald Sorin, *The Nurturing Neighborhood: The Brownsville Boys Club and Jewish Community in Urban America, 1940–1990* (New York: New York University Press, 1990).

18. After World War II, track star Jesse Owens became the club's executive director. In 1956, the South Side Boys Club merged with the American Boys Commonwealth and Boys Brotherhood Republic to create the Chicago Youth Centers. The 3947 South Michigan Avenue location was renamed the Elliott Donnelly Youth Center in 1959 and continues today to serve the neighborhood.

19. Richard Wright, "How 'Bigger' Was Born," *Native Son* (New York: Perennial, 2001), xxvi-xxvii.

20. After a fire damaged the school at East Pershing Road and Indiana Avenue in January 1935, a second all-black high school, the "new Phillips," opened seven months ahead of schedule. For half a year, students from both schools used the new building at 4934 South Wabash Avenue (six blocks west of Corpus Christi). It was renamed Jean Baptiste Pointe DuSable High School in 1936; Demsey J. Travis, *An Autobiography of Black Chicago* (Chicago: Urban Research Institute, 1981), 70. A generation later, DuSable's 1954 basketball squad garnered fame for advancing to the finals of the Illinois State basketball tournament. In 1942, a third all-black school, Paul L. Dunbar High School, opened at 30th Street and South Parkway (Martin Luther King Drive after 1968).

21. For a brief biographical sketch of Saperstein, see Zachary Davis, "Saperstein, Abraham M.," in Kirsch et al., *Encyclopedia of Ethnicity and Sports in the United States*, 399–400. For more on the Harlem Globetrotters, see George B. Kirsch, "Harlem Globetrotters," in Kirsch et al., *Encyclopedia of Ethnicity and Sports in the United States*, 206–7; Robert W. Peterson, *Cages to Jumpshots: Pro Basketball's Early Years* (New York: Oxford, 1990); Josh Wilker, *The Harlem Globetrotters* (Philadelphia: Chelsea House, 1997).

22. Robert Pruter, "Early Phillips High School Basketball Teams," Illinois High School Association, http://www.ihsa.org/NewsMedia/IllinoisHStoric/ IllinoisHStoricArticle.aspx?url=/archive/hstoric/basketball_phillips .htm, accessed 14 May 2014.

23. Cleveland Bray (St. Elizabeth), Tilford Cole, Charles Gant (Corpus Christi), William McQuitter (Corpus Christi), and Leroy Rhodes (St. Elizabeth) were Phillips alumni and Xavier starters; Pruter, "Early Phillips High School Basketball Teams."

24. Nathaniel "Sweetwater" Clifton graduated from DuSable High School and played for Xavier before entering the U.S. Army in 1943. He played in the NBA between 1950 and 1958. William C. Robinzine, Sr., graduated from Phillips High School and played for Xavier before transferring to DePaul in 1955; Sam Smith, "'Sweetwater' Keeps Rollin': First Black To Sign in NBA Now on Taxi Squad," *Chicago Tribune*, 9 June 1985; John W. Fountain, "'Sweetwater' Clifton, Former Globetrotter," *Chicago Tribune*,

2 September 1990; Fred Mitchell, "Robinzine Remembered at DePaul," *Chicago Tribune*, 25 July 2000.

25. Pruter, "Early Phillips High School Basketball Teams."

26. On racial discrimination against African Americans in college athletics, see Ocania Chalk, *Black College Sport* (New York: Dodd, Mead, 1976); David Kenneth Wiggins, *Black Athletes in White America* (Syracuse, NY: Syracuse University Press, 1997), chap. 7.

27. Larry Hawkins, former Public League coach and director of Special Programs at the University of Chicago dubbed the three institutions only blocks apart a "golden triangle"; Pruter, "Early Phillips High School Basketball Teams."

28. Eugene Saffold, interview by author, Hazel Crest, Illinois, 8 November 2001.

29. John Woodford, an African American Catholic born in 1914, recalled Bishop Sheil coming to St. Elizabeth parish in the early 1930s to recruit African American participants for CYO activities; John Woodford, interview by author, Chicago, Illinois, 26 April 2002.

30. George Phillips, interview by author, Chicago, Illinois, 8 August 2001.

31. The building opened on Thanksgiving Day, 1892; "Minor Locals," *Chicago Daily Sun*, 31 October 1892.

32. Another South Side mansion associated with the Swift family was completed the same year as the Sheridan Club. The Swift House—four blocks to the north of the Sheridan Club at 4500 South Michigan Avenue—was built by meatpacker Gustavus Swift's daughter and her husband. On the National Register of Historic Places, Swift House is now part of the headquarters for the Chicago Urban League; Wilbert R. Hasbrouck, *National Register of Historic Places Inventory—Nomination Form*, 9 June 1978; Bob Gendron, "Open House Chicago: Bronzeville—2 Treasures Escape Ravages of 'Progress': Mansion was Wedding Gift, Art Center Kept Rare Feature," *Chicago Tribune*, 13 October 2011, http://articles.chicagotribune.com/2011-10-13/site/ct-ent-1013 -openhouse-bronzeville-20111011_1_wedding-gift-art-center-bronzeville, accessed 14 May 2014.

33. "St. Elizabeth's Club House Remodeled," *New World*, 16 September 1938; Duncan E. Roudette, "St. Elizabeth Branch," *New World*, 1 September 1939.

34. The building at 4062 South Michigan Avenue was the former LaSalle University Extension.

35. Edwin W. Leaner, III, interview by author, Chicago, Illinois, 27 June 2001.

36. The Welfare Council of Chicago approved the transition from parish house to community center in February 1945; Chronology beginning "August to December, 1938," box 257, folder 3, Welfare Council of Metropolitan Chicago Papers, Chicago History Museum.

37. "Of course they had a balcony there [above the gymnasium floor]. That's where the nuns sat [during dances] and watched and made sure you stayed twelve inches apart," recalled St. Elizabeth alumna Marie Davis; Marie C. Davis, interview by author, Chicago, Illinois, 6 July 2001; Leaner interview; Phillips interview; Saffold interview; Warner Saunders, interview by author, Chicago, Illinois, 24 August 2001.

38. Leaner interview.

39. Treat, *Bishop Sheil and the CYO*, 130–34; "Joseph J. Robichaux Dies at 54;

Political Figure, Molder of Athletes," *Chicago Sun-Times*, 27 April 1971; "Athletic-Political Activist Succumbs," *Jet*, 13 May 1971, 12; A.S. "Doc" Young, *Negro Firsts in Sports* (Chicago: Johnson, 1963), 197.

40. On Louis, see Anthony O. Edmonds, "Louis, Joe (Barrow)," in Kirsch et al., *Encyclopedia of Ethnicity and Sports in the United States*, 297–98; Richard Bak, *Joe Louis: The Great Black Hope* (Dallas: Taylor, 1996); Joe Louis Barrow, Jr., and Barbara Munder, *Joe Louis: 50 Years an American Hero* (New York: McGraw-Hill, 1988); Anthony O. Edmonds, *Joe Louis* (Grand Rapids, MI: Eerdmans, 1973); Lewis A. Erenberg, *The Greatest Fight of Our Generation: Louis vs. Schmeling* (New York: Oxford University Press, 2006); Joe Louis, *My Life Story: An Autobiography* (Brighton, UK: Angus and Robertson, 1978); Chris Mead, *Champion: Joe Louis, Black Hero in White America* (New York: Scribner, 1985); Jeffrey T. Sammons, *Beyond the Ring: The Role of Boxing in American Society* (Urbana: University of Illinois Press, 1988).

41. Sammons, *Beyond the Ring*, 101–2.

42. The historian Timuel Black, a Bronzeville native, recalled the victory's impact on Chicago's African American community: "When we heard that Louis had knocked out Braddock in the eighth round, we went crazy . . . It was even sweeter because his victory came only a year after Louis' defeat by Max Schmeling, a product of Hitler's Germany"; Black, "1937: A Night to Remember," *Chicago Sun-Times*, 29 October 1999.

43. Wilfred Smith, "C.Y.O. Boxers Defeat Irish, Six Bouts to Four: Retain Perfect 7 Year Record Before 30,000," *Chicago Tribune*, 15 July 1938.

44. Richard Wright, "High Tide in Harlem: Joe Louis as Symbol of Freedom," *New Masses*, 5 July 1938, 18–20, reprinted in David K. Wiggins and Patrick B. Miller, eds., *The Unlevel Playing Field: A Documentary History of the African American Experience in Sport* (Urbana: University of Illinois Press, 2003), 169–74; Alex Haley and Malcolm X, *The Autobiography of Malcolm X* (New York: Ballantine, 1999), 25.

45. Sammons, *Beyond the Ring*, 102. Erenberg, *The Greatest Fight of Our Generation*, 159.

46. Erenberg, *The Greatest Fight of Our Generation*, 161.

47. Gary Gerstle, *American Crucible: Race and Nation in the Twentieth Century* (Princeton, NJ: Princeton University Press, 2001), 46–47.

48. "Lorenzo Lovings," *New World*, 21 April 1935.

49. "C.Y.O. Boxing Notes," *New World*, 7 September 1934.

50. "C.Y.O. Boxing Notes, *New World*, 23 August 1935.

51. Ralph C. Leo, "Looking 'Em Over," *New World*, 31 May 1935. Leo continued the metaphor a few months later to describe the Italian-Ethiopian conflict: "Haile Selassie steps into the ring against Mussolini . . . Haile and Il Duce . . . are still scowling at each other"; Leo, "Looking 'Em Over," *New World*, 13 September 1935.

52. The three CYO boxers on the eight-man U.S. team were: 118-pound Johnny Brown from Holy Angels, an Irish American parish on the South Side; 135-pound Andy Scrivani from St. Charles Borromeo, an Italian American parish on the West Side; and 147-pound Chester Rutecki from St. Michael's, a Polish American parish on the Far South Side. After the games ended, Bishop Sheil paid for Rutecki to fly to Poland, where he visited his grandmother and other relatives; Leo, "Looking 'Em Over," *New World*, 21 August 1936.

53. For discussion of the racial implications of the 1936 summer Olympic Games in Berlin, see Duff Hart-Davis, *Hitler's Games: The 1936 Olympics* (New York: Harper & Row, 1986); Arnd Krüger and William J. Murray, eds., *The Nazi Olympics: Sport, Politics and Appeasement in the 1930s* (Urbana: University of Illinois Press, 2003); David Clay Large, *Nazi Games: The Olympics of 1936* (New York: W. W. Norton, 2007); Richard D. Mandell, *The Nazi Olympics* (New York: Macmillan, 1971); David Kenneth Wiggins, *Black Athletes in White America*, chap. 4.

54. "Colored Boys to Take Part in C.Y.O. Glove Tournament: Catholic Boys of Colored Race Invited to Enter Great Boxing Tournament," *New World*, 23 October 1931.

55. "Youth Organization to Back a Giant Program of Athletic Bouts: Interview with M. Price Jones, Field Director, Gives Hint of a Busy Period of Activity for Chicago and Suburbs," *New World*, 9 October 1931.

56. The South District included St. Elizabeth and three white parishes: St. Laurence's on South Dorchester Avenue in the Grand Crossing neighborhood, St. Rita's on South Fairfield Avenue in the Marquette Park neighborhood, and Visitation on West Garfield Boulevard in the Back of the Yards and Englewood neighborhoods; M. Price Jones, "Many Applications for C.Y.O. Athletic Event Are Received: Entries Must Be Filed by October 5. Every Branch of Holy Name Society is Supporting This Event," *New World*, 2 October 1931.

57. Pacyga, "Chicago's 1919 Race Riot," 194. For forty-three consecutive years during the mid-twentieth century, the mayor of Chicago was an Irish Catholic graduate of De La Salle—Edward J. Kelly (1933–1946), Martin H. Kennelly (1946–1955), and Richard J. Daley (1955–1976). Chicago's longest-serving mayor, Richard M. Daley (son of Richard J., mayor for twenty-two years between 1989 and 2011) also graduated from De La Salle. Other influential politicians, like Democratic Party leader Dan Ryan (Cook County board president, 1954–1961) also graduated from the all-boys Catholic school.

58. "Corpus Christi to Hold Pageant Jan. Thirteenth," *Chicago Defender*, 9 January 1937. See also "Corpus Christi C.Y.O. Makes Plan for Pageant Jan. 13," *New World*, 8 January 1937.

59. "C.Y.O. Sports Summary: Week of March 8 to 15," *New World*, 8 March 1935.

60. Boxers Hiner Thomas and Jimmy Martin served as vice president and marshal, respectively; "Corpus Christi Young Men's Branch Selects New Officers for Year," *New World*, 8 January 1937.

61. "C.Y.O. Boxers Win in I.A.C. Tournament," *New World*, 2 February 1934; "All-Star Entertainment for Bishop Sheil Dinner," *New World*, 17 January 1936; "Capacity Crowd at St. Andrew's C.Y.O. Bouts," *New World*, 23 August 1935; "C.Y.O. Boxers in Benefit At Statesville, Ill., April 16," *New World*, 15 April 1932.

62. "C.Y.O. Boxers Give Exhibition at the Fair This Week," *New World*, 13 July 1934; "The Irish Village at A Century of Progress" [advertisement], *New World*, 20 July 1934; "Make Irish Village Irish," *New World*, 3 August 1934.

63. Amateur boxing has long been associated with the Mercy Home. Founded in 1887, the orphanage moved into its present location at 1140 West Jackson Boulevard in 1909. During the 1930s, operations fell under the CYO umbrella. Today, the Mercy Home for Boys and Girls continues to hold annual amateur boxing shows as fundraisers.

64. "C.Y.O. Boxing Notes," *New World*, 7 September 1934; "C.Y.O. Boxing Notes," 14 June 1935; Leo, "Looking 'Em Over," 28 June 1935.

65. "C.Y.O. Boxing Notes," *New World*, 21 December 1934, p. 16.

66. "Young, Canadeo and Dade, of C.Y.O., Win Golden Glove Titles," *New World*, 15 March 1940; Treat, *Bishop Sheil and the CYO*, 88.

67. "Former CYO Boxer Wins World Title," *C.Y.O. Voice*, February 1947, 1, 8, box 11, folder 11, Edward Victor Cardinal Papers (hereafter, CCRD), University of Notre Dame Archives, Notre Dame, Indiana.

68. *New World*, 1 January 1932, 7.

69. *New World*, 15 January 1932, 9; *New World*, 22 January 1932, 9; *New World*, 29 January 1932, 9; *New World*, 5 February 1932, 9; *New World*, 12 February 1932, 9; *New World*, 19 February 1932, 9; *New World*, 26 February 1932, 9; *New World*, 4 March 1932, 9.

70. *New World*, 6 January 1933, 9; "St. Elizabeth's Gym Center of C.Y.O. Games," *New World*, 2 December 1932. Corpus Christi also played games at St. Augustine's in the white Back of the Yards neighborhood; *New World*, 9 December 1932, 10.

71. St. Agnes was an Irish American parish in the white neighborhood of Brighton Park; St. Carthage an Irish American parish in the white neighborhood of Park Manor; St. Mary of Perpetual Help a Polish American parish in the white neighborhood of Bridgeport; St. Rose of Lima an Irish American parish in the white Back of the Yards neighborhood; and Visitation an Irish American parish in the white Englewood and Back of the Yards neighborhoods; "Boys' Division Scores," *New World*, 27 January 1933; "Boys Division Scores," *New World*, 20 January 1933. The 1933-1934 season witnessed similar dynamics. White teams—St. John the Baptist (an Irish American parish in the Back of the Yards), St. Gabriel's (an Irish American parish in Canaryville), and Sacred Heart (a Jesuit parish in the Czech neighborhood of Pilsen)—competed at St. Elizabeth's gymnasium with black teams from St. Anselm, Corpus Christi, and St. Elizabeth, as well as against the other white teams; "C.Y.O. Men's Basketball Divisions, 1933-1934," *New World*, 8 December 1933.

72. For an account of the 1949 rioting, see John T. McGreevy, *Parish Boundaries: The Catholic Encounter with Race in the Twentieth-Century Urban North* (Chicago: University of Chicago Press, 1996), 94–97.

73. St. Rita's later became infamous for white racist resistance to African Americans. In the 1960s, Francis X. Lawlor, an Augustinian priest at St. Rita High School (77th and Western Avenue) spoke out about "holding the line" against black encroachment; McGreevy, *Parish Boundaries*, 232. Lawlor became a hero to white ethnic Catholics who feared "losing" their neighborhoods to African Americans. Chicago Cardinal John Cody relieved the controversial Lawlor of his priestly duties in 1968. Lawlor then became the only Catholic priest ever to serve on the Chicago City Council, representing the Fifteenth Ward from 1971 to 1975. For more on Lawlor, see Megan Graydon, "The Rev. Francis X. Lawlor, 1917–2013: Catholic Priest Won Term as Alderman, Drew Controversy for Efforts to Slow Black Migration in 1960s and '70s," *Chicago Tribune*, 13 November 2013; Maureen O'Donnell, "The Rev. Francis X. Lawlor, 1917–2013: Controversial Priest Was Elected to City Council," *Chicago Sun-Times*, 8 November 2013.

74. "C.Y.O. Boys' Standings," *New World*, 20 February 1933; "Field of Undefeated

Teams in C.Y.O. Race Cut to Twelve," *New World*, 9 February 1934; *New World*, 13 December 1935, 17; *New World* sports schedules, 1937 and 1938; *New World*, 6 January 1939; *New World*, 20 January 1939, 12; *New World*, 27 January 1939, 12; *New World*, 3 February 1939, 10; *New World*, 10 February 1939, 12; *New World*, 17 February 1939, 16; "Final Week of Sectional Play Remains in Cage Tourney," *New World*, 24 February 1939; *New World* sports schedules, 1939–1940.

75. Harry C. Koenig, *A History of the Archdiocese of Chicago* (Chicago: Archdiocese of Chicago, 1980), 860.

76. Amateur sports enthusiasts established the AAU in 1888. The nonsectarian organization set uniform standards for amateur athletics, sponsored tournaments, and prepared U.S. athletes for the Olympic Games. St. Elizabeth played in St. Sabina's first AAU tournament. "St. Sabina Cage Tourney Finals Sunday Afternoon: Capacity Crowd Expected to See Climax of Colorful Cage Tournament," *New World*, 18 March 1938.

77. "Third Annual A.A.U. Cage Tourney Opens at St. Sabina's Gym," *New World*, 15 March 1940.

78. "St. Sabina Cage Tourney Slated for Dec. 4–13," *New World*, 2 December 1949.

79. Timothy B. Neary, "'An Inalienable Right to Play,'" *Chicago Tribune*, 17 June 2001.

80. "C.Y.O. Crowns 3 New Champs in Basketball: Cicero Five Wins Title in Heavyweight Class," *New World*, 12 March 1934. Ralph Leo described the crowd of 3,500 fans, who "cheered and screeched and screamed their heads off as the colored lads representing Corpus Christi defeated the heretofore invincible Sacred Heart lightweight machine . . . pandemonium was caused by the sensational playing of Corpus Christi in dethroning Sacred Heart." Leo, "1933–34 is Most Successful Season in C.Y.O. Basketball," *New World*, 23 March 1934.

81. Phillips, Saffold, and Saunders interviews.

82. Jack Elder, "Eight Teams Battle for Chicago C.Y.O. Titles at 132nd Infantry Armory," *New World*, 6 March 1936.

83. Gene Kent, "De Paul U. to Meet Loyola: Both Teams Boast Great Cage Records," *New World*, 26 March 1937.

84. Brown, for instance, was named AAU outstanding player of the Midwest in 1937; "Chicago Centennial Basketball Classic," *New World*, 26 March 1937.

85. Gene Kent, "400 Quintets Entered for 1937–38 Play," *New World*, 19 December 1937; "C.Y.O. Quints in Torrid Race for Cage Supremacy," *New World*, 13 January 1939.

86. "St. Elizabeth Again Wins C.Y.O. Title," *Chicago Tribune*, 7 March 1938.

87. Gene Kent, "6,500 Fans See Final of C.Y.O. Cage Tourney: St. Elizabeth, St. Dorothy and Sacred Heart Take 1938 Crowns," *New World*, 11 March 1938.

88. "Chicago Centennial Basketball Classic," *New World*, 26 March 1937; Gene Kent, "Loyola University Beats DePaul, 46–43," 2 April 1937.

89. "St. Elizabeth Again Wins C.Y.O. Title." In Denver, St. Elizabeth made it to the quarterfinals, where it lost to a team from Cicero, Illinois; "C.Y.O. Champions, 29 to 20, in A.A.U. Tourney," 8 March 1938; "Demons Defeat Cicero for A.A.U. Title, 31–27," 10 March 1938.

90. Mike Murphy, "C.Y.O. Jewish All-Stars in Cage Classic," *New World*, 31 March 1939.

91. Ibid.; "C.Y.O. All-Stars Nip Jewish Aces 39–34," *New World*, 7 April 1939.

92. Kent, "Loyola University Beats DePaul." St. Elizabeth defeated the Universal Pictures team from Hollywood, California, composed mostly of standout players from the University of California at Los Angeles. The Universal team went on to make up one half of the gold medal–winning U.S. team in Berlin at the first Olympic basketball competition in 1936; USA Basketball, http://www.usab.com/mens/national/moly_1936 .html, accessed 14 May 2014.

93. Dan Ryan, "Six Squads Await Climax of C.Y.O. Cage Meet Sunday," *New World*, 17 March 1939. St. Elizabeth's returned to the CYO finals in 1946 but lost to Annunciation, an Irish American parish on the North Side; "Annunciation Takes Senior Basketball Title," *The C.Y.O. Voice*, February–March 1946, box 11, folder 18, CCRD.

94. St. Sylvester's had won thirty-one straight games and had beaten St. Anselm earlier in the season; Mike Murphy, "St. Columbanus, St. Anselm Win C.Y.O. Basketball Titles," *New World*, 22 March 1940.

95. Mike Murphy, "C.Y.O. Cage Champs Meet Detroit at St. Sabina Gym," *New World*, 5 April 1940. St. Anselm defeated St. Hedwig, a Polish team from Detroit, 44–24; "Chicago C.Y.O. Basket Teams Defeat Detroit," *New World*, 8 April 1940. St. Anselm defeated the BBYO team by one point in the last minute; Mike Murphy, "C.Y.O. Champs Meet Cleveland Sunday: St. Columbanus, St. Anselm Journey to Ohio City for Title," 12 April 1940.

96. McGreevy, *Parish Boundaries*, 93; Vernon Jarrett, "Church Myths vs New Sabina," *Chicago Defender*, 20 June 2001.

97. "Try for Division Championship in C.Y.O. Girls' League," *New World*, 26 February 1932.

98. The St. Elizabeth girls competed against white teams from Our Lady of Good Counsel, Sacred Heart (a Jesuit parish in Pilsen), St. Augustine's (in the Back of the Yards), St. Anthony's (a German parish in Bridgeport), and St. George's (a German American parish); *New World*, 9 December 1932, 10; *New World*, 24 February 1933, 7.

99. New World, 16 February 1934, 14. In 1931, St. Agnes's had completed a new parish center with a gymnasium seating 1,800; "Mrgr. [sic] D. Byrnes Begins Modern Parish Center: New Structure Will Be Ready for June Commencement, It is Expected," *New World*, 3 April 1931.

100. Woodford interview.

101. Jack Elder, "C.Y.O. Track Meet Begins Tomorrow," *New World*, 12 August 1932; "Leonas and Bodeau Win C.Y.O. Titles: New Records Set in the Fifth Annual Meet at Loyola Field," *New World*, 3 July 1936; "C.Y.O. Track, Field Meet at Loyola Field: Marquardt, Gill, Bray, Brunton to Run," *New World*, 30 July 1937; "St. Elizabeth, St. Thomas Win in C.Y.O. Track: Marquardt, Brunton, Bowles, Star," *New World*, 6 August 1937; "Shatter 5 Records in C.Y.O. Track and Field Title," *New World*, 24 June 1938.

102. Girls, however, were welcome to use some parts of the downtown CYO Center during its first decade of operation. A 1934 advertisement invited girls to make use of the bowling alleys and meeting spaces on the second floor of the center; *Chicago Daily News Almanac and Yearbook* (1934): A2. I thank historian Ellen Skerrett for sharing this source with me.

103. Treat, *Bishop Sheil and the CYO*, 139.

104. Landry won the long jump in 1949, 1950, 1952, and 1953. She won the 50 meters in 1953 and 1954. Jones won the 100 meters in 1953 and 1954. USA Track and Field, the sport's national governing body, http://www.usatf.org/statistics/champions/outdoor/women.shtml, accessed 1 April 2004.

105. J. S. Fuerst and D. Bradford Hunt, eds., *When Public Housing Was Paradise: Building Community in Chicago* (Westport, CT: Praeger, 2003), 170. Robichaux's successful run continued after the CYO downsized and Sheil House closed in the mid-1950s. At the time of his death, he was coach of the 1972 U.S. women's Olympic track and field team; "Athletic-Political Activist Succumbs," *Jet,* 13 May 1971, 12.

106. Melissa Isaacson, "Finally on the Right Track," *Chicago Tribune,* 15 May 2008.

107. DePaul University, "Staton's Legacy: She Reached for the Sky—The 1952 Olympian Gets Inducted Sunday into DePaul's Athletic Hall of Fame," 17 January 2011, http://www.depaulbluedemons.com/sports/c-track/spec-rel/011711aaa.html, accessed 14 May 2014.

108. Isaacson, "Finally on the Right Track."

109. James Lampkins, telephone interview by author, Chicago, Illinois, 29 July 2002.

110. Phillips interview.

111. St. Elizabeth's senior girls competed in the South Section. In spring of 1939, they played in a playoff match against St. George's (a Slovenian parish in Far Southeast Chicago) at nearby Calumet Park gymnasium; "Girls' Volleyball Playoffs Open Next Sunday Afternoon," *New World,* 21 April 1939; "Playoffs in the C.Y.O. Horseshoe Meet Tomorrow: Lincoln Park is Scene of Event as Finalists Vie for Coveted Divisional Crowns," *New World,* 16 September 1938.

112. Gene Kent, "First Annual Meet Finals Near: District Playoffs to Be Held at Wells and Jackson Parks Tomorrow," *New World,* 29 April 1938; "Await Divisional Playoffs of C.Y.O. Marble Tourney," *New World,* 22 April 1938; Gene Kent, "Marble Meet Finis at Grant Park Tomorrow: Four Finalists Vie for Title of Colorful First Annual Marble Tournament," *New World,* 6 May 1938; "First Annual C.Y.O. Marble Tourney," *New World,* 11 March 1938.

113. "'People's Bishop' Has a Silver Jubilee: Chicago Gives Its Beloved 'Benny' Sheil a Well-Earned Celebration," *Life,* 18 May 1953, 63.

114. "Keen Competition Features Checker Finals at the C.Y.O.," *New World,* 3 February 1939.

115. Jack Elder, "Swimming, Volleyball and Table Tennis to the Fore in C.Y.O. Program," *New World,* 15 March 1935.

116. St. Anselm's Willa Gant won the female singles title against a girl from St. Hyacinth's—a Polish American parish in the Avondale neighborhood on the Northwest Side. Gant and Dunnings won women's doubles against a pair from St. Hyacinth's. Gant and James Green from St. Anselm won the mixed doubles against a pair from St. Theodore's—a parish in the West Englewood neighborhood; "Bartolini, Gant Snare Individual Honors of Table Tennis Meet," *New World,* 17 March 1939.

117. See Jeff Wiltse, *Contested Waters: A Social History of Swimming Pools in America* (Chapel Hill: University of North Carolina Press, 2007).

118. For example, blacks in Marion, Indiana, traveled thirty miles to swim until

a federal district court desegregated the town's public pool in the summer of 1954;
James H. Madison, *A Lynching in the Heartland: Race and Memory in America* (New
York: Palgrave, 2001), 130–38.

119. "St. Viator Takes C.Y.O. Swimming Championship," *New World*, 1 May 1936.

120. "C.Y.O. Swimming Meet Entries Being Accepted," *New World*, 8 April 1938.

121. Davis interview.

122. "CYO Open Swim Meet Slated for Aug. 12–13: Mermaids Set to Splash," *New
World*, 11 August 1950.

123. In 1966, white mobs confronted Martin Luther King, Jr., when he led marches
in the Gage Park neighborhood, 55th Street and Western Avenue. Only 2 of Gage Park's
28,244 residents were African American, and 62 percent of the residents were Catholic
(according to a 1952 survey), making it the "most heavily Catholic neighborhood in the
city." McGreevy, *Parish Boundaries*, 187–88.

124. "12-Year-Old Marilyn Stars in Swim Meet: Lake Shore Wins Title," *New
World*, 18 August 1950.

125. Wilfred Smith, "C.Y.O. Boxers Defeat Irish, Six Bouts to Four: Retain Perfect
7 Year Record Before 30,000," *Chicago Tribune*, 15 July 1938.

126. *New World*, 22 July 1938.

127. Phillips interview.

128. For example, the St. Elizabeth's high school basketball teams of the early 1950s
traveled to Mt. Carmel, Leo, Weber, Holy Trinity, St. Patrick's, St. George's, St. Rita's,
St. Mel's, and St. Ignatius; Phillips interview.

129. There are numerous examples of interracial competition in both black and
white neighborhoods. In the 1932 district championships, Harry Booker faced a boxer
from St. Anthony's (24th and Canal streets in the South Loop) at the CYO gymnasium in
the downtown Loop; *New World*, 4 November 1932, 10. In November 1935, two St. Anselm athletes (175-pound Paul Bracke and heavyweight Jules Bracke) boxed in the gymnasium at St. Bernard's, 65th Street and Harvard Avenue in the white Hamilton Park
neighborhood; *New World*, 15 November 1935, 10. In June 1937, three Corpus Christi
boxers fought in the auditorium of Sacred Heart, a Jesuit parish in Pilsen; "Review of
C.Y.O. Boxing in Recent Weeks," *New World*, 4 June 1937. In one week during January
1937, boxing shows were held on Monday at St. George's Catholic high school in north
suburban Evanston, on Tuesday at St. Pius parish in Pilsen, and on Wednesday at Corpus
Christi in Bronzeville; "C.Y.O. Boxers Face Busy Month," *New World*, 8 January 1937.

130. Phillips interview; Stephen L. Carter, Sr., interview by author, Chicago, Illinois, 11 July 2001.

131. Campbell Gibson and Kay Jung, *Historical Census Statistics On Population
Totals By Race, 1790 to 1990, and By Hispanic Origin, 1970 to 1990, For Large Cities
And Other Urban Places In The United States*, Popular Division Working Paper No. 76,
February (Washington, DC: U.S. Census Bureau, 2005), Table 14, http://www.census
.gov/population/www/documentation/twps0076/ILtab.pdf, accessed 14 May 2014.

132. "The primary 'race' problem for American Catholics before the 1940s," writes
John McGreevy, "was the physical and cultural integration of the various Euro-
American groups into parishes and neighborhoods of the urban North, not conflicts
between 'blacks' and 'whites.'" McGreevy, *Parish Boundaries*, 9.

133. Box 4263, "CYO History and Information" folder, CYO Papers, Archdiocese of Chicago's Joseph Cardinal Bernardin Archives and Records Center.

134. "'Hail the Victors!' C.Y.O. Presents 1938 Crop of Champs," *New World*, 6 January 1939.

135. Frank Mastro, "Nine St. Francis Boxers Fight Way to C.Y.O. Final," *Chicago Tribune*, 1 December 1948.

136. Ibid.; "South Boxers Beat North in C.Y.O. Finals," *Chicago Tribune*, 10 December 1948.

137. "Roman Catholics: Winning the Kingdom of God," *Time*, 26 September 1969, 63.

138. This phrase is taken from the CYO pledge; Treat, *Bishop Sheil and the CYO*, 70–71.

139. "Club of Champions Award Given to 6 by Bishop Sheil," *New World*, 31 May 1940.

140. Leo, "Looking 'Em Over," *New World*, 1 May 1936.

141. See chap. 2, note 50.

142. "This Week in Black History: Ralph Metcalfe: October 10, 1978," *Jet*, 10 October 1994, 29.

143. "Metcalfe, Sprint Star, Olympic Hope, Baptized Catholic," *New World*, 24 June 1932; "Metcalfe at Marquette," *New World*, 9 September 1932; "Colored College Man Elected," *New World*, 12 May 1933; "Ralph Metcalfe: Hopes for National Championship Here," *New World*, 16 June 1933; "Metcalfe Out for Law," *New World*, 22 September 1933; "Metcalfe Honored for Oratory," *New World*, 2 February 1934; "Metcalfe to Defend Title," *New World*, 20 April 1934; "Metcalfe Returns," *New World*, 1 February 1935; "Metcalfe Starts Summer Training," *New World*, 10 May 1935. Paul Robeson (1898–1976) was an exceptional African American student and athlete at Rutgers University where he became a member of Phi Beta Kappa and earned All-American football honors, serving as valedictorian for the Class of 1919. He then studied law at Columbia University while playing in the National Football League. A talented singer and actor, he was a part of the Harlem Renaissance of the 1920s and became a civil rights activist in the 1930s. During the late 1940s and 1950s he became a victim of McCarthyism. On Robeson, see Martin Duberman, *Paul Robeson: A Biography* (New York: New Press, 1995); Jordan Goodman, *Paul Robeson: A Watched Man* (London: Verso, 2013).

144. "C.Y.O. Track and Field Meet: Metcalfe to Run in Invitational Hundred," *New World*, 29 July 1932; Jack Elder, "St. Brenda's Boys Declared Winners in Sunday's Track Meet," *New World*, 26 August 1932.

145. "Sign of Cross Made by Athlete, Winner of Olympic Race: Metcalfe, American Star, Received Communion Before Victory," *New World*, 28 August 1936.

146. William J. Grimshaw, *Bitter Fruit: Black Politics and the Chicago Machine, 1931–1991* (Chicago: University of Chicago Press, 1992), 118.

147. Honorable John H. Stroger, Jr., interview by author, Chicago, Illinois, 8 April 2002.

148. "National Negro Title Goes to St. Elizabeth," *New World*, 31 March 1950.

149. Jason Bertrand, interview by author, Chicago, Illinois, 4 November 2000. Bertrand served as an administrative consultant of Vicariates III and IV for the Archdiocese

of Chicago and chief financial officer for Speedy Redi-Mix. Speedy was a minority-owned firm that received a profitable contract from Mayor Richard M. Daley's admin-istration in 2003. Bertrand's brother, Julian, was the company's vice president; "Native Son," *Catholic New World*, 1–7 October 2000, 19; Gary Washburn, "City Funds Firm, Gives It Big Pact: Minority Company to Get $3 Million More than Low Bid," *Chicago Tribune*, 20 May 2003; Washburn, "Daley Says Minority Pact Was Good Deal," *Chicago Tribune*, 22 May 2003.

150. Saffold interview; Barbara Sherlock, "Beer Company Exec, Coach Was Inspi-rational to Many: Eugene Saffold, 86," *Chicago Tribune*, 19 December 2003; Bridget Doyle, "Gene Saffold, 1955–2012: Investment Banker, Former Chicago Financial Chief Under Mayor Daley," *Chicago Tribune*, 11 October 2012. Other black Catholic suc-cess stories included the newscaster Warner Saunders of Chicago's NBC affiliate, who graduated from Corpus Christi in 1953 and attended Xavier University in New Orleans on a basketball scholarship, and Mitchell Ware, founder of the largest minority-owned law firm in the United States and Cook County judge. Ware was a standout athlete at St. Elizabeth High School who attended St. Ambrose College in Davenport, Iowa, and DePaul University's school of law in Chicago.

151. Elliott J. Gorn and Michael Oriard argue that sports are essential to under-standing twentieth-century African American history and culture; Gorn and Oriard, "Taking Sports Seriously," *Chronicle of Higher Education* 41.28 (1995): A52. A grow-ing body of scholarship over the past thirty years has examined the intersection of sports and race in U.S. history. For examples, see Gerald L. Early, *A Level Playing Field: African American Athletes and the Republic of Sports* (Cambridge, MA: Harvard Uni-versity Press, 2011); Erenberg, *The Greatest Fight of Our Generation*; Gerald R. Gems, *Windy City Wars: Labor, Leisure, and Sport in the Making of Chicago* (Lanham, MD: Scarecrow, 1997); Gorn and Warren Goldstein, *A Brief History of American Sports*, 2nd ed. (Urbana: University of Illinois Press, 2013); Gorn, *The Manly Art: Bare-Knuckle Prize Fighting in America* (Ithaca, NY: Cornell University Press, 1986); Gorn, ed., *Mu-hammad Ali: The People's Champ* (Urbana: University of Illinois Press, 1995); Steven A. Riess, *City Games: The Evolution of American Urban Society and the Rise of Sports* (Urbana: University of Illinois Press, 1991); Theresa Runstedtler, *Jack Johnson, Rebel Sojourner: Boxing in the Shadow of the Global Color Line* (Berkeley: University of Cali-fornia Press, 2012); Sammons, *Beyond the Ring*.

152. Bertrand, Carter, Davis, Lampkins, Leaner, Phillips, Saffold, Saunders, Wil-liams, and Woodford interviews.

153. St. Clair Drake and Horace Cayton, *Black Metropolis: A Study of Negro Life in a Northern City*, vol. 1 (New York: Harcourt, Brace & World, 1970), 123.

154. Sheil, "Speech to Negro Press Association," 14 October 1943.

CHAPTER FIVE

1. George Phillips, interview by author, Chicago, Illinois, 8 August 2001.

2. "Historical Survey of the Catholic Youth Organization," 1943, p. 7, box 11, folder 9, Edward Victor Cardinal Papers (hereafter, CCRD), University of Notre Dame Archives, Notre Dame, Indiana (hereafter, UNDA).

3. Catholic Youth Organization's Application for Membership in the Council of Social Agencies of Chicago, 22 August 1938, box 257, folder 3, Welfare Council of Metropolitan Chicago Papers (hereafter, WCMC), Chicago History Museum (hereafter, CHM). At the time of application, the CYO network included the following institutions: Mission of Our Lady of Mercy and Big Brothers of the Holy Name Society, 1140 West Jackson Boulevard; Catholic Youth Organization Homes, 2944 South Michigan Avenue; Lewis Holy Name School of Aeronautics, Lockport, Illinois; West Side Community Center, 1145 West Vernon Park Place; and the CYO Center, 31 East Congress Street. The Welfare Council accepted the CYO into membership in 1939; Wilfred S. Reynolds, Director of the Welfare Council of Metropolitan Chicago, to William Campbell, 20 April 1939, box 257, folder 3, WCMC, CHM.

4. See nos. 151, 151A, and 151B of *A Catechism of Christian Doctrine, No. 2*, rev. ed. of the Baltimore Catechism (Peterson, NJ: St. Anthony Guild Press, 1941).

5. Bishop Sheil received the first annual Msgr. John A. Ryan Award in 1945. The Committee of Catholics for Human Rights recognized him as "the Catholic clergyman who has contributed the most to the defense of human rights and furtherance of interracial amity"; "Religious News Notes," *Chicago Tribune*, 3 November 1945.

6. Gary Gerstle, *Working-Class Americanism: The Politics of Labor in a Textile City, 1914–1960* (Princeton, NJ: Princeton University Press, 2002), 247–48.

7. David J. O'Brien, *American Catholics and Social Reform: The New Deal Years* (New York: Oxford University Press, 1968), 40, 79.

8. Gerstle, *Working-Class Americanism*, 248.

9. "The Summer School of Catholic Action—1943, Stunts and Games Without Music," box 1, folder 2, Catholic Council on Working Life Papers (hereafter, CCWL), CHM.

10. Two of Hillenbrand's most important students were Daniel M. Cantwell and John J. "Jack" Egan. On Catholic Social Action in Chicago during the 1930s and 1940s, see Steven M. Avella, "Reynold Hillenbrand and Chicago Catholicism," *U.S. Catholic Historian* 9.4 (fall 1990): 353–70; Avella, "Hillenbrand and His Disciples," chap. 5 in *This Confident Church: Leadership and Life in Chicago, 1940–1965* (Notre Dame, IN: University of Notre Dame Press, 1992), 151–86; John Hill, "Reynold Hillenbrand: Priestly Rabble Rouser, Obedient Son of the Church," *Commonweal*, March 10, 2000, 15–19; Karen Joy Johnson, "The Universal Church in the Segregated City: Doing Catholic Interracialism in Chicago, 1915–1963" (PhD diss., University of Illinois at Chicago, 2013), chaps. 3–8; Edward R. Kantowicz, "Varieties of Catholic Action," chap. 13 in *Corporation Sole: Cardinal Mundelein and Chicago Catholicism* (Notre Dame, IN: University of Notre Dame Press, 1983), 189–202; Albert Schorsch III, "'Uncommon Women and Others': Memoirs and Lessons from Radical Catholics at Friendship House," *U.S. Catholic Historian* 9.4 (fall 1990): 371–86; Robert L. Tuzik, *Reynold Hillenbrand: The Reform of the Catholic Liturgy and the Call to Social Action* (Chicago: Hillenbrand/ Liturgy Training, 2010); Mary Irene Zotti, "The Young Christian Workers," *U.S. Catholic Historian* 9.4 (fall 1990): 387–400; Zotti, *A Time of Awakening: The Young Christian Worker Story in the United States, 1938 to 1970* (Chicago: Loyola University Press, 1991).

11. "Solving the Youth Problem in the Chicago Archdiocese," *Catholic Action: Official Organ of the National Catholic Welfare Conference* 16.2 (February 1934): 4. In

1938, the CYO Juvenile Delinquency Service served 11,459 youngsters; 10,007 of those did not have to go to court. The CYO also received referrals from the Chicago Police Department. Between September 1, 1940 and August 31, 1941, the CYO received 1,300 referrals from the police; "Juvenile Delinquency Prevention Service," 1943, box 257, folder 3, WCMC, CHM.

12. Ruth S. Kerr, "See Federal Housing as Aid to Colored Poor," *New World*, 5 November 1937.

13. The eight resolutions included treating African Americans courteously, giving to charities that served blacks, and including African Americans in the Mystical Body of Christ; "Catholic Action for the Negro," *America*, 10 June 1933, 221.

14. "Social Justice and Peace Are Debated: Consider Racial Justice and Avoidance of War," *New World*, 3 June 1938.

15. After graduating from Chicago's Mundelein Seminary in 1949, Rollins E. Lambert became the first African American ordained to the priesthood by the Archdiocese of Chicago.

16. For more on Catholic interracialism in Chicago, see Johnson, "The Universal Church in the Segregated City."

17. John T. McGreevy, *Parish Boundaries: The Catholic Encounter with Race in the Twentieth-Century Urban North* (Chicago: University of Chicago Press, 1996), 44.

18. "Catholic Leaders Urge 'Organized Social Justice,'" *New World*, 6 December 1935.

19. Sheil first used the phrase in a 1936 speech, "Problems of Youth," in Washington, DC; Bernard J. Sheil, "Problems of Youth," *Catholic Mind* (22 September 1936): 368.

20. On the history of Catholic Charities in the United States, see Dorothy M. Brown and Elizabeth McKeown, *The Poor Belong to Us: Catholic Charities and American Welfare* (Cambridge, MA: Harvard University Press, 1997). On women's leadership in the U.S. Catholic Church during the Progressive Era, see Kathleen Sprows Cummings, *New Women of the Old Faith: Gender and American Catholicism in the Progressive Era* (Chapel Hill: University of North Carolina Press, 2009).

21. On middle-class ideologies in professional social work, see Daniel J. Walkowitz, *Social Workers and the Politics of Middle-Class Identity* (Chapel Hill: University of North Carolina Press, 1999).

22. Sheil reorganized the program in December 1945. It was renamed Sheil Guidance Service in August 1948; Joseph Charles Vlasak, Jr., "A Statistical Study of One Hundred Cases Known to the Sheil Guidance Service, Social Service Department, Catholic Youth Organization, Chicago, Illinois, and Closed During the Period, July, 1949, to January, 1952" (MSW thesis, Loyola University Chicago, 1952), 5–6.

23. The Chicago Area Project was an affiliation of neighborhood-based community groups founded in 1932 by Clifford Shaw, a sociologist trained at the University of Chicago.

24. "West Side Community Center," 20–21, 24 January 1954, box 257, folder 3, WCMC, CHM; "New C.Y.O. Project," *New World*, 10 June 1938. The building at 1145 West Vernon Park Place was demolished to make way for post–World War II urban renewal. The property is now part of the campus of the University of Illinois at Chicago.

25. "Bishop Sheil Will Bless West Side C.Y.O. Center Nov. 9," *New World*, 3 November 1939.

26. "West Side Center," box 257, folder 3, WCMC, CHM.

27. Ernest Giovangelo, telephone interview by author, 11 February 2002.

28. O'Brien, *American Catholics and Social Reform*, 39.

29. "New Director at C.Y.O.," clipping from unnamed newspaper, box 257, folder 3, WCMC, CHM.

30. The staff included two students from the American College of Physical Education, one student from the School of the Art Institute of Chicago, and Florence Giovangelo Scala, Ernie's sister, who taught theater using techniques she learned while a member of the WPA Federal Theater Project; Giovangelo interview. In the late 1950s and early 1960s, Florence Scala led neighborhood opposition to urban renewal on the Near West Side, specifically, the construction of a campus of the University of Illinois. On Scala, see Carolyn Eastwood, *Near West Side Stories: Struggles for Community in Chicago's Maxwell Street Neighborhood* (Chicago: Lake Claremont, 2002), chaps. 5 and 6, 119–200.

31. Dora B. Somerville, "A Study of the Juvenile Delinquency Prevention Service of the Social Service Department: Catholic Youth Organization, Chicago, Illinois" (MSW thesis, Loyola University Chicago, 1947), 36.

32. Ibid., 46.

33. Mary Jo Carroll, Paul Kalinauskas, and George E. Ryan, "An Analysis of the Cases Known to the Juvenile Delinquency Prevention Service, Catholic Youth Organization, Chicago, December 1945 to June 1947" (MSW thesis, Loyola University Chicago, 1949), 24, 25.

34. Between 1945 and 1947, the Social Service Department served seven individuals from St. Anselm, two from Corpus Christi, one from St. Elizabeth, and two from St. James's; ibid., 70–72.

35. Robert E. Burns interview by Steven Avella, tape recording, Montello, Wisconsin, 4 January 1988, box 1, tape 1, Rev. Steven Avella Oral History Project, Archdiocese of Chicago's Joseph Cardinal Bernardin Archives and Records Center (hereafter, AAC).

36. Quotation from Giovangelo interview.

37. Dora Somerville, interview by Steven Avella, tape recording, Chicago, Illinois, 11 March 1989, box 4, Rev. Steven Avella Oral History Project, AAC; "Dora B. Somerville Named Director of C.Y.O. Social Work," *Chicago Tribune*, 18 August 1948. Somerville left the CYO in 1950 to pursue Chicago and Illinois government positions. Somerville's two master's theses were: Dora B. Somerville, "A Study of a Group of Negro Children Living in An Alley Culture" (MSW thesis, Catholic University of America, 1940); Somerville, "A Study of the Juvenile Delinquency Prevention Service."

38. "Summary of Statistics: Sheil Guidance Service, August 1, 1952–July 31, 1953," box 257, folder 3, WCMC, CHM.

39. Somerville interview. After leaving the CYO, Somerville went on to a successful career in rehabilitative social work. She was the first woman named to the Illinois Parole and Pardon Board in 1969, and became a program executive with the Illinois Department of Corrections in 1971.

40. Burns interview.

41. Avella, *This Confident Church*, 130–32; 134.

42. On the social/economic rise of Irish Americans, see Jay P. Dolan, *The Irish Americans: A History* (New York: Bloomsbury, 2008), and *The American Catholic Experience: A History from Colonial Times to the Present* (Notre Dame, IN: University of Notre Dame Press, 1985), 147–48.

43. This phenomenon dates to the antebellum period, when Irish immigrants felt threatened by the prospect of free black labor. Nevertheless, some Irish Americans in the antebellum period expressed sympathy for African American slaves. For example, see Frederick Douglass, "The Two Irishmen on the Wharf," in *My Bondage and My Freedom* (New York: Arno, 1968), 169–70.

44. Rev. James M. Gillis, CSP, "Sursum Corda . . . What's Right with the World: Waking Up to the Negro Problem," *New World*, 13 May 1938.

45. Bernard J. Sheil, "A Bishop Looks at Race Bias," *Negro Digest*, November 1942, 59.

46. Bernard J. Sheil, "If I Were a Negro: Eyes on the Future," *Negro Digest*, February 1943, back cover and inside back cover. The article was also partially reprinted in a national news magazine; "To the Negro," *Time*, 22 February 1943, 48.

47. Mark B. Sorvillo, "Bishop Bernard J. Sheil: Hero of the Catholic Left" (PhD diss., University of Chicago, 1990), 275, 277.

48. Zack J. Weston, "Bishop Sheil, Mrs. Bethune Presented Abbott Awards," *Chicago Defender*, 23 May 1953.

49. Lizabeth Cohen, *Making a New Deal: Industrial Workers in Chicago, 1919–1939* (New York: Cambridge University Press, 1990).

50. O'Brien, *American Catholics and Social Reform*, 14.

51. On African American Communists, see Robin D. G. Kelley, *Hammer and Hoe: Alabama Communists during the Great Depression* (Chapel Hill: University of North Carolina Press, 1990); Wilson Record, *The Negro and the Communist Party* (New York: Atheneum, 1971).

52. On 25 March 1931, nine African American teenage males, along with two white teenage females, were arrested near Scottsboro, Alabama, for stealing a ride on a freight train and getting into an altercation with some white hoboes. The two white girls accused the black boys of rape, and angry mobs began to call for the boys' executions. A three-day trial in an obviously unsympathetic courtroom found all nine youths guilty, sentencing eight of them to death. The IDF took the case to the U.S. Supreme Court, which overturned the verdict. On the Scottsboro case, see Dan T. Carter, *Scottsboro: A Tragedy of the American South* (Baton Rouge: Louisiana State University Press, 1969); James Goodman, *Stories of Scottsboro* (New York: Pantheon, 1994).

53. Advertisement for Catholic Action lectures at Chicago's Holy Name Cathedral, *New World*, 1 April 1938.

54. Thomas Gavin, "Five Years of *Work*," p. 6, unpublished paper, Medill School of Journalism, Northwestern University, 1948, box 2, CCWL, CHM.

55. "Proposals for Policies to be Adopted By the CLA," 28 November 1944, box 1, folder 3; "A Tentative Statement of Policy," 18 February 1945, box 1, folder 1, CCWL, CHM.

56. Robert Lasch, "Bishop in the Stockyards: Sheil of Chicago Runs a Cartel—of Charitable, Social-Service, Educational, Pro-Labor Enterprises," *Reporter* 1.6 (5 July 1949): 27.

57. Avella, *This Confident Church*, 124, 368n34.

58. Arvah E. Strickland, *History of the Chicago Urban League* (Urbana: University of Illinois Press, 1966), 144–45, 168.

59. Comments by Charles R. Swibel, Chairman, Chicago Housing Authority Board of Commissioners, board meeting, p. 2, 8 June 1972, box 38, folder 2, Daniel Cantwell Papers, CHM.

60. John LaFarge, SJ, to John L. Yancey, 4 April 1945, LaFarge correspondence, Rev./ John LaFarge, SJ Papers, Georgetown University Special Collections and Research Center, Washington, DC.

61. Leon Despres, interview by author, 27 February 2003, Chicago, Illinois. Despres (1908–2009), who represented the Hyde Park neighborhood on the Chicago City Council from 1955 to 1975, was a Democrat who operated independently of Richard J. Daley's political machine; Leon M. Despres with Kenan Heise, *Challenging the Daley Machine: A Chicago Alderman's Memoir* (Evanston, IL: Northwestern University Press, 2005).

62. Yancey served on the boards of the National Catholic Council of Interracial Justice, Lewis College (founded by Sheil), and Roosevelt University. He also sat on the Illinois Commission of Human Relations; Swibel, Chicago Housing Authority Board of Commissioners, board meeting, pp. 1–2, 8 June 1972.

63. "CHA to Dedicate Community Center," *Chicago Daily News*, 8 June 1972.

64. Bernard J. Sheil, "Racism," 24 June 1943, box 2, folder "Undated Speeches," Bishop Bernard J. Sheil Papers, CHM; copy of speech also in box 1, folder 36, Bishop Bernard J. Sheil Papers, AAC (original emphasis).

65. "Statement of Bishop Bernard J. Sheil read by Rev. William Gordon, OSA, Economics Department, Catholic University [of America], before U.S. House of Representatives sub-committee on Education and Labor," 9 July 1947, box 1, folder "Speeches 1947–49," Bishop Bernard J. Sheil Papers, CHM; "Statement of the Most Reverend Bernard J. Sheil, D.D., Senior Auxiliary Bishop of Chicago and Chairman of the National Emergency meeting on Jobs and Security: Session on Economic Problems," Washington, DC, December 7, 1945, box 1, folder "Speeches 1944–46," Sheil Papers, CHM.

66. Burns interview.

67. Saul Alinsky, "Prelate of the People," *Progressive* 15.6 (1 June 1951): 10.

68. Youngsters from the Jewish People's Institute competed with CYO boxers; "Boxing Each Wednesday Night at CYO Center," *New World*, 27 January 1933. CYO and BBYO basketball all stars met annually from 1937 to the early 1950s; Mike Murphy, "C.Y.O.-Jewish All-Star Cagers Meet Wednesday: Dream Teams of Youth Groups Mix at Lane Tech," *New World*, 29 March 1940; *The C.Y.O Voice* 3.2 (February–March 1946), Box 136, Folder 11, Reynold Hillenbrand Printed Materials (hereafter, PMRH), UNDA; "History Lesson," *Chicago Tribune*, 27 March 1992.

69. "Dedication of the St. Charles' C.Y.O. Center, October 9: Bishop Sheil to Officiate; Mayor Kelly and Other Civic Leaders to Attend," *New World*, 6 October 1933.

70. "Jew Baiters," *New World*, 23 September 1932.

71. "Catholic Protests," *New World*, 3 December 1938.

72. O'Brien, *American Catholics and Social Reform*, 62. On Coughlin, see Alan Brinkley, *Voices of Protest: Huey Long, Father Coughlin and the Great Depression* (New York: Vintage, 1982); Marcus Sheldon, *Father Coughlin: The Tumultuous Life of the Priest of the Little Flower* (Boston: Little, Brown, 1973); Donald I. Warren, *Radio Priest: Charles Coughlin, The Father of Hate Radio* (New York: Free, 1996); Ronald H. Carpenter, *Father Charles E. Coughlin: Surrogate Spokesman for the Dispossessed* (Westport, CT: Greenwood, 1998).

73. Eric Norden, "Saul Alinsky: A Candid Conversation with the Feisty Radical Organizer," *Playboy*, March 1972, 72. Sheil and Mundelein were not alone among Catholics who worked against anti-Semitism and supported Jewish causes. In 1935, the Roman Catholic former governor of New York and two-time presidential candidate Al Smith raised money for the United Jewish appeal to assist persecuted Jews in Nazi Germany and Eastern Europe; "Alfred E. Smith Joins in Jewish Aid Appeal," *New World*, 10 May 1935. Locally, members of Chicago's Catholic Worker house formed a committee against anti-Semitism; "Committee to Combat Anti-Semitism to be Formed Here July 23," *New World*, 21 July 1939; "Chicagoans Join to Combat Anti-Semitism Here: Initial Meeting of Chicago Committee of Catholics to Fight Anti-Semitism Held Sunday," *New World*, 28 July 1939.

74. O'Brien, *American Catholics and Social Reform*, 62.

75. "Cardinal Issues Stern Rebuke to Father Coughlin: He Doesn't Speak for the Church, Says Mundelein," *Chicago Tribune*, 12 December 1938; "Mundelein Denies Views of Coughlin Represent Church," *New York Times*, 12 December 1938.

76. Bernard J. Sheil, speech at Temple Shalom, Chicago, Illinois, 21 October 1942, box 1, folder "Speeches 1931–43," Bishop Bernard J. Sheil Papers, CHM.

77. Mundelein said of Hitler that he was an "Austrian paperhanger, and a poor one at that, I am told." See Kantowicz, "Varieties of Catholic Action," 224–27; "Mundelein Rips into Hitler for Church Attacks: Accuses Nazis of Plot to Secularize Children," *Chicago Tribune*, 19 May 1937; "Germany: Holy War," *Time*, 31 May 1937, 23.

78. "Mundelein Quoted for Arms Ban End: Bishop Sheil Delivers Radio Address Approved by the Cardinal Before His Death," *New York Times*, 3 October 1939; see also Avella, *This Confident Church*, 28.

79. "U.S. Jewish Group Gets Pope's Thanks: United Appeal's Donation for Catholic Refugees Called an Example of Good-Will," *New York Times*, 3 March 1940; "Interfaith Plea Asks United Refugee Aid: Protestants, Catholics and Jews Enlisted in War Relief Drives," 10 March 1947.

80. Jewish stockbroker Barnet Rosset donated the land for the Sheil Center. Burns interview; Avella, *This Confident Church*, 133.

81. Burns interview.

82. "Year in Palestine for Pastors Urged," *New York Times*, 9 June 1947.

83. "B'nai B'rith Honors Bishop," *New York Times*, 13 July 1951.

84. Brown v. Board of Education of Topeka 347 U.S. 483 (1954); Sheil, speech to B'nai B'rith, Chicago, 10 July 1951, box 1, folder "Speeches 1950–59," Bishop Bernard J. Sheil Papers, CHM.

85. "C.Y.O. Boxers in Benefit at Statesville, Ill., April 16," *New World*, 15 April 1932.

86. Somerville, "A Study of the Juvenile Delinquency Prevention Service of the Social Service Department," 12.

87. Harold L. Ickes, *The Secret Diary of Harold L. Ickes: Volume III The Lowering Clouds, 1939–1941* (New York: Simon and Schuster, 1954), 63; "Roman Catholics," *Time*, 26 September 1969, 63.

88. O'Brien, *American Catholics and Social Reform*, 86, 89.

89. Bernard J. Sheil, "A World a Man Can Live In," speech at the Social Science Forum, Siena College, Loudonville, NY, 15 June 1945, box 158, folder 7, Ann Harrigan Makletzoff Papers (hereafter, CMAK), UNDA.

90. Mary Braggiotti, "Fascists Hate This Man," *New York Post*, 23 November 1945.

91. Sheil, "Racism." In the summer of 1943, race riots took place in Baltimore; Beaumont, Texas; Detroit; Indianapolis; New York City; Los Angeles; Mobile, Alabama, Philadelphia; St. Louis; and Washington, DC.

92. On the Double V campaign, see Beth Bailey and David Farber, "The 'Double-V' Campaign in World War II Hawaii: African-Americans, Racial Ideology, and Federal Power," *Journal of Social History* 26.4 (1993): 817–43; Lee Finkle, "The Conservative Aims of Militant Rhetoric: Black Protest During World War II," *Journal of American History* 60.3 (1973): 692–713; Joyce Thomas, "The 'Double V' Was for Victory: Black Soldiers, the Black Protest, and World War II" (PhD diss., Ohio State University, 1993); Kevin Mumford, "Double V in New Jersey: African American Civic Culture and Rising Consciousness Against Jim Crow, 1938–1966," *New Jersey History* 119.3–4 (2001): 22–56; Byron R. Skinner, "The Double 'V': The Impact of World War II on Black America" (PhD diss., University of California, Berkeley, 1979).

93. "Bishop Sheil Urges Rights for Negroes: He Tells Conference That Discrimination Should Stop," *New York Times*, 29 September 1942.

94. Bernard J. Sheil, "The American Society," speech at Xavier University, Cincinnati, 8 April 1945, box 158, folder 7, PMRH, UNDA. See also Bernard J. Sheil, "What Are We Fighting For?" box 1, folder "Speeches 1931–43," Bishop Bernard J. Sheil Papers, CHM.

95. Sheil, "A World a Man Can Live In."

96. See Antonio Gramsci, *The Prison Notebooks* (New York: Columbia University Press, 2011). I thank Gerald Gems for suggesting this characterization of Sheil.

97. Burns interview.

98. Bernard J. Sheil, "The Bishop Writes: The Crisis of Today," *Novena Notes*, 25 June 1943, 3.

99. Lasch, "Bishop in the Stockyards," 26; Sheil, "The American Society."

100. Sheil, "Delinquency and Racial Minority Groups."

101. "Catherine Doherty, 85, Benefactor of the Poor," *Chicago Tribune*, 18 December 1985. For more on Friendship House, see Catherine de Hueck, *Friendship House Staff Workers* (New York: Friendship House, 1945) and *The Story of Friendship House* (New York: Blessed Martin Guild, 1939); Catherine de Hueck Doherty, *Fragments of My Life* (Notre Dame, IN: Ave Maria, 1979) and *Friendship House* (New York: Sheed and Ward, 1947); Lorene Hanley Duquinn, *They Called Her the Baroness: The Life of Catherine de Hueck Doherty* (Staten Island, NY: Alba House, 2000); Ann Harrigan,

"Invading the South Side: A Friendship House Comes to Chicago," *Commonweal*, 19 May 1944, 106–8; Johnson, "The Universal Church in the Segregated City"; Ann Harrigan Makletzoff, "Friendship House—40 Years After," unpublished paper, c. 1978, box 1, folder 5, Nina Polcyn Moore Papers, UNDA; Maryellen Muckenhirn, "Forty-Third Street Summer," *Chimes*, Fall 1944, 22–24, box 3, folder 27, CMAK, UNDA; "The Sheil Era," unpublished paper, box 3, folder 20, CMAK, UNDA; Schorsch, "'Uncommon Women and Others'"; Elizabeth Louise Sharum, "A Strange Fire Burning: A History of the Friendship House Movement" (PhD diss., Texas Tech University, 1977); Betty Schneider, interview by Steven Avella, St. Francis Seminary, Wisconsin, 12 February 1988, Rev. Steven Avella Oral History Project, AAC; Ellen Tarry, *The Third Door: The Autobiography of an American Negro Woman* (Tuscaloosa: University of Alabama Press, 1992), 127–212.

102. "Friendship House Opening Colorful Event," *Pittsburgh Courier*, 14 November 1942.

103. Harrigan, "Invading the South Side," 108.

104. See, for example, Edward Doherty, "The Bishop and the Wolves: A Heart-Warming True Story of Drama and a Death House That Gave Rise to a Stirring Adventure in Human Salvage," *Liberty*, 26 March 1938, 18–20.

105. Schorsch, "'Uncommon Women and Others,'" 378.

106. "Jail Chaplain Russell L. Marshall, 94," *Chicago Tribune*, 7 October 1999.

107. Eugene Saffold, interview by author, 8 November 2001; Treat, *Bishop Sheil and the CYO: The Story of the Catholic Youth Organization and the Man Who Influenced a Generation of Americans* (New York: Messner, 1951), 138.

108. Saffold interview.

109. "Sheil House Day Nursery," 29–31, January 1954, box 257, folder 3, WCMC, CHM; Treat, *Bishop Sheil and the CYO*, 135.

110. Treat, *Bishop Sheil and the CYO*, 136. Other staff members included Myrtle Wilson and basketball coach Clarence Cash; Phillips interview.

111. "Sheil House Day Nursery," 30.

112. "Catholic Youth Organization," 3, 25, January 1954, box 257, folder 3, WCMC, CHM.

113. On the St. Louis University controversy, see Philip Gleason, *Contending with Modernity: Catholic Higher Education in the Twentieth Century* (New York: Oxford University Press, 1995), 235–40. Dunne's uncle, Rev. Daniel J. Riordan, founded St. Elizabeth parish. Dunne lived in China as a missionary, received a doctorate in international relations from the University of Chicago, and served on the faculties of Georgetown University, Loyola Marymount University, St. Louis University, and Santa Clara University; George H. Dunne, *King's Pawn: The Memoirs of George H. Dunne, S.J.* (Chicago: Loyola Press, 1990).

114. George H. Dunne, "The Sin of Segregation: The Immorality of Racial Segregation," *Commonweal*, 21 September 1945, 542–45.

115. Philip Gleason, "The Erosion of Racism in Catholic Colleges in the 40's," *America*, 18 November 1995, 15.

116. Eric Pace, "George Dunne, 92, Priest and Ecumenist, Dies," *New York Times*, 14 July 1998.

117. Sheil School Bulletins, 1948, box 8, folder 6, CCRD, UNDA.

118. Mundelein College was one institution that hosted the play. Dunne and Sheil shared mutual admiration; the Jesuit even ghostwrote the bishop's speeches for a short time; Dunne, *King's Pawn*, 177–81.

119. On the Federal Arts Projects, see Rena Fraden, *Blueprints for a Black Federal Theatre, 1935–1939* (New York: Cambridge University Press, 1994); Glenda Eloise Gill, *White Grease Paint On Black Performers: A Study of the Federal Theatre of 1935–1939* (New York: P. Lang, 1988); Jerrold Hirsch, *Portrait of America: A Cultural History of the Federal Writers' Project* (Chapel Hill: University of North Carolina Press, 2003); Barbara Melosh, *Engendering Culture: Manhood and Womanhood in New Deal Public Art and Theater* (Washington, DC: Smithsonian Institution, 1991); Paul Sporn, *Against Itself: The Federal Theater and Writers' Projects in the Midwest* (Detroit: Wayne State University Press, 1995).

120. Curtis Lawrence, "Visionary Artists Brush Up the City," *Chicago Sun-Times*, 1 November 1999.

121. On Burroughs, see "Alumna Returns to St. Elizabeth," *New World*, 29 January 1993; Karen Schwartz, "Margaret Burroughs: 'When You Have Something You Want to Do, People Here Encourage You,'" *Chicago Tribune Sunday Magazine*, 11 October 1992, 6; William Grimes, "Margaret T. Burroughs, Archivist of Black History, Dies at 95," *New York Times*, 28 November 2010. On the South Side Community Art Center, see Bill V. Mullen, *Popular Fronts: Chicago and African American Cultural Politics, 1935–46* (Urbana: University of Illinois, 1999), 75–105.

122. Mullen, *Popular Fronts*, 101, 104. On Flory, see Tara Deering, "Ishmael Flory, 96: Communist Party Candidate for Governor and Senator," *Chicago Tribune*, 12 February 2004.

123. Catholic "labor schools" opened in cities across the country during the 1930s and 1940s; Colin J. Davis, "'Launch Out Into the Deep and Let Down Your Nets': Father John Corridan, S.J., and New York Longshoremen in the Post-World War II Era," *Catholic Historical Review* 86.1 (2000): 66–84; Joseph M. McShane, "Faith Seeking Justice: The Xavier Labor School of New York, 1936–1988," *Mid-America* 73.3 (1991): 243–72, and "'The Church is Not for the Cells and the Caves': The Working Spirituality of the Jesuit Labor Priests," *U.S. Catholic Historian* 9.3 (summer 1990): 289–304.

124. Sheil School Bulletins, 1943, box 8, folder, 1, CCRD, UNDA.

125. Annual Reports of the CYO Education Department, box 9, folder 10, CCRD, UNDA.

126. Sheil School Bulletins, 1943 and 1944, box 8, folders 1 and 2, CCRD, UNDA.

127. Sheil School Bulletins, 1945 and 1948, box 8, folders 3 and 6, CCRD, UNDA; Burns interview.

128. Extension classes were held at 2944 South Michigan Avenue; Sheil School Bulletins, 1947, box 8, folder 5, CCRD, UNDA. Dora Somerville's sister ran the South Side extension.

129. Annual Reports for Education Department, CYO, box 9, folder 9, CCRD, UNDA.

130. James O'Gara, "Chicago's 'Catholic Times Square,'" *America*, 28 January 1950, 492–95.

131. James Terrence Sparrow, "Fighting over the American Soldier: Moral Economy and National Citizenship in World War II" (PhD diss., Brown University, 2002), 21; see also James T. Sparrow, *Warfare State: World War II Americans and the Age of Big Government* (New York: Oxford University Press, 2011).

132. Sheil School Bulletin, 1945, box 8, folder 3, CCRD, UNDA.

133. Sheil School Bulletins, 1943 and 1944, box 8, folders 1 and 2, CCRD, UNDA.

134. On McKay, see Claude McKay, *A Long Way From Home* (New York: Arno, 1969); Wayne F. Cooper, *Claude McKay: Rebel Sojourner in the Harlem Renaissance, A Biography* (Baton Rouge: Louisiana State University Press, 1987); Cooper, *The Passion of Claude McKay: Selected Poetry and Prose, 1912–1948* (New York: Schocken, 1973); Winston James, *A Fierce Hatred of Injustice: Claude McKay's Jamaica and His Poetry of Rebellion* (London: Verso, 2001); Tyrone Tillery, *Claude McKay: A Black Poet's Struggle for Identity* (Amherst: University of Massachusetts Press, 1992).

135. McKay explains his conversion in "Right Turn to Catholicism," an unpublished typed manuscript, 1946, Schomburg Center for Research in Black Culture, New York Public Library. I thank Winston James for providing me with a photocopy of the manuscript.

136. Burns interview.

137. Tillery, *Claude McKay*, 182–83.

138. Ed Marciniak, interview by author, 11 April 2000; Cooper, *Rebel Sojourner*, 356–61; Burns interview. McKay died in Chicago at the age of fifty-seven on 22 May 1948, in Alexian Brothers Hospital; Cooper, *Rebel Sojourner*, 368.

139. Sheil House Bulletins, 1943 and 1945, box 8, folders 1 and 3, CCRD, UNDA.

140. Kantowicz, "Varieties of Catholic Action," 173–88.

141. "Moral Awakening Urged for Youth: Catholic Charities Speaker at Seattle Says Child Is Victim of 'Crazy-Quilt Civilization,'" *New York Times*, 4 August 1936; Frank S. Adams, "Thousands Worship in Mass for Youth: Capes and Caps of Children of Louisiana Enrich Gathering at Eucharistic Congress," *New York Times*, 20 October 1938; "Mundelein Quoted for Arms Ban End: Bishop Sheil Delivers Radio Address Approved by the Cardinal Before His Death," *New York Times*, 3 October 1939; "Vatican Paper Stresses Embargo Repeal Stand," *New York Times*, 5 October 1939; "The Press: Surprise," *Time*, 27 February 1939, 48; "National Affairs: Labor, Meat, and a Bishop," *Time*, 24 July 1939, 12.

142. "Vatican Newspaper Praises C.Y.O.," *New World*, 11 November 1938.

143. Samuel A. Stritch was born in Nashville, Tennessee, in 1887 (a year after Sheil). He received a PhD at the age of nineteen, became Bishop of Toledo, Ohio, at the age of thirty-four, and was consecrated archbishop of Milwaukee in 1930; "Milestones in a Great Career," *New World*, 12 January 1940. Stritch and Sheil were ordained on the same day in 1910; "Double Anniversary Day for Archbishop and Bishop," *New World*, 17 May 1940.

144. Mary Elizabeth Carroll, "Bishop Sheil: Prophet without Honor," *Harper's Magazine*, November 1955, 50.

145. Avella, *This Confident Church*, 112–14. In the summer of 1935, Sheil organized a meeting of 107 priests from 27 dioceses at the University of Notre Dame. They met to form a plan for the unification of Catholic youth organizations around the country;

"Plan to Unify C.Y.O. Work," *New World*, 19 July 1935; "Youth Leaders Map Program," *New World*, 26 July 1935. Again, in hopes of creating a national CYO program, the First Annual National Conference of C.Y.O. Leaders met in Chicago in 1938; Ralph C. Leo, "C.Y.O. Leaders Meet Here May 17–18: Scores of American and Canadian Delegates at Important Conference," *New World*, 13 May 1938. The group met again the next year in Cincinnati; "Bishop Sheil, Wm. J. Campbell to Speak at C.Y.O. Conference," *New World*, 8 September 1939.

146. The CYO public relations department aggressively promoted the Sheil brand. In the winter of 1936, *Chicago American* feature writer Charles E. Blake wrote "The Story of the CYO" in a series of articles over the course of three weeks; *Chicago American*, 27 January 1936. In August and September 1939, a ten-part series on the CYO aired on station WAAF; *New World*, 4, 18, 25 August and 8, 22 September 1939. Chicagoans also heard Sheil's story on WGN radio in 1946; "Birth of CYO is Described in Chicago Story: Young Priest Gets Idea at Execution," *Chicago Tribune*, 22 March 1946. Five years later, sportswriter Roger Treat published an expanded version of the legend; Treat, *Bishop Sheil and the CYO*.

147. For example, *Newsweek* learned "authoritatively" in 1946 that Sheil would be named Archbishop of St. Louis; "Religion: Labor's Bishop," *Newsweek*, 15 July 1946, 82. Steven Avella wrote that Sheil's "reckless jousting" with James Francis McIntyre, Cardinal Francis Spellman's auxiliary bishop of New York, "probably closed the doors to higher appointments in the Church"; Avella, *This Confident Church*, 141. Avella discovered evidence that Cardinal Stritch recommended to the Vatican that Sheil not be promoted and given his own diocese (ibid., 366–67n7). Sheil's assistant secretary at St. Andrew's from 1957 to 1966 said that Sheil's supporters continued to expect him to get his own archdiocese even into the 1950s; Anne Lyons, interview by author, Chicago, Illinois, 16 August 2000.

148. Bernard J. Sheil, "Restrictive Covenants vs. Brotherhood," 11 May 1946, speech to Chicago Council Against Racial Discrimination, box 158, folder 7, Monsignor Hillenbrand Papers, UNDA.

149. Shelley v. Kraemer 334 U.S. 1 (1948) deemed racially restrictive covenants unenforceable. On 26 July 1948, President Harry Truman signed Executive Order 9981 desegregating the U.S. armed forces.

150. Sorvillo, "Bishop Bernard J. Sheil," 236.

151. "Extend Rights of Labor, Sheil Tells Parley: Talks at Convention of Stage Workers," *Chicago Tribune*, 23 July 1946.

152. Hal Foust, "Aid of Hitler Questioned in Jail by Sheil," *Chicago Tribune*, 15 February 1946.

153. In 1951, Stritch did confront Sheil about excessive spending on a palatial addition to the rectory as well as repairs to the school and gymnasium at St. Andrew's parish where Sheil was pastor; Avella, *This Confident Church*, 138.

154. In May 1949, the CYO began broadcasting on the FM dial under the call letters WFJL (named for Catholic philanthropist and Sheil supporter Frank J. Lewis); Treat, *Bishop Sheil and the CYO*, 159; "New Design for Radio: WFJL-FM, Bishop Sheil Toast 167-Day 'Dream,'" *New World*, 4 November 1949. Sheil had a longtime interest in the media and entertainment. One of the first CYO programs outside of athletics was an

entertainment service; "Plan to Supply Programs for Catholic Events: Catholic Youth Organization to Open an Entertainment Service," *New World*, 30 January 1931. Two years later, the CYO began broadcasting a half-hour program on station WIBO; "Bishop Sheil Gives First Address Over C.Y.O. Radio Hour," *New World*, 17 February 1933. In 1936, the CYO began running a radio talent agency for youth, and the Balaban and Katz theater chain agreed to book CYO talent on its stages; "C.Y.O. to Sponsor Radio Talent Contest: First Auditions Jan. 28, 29 at Illinois Club for C.W.," 17 January 1936, *New World*; Leo, "Stage and Screen Await Radio Contest Winners: Balaban & Katz Theatres to Coöperate with C.Y.O.," 31 January 1936.

155. "Sheil Medal to Stritch: Chicago Cardinal Is Honored for 'Social Education,'" *New York Times*, 31 December 1949; "On Bishop Sheil," *Commonweal*, 3 March 1950, 558; Avella, *This Confident Church*, 123–24.

156. Frank Mastro, "North Beats South, 13–3, in C.Y.O. Boxing Final," *Chicago Tribune*, 25 October 1950.

157. Programs included the West Side Community Center and the Sheil House on the South Side; the Sheil School of Social Studies, which enrolled more than sixteen hundred adult students; a dental department serving six thousand children annually; a hundred-piece concert band; a literacy program evaluating the reading skills of more than seven thousand children annually; a Boy Scout program serving twelve thousand; a summer camp in Libertyville, Illinois; forty-eight summer vacation centers in city parks and parishes; a public relations department with four full-time staff members, a comprehensive social service program for Chicago's growing Puerto Rican population, a home for teenage boys on the Near West Side, and a psychiatric counseling service for emotionally disturbed children. Steven Avella writes that by 1954, the CYO included six departments employing ninety-five fulltime staffers; Avella, *This Confident Church*, 368n40.

158. The 1948 budget was $445,380; "Budget Comparison-Catholic Youth Organization," 1949, box 11, folder 1, CCRD, UNDA. The 1953 budget was $701,060; "Budget Comparison-Catholic Youth Organization," January 1954, box 257, folder 3, WCMC, CHM. Examples of Sheil's spendthrift approach included founding a university focused on international trade, finance, languages, business administration, and secretarial studies on Michigan Avenue in the Loop in 1947 and buying a polo pony farm in northwest suburban Chicago in 1953; "Full University Charter Given Sheil School," *Chicago Tribune*, 24 August 1950; Irene Power, "Bishop Sheil to Dedicate Polo Club," *Chicago Tribune*, 13 June 1953.

159. David Condon, "In the Wake of the News," *Chicago Tribune*, 15 September 1969.

160. "Bishop Sheil of Chicago Ill," *New York Times*, 9 November 1951; "Bishop Sheil Recovering," *New York Times*, 15 November 1951; Avella, *This Confident Church*, 141; Carroll, "Bishop Sheil," 51; Sorvillo, "Bishop Bernard J. Sheil," 398.

161. Carroll, "Bishop Sheil," 51.

162. "Statement of the Most Rev. Bernard J. Sheil, D.D. at the Conference on Pending Labor Legislation, Senate Office Building, Washington, DC, May 12, 1947"; "Address delivered by the Most Reverend Bernard J. Sheil, D.D. Auxiliary Bishop of Chicago, Over the American Broadcasting Company network, June 5, 1947"; "Address

given by the Most Reverend Bernard J. Sheil, D.D. on the Taft-Hartley Bill, in Madison Square Garden, 1947," box 1, folder "Speeches 1947–1949," Bishop Bernard J. Sheil Papers, CHM; "Statement of the Most Reverend Bernard J. Sheil, D.D., Senior Auxiliary Bishop of Chicago and Chairman for a Fair Minimum Wage. Delivered to the National Emergency Meeting on Jobs and Security: Session on Economic Problems, Washington, DC, December 7, 1945," box 1, folder "Speeches 1944–1946," CHM.

163. "Text of broadcast delivered by news commentator Upton Close on the Mutual Broadcasting System station KHJ, Los Angeles, attacking Bishop Sheil, August 27, 1946"; "Bishop Bernard J. Sheil's reply to Upton Close given over the Mutual Broadcasting System, September 3, 1946"; copy of telegram from Upton Close received by Sheil on September 3, 1946, 9:00 AM," box 1, folder "Speeches 1944–1946," Bishop Bernard J. Sheil Papers, CHM. Close was responding to a speech Sheil gave the American Veterans Committee in Des Moines in June 1946; Robert L. Tyler, "The American Veterans Committee," *American Quarterly* 18.3 (Autumn 1966): 423–24.

164. Sorvillo, "Bishop Bernard J. Sheil," 248.

165. Chronology of CYO participation in the Council of Social Agencies, p. 5, box 257, folder 3, WCMC, CHM.

166. "Bishop Sheil on McCarthy," (Detroit: UAW-CIO Education Department), Box 68, Folder 55, PMRH.

167. "For Joe: Phooey!" *Time*, 19 April 1954, 22–23; Foster Hailey, "A Catholic Bishop Berates M'Carthy: Sheil, in Chicago Talk, Calls Him 'Ineffective' Anti-Red Who Divides Country," *New York Times*, 10 April 1954; "Bishop Sheil Raps M'Carthy in Talk to UAW," *Chicago Tribune*, 10 April 1954. Edward R. Murrow produced a small film of Sheil's speech, which was aired on CBS television; "Murrow Rejects M'Carthy Lecture," *New York Times*, 14 April 1954. For more on Spellman's support of McCarthy, see John Cooney, *The American Pope: The Life and Times of Francis Cardinal Spellman* (New York: Times, 1984), 220–21.

168. "Reaction Mixed on Sheil Address: Wire Comments on His Attack on McCarthy Favorable—Legion Condemns Him," *New York Times*, 11 April 1954.

169. "Priest Defends M'Carthy Against Sheil: Calls Chicago Bishop's Views Uncharitable," *Chicago Tribune*, 12 April 1954.

170. Bernard J. Sheil, "Should a Clergyman Stay Out of Politics? Out of Partisan Politics, Yes; But on Moral Issues in Public Life, He Sometimes '*Must* Speak Out,'" *Look*, 10 August 1954, 66–69.

171. Carroll, "Bishop Sheil," 45, 51.

172. Roy M. Fisher, "Here's Why Sheil Quit the CYO: Church Politics, Health Involved; McCarthy Attack Not a Factor," *Chicago Daily News*, 24 January 1955 [reprinted as "Silent Bishop Sheil Sees Works Topple," *Washington Post*, 6 February 1955]. For an account of the day that Sheil unexpectedly announced his retirement, see Avella, *This Confident Church*, 109–10.

173. Avella, *This Confident Church*, 148.

174. Hollis Vick of the Welfare Council of Metropolitan Chicago reported in the summer of 1955, "The CYO program had gone through a process of decentralization to the parish level"; Chronology beginning "August to December, 1938," box 257, folder 3, WCMC, CHM.

175. Avella, *This Confident Church*, 146.

176. Letter from Robert H. MacRaye, Director of Welfare Council of Metropolitan Chicago, to Msgr. Edward J. Kelly, Director of the Catholic Youth Organization, 18 October 1955, box 257, folder 3, WCMC, CHM.

177. Leo, "Catholic Youth League to Centralize Athletics," *New World*, 14 November 1930.

178. Lyons interview.

179. When business leader Joe Kellman founded the Better Boys Foundation (BBF) in 1961 to fight juvenile delinquency in his native Lawndale neighborhood, he looked to Sheil for assistance. Sheil became honorary president of the BBF; Condon, "In the Wake of the News."

180. By the 1960s, for example, Sheil no longer administered the sacrament of Confirmation regularly, as was the expectation for auxiliary bishops; Richard Philbrick, "Sheil, 80, Is Replaced by New Pastor," *Chicago Tribune*, 10 May 1966. Sheil was invited to participate in the Second Vatican Council but failed to show; Avella, "Sheil, Bernard James (1886–1969)," in *The Encyclopedia of the Irish in America*, ed. Michael Glazier (Notre Dame, IN: University of Notre Dame Press, 1999), 857.

181. Avella, *This Confident Church*, 147.

182. "I got some fan mail all right," recalled Cody wryly; Wayne Thomas, "Controversy is No Stranger to Cardinal Cody: Cody's Efforts Draw Papal Praise, Laymen's Criticism," *Chicago Tribune*, 9 July 1967. The cardinal originally wished for Sheil to retain the title of pastor but hand over the daily operations of the parish to another priest. However, when an angry Sheil announced the private agreement to the press—"I didn't retire or anything else like that. This is a removal, and I want that made clear"— Cody withdrew his offer and named Sheil "pastor emeritus"; Philbrick, "Sheil, 80, Is Replaced by New Pastor."

183. Carroll, "Bishop Sheil," 50.

CHAPTER SIX

1. Edmund J. Rooney, "High, Lowly Mourn Sheil," *Chicago Daily News*, 16 September 1969. Many non-Catholics attended Sheil's funeral, where "the voices of his fellow priests were joined by those of Jews, Protestants, and possibly nonbelievers in singing the liturgy of the mass"; Patricia Krizmis, "Bishop Sheil Laid to Rest; Many Mourn: Church Leaders from All Faiths at Rites," *Chicago Tribune*, 18 September 1969.

2. "Chicago 'Apostle of Youth,' Archbishop Sheil, Mourned," *New World*, 19 September 1969. Arvey was Chicago's powerful Twenty-Fourth Ward alderman (1923–1941), Democratic committeeman (1934–1941), Cook County Democratic Committee chairman (1946–1950), and Chicago Park District commissioner (1945–1967). A Davis Park supervisor of recreation (1932–1937), Meegan sponsored CYO summer vacation schools and cofounded the Back of the Yards Neighborhood Council with Saul Alinsky. The NAACP awarded Lawless, a millionaire dermatologist and businessman from the South Side, its prestigious Spingarn Medal in 1954 for groundbreaking medical research and philanthropy.

3. On the same day Sheil's body lay in repose at St. Andrew's, for example, George

Clements, a black Catholic priest, held a press conference at St. Columbanus Church on the South Side. Clements charged white police officers with an unjust, racially motivated arrest of an African American police officer; John D. Vasilopulos, "Arrest Afro Police Leader; Charge 'Frame,'" *Chicago Daily Defender*, 16 September 1969.

4. Rooney, "High, Lowly, Mourn Sheil"; Wilfrid Smith, "20,000 See 16 C.Y.O. Champions Crowned: Kainrath Keeps Title Before Record Throng: John Noto Regains Championship" *Chicago Tribune*, 3 December 1936; Treat, *Bishop Sheil and the CYO: The Story of the Catholic Youth Organization and the Man Who Influenced a Generation of Americans* (New York: Messner, 1951), 136.

5. During his lifetime, Sheil was also known as the "Boys' Bishop" and "Labor's Bishop"; Edward R. Kantowicz, *Corporation Sole: Cardinal Mundelein and Chicago Catholicism* (Notre Dame, IN: University of Notre Dame Press, 1983), 174; "Labor's Bishop," *Newsweek* 15 July 1946, 28.

6. "Archbishop Sheil's Impact," *Chicago Daily News*, 16 September 1969.

7. "Arch Bishop [sic] Sheil, 'Apostle of Youth,'" *Chicago Defender*, 26 September 1969.

8. Carter Horsley, "Archbishop Bernard Sheil of Chicago Dies at 83; Controversial Prelate Was Outspoken Liberal; Founded the Catholic Youth Organization in 1930: 'Apostle of Youth,'" *New York Times*, 14 September 1969.

9. James H. Bowman, "'At Times, He Touched the Stars': In His Stormy Days as CYO Founder, 'Benny' Sheil Was Formidable Foe of McCarthyism and Bigotry," *Chicago Daily News*, 17 September 1969.

10. John T. McGreevy, *Parish Boundaries: The Catholic Encounter with Race in the Twentieth-Century Urban North* (Chicago: University of Chicago Press, 1996), 232.

11. Arnold Hirsch, "The Race Space Race," *Journal of Urban History* 26.4 (May 2000): 528.

12. Bernard J. Sheil, "Public and Private Charity," undated, box 2, folder 2, Bishop Bernard J. Sheil Papers, Chicago History Museum.

13. My conceptualization of open spaces has been influenced by Jürgen Habermas's analysis of civic discourse in *The Structural Transformation of the Public Sphere: An Inquiry into a Category of Bourgeois Society* (Cambridge, MA: MIT Press, 1991). In addition, Kevin Mumford's work on illicit urban settings where young white men sought out encounters with African American women are examples of different kinds of open spaces; Mumford, *Interzones: Black/White Sex Districts in Chicago and New York in the Early Twentieth Century* (New York: Columbia University Press, 1997).

14. Arnold Hirsch, *Making the Second Ghetto: Race and Housing in Chicago, 1940–1960* (Chicago: University of Chicago Press, 1998), 6.

15. "Mayor Denies 'Riot' Charge of FHA Chief," *Chicago Tribune*, 30 October 1954.

16. James W. Sanders, *The Education of an Urban Minority: Catholics in Chicago, 1833–1965* (New York: Oxford University Press, 1977), 219.

17. Alan Brinkley, *The End of Reform: New Deal Liberalism in Recession and War* (New York: Knopf, 1995); Eric Foner, *The Story of American Freedom* (New York: W. W. Norton, 1998), 249–273; Elaine Tyler May, *Homeward Bound: American Families in the Cold War Era* (New York: Basic, 1988). For a discussion of how these changes manifested themselves in Catholics leaving cities for the suburbs, see Andrew M. Greeley,

The Church and the Suburbs (New York: Sheed & Ward, 1959). Recent scholarship by Lila Corwin Berman complicates the narrative of postwar conservatism, white flight, and suburbanization going hand in hand. She demonstrates that most of Detroit's Jewish population remained politically liberal—including on issues of race—even as they engaged in white flight during the mid-twentieth century. See Berman, *Metropolitan Jews: Politics, Race, and Religion in Postwar Detroit* (Chicago: University of Chicago Press, 2015).

18. Kenneth T. Jackson, *Crabgrass Frontier: The Suburbanization of the United States* (New York: Oxford University Press, 1985).

19. *A Biography of the Most Reverend Bernard J. Sheil, DD, Auxiliary Bishop of Chicago, Founder of the Chicago Catholic Youth Organization*, February 1947, box 4, folder 20, Bishop Bernard J. Sheil Papers, Archdiocese of Chicago's Joseph Cardinal Bernardin Archives and Records Center.

20. For example, a deaf and blind nineteen-year-old from Bronzeville received a CYO guide dog in 1939; "Happiest Girl," *New World*, 13 January 1939; "Girl Aided by Students, C.Y.O. Can 'See' Now: 5,000 Pupils Help Bishop Sheil to Secure 'Master Eye' Dog for Blind Girl," *New World*, 20 January 1939; "Honor Bishop Sheil," *New World*, 9 June 1939.

21. "Education Urged for Handicapped," *New York Times*, 4 November 1947.

22. See Steven M. Avella, *This Confident Church: Catholic Leadership and Life in Chicago, 1940–1965* (Notre Dame, IN: University of Notre Dame Press, 1992), 134–39; Avella, "The Rise and Fall of Bernard Sheil," *Critic* 44.3 (spring 1990): 2–18.

23. Ira Katznelson, *City Trenches: Urban Politics and the Patterning of Class in the U.S.* (New York: Pantheon, 1981), 6.

24. Cathleen Falsani, "You Can't Play with Them: Black Catholic Grammar School Denied Membership in White League," *Chicago Sun-Times*, 31 May 2001. Auburn-Gresham was 98.4 percent African American in 2000; City of Chicago, Department of Planning and Development, Community Area 2000 Census Profile, http://www .cityofchicago.org/content/dam/city/depts/zlup/Zoning_Main_Page/Publications/ Census_2000_Community_Area_Profiles/PDF_71.pdf, accessed 14 May, 2014.

25. Allison Hantschel and Stephanie Gehring, "St. Sabina Raises Claims of Racism," *Daily Southtown*, 1 June 2001.

26. This account of events leading up to 31 May comes from the pastor of St. Denis Parish and SCC chaplain, Rev. Larry Dowling; Dowling, "The Lesson of St. Sabina," *Chicago Tribune*, 8 July 2001.

27. Cathleen Falsani, "Black School Can't Join Sports League," *Chicago Sun-Times*, 31 May 2001.

28. Don Terry, "Chicago Neighborhood Reveals an Ugly Side: Black Youth Badly Beaten in Bridgeport," *New York Times*, 27 March 1997.

29. Francis Cardinal George, O.M.I., *Dwell in My Love: A Pastoral Letter on Racism* (Chicago: Archdiocese of Chicago, 2001), 10.

30. Eileen M. McMahon, *What Parish Are You From? A Chicago Irish Community and Race Relations* (Lexington: University Press of Kentucky, 1995), 167.

31. On Pfleger, see Robert McClory, *Radical Disciple: Father Pfleger, St. Sabina Church, and the Fight for Social Justice* (Chicago: Chicago Review, 2010).

32. Alice Hohl and Allison Hantschel, "In Sight of St. Sabina," *Daily Southtown*, 3 June 2001; "Let St. Sabina's Kids Play," editorial, *Chicago Tribune*, 5 June 2001.

33. Allison Hantschel, "Hardliners Harden Foes: Some Parents are Upset That 'They're Making Such a Racial Issue Out of' Schools' Conflict," *Daily Southtown*, 29 July 2001.

34. Julia Lieblich, "2nd Sabina Vote Urged," *Chicago Tribune*, 6 June 2001; Cathleen Falsani, "St. Sabina's Athletes May Get to Play After All," *Chicago Sun-Times*, 6 June 2001; Allison Hantschel, "Resolution Near in St. Sabina Spat: Southside Pastors Have Faith New Ballot Will Admit Black Parish to Youth League," *Daily Southtown*, 6 June 2001; "Catholic School League Slates 2nd Vote on Sabina," *Chicago Tribune*, 8 June 2001; Falsani, "Catholic Schools to Vote Again," *Chicago Sun-Times*, 8 June 2001; Hantschel, "Conference Meeting Prompts Future Talks," *Daily Southtown*, 8 June 2001.

35. Francis George, "Corpus Christi: The Parish, the Feast and the Doctrine," *Catholic New World*, 24 June 2001. Ironically, a bitterly racist scene took place years later at Cardinal George's boyhood parish of St. Pascal's. On Palm Sunday in 1983, a vitriolic crowd of white Catholics cursed and spat at African American mayoral candidate Harold Washington as he visited St. Pascal's; Nathaniel Sheppard, Jr., "Mayoral Candidate Faces Angry Crowd At Chicago Church," *New York Times*, 28 March 1983.

36. Susan Kuczka, "George is Confident St. Sabina Will Play," *Chicago Tribune*, 18 June 2001.

37. Julia Lieblich, "This Time Door Opens to Sabina: No Dissenters in 2nd Vote by Catholic Schools," *Chicago Tribune*, 21 June 2001; Cathleen Falsani, "Sabina's Kids Get Back in the Game," *Chicago Sun-Times*, 21 June 2001; Allison Hantschel, "Conference Votes 21–0 to Let St. Sabina Play: Decision Overturns Vote After Allegations of Racism," *Daily Southtown*, 21 June 2001.

38. Bob Gorman, "Coach Says His Team Won't Play at St. Sabina," letter to the editor, *Daily Southtown*, 21 June 2001; Lieblich, "This Time Door Opens to Sabina."

39. Julia Lieblich and Karen Rivedal, "Sabina Pulls Out of Sports League," *Chicago Tribune*, 20 July 2001; Cathleen Falsani, "St. Sabina Kids Won't Play Ball," *Chicago Sun-Times*, 20 July 2001; Allison Hantschel and Alice Hohl, "St. Sabina Pulling Out of Athletic Conference: Pfleger Statement 'Shocks' League Officials Who Had Hoped for Accord," *Daily Southtown*, 20 July 2001.

40. Cathleen Falsani, "Bigots Jump into Sabina Fray," *Chicago Sun-Times*, 24 July 2001; Allison Hantschel, "White Supremacy Group Passes Out Fliers Against St. Sabina," *Daily Southtown*, 24 July 2001.

41. Other African American leaders assembled included Rev. Clay Evans of Fellowship Baptist Church, State Rep. Mary Flowers (D-Chicago), Rev. Walter Johnson of Near North Ministers Alliance, State Rep. Charles Morrow III (D-Chicago), Rev. Tyrone Crider of New Faith Baptist Church in south suburban Matteson, Leonard Muhammad, a representative of Minister Louis Farrakhan's Nation of Islam, and Rev. Walter Turner of the Baptist Ministers Conference of Chicago; Art Golab, "Pfleger Draws Key Support," *Chicago Sun-Times*, 25 July 2001.

42. Julia Lieblich, "Cardinal Backs Sabina: Parish's Demands for Athletic League Called Legitimate," *Chicago Tribune*, 26 July 2001; Janet Rausa Fuller, "Cardinal

Stands by St. Sabina," *Chicago Sun-Times*, 26 July 2001; Allison Hantschel, "'We Seek Redemption': Jackson, Ministers Meet at St. Sabina; Cardinal Endorses Parish's Demands," *Daily Southtown*, 26 July 2001; "St. Sabina-Southside Conference Talks Succeed," *Catholic New World*, 5 August 2001.

43. Julia Lieblich, "Sabina, League Reach Accord," *Chicago Tribune*, 2 August 2001; Annie Sweenie, "St. Sabina, Conference Reach Deal," *Chicago Sun-Times*, 2 August 2001; Allison Hantschel, "Sabina Compromise Cast," *Daily Southtown*, 2 August 2001.

44. Julia Lieblich, "St. Sabina to Remain in Sports Conference," *Chicago Tribune*, 10 August 2001; Allison Hantschel, "Sports, Prayers and Prejudice—SCC OKs New Rules: St. Sabina Claims Deceit and Balks at Forfeit Policy," *Daily Southtown*, 10 August 2001.

45. Julia Lieblich and Donna Freedman, "For St. Sabina, League, Games Are Small Victory," *Chicago Tribune*, 2 December 2001.

46. Southside Catholic Conference, http://www.MyTeam.com/go/scc, accessed 11 March 2002.

47. Julia Deardorff and Karen Rivedal, "St. Sabina Pulls Out of League: Parish Accuses Officials of 'Lack of Integrity,'" *Chicago Tribune*, 10 March 2002; Cathleen Falsani, "St. Sabina Quits League, Cites Clashes," *Chicago Sun-Times*, 10 March 2002; Allison Hantschel, "St. Sabina Quits On Athletic Conference: On Eve of the Basketball Playoffs, Church Decides Its Kids Won't Play Anymore," *Daily Southtown*, 9 March 2002.

48. John W. Fountain, "Team Leaves White Leagues in Silence Instead of Cheers," *New York Times*, 11 March 2002.

49. "St. Sabina Plays," *Catholic New World*, 14–28 September 2002.

50. "America in Black & White: Kids and Sports," *Nightline*, ABC, 6 May 2002, transcript, Burrelle's Information Services. For an account of the St. Sabina/SCC controversy, see Robert McClory, *Radical Disciple: Father Pfleger, St. Sabina Church, and the Fight for Social Justice* (Chicago: Chicago Review, 2010), 107–20. When former athletic directors Christopher Mallette (St. Sabina) and Tom Fitzgerald (SCC member St. Linus in Oak Lawn) met in 2012 for the first time since the controversy, they felt a sense of regret and loss about missed opportunities for Catholic interracial youth athletics; Chip Mitchell, "A Decade On, Coaches Try to Bridge Racial Divide: Their 2001 Encounter on a South Side Youth Basketball Court Added to Tensions that Had an African American Team Leaving a Mostly White League," WBEZ 91.5, Chicago Public Radio, http://www.wbez.org/series/race-out-loud/decade-coaches-try-bridge-racial-divide-101330, accessed 14 May 2014.

51. Martin Luther King, Jr., *Strength to Love* (New York: Harper & Row, 1963), 47.

52. Julia Lieblich, "For Kids, Sabina Vote a No-brainer: Blacks and Whites Who Play Together Say that Catholic Conference Should Accept School," *Chicago Tribune*, 19 June 2001.

BIBLIOGRAPHY

ARCHIVAL COLLECTIONS

Archdiocese of Chicago's Joseph Cardinal Bernardin Archives and Records Center,
    Chicago, Illinois
    Bishop Bernard J. Sheil Papers
    Catholic Youth Organization Papers
    George Cardinal Mundelein Personal Papers
    Madaj Collection
    New World Photographs Collection
    Parish Files
    Rev. Steven Avella Oral History Project
    Rev. Marty Zielinski Oral History Project/Clergy Exhibit
    Samuel Cardinal Stritch Personal Papers
Corpus Christi Church Archives, Chicago, Illinois
Chicago History Museum, Chicago, Illinois
    Bishop Bernard J. Sheil Papers
    Catholic Council on Working Life Papers
    Claude A. Barnett Papers
    Daniel Cantwell Papers
    Welfare Council of Metropolitan Chicago Papers
Chicago Park District Special Collections, Chicago, Illinois
Chicago Public Library, Special Collections and Preservation Division, Harold
    Washington Library Center, Chicago, Illinois
    Chicago City-Wide Collection
Georgetown University Special Collections Research Center, Washington, DC
    Rev. John LaFarge, SJ Papers
National Archives, College Park, Maryland
    Moving Images Collection
St. Elizabeth Convent Archives, Chicago, IL
University of Notre Dame Archives, Notre Dame, IN

Ann Harrigan Makletzoff Papers
Edward V. Cardinal Papers
Nina Polcyn Moore Papers
Parish History Collection
Reynold Hillenbrand Papers

INTERVIEWS BY THE AUTHOR

Jason Bertrand, Chicago, Illinois, 4 November 2000
Bob Bigott, taped interview, South Holland, Illinois, 9 March 2000
Timuel Black, Chicago, Illinois, 27 February 2003
Stephen L. Carter, Sr., taped interview, Chicago, Illinois, 11 July 2001
Marie C. Davis taped interview, Chicago, Illinois, 6 July 2001
Leon Despres, Chicago, Illinois, 27 February 2003
Ernest Giovangelo, telephone interview, 11 February 2002
Edwin W. Leaner, III, taped interview, Chicago, Illinois, 27 June 2001
George Phillips, taped interview, Chicago, Illinois, 10 August 2001
James Lampkins, telephone interview, Chicago, Illinois, 29 July 2002
Anne Lyons, taped interview, Chicago, Illinois, 16 August 2000
Ed Marciniak, taped interview, Chicago, Illinois, 11 April 2000
Eugene Saffold, taped interview, Hazel Crest, Illinois, 8 November 2001
Warner Saunders, taped interview, Chicago, Illinois, 24 August 2001
Rita Stalzer, CSJ, Chicago, Illinois, 3 May 2002
Honorable John H. Stroger, Jr., taped interview, Chicago, Illinois, 8 April 2002
James J. Williams, taped interview, Chicago, Illinois, 29 June 2001
John Woodford, taped interview, Chicago, Illinois, 26 April 2002

NEWSPAPERS

Chicago Daily News
Chicago Defender
Chicago Herald-Examiner
Chicago Sun-Times
Chicago Tribune
New World
New York Times
Pittsburgh Courier

JOURNALS AND MAGAZINES

America
Catholic Action
Catholic Digest
The Crisis
Commonweal

Esquire
Extension
Interracial Review
Look
Newsweek
Origins
Negro Digest
The Progressive
Time

SECONDARY SOURCES

Doctoral Dissertations

Applin, Albert G. II. "From Muscular Christianity to the Market Place: The History of Men's and Boys' Basketball in the United States, 1891–1957." PhD diss., University of Massachusetts, 1982.

Bielakowski, Rae, "You Are in the World: Catholic Campus Life at Loyola University Chicago, Mundelein College, and De Paul University, 1924–1950." PhD diss., Loyola University Chicago, 2009.

Carmode, D. Scott. "Faith and Affiliation: An Urban Religious History of Churches and Secular Voluntarism in Chicago's West Town, 1871–1914." PhD diss., Yale University, 1996.

Davis, Nancy Marie. "Integration, the 'New Negro,' and Community Building: Black Catholic Life in Four Catholic Churches in Detroit, 1911–1945." PhD diss., University of Michigan, 1996.

Dorey, Frank. "The Church and Segregation in Washington, DC, and Chicago, Ill.: A Prolegomenon to a Sociological Analysis of the Segregated Church," PhD diss., University of Chicago, 1950.

Frazier, E. Franklin. "The Negro Family in Chicago." PhD diss., University of Chicago, 1931.

Harrington, Henry Randolph. "Muscular Christianity: A Study of the Development of a Victorian Idea." PhD diss., Stanford University, 1971.

Johnson, Karen Joy. "The Universal Church in the Segregated City: Doing Catholic Interracialism in Chicago, 1915–1963." Ph.D. diss., University of Illinois at Chicago, 2013.

Kelliher, Thomas G., Jr. "Hispanic Catholics and the Archdiocese of Chicago, 1923–1970." PhD diss., University of Notre Dame, 1996.

Kerr, Louise Ano Nuevo. "The Chicano Experience in Chicago: 1920–1970." PhD diss., University of Illinois at Chicago, 1976.

McCarthy, Erin A. "Making Men: The Life and Career of Amos Alonzo Stagg, 1862–1933." PhD diss., Loyola University Chicago, 1994.

McCarthy, Joseph J. "History of Black Catholic Education in Chicago, 1871–1971." PhD diss., Loyola University Chicago, 1973.

McCarthy, Malachy R. "Which Christ Came to Chicago: Catholic and Protestant

Programs to Evangelize, Socialize, and Americanize the Mexican Immigrant, 1900–1940." PhD diss., Loyola University Chicago, 2002.

Prentiss, Craig R. "Taming Leviathan: The American Catholic Church and Economics, 1940–1960." PhD diss., University of Chicago, 1997.

Putney, Clifford Wallace. "Muscular Christianity: The Strenuous Mood in American Protestantism, 1880–1920." PhD diss., Brandeis University, 1995.

Rhodes, Helen Kathryn Marie. "An Historical Analysis of the Racial, Community and Religious Forces in the Establishment and Development of St. Monica's Parish Church, 1890–1930." EdD diss., Loyola University Chicago, 1993.

Sharum, Elizabeth Louise. "A Strange Fire Burning: A History of the Friendship House Movement." PhD diss., Texas Tech University, 1977.

Skinner, Byron R. "The Double 'V': The Impact of World War II on Black America." PhD diss., University of California, Berkeley, 1979.

Sorvillo, Mark B. "Bishop Bernard J. Sheil: Hero of the Catholic Left." PhD diss., University of Chicago, 1990.

Sparrow, James Terrence. "Fighting Over the American Soldier: Moral Economy and National Citizenship in World War II." PhD diss., Brown University, 2002.

Thomas, Joyce. "The 'Double V' Was for Victory: Black Soldiers, the Black Protest, and World War II." PhD diss., Ohio State University, 1993.

Wally, Julia Rath. "Faith, Hope, and Education: African-American Parents of Children in Catholic Schools and their Social and Religious Accommodation to Catholicism." PhD diss., University of Chicago, 1999.

Ward, Mary A. "From Mission to Mecca: An African American Catholic Church Redefines Itself." PhD diss., Fordham University, 1998.

MASTER'S THESES

Burns, Alice Mary. "A Study of the Catholic Youth Organization Home for Boys, 2944 South Michigan Avenue, Chicago, Illinois." MSW thesis, Loyola University Chicago, 1935.

Carroll, Mary Jo, Paul Kalinauskas, and George E. Ryan. "An Analysis of the Cases Known to the Juvenile Delinquency Prevention Service, Catholic Youth Organization, Chicago, December 1945 to June 1947." MSW thesis, Loyola University Chicago, 1949.

Debinski, Benjamin Joseph. "A Survey of the Opinions of Thirty-Two Parish Youth Directors of the Archdiocese of Baltimore on the Program of the Archdiocesan Catholic Youth Organization." MSW thesis, Catholic University, 1949.

Dennis, Sister Mary Robert, SBS. "St. Elizabeth's Parish and the Negro." MA thesis, Loyola University Chicago, 1940.

Doherty, James Francis. "A Study of the Catholic Youth Organization in the Twelve Catholic Parishes of Dorchester." MS thesis, Boston University, 1948.

Dougherty, Luke. "Catholic Youth Organization of the Archdiocese of San Francisco in the 1930s." MA thesis, Santa Clara University, 1965.

Gallagher, Raymond J. "A Study of One Hundred Children Known to the Social Service

Department of the Catholic Youth Organization of Chicago, During the First Year of its Operation." MSW thesis, Loyola University Chicago, 1948.

Krawczak, Arthur H. "The Opinions of Twenty-two Directors of the Qualifications for Lay Adult Leaders in the Baltimore Catholic Youth Organization." MSW thesis, Catholic University of America, 1951.

Luckey, Sr. Marie Clare. "Catholic Youth Organization." MA thesis, Marquette University, 1943.

Ly, John P. "A Comparative Study of the Young Men's Christian Association and the Catholic Youth Organization." MA thesis, Loyola University Chicago, 1951.

Marciniak, Ed. "The Racial Attitudes of Students in the Catholic Colleges of the Chicago Area." MA thesis, Loyola University Chicago, 1942.

Meyer, Sr. Mary Edward. "An Evaluation of the Catholic Youth Organization as a Guidance Program in Dayton." MA thesis, University of Dayton, 1943.

Moore, M. Mercedes. "The Social Role of the Catholic Girl Scout Movement: A Study of the Chicago Area." MSIR thesis, Loyola University Chicago, 1954.

Nick, David Harry. "A Comparison of Ratings and Qualifications of Basketball Officials in the Catholic Youth Organization Athletic Program of Johnson and Wyandotte Counties in Kansas." MS thesis, University of Kansas, 1976.

Pembroke, Margaret Mary. "The Vacation Schools of the Catholic Youth Organization of the Archdiocese of Chicago from the Summer of 1939: The History, Development, and Group Work Program of the Vacation Schools with Statistical Analysis of the Registration Cards." MSW thesis, Loyola University Chicago, 1940.

Rice, Eleanor Marie. "A Study of Vocational Guidance for Sodalities in the Catholic Youth Organization of Milwaukee, Wisconsin." MA thesis, Marquette University, 1940.

Sobczyk, Sr. Mary Claire, OSF. "A Survey of Catholic Education for the Negro in Five Parishes in Chicago." MA thesis, De Paul University, 1954.

Somerville, Dora B. "A Study of the Juvenile Delinquency Prevention Service of the Social Service Department, Catholic Youth Organization, Chicago, Illinois." MSW thesis, Loyola University Chicago, 1947.

Vader, Anthony J. "Racial Segregation within Catholic Institutions in Chicago: A Study in Behavior and Attitudes." AM thesis, University of Chicago, 1962.

Vlasak, Joseph Charles. "A Statistical Study of One Hundred Cases Known to the Sheil Guidance Service, Social Service Department, Catholic Youth Organization, Chicago, Illinois, and Closed During the Period, July, 1949 to January, 1952." MSW thesis, Loyola University Chicago, 1952.

BOOKS

Albrandt, Roger S. *Neighborhoods, People, and Community*. New York: Plenum, 1984.

Anderson, R. Bentley. *Black, White, and Catholic: New Orleans Interracialism, 1947–1956*. Nashville, TN: Vanderbilt University Press, 2008.

Appleby, R. Scott, and Kathleen Sprows Cummings, eds. *Catholics in the American*

Century: Recasting Narratives of U.S. History. Ithaca, NY: Cornell University Press, 2012.

Ash, Arthur. *A Hard Road to Glory—Boxing: The African-American Athlete in Boxing.* New York: Amistad/Penguin, 1993.

Avella, Steven M. *This Confident Church: Catholic Leadership and Life in Chicago, 1940–1965.* Notre Dame, IN: University of Notre Dame Press 1992.

Avella, Steven M., and Elizabeth McKeown, eds. *Public Voices: Catholics in the American Context.* Maryknoll, NY: Orbis, 1999.

Baier, Hans A. *African-American Religion in the Twentieth Century: Varieties of Protest and Accommodation.* Knoxville: University of Tennessee Press, 1992.

Bak, Richard. *Joe Louis: The Great Black Hope.* Dallas: Taylor, 1996.

Baker, William J. *Playing with God: Religion and Modern Sport.* Cambridge, MA: Harvard University Press, 2007.

Baldwin, Davarian L. *Chicago's New Negroes: Modernity, the Great Migration, and Black Urban Life.* Chapel Hill: University of North Carolina Press, 2007.

Barrett, James R. *The Irish Way: Becoming American in the Multiethnic City.* New York: Penguin, 2012.

Barrow, Joe Louis, Jr., and Barbara Munder. *Joe Louis: 50 Years an American Hero.* New York: McGraw-Hill, 1988.

Barton, Craig E., ed. *Sites of Memory: Perspectives on Architecture and Race.* New York: Princeton Architectural Press, 2001.

Bazzett, Mary. *The Life of Catherine de Hueck Doherty.* Combermere, ON: Madonna House, 1998.

Berman, Lila Corwin. *Metropolitan Jews: Politics, Race, and Religion in Postwar Detroit.* Chicago: University of Chicago Press, 2015.

Best, Wallace D. *"Passionately Human, No Less Divine": Religion and Culture in Black Chicago, 1915–1952.* Princeton, NJ: Princeton University Press, 2007.

Biondi, Martha. *To Stand and Fight: The Struggle for Civil Rights in Postwar New York City.* Cambridge, MA: Harvard University Press, 2006.

Blatnica, Dorothy Ann, V.S.C. *"At the Altar of Their God": African American Catholics in Cleveland, 1921–1961.* New York: Garland, 1995.

Blum, John Morton. *V Was for Victory: Politics and American Culture During World War II.* New York: Harcourt, Brace, Jovanovich, 1976.

Boyer, Paul. *Urban Masses and Moral Order in America, 1820–1920.* Cambridge, MA: Harvard University Press, 1978.

Brandewie, Ernest. *In the Light of the Word: Divine Word Missionaries of North America.* Maryknoll, NY: Oribs, 2000.

Bray, Rosemary L. *Unafraid of the Dark: A Memoir.* New York: Random House, 1998.

Brewer, Eileen Mary. *Nuns and the Education of American Catholic Women, 1860–1920.* Chicago: Loyola University Press, 1987.

Brinkley, Alan. *The End of Reform: New Deal Liberalism in Recession and War.* New York: Knopf, 1995.

———. *Voices of Protest: Huey Long, Father Coughlin and the Great Depression.* New York: Vintage, 1982.

Brooks, Gwendolyn. *A Street in Bronzeville.* New York: Harper, 1945.

Brown, Dorothy M., and Elizabeth McKeown. *The Poor Belong to Us: Catholic Charities and American Welfare*. Cambridge, MA: Harvard University Press, 1997.

Brown, Joseph A., SJ. *To Stand on the Rock: Meditation on Black Catholic Identity*. Maryknoll, NY: Orbis, 1998.

Brown, Roderick M., OP. *A Gathering at the River: 150 Years of Black Catholic History in the Diocese of Buffalo*. Buffalo: Catholic Diocese of Buffalo, 1997.

Bruns, Roger A. *Preacher: Billy Sunday and Big-Time American Evangelism*. New York: W. W. Norton, 1992.

Bukowski, Douglas. *Big Bill Thompson, Chicago, and the Politics of Image*. Urbana: University of Illinois Press, 1998.

Burns, Jeffrey M., Ellen Skerrett, and Joseph M. White, eds. *Keeping Faith: European and Asian Catholic Immigrants*. Maryknoll, NY: Orbis, 2000.

Butler, Loretta M. *History of Black Catholics in the Archdiocese of Washington, DC, 1634–1898: A Select Bibliography of Works Located in Maryland and Washington, DC Archives and Libraries*. Hyattsville, MD: Washington Archdiocese Pastoral Center, 1984.

Byrne, Julie. *O God of Players: The Story of the Immaculata Mighty Macs*. New York: Columbia University Press, 2003.

Carpenter, Ronald H. *Father Charles E. Coughlin: Surrogate Spokesman for the Dispossessed*. Westport, CT: Greenwood, 1998.

Carter, Dan T. *Scottsboro: A Tragedy of the American South*. Baton Rouge: Louisiana State University Press, 1969.

Cayton, Horace, and George Mitchell. *Black Workers and the New Unions*. Westport, CT: Negro Universities Press, 1970.

Chalk, Ocania. *Black College Sport*. New York: Dodd, Mead, 1976.

Chicago Commission on Race Relations. *The Negro in Chicago: A Study of Race Relations and a Race Riot*. Chicago: University of Chicago Press, 1922.

Chudacoff, Howard P. *Children at Play: An American History*. New York: New York University Press, 2007.

Cohen, Adam, and Elizabeth Taylor. *American Pharaoh: Mayor Richard J. Daley: His Battles for Chicago and the Nation*. Boston: Little, Brown, 2000.

Cohen, Lizabeth. *Making a New Deal: Industrial Workers in Chicago, 1919–1939*. New York: Cambridge University Press, 1990.

Congress of Colored Catholics of the United States. *Three Afro-American Congresses*. New York: Arno, 1978.

Cooney, John. *The American Pope: The Life and Times of Francis Cardinal Spellman*. New York: Times, 1984.

Cooper, Wayne F. *Claude McKay: Rebel Sojourner in the Harlem Renaissance—A Biography*. Baton Rouge: Louisiana State University Press, 1987.

———, ed. *The Passion of Claude McKay: Selected Poetry and Prose, 1912–1948*. New York: Schocken, 1973.

Cummings, Kathleen Sprows. *New Women of the Old Faith: Gender and American Catholicism in the Progressive Era*. Chapel Hill: University of North Carolina Press, 2009.

Davis, Cyprian, O.S.B. *The History of Black Catholics in the United States*. New York: Crossroad, 1990.

Dawes, Frank Victor. *A Cry from the Streets: The Boys' Club Movement in Britain from the 1850s to the Present Day*. Hove, UK: Wayland, 1975.

Dawley, Alan. *Struggles for Justice: Social Responsibility and the Liberal State*. Cambridge, MA: Harvard University Press, 1991.

de Hueck, Catherine. *Dear Bishop*. Buenos Aires: Ediciones C. Lohlé, 1954.

———. *Friendship House*. New York: Sheed and Ward, 1947.

———. *Friendship House Staff Workers*. New York: Friendship House, 1945.

———. *The Story of Friendship House*. New York: Blessed Martin Guild, 1939.

Delaney, John J. *Dictionary of American Catholic Biography*. New York: Doubleday, 1984.

Despres, Leon M., with Kenan Heise. *Challenging the Daley Machine: A Chicago Alderman's Memoir*. Evanston, IL: Northwestern University Press, 2005.

Dolan, Jay P. *The American Catholic Experience: A History from Colonial Times to the Present*. Garden City, NY: Doubleday, 1985.

———, ed. *The American Catholic Parish: A History from 1850 to the Present*. Vol. 1. New York: Paulist, 1987.

———, ed. *The American Catholic Parish: A History from 1850 to the Present*. Vol. 2. New York: Paulist, 1987.

———. *The Immigrant Church: New York's Irish and German Catholics*. Baltimore, MD: Johns Hopkins University Press, 1975.

———. *The Irish Americans: A History*. New York: Bloomsbury, 2008.

Dorinson, Joseph, and Joram Warmund, eds. *Jackie Robinson: Race, Sports, and the American Dream*. Armonk, NY: M.E. Sharpe, 1998.

Dorsett, Lyle W. *Billy Sunday and the Redemption of Urban America*. Grand Rapids, MI: William B. Eerdmans, 1991.

Douglass, Frederick. *My Bondage and My Freedom*. New York: Arno, 1968.

Drake, St. Clair. *Churches and Voluntary Associations in the Chicago Negro Community*. Chicago: Work Projects Administration, 1940.

Drake, St. Clair, and Horace Cayton. *Black Metropolis: A Study of Negro Life in a Northern City*. New York: Harcourt, Brace, 1945.

Du Bois, W. E. B. *The Souls of Black Folk*. New York: Vintage, 1990.

Dunne, George H. *King's Pawn: The Memoirs of George H. Dunne, S.J.* Chicago: Loyola University Press, 1990.

Duquin, Lorene Hanley. *They Called Her the Baroness: The Life of Catherine de Hueck Doherty*. New York: Alba House, 1995.

Early, Gerald L. *A Level Playing Field: African American Athletes and the Republic of Sports*. Cambridge, MA: Harvard University Press, 2011.

Edwards, E. J., SVD. *Herald of the Word*. Techny, IL: Mission, SVD, 1951.

Edmonds, Anthony O. *Joe Louis*. Grand Rapids, MI: Eerdmans, 1973.

Ehrenhalt, Alan. *The Lost City: The Forgotten Virtues of Community in America*. New York: Basic, 1995.

Eisen, George, and David K. Wiggins, eds. *Ethnicity and Sport in North American History and Culture*. Westport, CT: Greenwood, 1994.

Ellis, John Tracy. *Catholic Bishops: A Memoir*. Wilmington, DE: Michael Glazier, 1983.

Erenberg, Lewis A. *Greatest Fight of Our Generation: Louis vs. Schmeling*. New York: Oxford University Press, 2005.

———. *Swingin' the Dream: Big Band Jazz and the Rebirth of American Culture*. Chicago: University of Chicago Press, 1998.

Evans, Sara M., and Harry C. Boyte. *Free Spaces: The Sources of Democratic Change in America*. New York: Harper & Row, 1986.

Farrell, James T. *Studs Lonigan: A Trilogy Comprising* Young Lonigan, The Young Manhood of Studs Lonigan, *and* Judgment Day. New York: Penguin, 2001.

Ferraro, Thomas J., ed. *Catholic Lives, Contemporary America*. Durham, NC: Duke University Press, 1997.

Fischer, William C., David A. Gerber, Jorge M. Guitart, and Maxine S. Seller, eds. *Identity, Community, and Pluralism in American Life*. New York: Oxford University Press, 1987.

Fisher, James T. *The Catholic Counterculture in America, 1933–1962*. Chapel Hill: University of North Carolina Press, 1989.

Flanagan, Maureen A. *Seeing With Their Hearts: Chicago Women and the Vision of the Good City, 1871–1933*. Princeton, NJ: Princeton University Press, 2002.

Foley, Albert S. *God's Men of Color*. New York: Farrar, Straus, 1955.

Foner, Eric. *The Story of American Freedom*. New York: W. W. Norton, 1998.

Ford, George Barry. *A Degree of Difference*. New York: Farrar, Straus & Giroux, 1969.

Fraden, Rena. *Blueprints for a Black Federal Theatre, 1935–1939*. New York: Cambridge University Press, 1994.

Frazier, E. Franklin. *The Black Bourgeoisie*. New York: Free, 1957.

Froehle, Bryan T. and Mary L. Gautier. *Catholicism USA: A Portrait of the Catholic Church in the United States*. New York: Orbis, 2000.

Fuerst, J. S., and D. Bradford Hunt, eds. *When Public Housing Was Paradise: Building Community in Chicago*. Westport, CT: Praeger, 2003.

Fullinwider, Robert K., ed. *Civil Society, Democracy, and Civic Renewal*. Lanham, MD: Rowman & Littlefield, 1999.

Gamm, Gerald. *Urban Exodus: Why the Jews Left Boston and the Catholics Stayed*. Cambridge, MA: Harvard University Press, 1999.

Gems, Gerald R. *Windy City Wars: Labor, Leisure, and Sport in the Making of Chicago*. Lanham, MD: Scarecrow, 1997.

Genovese, Eugene. *Roll Jordan, Roll: The World the Slaves Made*. New York: Pantheon, 1974.

Gerstle, Gary. *American Crucible: Race and Nation in the Twentieth Century*. Princeton, NJ: Princeton University Press, 2001.

———. *Working-Class Americanism: The Politics of Labor in a Textile City, 1914–1960*. New York: Cambridge University Press, 1989.

Gill, Glenda Eloise. *White Grease Paint on Black Performers: A Study of the Federal Theatre of 1935–1939*. New York: P. Lang, 1988.

Gillard, John T. *The Catholic Church and the American Negro*. Baltimore, MD: St. Joseph's Society, 1929.

———. *Christ, Color and Communism*. Baltimore, MD: St. Joseph's Society, 1937.

———. *Colored Catholics in the United States*. Baltimore, MD: St. Joseph's Society, 1941.

Glazier, Michael, ed. *The Encyclopedia of the Irish in America*. Notre Dame, IN: University of Notre Dame Press, 1999.

Glazier, Michael, and Thomas J. Shelley, eds. *The Encyclopedia of American Catholic History*. Collegeville, MN: Liturgical, 1997.

Gleason, Philip. *Contending With Modernity: Catholic Higher Education in the Twentieth Century*. New York: Oxford University Press, 1995.

Godfried, Nathan. *WCFL: Chicago's Voice of Labor, 1926–78*. Urbana: University of Illinois Press, 1997.

Goodman, James. *Stories of Scottsboro*. New York: Pantheon, 1994.

Gordon, Linda. *Pitied But Not Entitled: Single Mothers and the History of Welfare, 1890–1935*. New York: Free, 1994.

Gorn, Elliott J. *The Manly Art: Bare-Knuckle Prize Fighting in America*. Ithaca, NY: Cornell University Press, 1986.

———, ed. *Muhammad Ali: The People's Champ*. Urbana: University of Illinois Press, 1995.

———, ed. *Sports in Chicago*. Urbana: University of Illinois Press, 2008.

Gorn, Elliott J., and Warren Goldstein. *A Brief History of American Sports*. 2nd ed. Urbana: University of Illinois Press, 2013.

Gosnell, Harold F. *Negro Politicians: The Rise of Negro Politicians in Chicago*. Chicago: University of Chicago Press, 1935.

Greeley, Andrew M. *The American Catholic: A Social Portrait*. New York: Basic, 1977.

———. *The Church and the Suburbs*. New York: Sheed & Ward, 1959.

Green, Adam. *Selling the Race: Culture, Community, and Black Chicago, 1940–1955*. Chicago: University of Chicago Press, 2007.

Green, Paul M., and Melvin G. Holli, eds. *The Mayors: The Chicago Political Tradition*. Carbondale: Southern Illinois University Press, 1987.

Grimshaw, William J. *Bitter Fruit: Black Politics and the Chicago Machine, 1931–1991*. Chicago: University of Chicago Press, 1992.

Grombach, John V. *The Saga of Sock: A Complete Story of Boxing*. New York: Barnes, 1949.

Grossman, James R. *Land of Hope: Chicago, Black Southerners, and the Great Migration*. Chicago: University of Chicago Press, 1989.

Guglielmo, Thomas A. *White on Arrival: Italians, Race, Color, and Power in Chicago*. New York: Oxford University Press, 2003.

Habermas, Jürgen. *The Structural Transformation of the Public Sphere: An Inquiry into a Category of Bourgeois Society*. Cambridge, MA: MIT Press, 1991.

Hall, Donald E., ed. *Muscular Christianity: Embodying the Victorian Age*. New York: Cambridge University Press, 1994.

Halperin, Rick. *Down on the Killing Floor: Black and White Workers in Chicago's Packinghouses, 1904–1954*. Urbana: University of Illinois Press, 1997.

Hampton, Lionel, with James Haskins. *Hamp: An Autobiography*. New York: Amistad/Penguin, 1993.

Harris, Abram L. *The Negro as Capitalist: A Study of Banking and Business among American Negroes*. College Park, MD: McGrath, 1936.

Harris, Frederick C. *Something Within: Religion in African-American Political Activism*. New York: Oxford University Press, 1999.

Hart-Davis, Duff. *Hitler's Games: The 1936 Olympics*. New York: Harper & Row, 1986.

Harte, Thomas J. *Catholic Organizations Promoting Negro-White Race Relations*. Washington, DC: Catholic University of America Press, 1947.

Hecht, Robert A. *An Unordinary Man: A Life of Father John LaFarge, S.J.* Lanham, MD: Scarecrow, 1996.

Helgeson, Jeffrey. *Crucibles of Black Empowerment: Chicago's Neighborhood Politics from the New Deal to Harold Washington*. Chicago: University of Chicago Press, 2014.

Heineman, Kenneth J. *A Catholic New Deal: Religion and Reform in Depression Pittsburgh*. College Station: Pennsylvania State University Press, 1999.

Hemesath, Caroline. *From Slave to Priest: A Biography of the Rev. Augustine Tolton (1854–1897), First Afro-American Priest of the United States*. Chicago: Franciscan Herald, 1973.

Higham, John. *Strangers in the Land: Patterns of American Nativism, 1860–1925*. New Brunswick, NJ: Rutgers University Press, 1955.

Hirsch, Arnold. *Making the Second Ghetto: Race and Housing in Chicago, 1940–1960*. Chicago: University of Chicago Press, 1998.

Hirsch, Jerrold, *Portrait of America: A Cultural History of the Federal Writers' Project*. Chapel Hill: University of North Carolina Press, 2003.

Hitchcock, James. *The Decline and Fall of Radical Catholicism*. New York: Herder and Herder, 1971.

Holli, Melvin G. and Peter d'A. Jones. *Ethnic Chicago: A Multicultural Portrait*. 4th ed. Grand Rapids, MI: William B. Eerdmans, 1995.

Holt, Glen E., and Dominic A. Pacyga. *Chicago: A Historical Guide to the Neighborhoods, The Loop and South Side*. Chicago: Chicago Historical Society, 1979.

Homel, Michael W. *Down from Equality: Black Chicagoans and the Public Schools*. Urbana: University of Illinois Press, 1984.

Horlick, Allan Stanley. *Country Boys and Merchant Princes: The Social Control of Young Men in New York*. Lewisburg, PA: Bucknell University Press, 1975.

Horwitt, Sanford D. *Let Them Call Me Rebel: Saul Alinsky—His Life and Legacy*. New York: Knopf, 1989.

Hoy, Suellen. *Good Hearts: Catholic Sisters in Chicago's Past*. Urbana: University of Illinois Press, 2006.

Hunter, Albert. *Symbolic Communities: The Persistence and Change of Chicago's Local Communities*. Chicago: University of Chicago Press, 1974.

Hunton, George K., with Gary MacEoin. *All of Which I Saw, Part of Which I Was: The Autobiography of George K. Hunton*. Garden City, NY: Doubleday, 1967.

Ickes, Harold L. *The Secret Diary of Harold L. Ickes*. Vol. 3, *The Lowering Clouds, 1939–1941*. New York: Simon and Schuster, 1954.

Ignatiev, Noel. *How the Irish Became White*. New York: Routledge, 1996.

Irvine, Jacqueline J., and Michèle Foster. *Growing Up African American in Catholic Schools*. New York: Teachers College Press, 1996.

Issel, William. *Church and State in the City: Catholics and Politics in Twentieth-Century San Francisco*. Philadelphia: Temple University Press, 2012.

———. *For Both Cross and Flag: Catholic Action, Anti-Catholicism, and National Security Politics in World War II San Francisco*. Philadelphia: Temple University Press, 2010.

Jackson, Kenneth T. *Crabgrass Frontier: The Suburbanization of the United States*. New York: Oxford University Press, 1985.

Jacobson, Matthew Frye. *Whiteness of a Different Color: European Immigrants and the Alchemy of Race*. Cambridge, MA: Harvard University Press, 1999.

James, Winston. *A Fierce Hatred of Injustice: Claude McKay's Jamaica and His Poetry of Rebellion*. London: Verso, 2001.

Johnson, John H., with Lerone Bennett, Jr. *Succeeding Against the Odds: The Autobiography of a Great American Businessman*. New York: Amistad, 1989.

Johnson, May Lee. *Coming Up on the Rough Side: A Black Catholic Story*. South Orange, NJ: Pillar, 1988.

Johnson, Philip A. *Call Me Neighbor, Call Me Friend: The Case History of the Integration of a Neighborhood on Chicago's South Side*. Garden City, NY: Doubleday, 1965.

Kantowicz, Edward R. *Corporation Sole: Cardinal Mundelein and Chicago Catholicism*. Notre Dame, IN: University of Notre Dame Press, 1983.

Katz, Michael B. *In the Shadow of the Poorhouse: A Social History of Welfare in America*. New York: Basic, 1996.

Katznelson, Ira. *City Trenches: Urban Politics and the Patterning of Class in the United States*. New York: Pantheon, 1981.

———. *Fear Itself: The New Deal and the Origins of Our Time*. New York: W. W. Norton, 2013.

———. *When Affirmative Action Was White*. New York: W. W. Norton, 2006.

Kelley, Francis C. *The Story of Extension*. Chicago: Extension, 1922.

Kelley, Robin D. G. *Hammer and Hoe: Alabama Communists during the Great Depression*. Chapel Hill: University of North Carolina Press, 1990.

Kelly, Tom. *The Imperial Post: The Myers, the Grahams and the Paper that Rules Washington*. New York: William Morrow, 1983.

Kennedy, David M. *Freedom from Fear: The American People in Depression and War, 1929–1945*. New York: Oxford University Press, 1999.

King, Martin Luther, Jr. *Strength to Love*. New York: Harper & Row, 1963.

Kirsch, George B., Othello Harris, and Claire E. Nolte, eds. *Encyclopedia of Ethnicity and Sports in the United States*. Westport, CT: Greenwood, 2000.

Koenig, Rev. Msgr. Harry C. *A History of the Parishes of the Archdiocese of Chicago*. Chicago: Archdiocese of Chicago, 1980.

Kogan, Herman, and Rick Kogan. *Yesterday's Chicago*. Miami: E.A. Seemann, 1976.

Korstad, Robert Rodgers. *Civil Rights Unionism: Tobacco Workers and the Struggle for Democracy in the Mid-Twentieth-Century South*. Chapel Hill: University of North Carolina Press, 2003.

Kosmin, Barry A., and Seymour P. Lachman. *One Nation under God: Religion in Contemporary American Society*. New York: Harmony, 1993.

Krüger, Arnd, and William J. Murray, eds, *The Nazi Olympics: Sport, Politics and Appeasement in the 1930s*. Urbana: University of Illinois Press, 2003.

Ladd, Tony, and James A. Mathisen. *Muscular Christianity: Evangelical Protestants and the Development of American Sport*. Grand Rapids, MI: Baker, 1999.

LaFarge, John, SJ. *The Catholic Viewpoint on Race Relations*. Garden City, NY: Hanover House, 1956.

———. *Interracial Justice: A Study of the Catholic Doctrine of Race Relations*. New York: America, 1937.

———. *The Manner is Ordinary*. New York: Harcourt, Brace, 1954.

———. *No Postponement: U.S. Moral Leadership and the Problem of Racial Minorities*. New York: Longmans, Green and Co., 1950.

———. *The Race Question and the Negro: A Study of the Catholic Doctrine on Interracial Justice*. New York: Longmans, Green, 1943.

LaFarge, John, SJ, Thurston N. Davis, SJ, and Joseph Small, SJ, eds. *John Lafarge Reader*. New York: America, 1956.

Large, David Clay. *Nazi Games: The Olympics of 1936*. New York: W. W. Norton, 2007.

Lemann, Nicholas. *The Promised Land: The Great Black Migration and How It Changed America*. New York: Knopf, 1991.

Leuchtenburg, William E. *Franklin D. Roosevelt and the New Deal, 1932–1940*. New York: Harper & Row, 1963.

Littlewood, Thomas B. *Arch: A Promoter, Not a Poet: The Story of Arch Ward*. Ames: Iowa State University Press, 1990.

Livezey, Lowell W., ed. *Religious Organizations and Structural Change in Metropolitan Chicago: The Research Report of the Religion in Urban American Program*. Chicago: University of Illinois at Chicago, 1996.

Logan, Rayford W. *Betrayal of the Negro: From Rutherford B. Hayes to Woodrow Wilson*. New York: Collier, 1965.

Louis, Joe. *My Life Story: An Autobiography*. Brighton, UK: Angus and Robertson, 1978.

MacGregor, Morris J. *The Emergence of a Black Catholic Community: St. Augustine's in Washington*. Washington, DC: Catholic University of America Press, 1999.

Madison, James H. *A Lynching in the Heartland: Race and Memory in America*. New York: Palgrave, 2001.

Mandell, Richard D. *The Nazi Olympics*. New York: Macmillan, 1971.

Martin, Robert Francis. *Hero of the Heartland: Billy Sunday and the Transformation of American Society, 1862–1935*. Bloomington: Indiana University Press, 2002.

May, Elaine Tyler. *Homeward Bound: American Families in the Cold War Era*. New York: Basic, 1988.

McCaffrey, Lawrence, Ellen Skerrett, Michael F. Funchion, and Charles Fanning. *The Irish in Chicago*. Urbana: University of Illinois Press, 1987.

McClory, Robert. *Radical Disciple: Father Pfleger, St. Sabina Church, and the Fight for Social Justice*. Chicago: Chicago Review, 2010.

McDonogh, Gary Wray. *Black and Catholic in Savannah, Georgia*. Knoxville: University of Tennessee Press, 1993.

McGreevy, John T. *Catholicism and American Freedom: A History*. New York: W. W. Norton, 2003.

———. *Parish Boundaries: The Catholic Encounter with Race in the Twentieth-Century Urban North*. Chicago: University of Chicago Press, 1996.

McKay, Claude. *A Long Way from Home*. New York: Arno, 1969.

McLoughlin, William G., Jr. *Billy Sunday Was His Real Name*. Chicago: University of Chicago Press, 1955.

McMahon, Eileen. *What Parish Are You From? A Chicago Irish Community and Race Relations*. Lexington: University Press of Kentucky, 1995.

Mead, Chris. *Champion: Joe Louis, Black Hero in White America*. New York: Scribner, 1985.

Meagher, Timothy J. *From Paddy to Studs: Irish American Communities in the Turn of the Century Era, 1880 to 1920*. Westport, CT: Greenwood, 1986.

Melosh, Barbara. *Engendering Culture: Manhood and Womanhood in New Deal Public Art and Theater*. Washington, DC: Smithsonian Institution, 1991.

Miller, Alton. *Harold Washington: The Mayor, The Man*. Chicago: Bonus, 1989.

Miller, Donald L. *City of the Century: The Epic of Chicago and the Making of America*. New York: Simon and Schuster, 1996.

Miller, Wayne F. *Chicago's South Side, 1946–1948*. Berkeley: University of California Press, 2000.

Mjagkij, Nina. *Light in the Darkness: African Americans and the YMCA, 1852–1946*. Lexington: University Press of Kentucky, 1994.

Mjagkij, Nina, and Margaret Spratt, eds., *Men and Women Adrift: The YMCA and the YWCA in the City*. New York: New York University Press, 1997.

Moore, Deborah Dash. *B'nai B'rith and the Challenge of Ethnic Leadership*. Albany: State University of New York Press, 1981.

Morgan, Thomas B. *Speaking of Cardinals*. New York: G. P. Putnam's Sons, 1946.

Morrow, Diane Batts. *Persons of Color and Religious at the Same Time*. Chapel Hill: University of North Carolina Press, 2002.

Mulder, Mark T. *Shades of White Flight: Evangelical Congregations and Urban Departure*. New Brunswick, NJ: Rutgers University Press, 2015.

Mullen, Bill V. *Popular Fronts: Chicago and African-American Cultural Politics, 1935–46*. Urbana: University of Illinois, 1999.

Mumford, Kevin. *Interzones: Black/White Sex Districts in Chicago and New York in the Early Twentieth Century*. New York: Columbia University Press, 1997.

Mundelein, George W. *Letters of a Bishop to His Flock, By His Eminence George Cardinal Mundelein*. New York: Benziger, 1927.

———. *Two Crowded Years: Being Selected Addresses, Pastorals, and Letters Issued During the First Twenty-Four Months of the Episcopate of the Most Rev. George Mundelein, D.D., As Archbishop of Chicago*. Chicago: Extension, 1918.

Myrdal, Gunnar. *An American Dilemma: The Negro Problem and Modern Democracy*. New York: Harper & Row, 1944.

National Conference of Catholic Bishops—Secretariat of Black Catholics. *Keep Your Hand on the Plow: The African American Presence in the Catholic Church*. Washington, DC: United States Catholic Conference, 1996.

———. *Many Rains Ago: A Historical and Theological Reflection on the Role of the Episcopate in the Evangelization of African American Catholics*. Washington, DC: United States Catholic Conference, 1990.

Newell, Barbara Warne. *Chicago and the Labor Movement: Metropolitan Unionism in the 1930s*. Urbana: University of Illinois Press, 1961.

Nickels, Marilyn Wenzke. *Black Catholic Protest and the Federated Colored Catholics, 1917–1933: Three Perspectives on Racial Justice*. New York: Garland, 1988.

Nolan, Hugh J., ed. *Pastoral Letters of the United States Catholic Bishops*. Vol. 1: 1792–1940. Washington, DC: National Conference of Catholic Bishops, United States Catholic Conference, 1984.

O'Brien, David J. *American Catholics and Social Reform: The New Deal Years*. New York: Oxford University Press, 1968.

O'Brien, John A., ed. *The White Harvest: A Symposium on Methods of Convert Making*. New York: Longmans, Green, 1927.

Ochs, Stephen J. *A Black Patriot and a White Priest: André Cailloux and Claude Paschal Maistre in Civil War New Orleans*. Baton Rouge: Louisiana State University Press, 2000.

———. *Desegregating the Altar: The Josephites and the Struggle for Black Priests, 1871–1960*. Baton Rouge: Louisiana State University Press, 1990.

Osborne, William Audley. *The Segregated Covenant: Race Relations and American Catholics*. New York: Herder and Herder, 1967.

O'Toole, James M. *Passing for White: Race, Religion, and the Healy Family, 1820–1920*. Amherst: University of Massachusetts Press, 2002.

Ottley, Roi. *The Lonely Warrior: The Life and Times of Robert S. Abbott*. Chicago: H. Regnery, 1955.

Pacyga, Dominic A. and Ellen Skerrett. *Chicago: City of Neighborhoods, Histories and Tours*. Chicago: Loyola University Press, 1986.

Parot, Joseph John. *Polish Catholics in Chicago, 1850–1920: A Religious History*. DeKalb: Northern Illinois Press, 1981.

Phelps, Jamie T., ed. *Black and Catholic: The Challenge and Gift of Black Folk—Contributions of African American Experience and Thought to Catholic Theology*. Milwaukee, WI: Marquette University Press, 1997.

Philpott, Thomas L. *The Slum and the Ghetto: Neighborhood Deterioration and Middle-Class Reform, 1890–1930*. New York: Oxford University Press, 1978.

Pruter, Robert. *The Rise of American High School Sports and the Search for Control, 1880–1930*. Syracuse, NY: Syracuse University Press, 2013.

Putnam, Robert. *Bowling Alone: The Collapse and Revival of American Community*. New York: Simon and Schuster, 2000.

Raboteau, Albert J. *A Fire in the Bones: Reflections on African-American Religious History*. Boston: Beacon, 1995.

Record, Wilson. *The Negro and the Communist Party*. New York: Atheneum, 1971.

Reed, Christopher Robert. *The Chicago NAACP and the Rise of Black Professional Leadership, 1910–1966*. Bloomington: Indiana University Press, 1997.

———. *The Rise of Chicago's Black Metropolis, 1920–1929*. Urbana: University of Illinois Press, 2011.

Reese, Thomas J. *Archbishop: Inside the Power Structure of the American Catholic Church*. San Francisco: Harper & Row, 1989.

Reiss, Steven. *City Games: The Evolution of American Urban Society and the Rise of Sports*. Urbana: University of Illinois Press, 1989.

Rex, Frederick. *Centennial List of Mayors, City Clerks, City Attorney, City Treasurer, and Aldermen, Elected by the People of the City of Chicago, From Incorporation of the City on March 4, 1837 to March 4, 1937, Arranged in Alphabetical Order Showing the Years During which Each Official Held Office*. Chicago: Municipal Reference Library, 1937.

Reynolds, Edward D. *Jesuits for the Negro*. New York: America, 1949.

Rhodes, Chip. *Structures of the Jazz Age: Mass Culture, Progressive Education, and Racial Discourse in American Modernism*. London: Verso, 1998.

Roche, Richard J. *Catholic Colleges and the Negro Student*. Washington, DC: Catholic University of America Press, 1948.

Roediger, David R. *The Wages of Whiteness: Race and the Making of the American Working Class*. New York: Verso, 1991.

———. *Working toward Whiteness: How America's Immigrants Became White: The Strange Journey from Ellis Island to the Suburbs*. New York: Basic, 2005.

Rosswurm, Steve, ed. *The CIO's Left-Led Unions*. New Brunswick, NJ: Rutgers University Press, 1992.

———. *The FBI and the Catholic Church, 1935–1962*. Amherst: University of Massachusetts Press, 2009.

Runstedtler, Theresa. *Jack Johnson, Rebel Sojourner: Boxing in the Shadow of the Global Color Line*. Berkeley: University of California Press, 2012.

Sammons, Jeffrey T. *Beyond the Ring: The Role of Boxing in American Society*. Urbana: University of Illinois Press, 1988.

Sanders, James W. *The Education of an Urban Minority: Catholics in Chicago, 1833–1965*. New York: Oxford University Press, 1977.

Scherzer, Kenneth A. *The Unbounded Community: Neighborhood Life and Social Structure in New York City, 1830–1875*. Durham, NC: Duke University Press, 1992.

Schneirov, Richard. *Labor and Urban Politics: Class Conflict and the Origins of Modern Liberalism in Chicago, 1864–1897*. Urbana: University of Illinois Press, 1998.

Schultz, Kevin M. *Tri-Faith America: How Catholics and Jews Held Postwar American to Its Protestant Promise*. New York: Oxford University Press, 2011.

Selby, Earl, and Miriam Selby. *Odyssey: Journey through Black America*. New York: G. P. Putman's Sons, 1971.

Shanabruch, Charles. *Chicago's Catholics: The Evolution of an American Identity*. Notre Dame, IN: University of Notre Dame Press, 1981.

Shaw, Stephen J. *The Catholic Parish as a Way-Station of Ethnicity and Americanization: Chicago's Germans and Italians, 1903–1939*. Brooklyn: Carlson, 1991.

Sheldon, Marcus. *Father Coughlin: The Tumultuous Life of the Priest of the Little Flower*. Boston: Little, Brown, 1973.

Shuster, George, SSJ, and Robert M. Kearns, SSJ. *Statistical Profile of Black Catholics*. Washington, DC: Josephite Pastoral Center, 1976.

Sicius, Francis J. *The Word Made Flesh: The Chicago Catholic Worker and the Emergence of Lay Activism in the Church*. Lanham, MD: University Press of America, 1990.

Sinkevitch, Alice, ed. *AIA Guide to Chicago*. New York: Harcourt, Brace, 1993.

Sitkoff, Harvard. *A New Deal for Blacks: The Emergence of a National Issue: The Depression Decade*. New York: Oxford University Press, 1978.

Skerrett, Ellen. *At the Crossroads: Old St. Patrick's and the Chicago Irish*. Chicago: Wild Onion, 1997.

———. *Born in Chicago: A History of Chicago's Jesuit University*. Chicago: Loyola, 2008.

Skerrett, Ellen, Edward R. Kantowicz, and Steven M. Avella. *Catholicism, Chicago Style*. Chicago: Loyola University Press, 1993.

Slayton, Robert A. *Back of the Yards: The Making of a Local Democracy*. Chicago: University of Chicago Press, 1986.

Smith, Anthony Burke. *The Look of Catholics: Portrayals in Popular Culture from the Great Depression to the Cold War*. Lawrence: University Press of Kansas, 2010.

Smithson, Sandra O., OSF. *To Be the Bridge: A Commentary on Black/White Catholicism in America*. Nashville: Winston-Derek, 1984.

Spear, Alan. *Black Chicago: Making of a Negro Ghetto, 1890–1920*. Chicago: University of Chicago Press, 1967.

Sisters of the Blessed Sacrament. *Century Book: Sharing the Bread in Service, 1891–1991*. Bensalem, PA: Sisters of the Blessed Sacrament, 1991.

Sorin, Gerald. *The Nurturing Neighborhood: The Brownsville Boys Club and Jewish Community in Urban America, 1940–1990*. New York: New York University Press, 1990.

Sorrentino, Anthony. *Organizing Against Crime: Redeveloping the Neighborhood*. New York: Human Science, 1977.

Southern, David W. *John LaFarge and the Limits of Catholic Interracialism, 1911–1963*. Baton Rouge: Louisiana State University Press, 1996.

Sparrow, James T. *Warfare State: World War II Americans and the Age of Big Government*. New York: Oxford University Press, 2011.

Sporn, Paul. *Against Itself: The Federal Theater and Writers' Projects in the Midwest*. Detroit: Wayne State University Press, 1995.

Stackhouse, Perry J. *Chicago and the Baptists*. Chicago: University of Chicago Press, 1933.

Stange, Maren, ed. *Bronzeville: Black Chicago in Pictures, 1941–1943*. New York: New, 2003.

Sterne, Evelyn Savidge. *Ballots and Bibles: Ethnic Politics and the Catholic Church in Providence*. Ithaca, NY: Cornell University Press, 2003.

Strickland, Arvarh E. *History of the Chicago Urban League*. Urbana: University of Illinois Press, 1966.

Stuckey, Sterling. *Slave Culture and the Foundations of Black America*. New York: Oxford University Press, 1987.

Sugrue, Thomas J. *The Origins of the New Urban Crisis: Race and Inequality in Postwar Detroit*. Princeton, NJ: Princeton University Press, 1996.

———. *Sweet Land of Liberty: The Forgotten Struggle for Civil Rights in the North.* New York: Random House, 2008.

Tarry, Ellen. *Katharine Drexel: Friend of the Oppressed.* Nashville: Winston-Derek, 1990.

———. *The Third Door: The Autobiography of an American Negro Woman.* Tuscaloosa: University of Alabama Press, 1992.

Tentler, Leslie Woodcock, *Seasons of Grace: A History of the Catholic Archdiocese of Detroit.* Detroit, MI: Wayne State University Press, 1990.

Thompson, Joseph J. *The Archdiocese of Chicago: Antecedents and Development.* Des Plaines, IL: St. Mary's Training School, 1920.

Thrasher, Frederic Milton. *The Gang: A Study of 1,313 Gangs in Chicago.* Chicago: University of Chicago Press, 1927.

Tillery, Tyrone. *Claude McKay: A Black Poet's Struggle for Identity.* Amherst: University of Massachusetts Press, 1992.

Travis, Dempsey. *An Autobiography of Black Chicago.* Chicago: Urban Research Institute, 1981.

———. *An Autobiography of Black Jazz.* Chicago: Urban Research Institute, 1983.

———. *An Autobiography of Black Politics.* Chicago: Urban Research Institute, 1987.

———. *"Harold," The People's Mayor: The Authorized Biography of Mayor Harold Washington.* Chicago: Urban Research Institute, 1989.

Treat, Roger L. *Bishop Sheil and the CYO: The Story of the Catholic Youth Organization and the Man Who Influenced a Generation of Americans.* New York: Messner, 1951.

Tuttle, William M., Jr. *Race Riot: Chicago in the Red Summer of 1919.* New York: Atheneum, 1970.

Tuzik, Robert L. *Reynold Hillenbrand: The Reform of the Catholic Liturgy and the Call to Social Action.* Chicago: Hillenbrand/Liturgy Training, 2010.

von Hoffman, Alexander. *Local Attachments: The Making of an American Urban Neighborhood, 1850–1920.* Baltimore, MD: Johns Hopkins University Press, 1994.

Walkowitz, Daniel J. *Working with Class: Social Workers and the Politics of Middle-Class Identity.* Chapel Hill: University of North Carolina Press, 1999.

Ward, Mary A. *A Mission for Justice: The History of the First African American Catholic Church in Newark, New Jersey.* Knoxville: University of Tennessee Press, 2002.

Warren, Donald I. *Radio Priest: Charles Coughlin, the Father of Hate Radio.* New York: Free, 1996.

Weisenfeld, Judith. *African American Women and Christian Activism: New York's Black YWCA, 1905–1945.* Cambridge, MA: Harvard University Press, 1997.

Weisenfeld, Judith, and Richard Newman, eds. *This Far by Faith: Readings in African-American Women's Religious Biography.* New York: Routledge, 1996.

Weiss, Nancy J. *Farewell to the Party of Lincoln: Black Politics in the Age of FDR.* Princeton, NJ: Princeton University Press, 1983.

Wiggins, David. *Black Athletes in White America.* Syracuse, NY: Syracuse University Press, 1997.

Wiggins, David, and Patrick B. Miller, eds. *The Unlevel Playing Field: A Documentary*

History of African American Experience in Sport. Urbana: University of Illinois Press, 2003.

Wiltse, Jeff. *Contested Waters: A Social History of Swimming Pools in America*. Chapel Hill: University of North Carolina Press, 2007.

Wright, Richard. *Native Son*. New York: Harper, 1940.

Young, Julie. *The CYO in Indianapolis and Central Indiana*. Charleston, SC: History, 2011.

Zoti, Mary Irene. *A Time of Awakening: The Young Christian Worker Story in the United States, 1938–1970*. Chicago: Loyola University Press, 1991.

INDEX

Page numbers in italics refer to figures and tables.

HISTORICAL STUDIES OF URBAN AMERICA

Edited by Lilia Fernández, Timothy J. Gilfoyle, Becky M. Nicolaides, and Amanda I. Seligman
James R. Grossman, editor emeritus

SERIES TITLES, CONTINUED FROM FRONTMATTER